10/96

Daughters of the Great Depression

Daughters

of the Great Depression

Women, Work, and Fiction
in the American 1930s ■

BY LAURA HAPKE

The University of Georgia Press ■ Athens and London

© 1995 by the University of Georgia Press
Athens, Georgia 30602
All rights reserved
Designed by Sandra Strother Hudson
Set in 10.5/14 Bembo by Tseng Information Systems, Inc.
Printed and bound by Thomson-Shore
The paper in this book meets the guidelines
for permanence and durability of the Committee on
Production Guidelines for Book Longevity
of the Council on Library Resources.

Printed in the United States of America
99 98 97 96 95 C 5 4 3 2 1

Library of Congress Cataloging in Publication Data

Hapke, Laura.
Daughters of the Great Depression : women, work, and
fiction in the American 1930s / Laura Hapke.
p. cm.
Includes bibliographical references (p.) and index.
ISBN 0-8203-1718-7 (alk. paper)
1. American fiction—20th century—History and
criticism.   2. Women and literature—United States—
History—20th century.   3. American fiction—Women
authors—History and criticism.   4. Women—
Employment—United States—Historiography.
5. Women employees in literature.   6. Depressions in
literature.   7. Work in literature.   I. Title.
PS374.W6H357   1995
813'.5209352042—dc20   94-40316

British Library Cataloging in Publication Data available
Title page illlustration: A Lewis Hine homage to
Depression Era working women, *Shelton Looms,* Shelton,
Connecticut, 1933. Courtesy of the Hine Collection,
George Eastman House.

To the memory of my father: writer, union man,
and son of the Great Depression

CONTENTS

LIST OF ILLUSTRATIONS

ACKNOWLEDGMENTS

I extend my thanks to Pace University, which helped support this project through Scholarly Research Committee and summer research grants. My gratitude is owed as well to the library staff, particularly Elisabeth Birnbaum, for great dedication in tracking down period sources.

Grateful acknowledgment is made to the Tamiment Library of New York University for permission to reproduce the *Working Woman* photograph; the Metropolitan Museum of Art, George A. Hearn Fund, for permission to reprint Edward Hopper's painting *Tables for Ladies;* the Museum of the City of New York for permission to reprint Eli Jacobi's lithograph *Maxi's Moose* and Vincent La Gambina's painting *The Life Cafeteria;* the Library of Congress for permission to reprint Marion Post Wolcott's photograph *A Woman Migrant Packinghouse Worker;* the Archives of Labor and Urban Affairs, Wayne State University, for permission to reproduce the photograph of the Gastonia textile strike; the Whitney Museum of American Art for permission to reproduce Raphael Soyer's painting *Office Girls;* the Art Gallery, University of Maryland at College Park, for permission to reproduce George Biddle's painting *Sweatshop;* and the George Eastman House for permission to reprint Lewis Hine's photo *Shelton Looms.*

THE
WORKING WOMAN

5¢

TO MAKE
MY BREAD
By GRACE LUMPKIN

•

YOUR
SON MAY BE
NEXT
By SASHA SMALL

•

POVERTY
BREAKS
HEALTH
By Dr. LONE

•

LETTERS FROM
WORKERS

ON TO
WASHINGTON

TO

UNEMPLOYED WOMEN ON THE MARCH
New York homeless and jobless women in demonstration for work and shelter.

Unemployed Convention FEB. 3-4-5

The female breadwinner, envisioned for the December 1933 cover of the
Communist Party journal *Working Woman*. Tamiment Library,
New York University.

PREFACE

Until recent scholars of women's history resurrected the eleven-million-strong army of working women who were the female foot soldiers of the Great Depression, studies of the 1930s centered on men.[1] For decades after the Great Crash of 1929, historians wrote eloquently about the forgotten men and working stiffs who rode the rails as "boes," peopled Hoovervilles, despaired of feeding themselves and their children, and sought out work relief programs.[2] The same chroniclers erased or minimized the more than two million women, including heads of households, who faced the specters of homelessness and joblessness; gathered in unemployment offices; slept in vacant lots, city subways, and Bertha-like in boxcars; wrote pleading letters to the Roosevelts and Labor Secretary Frances Perkins; and hoped for rescue by New Deal agencies.[3]

Again until recently, many anthologist-critics have been similarly inattentive to the era's working women. Following a trend in 1930s anthologies, their collections of reprints consistently omitted all but token selections about the one-quarter of all American women who went out to work in this decade, much less the labor-class mothers, wives, and daughters who did "women's work" at home.[4] Critics' retrospective pieces in the 1970s and early 1980s sidestepped female wage earners as literary subjects. Such pieces excluded as well the predominantly radical women writers who, by the Depression Era, were more likely to provide these representations.[5]

The renascence of interest in the era's female proletariat—a term the new scholarship extends to labor-class women—and its radical authors is aptly represented in editorial essays prefacing, as well as selections from, a well-received anthology including fiction and reportage by women associated with "red" causes and working-class themes.[6] Several other reprints of "lost" women writers, radical and otherwise, further redirect attention to the female of the 1930s.[7] In a series of parallel developments, revisionist biographies of such leftist authors as Josephine Herbst, Agnes Smedley, and Leane Zugsmith have appeared during the last few years; perhaps more important, leftist women's fiction in general and Tillie Olsen in particular are now the subjects of numerous studies.[8]

Using radical women's fiction as part of a larger discourse on women's work, new interpreters see an author such as Olsen as a bard of women's struggle for survival inside the home, that rough terrain of proletarian wife-, mother-, and daughterhood. This theme is certainly as crucial to her unfinished mid-1930s novel of packinghouse conditions, *Yonnondio*, as is its indictment of the repressive conditions in the meatpacking work-force and larger industrial society. The insight that many radical women's, and some men's, fiction contains a plea for a dramatically altered system of social relations illuminates reinterpretations of *Yonnondio*, Agnes Smedley's *Daughter of Earth* (1929), Catharine Brody's 1932 novel of blue-collar wife abuse, *Nobody Starves,* Tom Kromer's *Waiting for Nothing* (1935), Mike Gold's *Jews Without Money* (1930)—and, as we shall observe, Margaret Mitchell's *Gone with the Wind* (1936), Fannie Hurst's *Back Street* (1931), Sinclair Lewis's *Ann Vickers* (1933), and Christopher Morley's *Kitty Foyle* (1941) as well. By revisiting the Communist Party's debate on the "Woman Question" and on the economic value of housework, scholars have profitably widened traditional definitions of productive work to in-clude the female home-front and child-rearing experience, whether urban or rural, white or black—what Paula Rabinowitz terms "putting sexuality and maternity into working-class narrative" (*Labor,* 182).

My book continues the new approach to the laboring 1930s by analyz-ing literary and cultural depictions not only of domestic womanhood but of her breadwinning counterpart, the female wage earner. Such analy-ses, particularly applied to avidly read nonprotest fare of the time, can both establish continuities between unwaged and waged female labor and probe the difficulties created for the female breadwinner by a hard-pressed, women-resenting, masculine labor force. My reading of Olsen's vision of blue-collar motherhood, for example, has her fiction drawing on her experience as a veteran of midwestern meatpacking and food-processing jobs. For the individualistically autobiographical factory- and office-bound heroines of her apprentice and post-1930s short fiction join the job-site women who are after-hours neighbors of *Yonnondio's* Anna Holbrook, the packing town heroine/housewife, in going out to work. Instead, in the projected conclusion to the book, Olsen's alter ego, Mazie

Holbrook, is also poised to become a working, and working-class, writer (Pearlman and Werlock, 52).

Indeed, because the Depression was a time when wage-earning women were charged with stealing jobs from men, a scrutiny of Olsen and her sister (and brother) writers—which this study extends to best-selling fiction as well—profits from what one historian of feminine labor terms understanding the "dialectic between domesticity and workplace" in the lives of that one-quarter of American women who met the culture's definition of the wage worker.[9] In reality, only rarely did women and men compete for the same jobs. Nor did firing women ensure men access to jobs; it only contributed to the downfall of households supported by women. Nevertheless, working women, especially married ones, became the scapegoats of a movement to reassert the separate sphere thinking of past decades. One alarmed observer wrote as late as 1939 that a "widespread movement against working women is under way with ten million jobs at stake."[10] In women's history and the fiction that interpreted and imaginatively reshaped it, the campaign against this embattled female 25 percent was symbolic of attitudes that encumbered all women, laboring or not. How these views pervaded the novels and shorter fiction of the period, from popular to militant, is the chief subject of this book.

Building on what Ellen Wiley Todd terms the "ambiguous and problematic relationship between femininity and labor in the Depression" (272), this book also charts the extent to which this fiction dramatizes the lived experience of American women workers, what Patricia Cooper, a historian of female work culture, calls woman's outlook on her own work.[11] If, as most notably depicted in the works of male radical writers devoted to the comrade wife ideal, nondomestic work is unwomanly and potentially emasculating, what imaginative strategies convey that conviction? In fiction by nonleftist writers who were better known to a wider American audience, what constitute culturally palatable images of breadwinning womanhood? If jobholding womanhood survived in the masculine work world only by "adher[ing] to male goals" (Kessler-Harris, "Gender," 37), what forms did this adherence take in the various subgenres of period fiction? Given the erosion of gains made by women in the 1920s in the clerical and professional fields, what new hostilities burdened the white-collar girl of 1930s literature? Finally, did African-American writers, more likely to depict the varieties of (customarily low-rung) black female work than were their white colleagues, offer substantially different answers to these questions?

Without scanting what Janet Zandy calls the "double work lives" of labor-class women—job and family—[12] I seek to discover how the Depression, through its fiction and its fictions, inherited, combated, and transfigured a decades-old American debate about women's suitability for paid work outside the home. By 1930 women's labor force participation had more than doubled since their first mass entry in the 1890s. But, particularly given the burgeoning back-to-the-home movement of the 1930s, working women were carrying the baggage of a lingering Victorianism concerning their physical and moral fitness for work. For well over three decades, defenders had argued with detractors, who impugned the woman wage earner's fitness for wife- and motherhood, her unsavory companions, promiscuous ways, and desire to take men's jobs.[13] As the new opportunities for and acceptance of women in the workplace ushered in by the end of World War I were under assault in the breadline climate of the 1930s, many turned to the old argument that woman and work was a contradiction in terms.

Of central importance in evaluating what "cultural [and literary] discourses emerge[d] to take care of threatening social changes"[14] is the period's mountainous social documentation of women workers, some of which they compiled themselves. Breadwinning womanhood was analyzed by economic historians who supported protective rather than egalitarian legislation; interviewed and edited by the mostly middle-class employees of the Federal Writers' Project; and commiserated with by the philanthropic but fading Women's Trade Union League and by a constricted Women's Bureau of the Department of Labor. Women laborers were exhorted to political action by female organizers poised to recruit in mass industry for organizations such as the Trade Union Unity League (TUUL), Textile Workers Union (TWU), International Ladies' Garment Workers' Union (ILGWU), and, later in the decade, by the Popular Front laborites and unions of the Congress of Industrial Organizations (CIO). But the working woman was discouraged from feminist agitation—or executive board leadership—by both male party and union officials. Black laboring women were reduced to the worst of the bad jobs traditionally assigned them and defeated by the clamoring of hard-pressed white women, who often proved to be no labor sisters. For the few white and fewer black women at the other end of the job spectrum, among them teachers, lawyers, and businesswomen, there were the dangers of deskilling, incursions by jobless male professionals, and, like their labor-class counterparts, simple guilt at jobholding itself. In sum, from stenographers to assembly-liners to college teachers, women were denied equal pay for equal work under the provisions of the National Recovery Administration (NRA) code; if married, forbidden from government and other employment by a section of the Federal Economy Act; and similarly restricted by the agenda of mainstream periodical articles with titles such as "Do You Need Your Job?" They were accused of emasculation, promiscuity, or both if they resisted these constraints but praised if they complied with the dictates of the back-to-the-home movement.

Students of women's representation in literature, especially the strike novel, can find a further documentary context for such literature in the lived work history of women themselves: their participation as organizers in the Gastonia textile strike of 1929; as auxiliaries in the historic sit-down strikes in the rubber, steel, and automobile industries; as travelers in the mass Okie migration to California in search of field work; as fuelers of strike waves in northern and midwestern urban garment trades work; and, to a lesser degree, in the New York City protests of exploitation of department store, restaurant, and even clerical workers.

A study of attitudes toward and representations of the working woman of the 1930s best locates her within a Depression Era context by using fiction as reflector and reshaper of the attitudes and events described above. In this endeavor, though, the distinction between social protest and mainstream fiction can be somewhat blurred.[15] Militant fiction certainly employed popular stereotypes of femininity and masculinity; mainstream fiction likewise borrowed from social-consciousness plotting. Though with few exceptions proletarian works sold poorly, they received widespread critical attention and flourished more in the 1930s than in any other decade before or since. James T. Farrell is not being too idealistic when he has his eponymous Common Man, Studs Lonigan, scan a bookshop window and see such 1930's proletarian fare as Louis Colman's novel *Lumber* and Mike Gold's *Jews Without Money* alongside a prizefight yarn by W. R. Burnett, *Iron Man,* and, in Farrell's slap at the day's novelistic trivia, a probably invented title, *The Mystery of Madame Q.*[16] The early 1930s saw enough familiarity with labor titles that, unlike Studs, whose actual reading was restricted to scanning *True Confessions* in a drugstore, a bewildered matron in a *New Yorker* cartoon asks a clerk, "Have you a book that isn't about poor people?"[17]

The dowager's surface knowledge and rejection of texts on labor and the weakened economy aside, some of them, Farrell's and Gold's included, with John Steinbeck heading the list, did do well in the 1930s. But, like the affluent readers subscribing to and cartooned by the *New Yorker,* the public may well have found labor themes far more palatable as novelistic scenery. For instance, Dashiell Hammett's widely read tale of thugs brought in to defeat striking miners, *Red Harvest,* depicts Poisonville as "ripe for the harvest" of bloody labor struggle, but the reader's attention is on the gangster scenario.[18]

Readers also flocked to historical escape tales and to the romantic thralldom novel (Rabinowitz, *Labor,* 80). In the 1930s Louis Adamic was determining that workers themselves often disliked the proletarian books that purported to speak for them and applauded the trivial romantic fare that even the Gastonia strike organizer Vera Buch Weisbord read to while away the time in a southern prison.[19] Such fiction may have been less earnest than *Lumber* or *Daughter of Earth,* but it provided timely accounts of shared fears, values, and fantasies. Moreover, had Studs been a female browser, her bookshop window would certainly have included Hurst, Mitchell, Lewis, and Morley. Appealing to women readers on the romance/fantasy level, these crowd-pleasing authors nevertheless offered versions of the women and work controversy that have been overlooked in the rush to stigmatize their novels as superficial and to relegate them to the back rooms of literary history.

Chapter 1 is an overview of that controversy, a social and literary history of the debate on, and minimizing American attitude toward, female job seekers. Under scrutiny are the era's various propaganda campaigns to disfranchise women wage earners and professionals; these women's pinched salaries, "man-sized" joblessness, and ambiguous New Deal benefits; and their contested thrusts toward full participation in trade unionism and the Communist Party. Linking the above contestations over women and work to literary responses to the controversial female worker, the first chapter closes by considering her incarnation in three key authors, well-known to Depression audiences: apostle of the earth mother as field worker John Steinbeck, bard of the eroticized mill girl Erskine Caldwell, and radical challenger of such types Agnes Smedley.

The remainder of the book draws on period documents to probe other contrasts between and among men's and women's texts on the womanly work site as well as, in the first pair of chapters, the sweated terrain of the labor-class home. Chapter 2 contextualizes men's social protest novels within the left-Socialist cultural denial of women's work identity—in many ways a mirror of the wider culture also limned in the first chapter. Studying Steinbeck, Gold, and their numerous contemporaries, it examines the ambivalence surrounding their depictions of the female breadwinner and her submergence in the saintly—or carnally flawed—mother. Chapter 3 continues this scrutiny by contrasting masculine mother myths with the countervisions of three of the era's foremost radical novelists: Olsen, Meridel Le Sueur, and Smedley. In fiction likening paid female toil to overworked motherhood, these women revise the proletarian family by challenging the era's orthodoxies about housework and women's work alike.

Chapters 4 through 6 unveil a trio of further orthodoxies—romance-obsessed emotionalism, flawed militance, and guilt-ridden professionalism—that in crucial ways informed the negative construction of wage-earning women. The fourth chapter, considering a variety of male and female authors, from left-embracing to mass market, seen in romantic femininity a trope of working womanhood both validated and undercut by the narratives of women workers and the novels of Fannie Hurst, Zora Neale Hurston, and many others. Chapter 5, scanning the political novel, analyzes fictions of erasable militance: the novels of the important though failed Gastonia textile strike of 1929. Placing feminine and, to a greater extent, masculine novels' emphasis on Gastonia as male protest within the context of the mill women's actual role, it asks whose strike Gastonia really was. Finally, Chapter 6 looks at a host of novels by those from Tess Slesinger to Sinclair Lewis about more privileged, though no less embattled, women at work and applies to these works the surprisingly limited ideological alternatives embodied by the era's foremost female professionals, the New Deal's "social motherly" cabinet member, Frances Perkins, and the "New Womanly" international journalist, Dorothy Thompson. Neither provided the professional ballast needed by the remorseful (or culpable) careerists who are their fictive counterparts.

Although my method is selective rather than exhaustive, the texts chosen certainly reflect the varieties of public rhetoric that period writers employed to describe women wage earners. Throughout the book, the argument is that, whether by fervently left-wing authors, vaguely socialistic ones with more popular appeal, conservative apologists of the home, or best-selling explicators of the stagnating blue-collar and ambitious white-collar girl, fiction reflected the era's conflict between traditional expectations and the realities of feminine economic desperation, between the still-potent ideology of woman's separate sphere and her new roles as self-supporting or family breadwinner, whether by inclination or default.

Well over twenty years ago the scholar of literary naturalism Charles Child Walcutt reminded me that criticism should carry its own baggage. My valise is filled with details for those less conversant with the many forgotten texts under scrutiny, including, where relevant, their predecessors in the decades before the Depression. Included as well are works that, for a variety of reasons, relegate working women to the shadows of a subplot. Read carefully, texts passing over woman's job place identity become as important as those acknowledging it.

My bags are also packed with information less common to literary critiques. In the Depression's massive account of itself, I contend, novels need not be cordoned off from federal surveys, job seekers' letters, or women's work autobiographies, although distinctions, particularly between art and social document, are imperative. Because I read fictive texts as powerfully responsive to the Depression Era debate on women's labor, each chapter, especially the opening one, includes a substantial historical section and extensive notes in an effort to aid the reader. Whether it is a data-filled recounting of the resentments women workers caused and felt in mainstream and leftist cultures, a summary of the period's debate on women's labor fiction versus the "authentic" proletarian novel, or a chronicle of one of the foremost examples of working-class feminine militance, each chapter layers an analysis of the working heroine, from Mike Gold to Margaret Mitchell, with a study of how her real-life counterparts rebelled against or succumbed to the misogynistic laboring (or writing) environment of the 1930s. I thus attempt to contribute to the current reevaluation of 1930s writers; to make visible that host of feminine laboring personae often obscured by historians and critics; to synthesize masculinist and feminist critiques of both female and male authors; and to clarify the contesting ideologies of womanhood that shaped the actual and invented daughters of the Great Depression.

Daughters of the Great Depression

Chapter One

OLD WHINE, NEW BATTLES: MEN'S NEEDS, WOMEN'S JOBS

Edward Hopper, *Tables for Ladies,* on the isolation of the female workplace, 1930.
Metropolitan Museum of Art, George A. Hearn Fund (31.62).

After a while the faces of the watching men lost their bemused perplexity and became
hard and angry and resistant. Then the women knew that they were safe.
—John Steinbeck, *The Grapes of Wrath* (1939)

"[The job] means . . . that I can look people in the eye because I'm not on a dole. . . .
It isn't like relief. Being on relief just breaks me all up."
—"Florence B.," Minnesota WPA worker, 1941

"Oh, all the girls I knew worked."
—Man who worked as a bank clerk in the 1930s

The onset of the Great Depression ended the female job mobility
that accompanied or replaced women's aspirations in the 1920s. A
decades-old debate about the propriety of woman at work resurfaced, taking on a new form occasioned by the historical moment. That
debate affected and was affected by makers of fiction, from the left-wing
novelist hoping to rouse people to militance, to the historical romancer
who took their minds off their troubles. Whatever their literary or political stripe, and whether they mirrored, actively interpreted, or reshaped
that debate, these writers inevitably contributed to the cultural scrutiny
of Depression Era womanhood, in or out of the workplace. Perhaps more
than ever before in American fiction, the novel and short story became
mouthpieces for the economic and political concerns of their day. This is
not to deny that authors of the 1930s imposed artistic order upon social
themes. Rather, it is to argue that the configuration they imposed on
historical materials reinforced a disturbingly regressive perception of the
feminine role. Whether consciously or not, writers of various political
persuasions subjected the daughters of the Great Depression to a trial
that the men of the era, though prey to joblessness, economic insecurity,
and their attendant miseries, did not have to endure: the defense of the
right to waged work.

How the women and work controversy took shape in the years before
the Depression, the early working-girl novels it engendered, and its im-
print on Women's Bureau surveyors, women's magazine pundits, First
Lady Eleanor Roosevelt, CIO trade unionists, *Daily Worker* columnists,
and novelists as divergent as John Steinbeck, Erskine Caldwell, and Agnes
Smedley are the subjects of this chapter.

The Debate on Women's Labor

Americans had engaged in a lengthy and impassioned debate on women in the workplace well before the anxieties of the Great Depression rekindled the nation's interest in the subject and gave it a new urgency. From the time women entered industry en masse in the 1890s until well past World War I, when the growing numbers of "white-collar girls" gained relative acceptance for female wage earners, the controversy over feminine labor outside the domestic, or "natural," sphere informed low- to highbrow fiction, mass-circulation magazines and newspapers, and a wealth of reformist exposés and traditionalist studies. For more than three decades, advocates wrangled with critics over the social, moral, and physiological consequences of what one incensed foe, voicing a widespread prejudice, termed female wage earners' "warfare on home life."[1]

Such hostile observers saw not the defeated legions of underpaid females who typically toiled at dead-end jobs but an army of immigrants and first-generation invaders who threatened cherished notions of woman's role and, by their very presence in the male world of industrial work, courted immorality. American daughters, entrants in the burgeoning sales world and the newly feminized arena of the business office, also generated alarm, even if, as many in a nativist era agreed, these homegrown products were more likely than the Yettas, Rosas, and Kittys to evade corruption by seductive bosses and co-workers. Yet, at least to their conservative detractors, all wage-earning women, whether in sales or clerical work, in the ill-paid sweatshop, manufacturing, and lesser service jobs that made up the bulk of female employment, or even, in rare cases, the professions, implicitly challenged notions of feminine moral purity and the companion ideal of family-as-vocation.[2]

Debating the effect of the work site not only on the working woman's morality but also on her dress, diet, companions, after-hours activities, and reproductive abilities, her defenders and attackers warred with each other everywhere from widely read establishment periodicals to liberal journals to government surveys to mainstream and iconoclastic fiction. The working woman's reform-minded befrienders in literary and non-literary circles, though ambivalent themselves about her moral purity, pointed to the economic conditions that had driven her out to work in the first place. Some even defended her right to such limited economic freedom as her wages could provide before, or in the absence of, marriage.

Despite their belief in the division between marriage and work, these defenders, like their successors during the Depression Era, emphasized that for many women, particularly those who were poor and unwed—recent immigrants and their daughters or southern blacks and their migrant counterparts in the northern cities—work was a necessity. More enlightened advocates, by the 1920s most notably those connected with the recently founded Women's Bureau of the Labor Department, did their best to explode the "pin money theory" that a woman earned only to buy frivolities or, at best, to supplement an already adequate family income.[3] One veteran of the wage-earning world, Elizabeth Sears, asked: "What reasonable person will believe that a girl will crowd to work every morning, rain or shine, because she wants extra pin-money that she has no time to spend?"[4] It was a question that working-girl fiction before the Depression took seriously.

Early Working-Girl Fiction: From Sympathy to Empowerment

Writing in 1903 of her undercover work in a Pittsburgh bottling factory, the investigator Bessie Van Vorst summarized her experience: "Oh! . . . the never-ending supply of work to be begun and finished, begun and finished!"[5] Her sister-in-law Marie was one of several writers to echo that plaint in fiction. She created in the title character of *Amanda of the Mill* (1904) a composite portrait of the southern farm women who gave up their youth to the dusty air of the local textile mills. The Van Vorsts were writing in the social scientific spirit of the Progressive Era (1907–17) surveys, as were muckraking novelists of two landmark events in female labor history, the 1910–11 New York City shirtwaist strike, known as the Uprising of the 20,000, and the woman-fueled Lawrence, Massachusetts, textile strike of 1912. Novelists as socialistic as the onetime organizer Theresa Malkiel, who covered the shirtwaist strike for the *New York Call*, rebutted conservatives like American author Winston Churchill, in whose disapproving version of the strike the eyes of the female pickets "glittered like the points of daggers."[6] Malkiel joined James Oppenheim, Arthur Bullard, and other Socialists who demystified labor agitation for middlebrow audiences by featuring firebrand working girls in their novels and muckraking the deplorable conditions under which so many labored.

These early imaginers inaugurated a movement from sympathy (or censure) to admiration, from validation to empowerment. By the opening years of the new century, even so *grande* a literary dame as Edith Wharton paid attention to the woman worker, though with far less sympathy than she held for an aristocrat fallen to the working class. Joining a host of now-forgotten tenement, social protest, and quasi-feminist authors, Wharton, Theodore Dreiser, and O. Henry paved the way for the "upward mobility" writers of the 1920s, who defended the working girl as a valid subject for fiction by charting her romantic vicissitudes, if not her workplace relations.

As writers with some claim to art and much to popular attention, they had forged a tradition of sorts by the 1920s. Some, like outspoken Anzia Yezierska's immigrant protagonists, trumpeted the female right "to make myself for a person,"[7] though at the cost of renouncing workplace solidarity and embracing an "every girl for herself" philosophy. By now, too, American literature was offering the autonomy novels of Sinclair Lewis and Edna Ferber and the laments for dependence by Fannie Hurst. The point was largely to extract the working-class woman from her job rather than examine her in it. But best-selling authors from Ferber in her avidly read Emma McChesney stories, to Lewis in his novel of an astute office girl who carves out a real estate success, *The Job* (1917) (his Carol Kennicott in *Main Street* [1920] would not be as fortunate), joined Yezierska in celebrating economic ascension, propelling heroines from genteel homes (or uncouth sweatshops) to teaching (*Hungry Hearts* [1920]), or better still, their own businesses (*Salome of the Tenements* [1923]). Except for the rare novel like the socialist Elias Tobenkin's *The Road* (1922), in which, significantly, he can reward his politically radical trade union heroine in her search for a true labor collective only by sending her to live and work in the Soviet Union, the working woman in American fiction was depicted in terms of her aspiration to escape, not her desire to remain in her class and improve its lot. But what she lacked in social consciousness, she made up for in revelation of social change.[8]

By the mid-1920s, as a *New York Times* headline ungraciously phrased it, women had "invaded" nearly all occupations.[9] Indeed, in her survey of women's occupations, one less dedicated than the *Times* to the status quo, the anticapitalist critic Grace Hutchins found that by the beginning of the 1930s, women were employed in all but thirty of over five hundred occupation groups.[10] In fiction, even so genteel an idolator of the well-bred small-town girl as Booth Tarkington registered the social change: his eponymous 1921 heroine Alice Adams, disappointed in her hopes for economic security through marriage, faces facts and enters Frincke's Business College with the knowledge that doing so would ensure her livelihood. Such certainty the Great Depression would soon call into doubt.

Men's Needs, Women's Jobs: The New Austerity

By 1930, the national focus was on men's unemployment—two to three times that of women's during most, though not the last, of the Depression years—and not on women's job sufferings or joblessness.[11] Future labor secretary Frances Perkins, criticized by Women's Bureau chief Mary Anderson for her inattention to jobless women, was resuscitating the largely mythic pin-money worker and finding the wage-earning wife particularly culpable.[12] There was so much emphasis on male breadwinners that Lorena Hickok, FERA (Federal Emergency Relief Administration, 1933–35) czar Harry Hopkins's New Deal troubleshooter, complained as she toured the country investigating the administration of relief that jobless (single) women were "discards . . . just managing to keep alive."[13] Alluding to what she termed "the usual difficulty, wangling jobs for women" (145), she lamented that businessmen, for example, "won't believe there are any women who are absolutely self-supporting" (122), an idea on which period fiction would ring many changes.

Yet women's sufferings as the Depression set in were real enough. In only five industries surveyed by the Women's Bureau were white women making more than $18 per week at a time when a jersey dress cost $5 and a winter coat cost $40 (Kennedy, 167). The Department of Labor Women's Bureau was instituted to oversee wages and conditions in the feminine workplace. In a 1937 survey of women who worked "by the piece, by the hour, or by the week," the bureau found that more than two and one-half million women were out of work or underemployed; other estimates reached as high as four million (Hutchins, 181).[14] One-fifth of all white women workers still worked in factories and one-third as domestics; these occupations came notoriously short of providing a living wage. Many no doubt would have recognized themselves in this description of hotel work from a letter to Mrs. Roosevelt: "We are not fighting for a 30 hour week, we are breaking in health under 10 to 12 hours a day of fast hard work in a hot hot kitchen . . . and only beg for 8 hours [a day] and one day to lie in bed, and rest."[15]

Black women fared even worse: nine out of ten toiled as underpaid agricultural laborers, and two-thirds of domestic servants were black. Less than one-tenth of all black wage-earning women worked in manufacturing in the most unsavory jobs the meatpacking, cigar and cigarette, and textile industries, among others, had to supply.[16]

Professional women paid a price, too. Of the three million in business, the professions, nursing, social work, and teaching, many were simply in nonfactory jobs, or, at best, quasi-professional fields.[17] Nor were these fields easy to enter. In 1934 well-connected graduates of the Seven Sisters colleges took almost a year to find jobs, most in the traditional fields of education and social welfare, others in sales and clerical work, although, for these collegians at least, the latter included office positions that sometimes paid well (Ware, 67). Yet the very fact that a Smith or Vassar graduate sought such work suggests that clerical and sales posts gained at the cost of professional ones. What one historian of the family calls the "loss of status" was characteristic of aspiring women professionals.[18] It was a making-do situation that the novelist Tess Slesinger's rueful young heroines—"I signed thirty-seven curt letters Adolph Worthington and I crossed the t at thirty-seven different angles—"[19] dramatized well. Women were urged to view the office as an extension of home duties: she who wished to retain her job did well to meet the business needs of her employer-mate. In this new climate, it was not surprising to read a *New York Times* article headlined "Women Held Best Suited for Monotonous Jobs."[20] Yet the more seasoned—or the married—discovered, in the words of a Federation of Business and Professional Women survey, that "no woman, however trained and affluent, [was] secure against the avalanche of unemployment" (qtd. Ware 71).

Because of the varied pressures and the lack of aid for business and professional women from New Deal legislation, their proportion declined by the end of the Depression to a level hardly higher than it had been twenty years earlier. For their jobless sisters, from professors to domestics, as for the bulk of female workers, who, despite the gains of the 1920s, still congregated in low-level jobs, by the early 1930s, "the status of the woman . . . worker had reached a nadir" (Woloch, 47). Their pay never equal to men's in the first place, they longed for a feminine new deal.

A New Deal for Women?

Some of the women whose job conditions and wages were substandard did profit to an extent under the National Industrial Recovery Act (NIRA) of 1933, for it established industry-wide codes that included provisions for wages and hours worked.[21] Nevertheless, as was true of all New Deal programs, the record on women was uneven. Even under the NIRA codes (the voluntary guidelines declared unconstitutional by 1935), many employers found ways to avoid compliance. In the garment industry, with its long tradition of owners' strictures and workers' rebellion, in true sweatshop style learners and apprentices were fired before their NRA minimum was due, their places taken by newcomers.[22] From the violations that the ILGWU organizer Rose Pesotta found in operation among Mexican-American women in the dress factories of Los Angeles to those the watchdog journalist Amy Hewes heard of in interviews with northern seamstresses, the common sentiment was, as one woman lamented, "No matter how hard we worked, we couldn't make the code minimum of $2.60 a day."[23]

FERA field representative Lorena Hickok was outraged to find that a myriad of loopholes and "legalities" fenced in those in other "women's" work. When employing waitresses, "Childs wrote their own [NRA] code" for women's twenty-five-cents-an-hour, three-day-a-week jobs, the restaurant chain spokesmen "calmly" informed her (350). Needless to say, if the NRA condoned wage differentials for white men and women and failed to regulate code violations in the white feminine workplace, black women, 90 percent of whom worked in occupations not covered by the NRA codes or their more permanent successor, the Fair Labor Standards Act, were even worse served.[24] After 1937, when the rise of the CIO and the passage of the Wagner Act had put teeth into collective bargaining, as James R. Green observes in *The World of the Worker* (1980), "the CIO generally failed to halt patterns of discrimination against women in industry. . . . The new unions mobilized women . . . but they did not fight to change [their] status in the industries they organized."[25] Job categories remained gender-defined.

Government reluctance to give women equal access to work relief or equitable wages or to depart from prescribed modes of allotting work based on gender suggested what one vocal critic of the New Deal policies toward women termed the dubious "theory that in times of stress paid jobs belonged, by right, to men" (Weed, 179). Thus the bulk of relief work given to women merely replicated their home functions. Representative indeed was the title character of the roving reporter Martha Gellhorn's short story "Mrs. Maddison Makes Both Ends Meet" (1936), who mended in a southern warehouse at fifteen cents an hour, repaired old garments, or sewed new ones from surplus materials (Ware, 40).

Even so ardent an advocate of women's right to work relief as Eleanor Roosevelt called on women to use the Depression "to assert traditional feminine strengths, both as inspirations in the home and activists in public life" (Woloch, 435). She believed in work relief for poor women, but like many of the New Deal women activists whose careers she advanced, she "assumed most [women] wanted, and ought to concentrate on, homemaking and child rearing" (Cohen, 337).[26] She and those like Ellen Woodward, responsible for allocating jobs to women under the FERA and Civil Works Administration (CWA), in large part thought in terms of the traditional talents of women—sewing was the relief job most often suggested—not about providing vocational training or advancement, much less challenging sex segregation in the workplace.

It is all the more ironic that the women least helped by either New Deal measures or NRA codes were household workers, who went largely unnoticed by New Deal policymakers. Even the Works Progress Administration (WPA) gave no wages to women training as housekeepers, despite a general policy of paying trainees (Foner, 293). Both in federal programs and society in general, the treatment accorded them revealed that despite the pronouncements of back-to-the-home pundits, women's work—never accorded the status of men's—was less respected than other waged work when its locus was the home. On an unconscious level, it was easy to conflate women in domestic service with homemakers. But far from raising the respect given women "at home," this linkage lowered it. Race again exacerbated misogynist attitudes. One businessmen's group interviewed by Lorena Hickok "thought that all [Negro] women who refused to take living-in housemaid jobs at $3 a week should be cut off relief" (350). Whether the domestic worker was black or white, she was affected by the culture's minimizing attitude toward housework, an attitude exploitative women employers too often embraced.[27]

The Old Deal: Invisible Women

Although in her study of 1930s womanhood Lois Scharf remarks that the well-known magazines of the day addressed "all developments related to women and work" (218), elsewhere she acknowledges that "the needs of unemployed and underemployed women received much less attention and publicity than those of men" (120). It was far more common for the liberal *Nation* or *Forum* or, to a lesser extent, the genteel but socially conscious *Scribner's, Atlantic Monthly,* and *Harper's* to run pieces on the woman as supplemental rather than essential breadwinner or to take aim at married women workers by invoking the pin-money theory. Whereas in the 1890s, when working women first entered the workplace en masse, the *Forum* ran studies with such titles as "The Condition of Wage-Earning Women," by the mid-1930s, it was featuring articles like "Pin-Money Slaves," in which the author deplored the married female who forsook family responsibilities for a little extra cash and "call[ed] upon our job-bent women to . . . be true ladies of leisure, cultivating the graces of civilization." [28] To the author of another *Forum* piece, "You May Have My Job: A Feminist Discovers Her Home," not only did work outside the home threaten to defeminize by making women "narrow, hard, [and] efficiency bitten," but it distracted them from the lesson of True Womanhood: that children "are her immortality." [29] A rare magazine piece on factory women, "Working Girl" (1936), in which the narrator moves from tobacco sweatshop to white-collar sector, was an upward mobility tale in the tradition of Dorothy Richardson's 1905 classic *The Long Day: The Story of a New York Working Girl* and the Edna Ferber stories of the 1910s and 1920s; it hardly reflected the realities of the Depression Era. [30]

The women's magazines, whose attention had always been solidly focused on the satisfactions of middle-class domesticity, were even more removed from the financial plight of less affluent women. On occasion, *Good Housekeeping* and *Ladies' Home Journal* defended married women's work on general principles (Scharf, 59), but the reader of these wide-circulation periodicals might go for months without coming across any reference to feminine hard times. Tess Slesinger, who would soon publish her novel *The Unpossessed* on "the times in which [women] are living" [31] to counter the "Victorian Lady-Book" (125) world of the *Journal* and its ilk, remarked that, in their pages, "problems of national politics and economics do not exist" (127). In their rare allusions to the Depression, mostly in suggesting cost-trimming recipes, these periodicals collaborated in the trivialization of women's economic difficulties. A journal like *Independent Woman*, a magazine for the female business professional, obviously took the subject of work in the upper reaches of the job world far more seriously. But like so many other publications that were not allied to unions, the Left, or the Women's Bureau, it hardly noticed the blue-collar woman. On occasion the magazine reviewed a novel on department store workers, a vocation on the margins of the white-collar world. Yet the reviewer sanitized the menial jobs in a novel like Leane Zugsmith's *A Time to Remember* (1936) and praised the book as "pleasurable," completely sidestepping the militance of the plot.[32]

Outside the cloistered bourgeois world of *Good Housekeeping*, the *Ladies' Home Journal*, *McCall's*, and even *Collier's*, some journals were receptive to narratives of feminine job trials, but the focus was on the articulate college-educated woman. "How It Feels," in a 1932 issue of the professional journal *Survey*, was authored by a social worker; "The Return of the Lady" concerned the difficulties of professional women; and a 1934 *Scribner's* plaint, "We Live on Relief," by a music teacher who with her orchestra conductor husband was barely scraping by on relief, was a representative title.[33] Such pieces seemed to interest the public at large as much as those that emphasized male economic woes. Although including white-collar women in the lower echelon of female professionals does make the spate of articles and books about the difficulties of professional women more relevant, the fact remains that the roughly five million women in industry (Foner, 299), not including those in domestic work, received short shrift.

In trying to account for the invisibility in the media of jobless females, Meridel Le Sueur, whose fiction would expand on her insights, explained: "You don't see women in bread lines. . . . A woman, ten to one, will starve alone in a hall bedroom until she is thrown out, and then she will sleep alone in some alley."[34] To the editors of the *New York Times*, women were an afterthought. One representative headline declaimed "[City] Finds Homeless Men Face Hard Winter." Only one sentence in the article beneath it alluded to the female homeless. A similar inattentiveness characterized the writings of sociologists. More than 140,000 homeless girls were wandering from city to city (Parkhurst, 744), but even the author of *Boy and Girl Tramps of America* minimized that number.[35] Although the title of an important study, *Citizens Without Work* (1940), was gender-free, the first sentence of the preface describes the book as a companion volume to *The Unemployed Man,* published seven years earlier.[36]

If many studies assumed unemployment was a masculine problem, women's job difficulties were compounded because less percipient observers thought women were taking male breadwinners' jobs. The author of "Will Women Lose Jobs?" worried that to "simply fire the women, and hire the men" would constitute "the greatest assault on women's rights in two decades."[37] It is true that at the beginning of the Depression women worked either in industries less affected by the job shortage or in routinized mechanical tasks men would not take. Thus James T. Farrell's hapless Studs Lonigan, scanning the Chicago papers in the early 1930s, finds more jobs for women than men. Studs resents the female clerical workers he finds in outer offices when he goes to apply for selling jobs, but like many of his real-life counterparts he never considers doing that work himself. Still, the logic of those who reminded Americans that "a coal miner or steel worker cannot very well fill the jobs of our nursemaids, cleaning women, or the factory and clerical occupations now occupied by women" (qtd. Ware, 28) did little to abate male hostility to female "competitors."

Assembly Line and Picket Line

The era's male anger against female job competitors was articulated by the jobless Jim Brogan in the 1935 Detroit auto industry novel *Conveyor:* "What chance had he of getting a job? There were thousands of men—and women too—just praying for a job . . . guys from Kentucky and Tennessee. . . . And them women, too."[38] In fact, more women worked in automobile factories than in any other industry in Detroit; but as in much of the country, they took jobs traditionally assigned to their sex: sewing upholstery and tedious assembly-line work like making spark plugs. Sometimes they took over jobs previously held by men, but they invariably received less pay. Far more common was the introduction of a new technology that, as in the cigar and cigarette industry, ushered in simpler machine operations and far lower wage rates, alienating male workers from such employment.[39]

The wife of *Conveyor*'s Jim Brogan, Marie, does metal stamping, earning $1.98 for a ten-hour day—not the fairly well-paid body work her husband has been unable to secure. Too, Marie has returned to the workplace to help the family, which only increases Brogan's ire that she is abandoning her "duty" (138–39), a feeling many of his real-life counterparts may have shared. Her anxiety that the family could not survive on the newly reemployed husband's meager earnings, the novel intones, has destroyed the family unit. To restore the fundamental rightness of things, at novel's end Marie, chastised for her insurrection, proves unable to summon the strength for her factory job. She deserts Jim, who goes off to help organize for the United Auto Workers.

The message of *Conveyor* and a plethora of 1930s strike novels notwithstanding, women in industry had engaged in a fair amount of organizing action throughout the nation by the middle of the decade. Before the drives of the mid-decade, spearheaded by the American Federation of Labor (AFL) breakaway group, the CIO, more women workers were members of the YWCA than of unions affiliated with the AFL (Hutchins, 260). Yet even in those early years, women frequently made up in determination what they lacked in numbers.[40] From 1929 to 1933, needle trades workers "carried on their militant tradition on the picket lines" (Hutchins, 247), culminating in 1933, in a Depression Era version of the 1911 Uprising of the 20,000, in a strike of sixty thousand New York City dressmakers, most of them women, at the management's busiest time of the year (Foner, 282). It was the prelude to a nationwide drive in 1934 (and, under the CIO aegis, in 1937) to organize dress shops, the majority of whose workers were unskilled females. Indeed, the pre-CIO years saw labor unrest, to choose from a wealth of examples, among Pennsylvania garment workers, St. Louis laundresses and nut factory workers— both black and white—and women in midwestern hosiery mills (Scharf, 118). Women employees played a courageous part in the "men's strikes" in the auto trades from the early 1930s onward. Often among the most determined of the picketers, they were highly visible in the wave of important—though, like most textile strikes, unsuccessful—1934 strikes in states such as Rhode Island, Pennsylvania, and North Carolina and apparently, noted the *New York Times* fearfully of the southern women, were "prepared to stop at nothing to gain their objectives."[41]

By the CIO years, women strikers even in the heavy industries—auto, steel, rubber, mining—were a fixture on the labor landscape.[42] Still, in the years before the founding of the CIO, AFL affiliates, craft-based unions representing the skilled trades (McElvaine, 184), excluded women or discouraged them from joining, often with the tacit blessing of union wives threatened by the idea of female workers. The female strikers in the largely unorganized textile trades who led the charge at Gastonia in a futile bid for AFL support unsuccessfully called on it to widen its scope to include southern labor (Foner, 230). AFL leaders voiced a similar opposition to southern women attending a summer school for women workers to bring them into the labor movement, accusing a small group of Alabama women garment workers in 1935 of being "radicals and agitators."[43] Many in the AFL advocated that married women "should be discriminated against in hiring" (qtd. Woloch, 441). They shrugged off the charge of one 1933 convention delegate from an affiliated women's organization that the AFL was patently unfair to the over five million women eligible to be union members (Hutchins, 261).

Women were better served by the newly emerging Committee on (and by 1937, Congress of) Industrial Organizations, born in a breakaway spirit at a 1935 AFL convention. At the decade's end, largely owing to CIO organizing work, there were 800,000 women in unions, a 300 percent increase over ten years earlier, though they were less than 10 percent of all women workers (Ware, 42). Certainly the two clothing trades leaders represented industries in which substantial numbers of women labored; during the mid-1930s in the textile industry alone, almost 40 percent, or 420,000 workers, were female.[44] The Communist Party (CP), in service to its dual union philosophy, sent female organizers like the National Textile Workers Union (NTWU) leader Ann Burlak on drives and the party member and "colonizer" Stella Nowicki to the Chicago meatpacking factories. Nonparty women such as Dorothy Bellanca of the Amalgamated Clothing Workers (ACW) were active in most of the major battles for women textile workers in the 1930s.

Although the trade union movement gained momentum in part thanks to these women, many male colleagues opposed the idea of female organizers, as the reminiscences of those including lone ILGWU executive Rose Pesotta and meatpackers' local union officer Stella Nowicki attest.[45] Nor was the female labor leader the only one to experience discriminatory treatment by male colleagues.[46] The 1939 *CIO News* approvingly cited a male picketer protesting "girl's wages" who dressed in drag and carried signs reading "Restore Our Manhood" (Strom, 370). More important, CIO unions "continued the . . . AFL . . . tradition of setting lower wages for women's jobs than for men's jobs in their contracts" (Strom, 369). The dominant perception was that inside as well as outside the union movement, women were still thought of as transients in the labor force. They might be given protection, but they did not enjoy the same treatment or consideration as men.

The Communist Party's Girls

In the Communist Party, in which during the Depression decade the percentage of female members rose considerably, women's concerns were again subordinated to a broader goal: the revolutionary struggle for social justice for the working class and against fascism. The party maverick Mary Inman called male ideologues to task for failing to recognize women's special oppression and urged them to fight both for socialism and for women but, significantly, the party refused to publish her manuscript, and she eventually broke with it.[47] In fact, both Communist ideology and practice opposed feminism, fundamentally on the ground that it "drew working-class women away from their male working-class allies and into the orbit of bourgeois women."[48] Thus one female contributor to *Party Organizer,* a journal for party functionaries, typically defined her task as building socialism in a proletarian homeland with women as equal members of society.[49] There "were so many things to work for," commented "red" missionary Stella Nowicki, "they couldn't worry about these things in relation to women" (Lynd and Lynd, 84). Tillie Olsen was more generous when she remarked, in her coverage of the 1934 San Francisco general strike, that the women were with the men to the finish.[50]

Issues related to working-class women to a lesser extent concerned the *Daily Worker* itself, as well as party organs such as the *Labor Defender,* published by the CP's legal arm, the International Labor Defense.[51] That magazine used articles on the hunger striker Edith Berkman, who was arrested for labor agitation in the textile trades, in its plea for women to work along with men in the class struggle.[52] Nor can it be denied that the party served as a forum for the discussion of women's issues such as day care and birth control, that both white and black women were promoted to positions of leadership,[53] or that the party was among the most inventive in using working-class women, whether workers or housewives, in a variety of protest activities from eviction resistance and relief bureau sit-ins to rent strikes. In the words of one modern student of the subject, however, if "the experience of Party membership, of organizing women's auxiliaries, consumer boycotts, and picket lines gave many a female Communist the organizing experience and self-respect she needed to become an independent woman . . . standing up for women, working with women, or becoming independent of men was not the same as possessing a feminist consciousness" (Strom, 368). Furthermore, the party press highlighted women's auxiliaries, most of which were dedicated to buttressing male unions or male-dominated heavy industries, rather than women's unions. Though the CP routinely lamented the plight of jobless women, it both channeled its energies into largely masculine industries (Dixler, 209) and refrained from criticizing the CIO's exclusionary policies. Communists in the labor movement, then, were more concerned with gaining power in men's unions than in empowering women. Particularly during the Popular Front period (1936–39), when the party leadership was trying to make it more accessible to average Americans, it stressed the value of traditional femininity, and Communists increasingly "appealed to women in their roles as wives, housekeepers, and mothers, rather than as people in their own right" (Dixler, ii).[54]

The idea of subordination, whether in the party hierarchy, in the party-influenced trade union, or as a home-front party loyalist whose goals in no way diverged from her working-class mate's, bespoke the imposition of a non- or secondary work identity on women. From the guidance-craving girl-wives and docile country helpmeets of *This Is Your Day* (1937), Edward Newhouse's novel of a male party organizer, to the real-life party wife (ironically, a common-law one) Peggy Dennis, author of the retrospective *Autobiography of an American Communist* (1977), women were foot soldiers, never officers. Because the party rejected out of hand the iconoclast Mary Inman's argument that working-class men had much the same control over their wives as did men in any other class, married women were essentially instructed to take their orders from men. This is not to equate party ideology with the back-to-the-home pronouncements of the dominant culture. The party never opposed women working or issued ominous warnings about women stealing jobs from male breadwinners. Nor did it openly discriminate between married and single women workers. But as in society as a whole, there seemed to be a separate agenda for married women, workers or not, and a motherly one at that.[55]

Bringing It All Back Home: Depression Era Fiction

Often cited by analysts of the time as a model for strengthening the home in time of national need, Ma Joad in the hugely popular *Grapes of Wrath* (1939) is instructive.[56] Modern interpreters have ascribed the book's best-seller status to the fact that, although the central character takes up a vaguely defined organizing mission, unlike the host of avowedly pro-letarian fiction the book "steers clear of any international revolutionary implications" by "retreat[ing] from precise political solutions."[57] By offering the plight of the Okies as an "ecological catastrophe" (Cook, 160–61) and following a poor white family in its struggles to maintain itself, the novel mirrors the period's concern for the difficulties of the rural "forgotten man" who is disfranchised by the vast, impersonal forces of nature and economics. In service to this naturalistic task, it demonstrates the re-assuring gender division challenged by working women in real life and some women writers in defiance of the party line. Much has been made of "supermother" Ma Joad's manly strength; one period critic proclaimed that she is the "best man of the lot."[58] But Sylvia Jenkins Cook rightly points out that Ma is fully aware that hers is an "emergency role" (180). The Okie matriarch passes on to her oldest girl her own belief in deferring to male authority. She not only reminds Rose of Sharon that her husband would be right to strike the young (and pregnant) woman to keep her in line—"You got it comin'" (Steinbeck, 345)—but she twice agrees with an incensed though increasingly ineffectual Pa Joad that she deserves a whipping for undermining his authority. On only one occasion, offered as unusual, is she pictured, with her younger children, working in the California peach fields, hardly a sharing of the breadwinning role with the Joad men. Because this brief stint in the fields interrupts what she and Steinbeck perceive as her real duties, her only response to her picker's day is to soothe the children who complain they are tired. What may appear as Ma's much-discussed stoicism is also a signal that her waged work, and presumably that of Okie and Arkie womenfolk in general, in no way defines her identity; it is as if the day in the fields never occurred.

Apart from an ambiguous reference or two to women alongside the men waiting for pay (their own? their men's?) from a day's work in the fields, the novel's few other references to female farm workers underscore the unnaturalness of the womanly wage earner. Near the end of the tale, a very pregnant Rose of Sharon toils in a cotton field for a day and quickly becomes ill for defying biology. The other woman noted, in an interchapter segment featuring a salacious anecdote that migrant workers tell one another, is a laughable type from "back home" whose wayward habits are legendary. But she is "a good picker" (Steinbeck, 521), a linkage that suggests a woman habitually out in the fields goes to the bad by shunning the domesticity of a Ma Joad.

The Grapes of Wrath appeared at a time when a substantial number of the 750,000 agrarian women (the majority of them tenants' and sharecroppers' wives) and of the more than 170,000 females classed as wage-earning farm laborers (Hutchins, 61) had relocated to places within their home state or territory or, as did the Joad clan, had left the South and Southwest altogether.[59] Often enough, the southern women who accompanied their men from farm to town also joined them, for less pay, on the textile mill shop floor. At the Manville-Jenckes factory in notorious Gastonia, North Carolina, for instance, men were given employment only on the condition that their wives worked (Foner, 232). The female members of Dust Bowl families, though following a wider migrant path, were also transformed into laborers with their husbands. The handbill inspiring the Joads to pick oranges and peaches in California may have read "men needed" (Steinbeck, 252), a refrain reiterated when, later in the novel, the bosses' men come to migrant camps asking, "You men want to work?" (337). But the Labor Department's Women's Bureau discovered a different truth.

Investigators found it common for whole families to follow the crops, working together in fields and orchards on the Pacific coast and in the Washington apple and pear orchards, bureau chief Mary Anderson learned. Women were even paid at the same rate for the same work,[60] a practice the Joad men, seeking work in the fruit fields and canneries of the Santa Clara Valley, certainly would have resented despite their poverty. Continuing "on the trail of the migrant," the title of one of her articles, Anderson also observed that in addition to migrant worker-wives or companions, there were numbers of single "women casuals," who returned home at the close of the season or drifted around as fruit tramps, with "no address other than the immediate one" (776–77). Furthermore, in contrast to the male militants of Steinbeck's scenario, two distinct groups of female migrant fruit workers, Mexican and Filipino women, acted as protesters and looked up to party-affiliated women organizers like Dorothy Ray Healey and Caroline Decker. Decker inspired no less a talent than Langston Hughes to write a play on her heroism, *Blood on the Fields* (1934), concerning an important 1933 strike engineered by the leftist California Cannery and Agricultural Workers Union (CAWU) and involving eighteen thousand farmworkers (Hutchins, 69, 272). In 1934, at the first CAWU convention, women were included in a platform that advocated equal pay for workers regardless of gender. At later conventions, women labor organizers, including Latinas, launched campaigns aimed at female and other minority field and cannery workers.[61]

Although no artist can be faulted for altering reality, William Stott echoes an enduring sentiment in calling Steinbeck's "the thirties' novel most closely related to documentary."[62] Furthermore, Steinbeck's own letters on his data gathering at the California Okie camps attest to a determination to reproduce in fiction what his colleague Ernest Hemingway called "things as they are."[63] For his own reasons, Steinbeck evades a truth evident to anyone touring the camps. He erases women field workers from his 1930s correspondence and relegates them to the labor shadows in both his California strike novel *In Dubious Battle* (1936) and in *The Grapes of Wrath*.

A similar evasiveness characterized the fiction of his contemporary Erskine Caldwell. In the photo-narrative *You Have Seen Their Faces* (1937), on which he collaborated with his photographer-wife Margaret Bourke-White, Caldwell included references to hard-hit southern women sharecroppers; yet his fiction offers at best a fretful response to women's work. His early novels concern those who chose to eke out a living in the Depression. In *God's Little Acre* (1933), they are starved Georgia sharecroppers and the disempowered Carolina mill strikers scornfully called "lintheads."[64] As a saga of family lust and revenge, *God's Little Acre* was as avidly read as it was castigated for eroticism and even unsuccessfully taken to court by the Society for the Suppression of Vice. Neither critics nor public failed to respond to Darling Jill and Griselda, the overripe women of the Walter family, the patriarchal farming clan that is the fictional center of the work. A cardboard femme fatale, the daughter, nubile, amoral Darling Jill, is ready to fornicate with a brother-in-law. "Take me, Will," this fantasy woman "beg[s]" her sister's husband. "Please, Will, right now" (56). Equally one-dimensional is the tantalizing Griselda, the Walter clan daughter-in-law, monogamous for the moment but casting a spell on the Walter brothers, whose lust for her erupts in murder and suicide.

In Caldwell's down-home reenactment of the Garden of Eden, woman's carnality, not men's, is the disruptive force. Her relation to work signifies a seduction and castration of the men whose energy is sapped by her presence in the workplace: "The men who worked in the mill looked tired and worn, but the girls were in love with the looms and spindles and the flying lint. The wild-eyed girls on the inside of the ivy-walled mill looked like potted plants in bloom" (69).

These "firm-bodied girls with eyes like morning glories" (69) are the spiritual descendants of Nathaniel Hawthorne's Rappaccini's daughter, serpents in a new poisonous garden, that of industry. A recent commentator has argued that the key to the puzzling passage above, one of the novel's few on mill work, is that "machinery replaces the earth as the dynamic and sustaining power equated with sexual energy." It is a "male rather than a female force," and it "exerts a strange power over the factory girls . . . so that they regard both the machines and the mill with a kind of passionate awe" (Cook, 73). Yet such a view does not fully account for Caldwell's negative associations with female mill work, a vocation viewed far more positively by real-life southern factory women. One of the few coherent thoughts sustained by the played-out matriarch in *Tobacco Road* (1932), published the year before *Acre,* was her wish that her young daughter Pearl follow daughter Lizzie Belle into the Augusta cotton mill and out of the bondage Lizzie could expect as a tenant farm wife. Touring Caldwell's home state of Georgia as a New Deal investigator, Margaret Hagood, the author of *Mothers of the South: Portraiture of the White Tenant Farm Woman* (1939), interviewed "Mollie." The woman had worked in a tobacco factory and exulted in making $20 a week in the late 1920s. It proved an idyllic period cut short by the demands of her sickly rural family and, too soon, marriage and the necessities of childbearing.[65]

Viewed in light of the thwarted aspirations of such women—so far from Caldwell's mill girls who prefer the machines to men as sexual surrogates—the above passage acquires clarity if read as a grudging acknowledgment of the feminine preference for waged work over the attentions of the unemployed mill men protesting harsh conditions. Resenting the sexual allure as much as the employed status of these girls, who, Caldwell writes pointedly, "never rebelled against the harder work, the stretching-out, or the cutting of pay," the male strikers subordinate their resentment of scabs to a defeated lust. They watch the energized women enter and leave the mill or walk the streets of the Valley town, their "breasts firm and erect" (Caldwell, *Acre,* 69).

In so eroticized a world, Caldwell metamorphoses the feminine preference for wages over subordination to workless men into a tool of seduction. On an economic level, women's scab wages wrongly ensure their independence at the cost of men's freedom; on a mythological one, these witchlike daughters of Eve thrive on the dust-filled environment that weakens the males, sinister proof that women threaten men's very existence.

Despite their differing attitudes toward female sexuality, both the creators of Darling Jill and Ma Joad embraced their decade's widespread conviction that women were intruders in the workplace. In her autobiographical novel *Daughter of Earth,* published in 1929 and reissued in a shorter form in 1935, the veteran journalist Agnes Smedley, by the height of the Depression well known for her dispatches on the Chinese Communist revolution, was one of the rare authors to offer an alternative view of the female role in the workplace. Superficially, *Daughter of Earth* shares characteristics of the feminine autonomy novel of the late 1910s and early 1920s. Marie Rogers climbs from rural poverty in 1890s Missouri to teaching in an isolated New Mexico schoolhouse to a foothold in the white-collar world. With her new stenographic skills—an advance on the drudgery of her mother's work as a laundress—she pays her way through a university in California and, finally, in New York City. To better herself, she has "buried [her] head in books and studied until [her] brain whirled."[66] But Marie's goal, unlike that of a Lewis or Ferber heroine, is not to gain a foothold in the upper reaches of the commercial workplace. Still in college at the onset of World War I, she embarks on pacifist speaking tours and brings the fervor of a devotee to the cause of Indian independence from British rule.

Because the lengthy final portion of the book detailing her anticolonial activities was omitted from the 1935 edition, it was her graphic presentation of the Rogers family's suffering on a Missouri farm and in a

Rockefeller-owned mining camp that gave the novel a renewed relevance for 1930s audiences. Smedley locates Marie's philosophy, "escape I determined to" (125), in a portrait of the difficulties sabotaging the father, an unskilled worker cheated by mining camp operators, and the mother, a washerwoman and boardinghouse keeper ground down by her alcoholic husband's desertions and brutalities and by her own ceaseless toil.

In a challenge to 1930s ideologies of women, Smedley repudiates the mothering ideal. Despite, or because of, the male-identified protagonist's quest for manly independence, it is the mother figure who is contemptuous—of her own child. Mrs. Rogers is a cruel antithesis of Ma Joad and lacks even the low-level maternal feeling of an Erskine Caldwell sharecropper's wife. She beats, taunts, and ridicules Marie and engages in an Oedipal struggle for the attentions of the seductive but elusive father. Observes the narrator, she only "talked to me as if we were friends . . . when my father was not there" (41). She is rarely tender, and then only when she is not afraid her child is her rival.

What Caldwell castigated and Steinbeck refused to consider, Smedley holds up as a model of feminine conduct: the woman on her own, doing work of her choosing, to escape both the mother's manipulations and her fate. Marie's repudiation of her early unhappy marriage and the abortions she preferred to mothering are offered as aspects of the struggle for autonomy, for separation from the naysaying mother. What the culture accepted as at best a necessary evil emerges as her own salvation.

Conclusion

Smedley, whose voice of opposition to the era's mother myths was fainter because she spent the Depression years outside the country (though in equally pinched circumstances), was a lone dissenter. Just as the public debate focused on what Ruth McKenney called the "phony problem,"[67] in fiction there was a parallel return to minimizing women workers. It is not surprising to find that attitude in the mega-selling *Gone with the Wind* (1936), in which feminine business acumen is allied with ruthlessness and the inability to love, or in author Viña Delmar's weeper, *Bad Girl* (1928), in which a working woman turned wife cannot understand why her depression increases the more she stays home alone. But the minimizing tradition informs even the proletarian novel, with its supposedly antiauthoritarian mission, and social fiction, which, though less critical of government, espoused a communal ethos. All of this fiction carried Victorian baggage. From John Steinbeck to the black novelist William Attaway (the chronicler of racial tensions in the Pittsburgh steel mills), to the Chicago James Joyce, James T. Farrell, to, despite the revisionist view of her, Meridel Le Sueur, women workers are subordinate in the times that tried only men's souls.

As the following chapters demonstrate, literary responses to women in the workplace were varied. Nevertheless, all the texts under scrutiny were preoccupied with—or, in the minority of dissenting voices, vexed by—woman as family or society nurturer rather than productive worker, a consoler rather than a producer, a helpmeet rather than an independent entity. Many fictions transformed women workers into literal or figurative mothers, who are moved to downplay their breadwinning role. Often writers grafted the mother onto the unlikely person of the prostitute or castigated any woman deemed "wayward" for her absence of maternal qualities. All of this suggested what modern critics have variously labeled a need for "social solace," a feeling of "lost . . . hope and authority" (Cook, 178), or a search for "new fathers."[68] Whatever the label, central to this quest is the impulse to minimize and restrict woman's nondomestic work during an economic crisis viewed as male. In any case, the assumption was that women, because they were women, merited less than men.

Yet "dutiful daughter[s] and malleable matron[s],"[69] as well as their flawed (that is, sexually wayward) antitheses, displacing their sexuality onto political action in a way that made them suspect, surface repeatedly in the Depression Era texts. All of these women generate more questions than answers. David Peeler has contended that in resolving the conflict between the need for social solace and social criticism, literary artists of the 1930s embraced hope against hope, an optimism that, in words he quotes from James Agee, "cut the roots of reason" (3). Woman, traditionally split into maternal and carnally threatening presence, played an important role in producing this desperate hopefulness. Her own economic victimization, as worker, family member dependent on male earnings, or both, was routinely denied in the focus on male frustration and despair. When she was scapegoated—underpaid or told not to "steal men's jobs"—such hostility colored literary depictions. Conversely, when she "manned" the labor barricades, it was as a labor mother or, as some contended, an unwomanly or promiscuous rebel. And when, pro-strike or not, she simply held down a job, she was most often explained away as a woman looking for romance, her priorities emotional rather than political. In a variant on punishing the woman breadwinner, however, her romantic prospects dimmed if she ascended to the professions. In any event, what was viewed as her refusal to mother produced resentment in most male authors and a corresponding critique of the burdens of mothering in female ones, and for somewhat different reasons, in a handful of black writers of both genders. No matter how divergent the authors or depictions, there was a common tendency to cast woman as social mother. Female and black writers depicted the flawed mother victimized by family and economic burdens, whereas male writers either constructed a wife, daughter, or similarly ministering female with saintly qualities or deplored their lack.

We begin, then, with the texts themselves: works by major male authors such as Steinbeck and Henry Roth; lesser lights, of the "Bottom Dogs" school, such as Daniel Fuchs, James T. Farrell, and Mike Gold; the numerous but largely forgotten strike chroniclers, including Robert Cantwell, Edward Newhouse, and William Rollins; the rediscovered feminist foremothers Tillie Olsen and Meridel Le Sueur; the strike journalist-novelist Mary Heaton Vorse; the "lost" party-line female authors such as the *New Masses* contributor Clara Weatherwax; those like Sinclair Lewis who straddled "serious" and popular fiction; the popularizers Margaret Mitchell, Viña Delmar, Fannie Hurst, and onetime Book-of-the-Month Club board member Christopher Morley, author of *Kitty Foyle;* Josephine Herbst and Tess Slesinger, amalgams of radicals and 1930s-style "New Women"; writers on the black experience such as Zora Neale Hurston; the late-Depression author and onetime party sympathizer Richard Wright and other male luminaries of the Harlem Renaissance, Claude McKay, Wallace Thurman, and Langston Hughes. All of their works embody the attempt to reconcile the masculine struggle for the dignity of labor with that of a needy feminine workforce that, in so many literary and nonliterary quarters, was accused of undermining it.

Chapter Two

EARTH MOTHERS, STREETWALKERS, AND MASCULINE SOCIAL PROTEST FICTION

The proletarian as male in Eli Jacobi's linoleum cut, *Maxi's Moose,* ca. 1940. Museum of the City of New York.

"So that's how it is in the restaurant [where I work]. They call me Momma."
—Mike Gold, *Jews Without Money* (1930)

"I have as much respect for a woman who sells her body for pleasure as I do for these sweatshop slaves and these girls in these cheap department stores. Take all these women running back and forth from these offices. They are prostituting their minds and their hands to make some man richer."
—Edward Anderson, *Hungry Men* (1935)

"She's only a gal and you're a person."
—Edward Newhouse, *You Can't Sleep Here* (1934)

A t the height of national sympathy for the rural poor who were vivid casualties of the Depression, the Farm Security Administration (FSA), 1935–42, photographer Dorothea Lange captured a "hungry and desperate" woman and her needy offspring in a series on a Nipomo, California, pea pickers' camp.[1] In most of these 1936 renderings, the woman seems remote, even when she suckles her child. But there is one unusual photo of her, worried but stalwart, an infant on her lap, one child nestled against her right shoulder and another against her left, her gaze fixed as if on a bleak future. "She has all of the suffering of mankind in her but all of the perseverance too," the FSA Historical Section head Roy Stryker said of the picture that retains its transcendence to this day.[2] Like the series as a whole, the photograph was labeled *Migrant Mother,* most likely by Lange's traveling companion and husband, Paul Taylor, who was studying squatter camps for the FSA, or possibly by Stryker himself, who routinely supplied captions if his photographers omitted them.[3] *Migrant Mother* quickly came to represent the travails of the rural family dislocated by the Great Depression. John Steinbeck studied it as he constructed his best-selling fictional protest against the migrant situation, *The Grapes of Wrath.*[4] Interestingly, his 1938 pamphlet *Their Blood Is Strong,* which exposed the migrant plight by describing Nipomo and other camps, features a cover with a far less arresting Lange migrant mother, a conventionally pretty woman suckling an apparently healthy child. Perhaps the subject of Lange's more celebrated and troubling picture would have sent too powerful a message of womanly strength in adversity.[5]

Migrant Mother no doubt helped inspire impassioned muckraking by social protest writers such as Steinbeck. But many more perceived it as a paean to enduring motherhood—an interpretation of the picture in the "timeless tradition of art whose theme is Mother and Child," echoed in modern assessments.[6] Indeed, so linked in the consciousness of the 1930s was the subject matter to ideal maternal imagery that an alternative title for the arresting picture—again, one not chosen by Lange—was *Migrant Madonna.*[7] Lange herself did not fill in the details until years later, and apparently no one inquired about the person behind the photo: Florence Thompson, a transient farmworker, aged thirty-two, and the sole support of six. As years passed and acclaim swelled—Irving Bernstein has, with little exaggeration, called it the most famous photograph in the world (261)—historians continued to erase the fact that the solicitous mother photographed was an anxiety-ridden breadwinner. Finally, in a 1960 reminiscence, Lange pointed out that the woman looks harried because the pea fields where she worked had frozen over, she had sold her possessions for food, and "there was no work for anybody" (126); she did not know where to turn. When Steinbeck alluded to the Nipomo migrants' plight in *Their Blood Is Strong,* he mentioned only jobless men.

Lange, like her gifted FSA colleague Marion Post Wolcott and the important WPA photographers Lewis Hine and Eudora Welty, routinely gave visual expression to the hard-up woman worker, as one San Francisco newspaper acknowledged when it called her subjects "Ragged, Hungry, Broke Harvest Workers" and ran two of her other Nipomo mother-child photos below this headline.[8] Certainly, like all of the women Lange captured at Nipomo, her unnamed migrant mother represented the almost one million agrarian women whose family lives were disrupted by the Depression. But she also represented between two and three million feminine unemployed; the one-tenth of all women who, when employed, did farm labor; the almost four million women homemakers who doubled as wage earners; the more than one-third of all American working women whose families were dependent for support on them alone; the one million deserted wives; and the almost two million divorcees and widows. Many of these women, like the widowed Thompson herself, had to scrounge for food to survive.[9]

None of these statistical truths has informed the reading of the celebrated picture. Many period observers responded at least as much to certain assumptions about women as to the fact that Lange, like other social documentary photographers of the time, often grouped women and children in poses depicting the family's economic hardship. Even the modern historian who supplies her name, age, family situation, and later work history (as a hospital worker, a bar worker, a cook, and a field hand), fails to identify her as a transient pea picker at the time the photograph was taken.[10] Most other modern (male) historians have assumed the subject was an offstage male "pea picker's family."[11] Or they have implied that the unknown woman is the female counterpart of the subject of another Lange photo, again not titled by Lange herself, the 1937 *Mexican Migrant Fieldworker*.[12] Although he is holding an infant in his arms, commentators perceive him not as a migrant father but as the quintessential "forgotten man" (Cashman, 195). Many of Lange's contemporaries, both inside and outside the FSA, bolstered the iconography of the woman at work. Wolcott, who carefully captioned mother-and-child photos with phrases such as "a woman migrant packing house worker and her oldest child preparing supper," also offered a late 1930s gallery of southern white women bean pickers and black female maids (*Domestic Servants Waiting for Street Car on Way to Work Early in the Morning, Mitchell Street, Atlanta, Georgia, May 1939*), field hands, and tobacco strippers. Eudora Welty took such period photos of women workers as *Saturday Off, Jackson*, and *Ex-Slave, Alabama*. Continuing his pre-1930s inquiry, Lewis Hine muckraked the feminine work site in his many industrial photos, particularly a series in 1936–37 of North Carolina textile workers in risky mill environments.[13] Despite this documentation, the dominant cultural impulse—to which Lange, who did not fill in the context of her *Migrant Mother* photograph until years later, contributed—was to remove woman from the labor landscape and sanctify her as a maternal figure.

Many of the important male visual artists also recast the heterosexual workplace so that groups of laborers, usually in factory settings or in the fields, did not include women.[14] In their social realist murals, the source of national wealth was "a heroic figure—large, muscular, strong, effective."[15] In more complicated ways involving a variety of literary strategies, a similar misreading of Depression Era women is evident in white and, to some extent, black authors from Steinbeck to Farrell, Wright to Gold,

Attaway to Kromer. For these practitioners of either social or proletarian fiction, their need for migrant mothers amid needy children obscures as many feminine economic difficulties as it reveals.

Misreading Womanhood: Social and Proletarian Novels

What David Peeler aptly classifies as the social novel of Steinbeck and James T. Farrell celebrates the common man but resists "politically dogmatic solutions to workers' problems . . . neither proletarian nor individualistic [but] united in a common approach that resembled literary naturalism."[16] In contrast, the school broadly termed proletarian exhibits sympathy (though often wavering or muted) to party ideology and its interest, though not an exclusive one, in "strikes, conversions to a collectivist vision, life among the proletariat . . . death in the mines . . . labor history."[17] The social novel shared the proletarian novel's interest in workers' discontents at home and on the job, in oppressive institutions, and in failed American dreams, groups, and events. Despite the continued disagreement over which works are "social" and which "proletarian," the two forms do overlap.[18] Regardless of disputes about individual texts or authors, the novels of radical male writers are marked by the centrality of the workingman and the rise of (or obstacles in the way of) the heroic proletarian.[19]

This does not mean there were no distortions of male workers. Whether in farm, field, mill, mine, or factory, excepting books with a completely "lower depths" slant, the social protest genre routinely idealized the nobility or potential greatness of the common man or exaggerated the numbers and commitment of the rank-and-file militant. As one eyewitness historian remembered, "The tire builders I [worked with] did not want to remain proletarians."[20] Like much social protest fiction before and since, these works suffer from dogmatism, the conflation of social classes with their individual members, and unrelenting grimness, problems noted in their day by mainstream and anti- (sometimes former) leftists. Among their supporters, of course, such flaws were merits, for, as Edwin Seaver wrote in *New Masses,* one of the chief journals dedicated to advancing proletarian fiction, creative writers were now under the "necessity of personally helping to accelerate the destruction of capitalism and the establishment of a workers' government."[21] To the *New*

Masses editor Mike Gold, the "chief critical exponent of all proletarian literature" (Rideout, 150), even a worker-author like Jack Conroy, whose proletarian credentials were impressive, was faulted for permitting his protagonist to embrace strictly nonmilitant labor organizing and that only at novel's end.[22] Still, Conroy appeared to follow Mike Gold's prescriptions to write of "life in mine, mill and farm," to gain "a knowledge of working-class life . . . from first-hand contacts," to renounce bourgeois or genteel literary traditions, and, in sum, to "go left."[23]

In a spurt of literary resurrection dating from the late 1960s, analysts have attempted to rescue forgotten social and proletarian novels to prove that "art and politics [could] mix."[24] This small critical group has defended the novels' documentary power and their fidelity to the rhythms of blue-collar speech, as well as to the "problems of the worker and *his* family, the conditions of the workplace, the terrors of joblessness and poverty" (Bernstein, 192, emphasis added). Those from Steinbeck to the practitioners of proletarian fiction as aptly characterized by Walter Rideout—Nelson Algren and black author William Attaway ("Bottom Dogs," a label inspired by Edward Dahlberg's 1930 novel), Jack Conroy and Mike Gold (conversion), and Robert Cantwell and Albert Halper (strike)—are praised for taking on the artistic problems of portraying working-class life (even if, as in Steinbeck's unflattering response to strike fiction, *In Dubious Battle* [1936], his loyalty to workers is vitiated by contempt for their herd mentality).[25]

This praise for realistic chronicles of the worker and his problems is what irritates those searching in social and proletarian fiction for balanced portrayals of labor-class women. Paula Rabinowitz sees the female working class as a subject not recognized within proletarian realism.[26] By making women invisible members of the workforce or denying the family the locus of the site of struggle (83), and thus minimizing the importance of marriage, the family, and sexuality, such texts in effect remove women from history. Barbara Foley finds that while some male texts attend to gender issues, male writers offer a (masculine) bildungsroman of bourgeois individualism, for in the conversion to radicalism many of the worker-hero's "exemplary traits express his superior personal qualities rather than the formation of a militant consciousness."[27] Needless to say, when the subject is the coming of age of the hero, even if, as is more often the case in 1930s plots, he represents the group's coming to maturity as well, there is little room for a discussion of women's oppression within the family or the workplace. Amy Godine, who adds the social novelist to the proletarian discussed in Rabinowitz and Foley, finds a similar "relation between . . . virility and political consciousness" in the form of a "quest for new fathers . . . leaders . . . revolutionary preachers . . . labor organizers . . . outside agitators."[28] In this search for the father, she sees a corresponding resentment of female hegemony (212).

Both feminists who elucidate male bias and those who defend the democratic realism of social and proletarian fiction make telling points. The biases are there, but so is the attention to the experience of the common man and, albeit far less often, to the common woman as well. Yet perhaps because of their interest in countering the misogyny of the 1930s or, conversely, in polishing the tarnished (that is, antifeminine) image of male writers, perhaps neither group has fully considered the working women who do people masculine fiction or answered the critical questions raised by their presence. What happens when, under the sway of a documentary impulse, writers from Steinbeck to Gold to Wright do limn female workers? How does this male fiction embody period fears about the female working class? In what ways does it reflect the tension between the historical moment, in which women shared or "usurped" the breadwinning role and were thus very much "in history," and the thrust to fend off feminine economic dominance (as discussed in the first chapter)? How is the familiar maternal ideal invoked? Violated? Questioned? Reversed, however tentatively? Finally, what are the costs to verisimilitude when no questioning or reversal occurs?

To answer such questions, this chapter locates male literary distortions of feminine work in the resistance to workplace womanhood that erased the *Migrant Mother*'s labor identity. It analyzes how social and proletarian writers, in principle opposed to such sexual stereotyping, wrestled with responses to the decade's womanly workforce. As we shall observe, social novelists, by their glorification of the maternal function and implicit condemnation of women—particularly breadwinners—who did not fulfill it, articulated a philosophy that was given more diverse expression in proletarian texts, thus marking the very fiction that claimed to reach beyond that limiting view.

Social Novels/Mother Myths

No writer of his time was more dedicated to the centrality of the mother myth than Steinbeck. The only peaceful scene in *In Dubious Battle,* a novel filled with manipulative CP field organizers, unattractive strikers, merciless growers, and a group turned mindless or violent mob, is the birth of a young woman's child. (Perhaps, also, Jim Nolan is looking for a substitute family, unlike Tom Joad, who wants to apply lessons of humanity learned in his family to his mission to help replace preacher Casy, slain by the police.) Women are so invisible in *In Dubious Batttle,* though, that their redemptive power cannot be exercised, a situation Steinbeck rectified in his hymn to the family of woman, *The Grapes of Wrath.*

Much of the novel's popularity rested on the fact that it "called on men to remember their roots and protect what they had."[29] In other words, it offered comfort, a way for men demoralized by Depression indignities to keep their self-respect by remaining faithful to family values and their role as head. In an early passage, before the Joads are driven from their land, the women "studied the men's faces" (6) to see if "this time the men would break." Just before the "tractoring off," the women again "watched the men" (45) to determine the mental state of the family. At the novel's end, when the Joads are little better off in the fields filled with surplus labor, much the same language is used: the women "watched the men . . . to see whether the break had come at last" (556).

Apart from tracking the resilience of the Joads in particular and the migrants in general, such reiteration also establishes the rigid world of gender relations that apparently assured a wide readership. That subordination obtains on every level of migrant life: whether its overarching functions—males at or in search of field work, women in the camp tent— or the apparently incidental ones, as when, in a peaceful moment at a camp, the men "sang the words, and the women hummed the tunes" (250).

The rigidity of gender relations in the migrant camps is not in dispute. A recent study, *American Exodus: The Dust Bowl Migration and Okie Culture in California* (1989), points out that real-life Ma Joads, whether devotees or casualties of the division of labor, and rarely, if ever, doing "men's work," constituted the almost 90 percent of married women who did no waged work (Gregory, 47). It was no accident that, as Steinbeck found in his research visits and as his novel chronicles, area camps were divided into male governing and female Good Neighbors committees (*Blood,* 16). But it was also true that single, divorced, and widowed migrants were citizens of the camps, although New Deal studies made only oblique references to them, concentrating on the health of all migrant women, farmworkers presumably included, but not on the rough work that may have affected it.[30] Nevertheless, almost 40 percent of the single, widowed, or divorced women migrants did field or cannery work (Gregory, 47). As Steinbeck himself acknowledged in researching the book, women worked alongside men in the fields in case of dire need, and women and girls, Mexican and Filipino migrants in the main, routinely did low-level food-processing work in nearby canneries (*Blood,* 32, 31), truths he alluded to in passing on the opening pages of *Cannery Row* (1945), years after the Depression. Nevertheless—possibly because of the freewheeling behavior attributed to such women—few were the fictional incarnations in their day, save for the sanitized title character of Morris Hull's lightly comic *Cannery Anne,* a negligible novel appearing three years before Steinbeck's.

Because the Okie version of the Holy Family, and not the free-spirited but virginal fruit gypsy of Hull's version, is what Steinbeck wishes to foreground, he does not complicate the identity of Ma Joad and the other materfamilias types she meets on the road and in the camps. To do so would be to desanctify her sex-ordained role and unwavering pro-family stance.

If woman's power issues from her caritative function, central to which is self-subordination, it is necessary to separate her from the potentially egalitarian wage-earning work that might imperil this gender-stratified world. Marion Post Wolcott's photographs of tobacco strippers on the home farm or in the cotton field often pointed to the heterosexual farm site, yet Steinbeck's descriptions of the pretransient Joads restrict the women to the home sphere while the men, soon to be tractored off and thus deprived of their farm labor, are standing or squatting disconsolately outside. As the banks move in ominously, it is the men who proclaim a despondent closeness to now-forfeited land; the women stand in (40) or near (44) the doorways, cordoned off by their domesticity. Despite the novel's myriad associations of women with mother earth, it is the man returned from jail, Tom, not the women who have lived so close to the land, who expresses an intuitive understanding of its value. Returning to the recently deserted Joad homestead, he recites the litany of farm life, pointing out to his companion, the preacher Casy, that the tools he once used were broken, the land misused, as he mourns the Joad men's forced alienation from the soil.

When, with Tom returned to them, the Joads reach the migrant camps, Steinbeck's references to women as paid harvesters of others' land are almost as grudging. Ma's waged work stint is restricted to one day, and references to the field labor of a handful of unnamed women are fleeting and ambiguous. Women in other menial work, though not as invisible, receive little notice as well. At the prototypical Route 66 truckstop cafe where the Joads naively ask to buy a loaf of bread, the author minutely describes the owner Al's expert hamburger frying, his boredom that of the lifetime short-order cook. But the same writer has only a satirical phrase for the waitress's (non-) labors, which he reduces to "smiling with all her might" at the drivers and "calling [orders] to the cook with a screech like a peacock" (197). Calling on the clichés of this female work type—she is, he is sure, "a Minnie or Susy or Mae" (197)—he sees no reason to individuate this description of the vulgar, aging waitress—indeed named Mae—with her "hair curled and rouge and powder on a sweating face" (197). He presents her as a woman who would give in to better impulses—in this case, to give the Okies food at reduced prices without telling them so and thus hurting their pride—only when inspired by her male customers.

It is doubly interesting that Steinbeck's truckstop vignette feeds on the period's association of the loose waitress and the prostitute.[31] Such moralizing contrasts with his tolerance of prostitutes in another California novel, *Tortilla Flat* (1935), and his humorous praise for them in *Cannery Row,* which even features a Monterey brothel-keeping Ma Joad, lauded, though comically, for "mothering" her girls. Viewed in this context, Mae's crime seems more to be that of masquerading as a worker when her real job is commercialized sex. Some proletarian writers play on this association: Conroy (*Disinherited*, 203) describes a Chicago coffee shop that fronts for a brothel; the "hostess" of the restaurant doubles as a madam who steers customers to the dive in the back. In any case, the Steinbeck waitresses are morally attractive when they relinquish their work role to be motherly: first toward the Okies, then toward the truck drivers who have reminded them of their duties as women rather than wage earners. It is notable that in the same scene Steinbeck briefly pillories another class of women who have forgotten the mother role. Though they do not commit the sin of earning a living, like the waitresses, by ogling the clients for better tips, rich women are also in a sense fallen women. They have sold themselves to wealthy men who bore them and, as Steinbeck makes clear in a sneer at their "jellies to make sexual intercourse safe, odorless, and unproductive" (199), they have abdicated family. In contrast to both classes of women, who have sacrificed true womanliness for economic power, the female Joads, neither blue-collar sluts nor leisure-class rejecters of the maternal, are migrant madonnas indeed.

If, particularly given the expectations of the Joad men, Ma is too old (and Rose of Sharon too encumbered by pregnancy) to work like a man, she does hold power of a noneconomic kind. To an extent, Ma is a controlling and even a manipulative personality, as in the chapter 16 scene in which she refuses to let Tom split off from the family, ultimately an act of futility in such compelling times for the workingman. But she is not a spiritually stifling presence. She does not force the oldest son to be furtive, scatter guilt, or demand compliance, dangers to the family always implicit in the type. She is not the maternal demon of Farrell's *Studs Lonigan* trilogy: mother as holy-rolling harpy. If, as Amy Godine observes, Steinbeck shares the "fear of female domination" (213) endemic to novels by men in a period fraught with challenges to male dominance, he allays it by directing Ma's formidable energies to male-empowering ends. Ma's cannot be a personal will to power; her drive is to extend mothering to the Joad men and their bruised psyches and, through Rose, at novel's end, to all mankind. Thus her attempt to prevent her oldest son from leaving the family is couched as a plea that he replace his listless father: "Pa's lost his place. He ain't the head no more. We're crackin' up, Tom. There ain't no family. . . . Don't go, Tom. Stay an' help" (503).

Though it is Rose of Sharon and not her mother who appears central to the last mothering act of the novel, that much-analyzed closing scene provides more evidence of feminine strength transmuted into a maternal agenda. Rose, her baby lost at birth, gives suck to alleviate another urgent kind of Depression helplessness: the starving forgotten man, in this case a fifty-year-old stranger who has to "have soup or milk" (580) lest he die. The scene has been called everything from sentimental to erotic. What has not been remarked, though, is that it is again Ma who stage-manages family unity in her newly awakened sense of the universal family. The many observers who have pointed out Ma's need to mother the human race (Peeler, 163) have not integrated it into this passage: "Now, as her eyes passed to Rose of Sharon's eyes, and came back to them" (580), she wills the girl to perform the one function she is too old to perform.

For Rose is Ma's surrogate, a symbol of the new generation of men-inspiriting women taking dire measures for dire times. On a symbolic level the scene was meant to suggest that the world has to be humanized for its economic waifs to survive. Yet it is noteworthy that Steinbeck defended the scene by downplaying the womanly act. For in a letter to his publisher, he undercuts his own description of the scene as an earth mother nursing by remarking that the Joad daughter's giving of the breast "has no more sentiment than the giving of a piece of bread" (178), a depersonalizing comment superficially opposed but actually reinforced by a diary entry on the scene as a "breast pump" one.[32] Paradoxically, this very objectification of woman, her reduction to a body part, bolsters the reading by one modern critic that the scene symbolizes "men's compassionate responsibility for one another."[33] Yet if anything, the symbolism of the final pages extends women's biological role to FDR's ill-fed, ill-housed, ill-clad Depression constituency.

Like Steinbeck, Farrell used an extended family portrait to limn the forces controlling the destinies of economically buffeted people, although his is a harsher indictment of their collaboration in their own downfall. For the subjects of his *Studs Lonigan* trilogy (1932–35), the petty-bourgeois Mary and Paddy Lonigan and their children, particularly their eldest son, Studs, stake their identity on individualistic separation from the worker class.[34] They consistently refuse to acknowledge the gravity of an economic crisis that binds them to their fellow sufferers. Farrell's underlying belief that capitalist democracy was "impermanent" (*Note,* 77) informed his critique of the financially beaten Lonigans, floundering in valueless stocks and unpaid mortgage notes. His final and most powerful volume, *Judgment Day* (1935), even features a parade whose optimistic far-left marchers are glowingly contrasted to Studs's downcast father, who has been bankrupted by his twinned faith in capitalism and Catholicism ("mortal men . . . cannot see the ways of the Almighty," he passively responds as he loses his capital [422]) and is drunkenly en route to his played-out son Studs's deathbed. Yet, that scene excepted, Farrell's was no ode to the new proletariat but a naturalistic work that generated widespread readers—and the commercially valuable Book-of-the-Month-Club mark of approval—for its meticulous indictment of the "banalities, commonplaces, formal religious fanaticism, [and] spiritual emptiness" of the bigoted Lonigan clan.[35]

Rejecting a purely determinist stance, Farrell once wrote that "free will is an achievement of men, gained individually and collectively, through knowledge and the acquisition of control, both over nature and over self."[36] Although his philosophy resembled Steinbeck's belief that the family trying to save itself must recognize deeper kinships than region, religion, or ethnicity and embrace life-affirming values, it is a foregone conclusion that the Irish-Catholic Chicago family of the trilogy, particularly his title character, lacks the spiritual currency to purchase such redemption. For the Lonigans founder in a blind adherence to the authority of the church in all matters; to the primacy of materialism and the (white, Catholic) self-made man; to the evils of sexual liberty; to the sin of questioning. In Farrell's own summation, parents and children alike, fearful of intellect and emotion, live in "a world without ideas" (qtd. Branch, 56). Farrell shines his authorial searchlight on a more reputable urban Irish group than Stephen Crane's sleazy Johnsons in *Maggie: A Girl of the Streets* (1893). Nevertheless, the "values of school, playground, church, and home"—and, one should add, popular culture, for Studs, like Maggie and her brother Jimmie, reveres mindlessly violent melodrama— "are revealed," remarks Charles Child Walcutt, "in their naked poverty."[37]

By *Judgment Day* the Lonigans, an increasingly wrangling, embittered bunch, have less in common emotionally with the put-upon Joads than with Crane's impoverished Bowery-dwelling Johnsons, a dysfunctional tenement family who prefer hard living (and hypocritically pious homilies to their children) to facing economic facts. Of course, Crane's police court habitué Mary Johnson, screaming hysterically at her ruffian son for tearing his clothes while, on her slide into drunken insensibility, she breaks the last bits of furniture in their slum flat, is superficially worlds apart from the strait-laced, repressed Lonigan matriarch (though not from the eponymous churchgoer of Crane's "George's Mother" [1896]). In an economic world she never made, this equally misnamed Mary whines, nags, and endlessly upholds religion and filial piety. "Be good, son, and come home early," she sniffles to the grown-up Studs (*Judgment,* 129). In short, she keeps the weak-willed Studs, who projects his guilt about the "dirty" sex act onto whorish or easily aroused women, squirming on her piety hook.

If the alcoholic, violence-prone Studs, like Crane's Rum Alley youths, longs inarticulately for a less brutal life but pursues what David Peeler eloquently calls the "chimeras of masculinity, property and heaven" (173), his is also a quest for the approval of the impossible mother. Although Mrs. Lonigan is one of many authority figures, both secular and religious, whose advice provokes confusion, self-laceration, and, as his drinking increases, self-destructive behavior in Studs, her pious belief that "a boy can never do a wrong thing if he is guided by his mother" (*Judgment,* 246) signals that she herself is a Ma Joad out of control. Her specialty is tearful proclamations of devotion, which Studs, in his final moments, transforms into her nightmarish chanting "No one loves you like your mother" (395).

Most discussions of *Judgment Day* center on the son's warped ideals, particularly his "tragic hope . . . to be a big shot," [38] not on his mother's deleterious effect on a family whose morale is already debilitated by declining fortunes, bad investments, and joblessness. But from her "shrill clamoring," in an earlier volume (Walcutt, 241), that Studs enter the priesthood to her struggle to break his engagement to Catherine in the final scenes of the trilogy, she appears to nurture in order to command. Infantilizing Studs, who is still living at home at thirty, she tells him how to eat his dinner, nags him to be cheerful, and cautions him to avoid relationships with women. Although she is traditionally passive when financial decisions need to be made, the family's economic troubles seem to empower her further. In the face of looming bankruptcy, her increased demands that the family remain a unit betoken the controlling mother and perpetuate childishness, not Steinbeck's family citadel.

Her maternal abuse of power culminates in the "gleam of apparent enjoyment" with which, in Studs's last moments, when the family is in emotional disarray, she asserts her supremacy "with a calculation made doubly vicious by her even voice" (*Judgment,* 416). She skewers his pregnant fiancée Catherine by lauding the narrow moralism that her son Studs—who absorbed her vision of the "decent girl" (195) while trying to seduce all women—had ambivalently attempted to flee. As her dying son hallucinates about his brainwashed childhood—he watches his mother step in front of President Wilson and intone that the "home is the most sacred thing on earth" (395)—she is busy acting out the final stage of her own transit from domestic lawgiver to jealous, obsessed, Oedipal manipulator. Fueled by a jealousy that makes her "envy" Catherine for having known Studs sexually (420), she finds a perverse pleasure at the death of her son, for "she was Studs' mother, and Studs was hers now" (403).

In her tight domestic rule, the monster mater of the Lonigan tale is but one of the forces sapping the vitality of Depression Era manhood, what Farrell termed "the . . . processes whereby society, through the instrumentality of social institutions, forms and molds characters, giving to the individual the very content of his consciousness" (qtd. Branch, 52). But if, as Donald Pizer suggests, Farrell's concern, with Joyce's literary model before him, was with the "inhospitality of Irish-American, lower-middle-class culture to the life of the mind and spirit,"[39] the mother's grip on her son's psyche has been neglected by most commentators. It is a neglect to which Farrell himself contributed, for though he devotes hundreds of pages to Studs's motives, he leaves the reader to speculate on Mary Lonigan's. There is, for instance, no hint that her conduct stems from a thwarted desire for self-actualization outside the home. Farrell's few working women want only to trade office work for marriage; nothing in her routine typing work alters her conventional fidelity as an engaged woman to marriage or, for that matter, suggests that she would break with the restrictively sterile home philosophy of her future mother-in-law. Nevertheless, though Farrell repudiates the unreality of Steinbeck's earth mother, *Studs Lonigan* is equally an indictment of the woman who could not live up to the myth.

Between them, with nods at morally dubious single women—Steinbeck's hoydenish waitresses, Farrell's "easy" working girls (even the prim Catherine succumbs to a passionate premarital sexuality)—the two authors, disdaining the much-favored militant-convert, strike, or down-and-outer plots of their contemporaries, examined the prototype and antitype of 1930s mothering: Ma Joad as family unifier, Mary Lonigan as sower of discord. But powerful as they were as signals to women, these portrayals were removed from the industrial arena. It was the task of the proletarians, alive to the presence of women in the workplace in a way that Steinbeck and Farrell were not, to extend, transform, and reverse the ideal mother and to cast the woman wage earner, the antithesis of the domestic nurturer, as a latter-day fallen woman. To varying degrees, male proletarians cataloged how women, including child-rearing ones, took on job identities and wrestled with family disunity, male resentment, and a host of other work-site traumas. In exploring these matters, however briefly, these authors posed the very questions social novelists skirted: Did a labor-class identity preclude a maternal one? If women were needed to swell the protest ranks, did they betray their womanliness in so doing? Although authors as diverse as Conroy, Gold, Algren, and Cantwell began the inquiry, all too often, in their apparent longing for the gender-stratified world of Steinbeck and Farrell, their answer was yes.

Novels: Mothers Under Siege

Two of the earliest proletarian novels to integrate women into the unfriendly industrial landscape came from the once-prominent Jack Conroy and one of his reviewers, Mike Gold, like Conroy an important author in his own right. For one thing, the subplots of the radical male bildungsromans *The Disinherited* (1933) and *Jews Without Money* (1930) subjected the home-loving mother to a new set of pressures.[40] Cast, variously, as widow or jobless husband's support, she now took on the martyrdom of work. For another, particularly in the Conroy work—which, with a wider canvas than the Jewish Lower East Side of Gold's envisioning, seemed to some the "first memorable proletarian novel of the decade"—there was a burgeoning attention to the single feminine breadwinner.[41] Yet, especially in light of the New Deal Era's minimization of working women (and the two writers' sentimentalization of their hardworking mothers, their childhood economic mainstays), such novels revealed the difficulties of a subject so freighted with controversy.

The disinherited group referred to in Conroy's title are those whom Larry Donovan, Conroy's stand-in, in his travels from the Monkey Nest mining camp in Missouri coal country through a series of hard Detroit factory and other Midwest manual laboring tasks comes to term those "from many a closed and crippled factory. . . . The cruel competition for bare existence had made rats of them" (236). Despite—or because of—the novel's penchant for such impassioned rhetoric, it painted, as the noted reviewer John Chamberlain wrote in the *New York Times,* the "world of the working stiff" in "remarkably vivid prose" (qtd. *Disinherited,* intro., vii).

Though *The Disinherited* is a story of both the male and female work experience, only the men toil in the industrial sphere: the father and brothers
in coal mines, the son employed in a railroad machine shop, steel mill,
rubber heel factory, automobile assembling plant, and, descending in the
job world, as beet pulp loader, high-iron day worker, ditchdigger, and
road paver. The mother becomes a laundress, and the younger women
are farm daughters, boardinghouse keepers, waitresses or lunch-wagon
girls, and prostitutes. This feminine exclusion from the world of factory
and male manual labor is more deliberate than documentary. In his own
introduction to a 1972 reprint of his novel, Conroy remembers gratefully
that his wife worked at a shoe factory while he was doing short-lived odd
jobs (vi). In the novel itself, his gratitude vanishes into ambivalence. His
protective and condemnatory impulses toward female wage earners are in
conflict, and both preclude gender-free labor solidarity.

In fact, only disturbing images of women at work dot the narrative.
Three vignettes, of Larry's mother, of Helen, an "easy" working girl he
is fitfully attracted to, and of his true love, Bonny Fern Haskin, illustrate
the problematic nature of women workers in what, Farrell's reservations
notwithstanding, was received by the *Saturday Review of Literature,* that
conduit to middlebrow readership, as a proletarian novel of "vigor . . . and
significance." [42] In his 1933 attack in the *Nation* on the Conroy novel, Farrell, though not one to talk, included the valid criticism that the women
characters were stereotypes (714). What he did not observe, perhaps because of his own tunnel vision on the subject, was how the stereotypes
reinforce the unsuitability of women at waged work. Mrs. Donovan, the
uncomplaining, family-welding widow of a victimized miner, is a saintly
precursor of Ma Joad but is bereft of her menfolk's earnings and forced
to take in washing. For the character of Larry Donovan's love interest,
Bonny Fern, Conroy seems to have dipped into the dime novels he read
and the romantic ballads he was fond of hearing as a child. As the daughter of a prosperous farmer before the hard times hit (the Depression sets
in as Larry grows to adulthood), this flowerlike girl is a rural princess,
blonde, with—archaic diction for a 1930s narrative!—"flaxen hair" (15)
and "gaudy ribbons" (15), she was born to be protected. In their pre-
Depression childhood, she is disdainful of the dirty-handed narrator. But
in a thinly veiled version of a turn-of-the-century sentimental romance,
by novel's end, having failed to survive in the city, she turns to her pro-

letarian knight for comfort and guidance. Indeed, the last scene spotlights the martyr mother, too old and weak to work, and the now home-centered Bonny. Both are bid farewell by Larry, who, newly converted to labor's cause, goes off to meet his destiny. Balladic folk tale becomes dime western when, in a bow to the solitary mission of the man who must effect labor change, he reflects that he "had to be free" of romantic encumbrance. Yet Bonny's "I'll be right here" (307) suggests an alternate finale when better times come. Bonny's submissive stance—how will she and the mother survive?—is all the more surprising in a novel of this kind in that she had gone to the city, entered school, become political herself, and initially rejected the callow Larry for more seasoned and case-hardened suitors. But as Larry comes into his labor-class own, there seems a narrative necessity that she pose no challenge and withdraw to the domestic sidelines.

An even more repressive authorial impulse is played out when Conroy considers the woman who refuses to stop working. There he rehearses the fallen woman myth, echoing the classist Victorian naysayers who warned of the morally corrupting effect of the factory. Wrote one of the chief moralizers in the early 1900s of the mass feminine entry into factory life: "[It] seems more adventurous to leave home, so the ignorant girls meet their wretched fate. Even if not entirely ruined, girls in factories and similar employments are usually coarsened, and their chances of marrying respectable husbands are diminished."[43] Helen Baker's cautionary tale is told in this spirit. When she first appears in the rubber heel factory, which is the narrator's (as it was Conroy's) initiation into the hell of the un-regulated work site, the lunch-wagon girl has already been tainted with the vulgarity of the workplace. She may wheel a lunch cart for pay, but she is well on the road to sexual ruin. In Conroy's hands, her very work becomes an erotic act. As she "speared a weinie . . . deposited it on a bun" and "chirped archly, 'ten cents!' " her "right eye screwed itself into a broad wink" (161). The comic element is there, for the virginal narrator's "retreat from such bold overtures" (162) need not replicate his creator's point of view. Yet, comedy aside, the youth in his innocence underscores the point of the scene: "It seemed indecent for her to be here" (161).

As in his handling of the two other worker females, Conroy's response to the problem of woman's work is to remove her from the conditions of waged labor, a stock device in "working girl" fiction well past World

War I. Of course, having thrust herself into the industrial heart of things, even if as lunchtime visitor rather than on-site laborer, the wayward Helen, unlike the sanctified mother and rural princess, is too far gone. Lacking the altruistic excuse of a Mrs. Donovan or the daughterly devotion of a Bonny Fern, who follows her father out of the city and back to the homestead, Helen is a type familiar to historians of prostitution. Like many of the real-life women interviewed by Henry Mayhew in *London Labour and the London Poor* (1862), Dr. William Sanger at mid-century in the United States, or those who testified in front of that preeminent fact-finding body, the Chicago Vice Commission of 1911, Helen encounters urban sexuality, unwanted pregnancy (or, in the Progressive revision, bad company), and the fatal easiness of entry into the world of sex work. Conroy's updating of the harlot's progress story is as reminiscent of the pathetic "fallen woman" tale as of the investigating interview. By the time Larry seeks her out—and cruelly offers to pay for her services—Helen tells a story that, however out of place in a 1930s worker narrative, was a staple of the "Ruined Maid" subgenre, from the British writer Elizabeth Gaskell's *Ruth* (1853) to Louisa May Alcott's *Work* (1873) to Dreiser's *Jennie Gerhardt* (1911). Languishing, she claims, from his apparent rejection of her, Helen despondently takes the first man who wants her and begins her transit to the gutter.

A further irony is that the prelapsarian Helen is too déclassé for Larry, who prefers fantasies of the pure Bonny Fern to the lunch-wagon girl's wagging hips and slangy come-ons. In the tones of a Crane jeering his cuff factory heroine's lowbrow tastes, and in deliberate contrast to her "Gee! That's keen!", Conroy describes Helen's debates "as to which was the most juicy brand of gum" and her "positive opinions as to the relative pulchritude of the movie stars, male and female" (172).

Ironically, the attitudes toward Helen these phrases reveal link Conroy to the late Victorian do-gooders whose greatest wish was to make ladies of working girls. These lady bountifuls paid lip service to changing the harsh conditions of employment but were far more interested in altering the uncouth social reality of working girls' subculture. Intoned one incognito investigator of the woman-filled factory: "Their conversation is vulgar and prosaic; there is nothing in the language they use that suggests any ideal or any conception of the abstract. . . . In all they say there is not one word of value."[44] To such reformers, the solution was the Protestant-run Working Girls' Club or settlement house and a ban on the lascivious amusement park and dance hall. (There was even a Progressive Era New York City Committee on the Amusement of Working Girls on which no working girls sat.) Conroy may well have scoffed at such elitist interference, but his portrait of Helen comes dangerously close to reflecting the sentiments that fueled it.

Conroy does not, as his "Bottom Dogs" contemporaries did, place his heroine's fate within the context of urban indifference: hers comes of her rootlessness. For that inability to remain with her own or find a surrogate family she pays dearly. Furthermore, the novel's respect for the working class clearly does not extend to girls who go wrong. Whatever ideals the Depression tarnishes, feminine purity is not one. Those like Mrs. Donovan and Bonny, therefore, are a moral world apart from the vulgar working girl. Imposing this angel/whore dichotomy on a novel so unsuited to it, however, is not without cost to the hearth angels. In severing Mrs. Donovan from her wage-earning past, the novel offers no real survival alternative for her. Bonny, who in Detroit with her father and Larry had been energized to listen to street-corner agitators and join political clubs, is even more disempowered by novel's end. Both she and her new role model, the long-suffering Mrs. Donovan, are relegated to a barren farm where there is no work, only dependence on a faraway son and lover out organizing workers for a better masculine day.

Jews Without Money, like *The Disinherited* a semiautobiographical exploration of city- and workscape, was duly noticed by and met greater acclaim in the *Times* and the *Saturday Review,* the latter jolted into a temporary abandonment of complacency by Gold's poetic treatment of poverty. The book "smells of the sewer. . . . [Gold] . . . means it to be so. . . . Surely only from the heart could it have been written," the journal explained.[45] Its eleven printings between February and October of 1930 testified to its ability to interest wide audiences in a lyrical ethnography of the ghetto, part Yiddish folk tale, part Jacob Riis exposé, part radical coming-of-age tract. As in Conroy, by the novel's close, Mikey, the son of an immigrant tenement family with a disabled father ("Twenty years in America and poorer than when I came," he laments [301]), has embraced the religion of militant change, while the women, who have labored to support the family in the economic void left by the men, have in various ways been denied the liberation of political insight. Yet, given Gold's fidelity to the

Lower East Side Jewish feminine experience of hard times (much of the narrative is set in the great era of female garment trade militance, 1900 to 1915, but is a parable of Depression Era trials), it attempts to resolve the contradiction between the documentary and the misogynistic in a manner that Conroy does not.

Well before the 1930s, Jewish women in both the Old World and the New had a solid work tradition. In Russia by the end of the nineteenth century, 15 percent of all artisans, 24 percent of all industrial workers, and almost half of all textile workers were female; that last statistic was even higher in the American garment trades.[46] Likewise, married Eastern European emigrants, accustomed to the role of scholar-supporting or small-business helpmeet, laid the groundwork for their own double identities as mothers and workers by taking in boarders or doing homework. Furthermore, interviews with women who, like Mikey's mother, Katie, took jobs outside the home to help sustain their hungry families reveal that by the Depression, a fair number perceived themselves, and were perceived by their children, as the dominant parent (Weinberg, 241). The narrative initially lauds this role—crows Katie to her bewildered husband, "I have time and strength for everything" (245)—but then undercuts it. Whether in real-life women's healthily self-proclaiming oral interviews or in Gold's ambivalent fictive memoir, though, Jewish women's work did not bear the taint of domestic service that the Irish-American Conroy and the larger culture gave Mrs. Donovan's laundry work. He has her son Larry remember, with bitter childhood shame, his mother "ironing away at midnight on someone else's clothes" (67) to support him and his young siblings. The ceaseless labor that in Conroy seems such a comedown is a badge of honor in *Jews Without Money,* a mark of heroism that the title extends to the entire ethnic group.

Gold, then, places Mikey's mother, who takes a job in a Broadway cafeteria peeling and scouring "tons of vegetables" (246), and his aunt Lena, who does piecework, within a distinct ethnic context. Her work notwithstanding, Katie is not deterred, in a by now familiar pattern, from unconflicted devotion to her family. In a 1935 introduction to the reissued novel, Gold locates both himself as a novelist and Katie as a representative character by extolling his own "beautiful proletarian mother" (iv). Her housepainter husband, Herman, a casualty of lead poisoning, becomes one more child she must take care of, and like a similarly idealized figure in Roth's *Call It Sleep* (1934), she bears his taunts cheerfully. She is thus a model of altruism, a fictive reproach to the phony martyr of Farrell's *Judgment Day*. And she begins to explore another self as well. Paula Rabinowitz points out that it is the women who are the workhorses and the militants—the mother organizes a rent strike, the aunt marches on a shirtwaist strike type of picket line—while the men are allied with dreamers, artists, and storytellers (187n). This is true to a point, but it overlooks the minimizing process in which the novel engages. The narrative structure implies that Katie's motherly workplace militance—she is both advocate for and mother of the other workers, a cross between Ma Joad and Mother Jones—and Lena's daily defiance of Italian gangsters and Irish policemen, whom the sweatshop bosses have hired to harass her—are symptomatic of an early phase in the revolutionary struggle. The women still protest within existing structures, without a coherent (masculine) political strategy for total change.

These acts of defiance are the political lessons of Mikey's childhood. But by the time he grows to labor manhood, condemned for a time to a hellish job in a chemical factory, his mother has been debilitated by the hit-and-run death of a daughter (an interesting inclusion, as Gold had no sisters), almost as if the narrator is meting out a punishment for her extrafamily militance. By narrative's end, too, no more is heard, no influence acknowledged, of the onetime activist Lena, who was fast becoming another Clara Lemlich, that force in the 1910 Uprising of the 20,000 women garment makers. Instead, in the Hades of Mikey's work at the chemical plant, only after the "men" are described are the "girls"—the spiritual descendants of the wraithlike paper mill girls in Herman Melville's "The Paradise of Bachelors and the Tartarus of Maids" (1855)—glimpsed in passing. If they have any other labor identity, it is as members of the mass who "dripped with sweat . . . haggard, as though in pain" (307). Along with the prostitutes Mikey now scornfully patronizes, they fade into the background as he seeks a manly answer to the problem of poverty. When, listening to a man on an East Side soapbox, he finds it in the workers' revolution, he no longer hears its echoes in his mother's dream of a promised land of American equality or her labor activity of decades before. Rather, he has replaced his discredited and weakened father with what Godine terms the "saintly surrogate paternalism" (211) of the Union Square orator.

There are other reasons for his doing this. His mother and Lena excepted, the majority of the women in the novel are grotesque. Their attempts at street-corner seductions, their witchlike powers, and their bourgeois crassness variously menace, frighten, or disgust Mikey. From the massive street prostitutes Rosie and Ida to the half-cracked self-styled "healer" Baba Sima to a friend's insane mother to Mrs. Zechariah Cohn, the morally monstrous wife of his father's grasping sometime employer, women threaten to shut out whatever light both sidewalk world and revolutionary activity afford. If by narrative's end he has kept these furies at bay, he has learned to do so without the benevolence of his female relatives as a talisman. Early in the novel Mikey can still thank the mother who taught him that the "world must be made gracious for the poor" (158) and who invited remorseful streetwalkers to her house almost in the communitarian spirit of Emma Goldman. By the denouement, however, he mirrors the self of his 1929 *New Masses* piece "Go Left, Young Writers!" Men make revolutions, literary and otherwise.

The "Bottom Dogs" Novel and Motherhood Betrayed

If to some extent the chief male representatives of the proletarian conversion novel disempower the female wage earner, locate her in a safely nostalgic past, or relegate her in passing to the status of a living corpse or hired sex partner, Conroy and Gold, in contrast to Steinbeck and Farrell, at least recognized a feminine presence in the workplace. In the "Bottom Dogs" subgenre, writers shift attention from proletarian families, holy or disintegrating, and carve out new terrain. Too grim to be popular with American audiences, "for the most part refusing the assistance of slogans, resolutions, and other revolutionary gestures," writes Walter Rideout of the form he categorized, "these novelists ambush the reader from behind a relentless description of life in the lower depths" (185). They also describe a gender democracy, though admittedly one of failure to work, a transient subculture of women and men always aimlessly on the move, too dispirited to find a job or keep it long, too alienated to have hope for anything more than "three hots and a flop."[47] But in so doing, such chroniclers of despair create a world in which, as one down-on-his-luck wanderer says of a woman he meets "on the skid road," "I can see that she is the same as me" (*Waiting*, 112–13). In that characterization from Tom

Kromer's aptly titled *Waiting for Nothing,* in Edward Anderson's depiction of the edgily hedonistic Corinne in *Hungry Men,* or Nelson Algren's of onetime dress worker Norah Egan in *Somebody in Boots,* men and women often experience the same degradation.[48] All three works appeared in 1935. The first two were inspired by on-the-road experiences of journalists who had doubled as migrant laborers to explore the subworld of the itinerant; Algren had sampled the hardships of migrant work in the Southwest before coming to the WPA in Chicago.

In these novels, homeless down-and-outers of both genders seek doorway shelter, cadge, lie, beg, con, and contemplate or carry out the sale of their bodies. (Anderson's luckless Acel Stecker has relations with a "Mrs. Carter" for a meal and a night's lodging.) The very matter-of-factness of the Mrs. Carter incident is in keeping with Anderson's refusal to condemn prostitution as an act of survival, particularly female prostitution. Many of the studies of the day carried on the Progressive Era exculpation of the streetwalker by emphasizing, as the liberal *New Republic* put it in 1936, that soliciting was "the best job these girls [could] get."[49] It joined the other reformist journals of the time in alluding to the scarcity of good jobs and the more tempting wages of illicit sex, criticizing not the girls but the powerful vice interests and the madams who catered to them, lamenting the sordid conditions of their trade, and deploring the lack of "preventive work" to reclaim women from it.[50]

The purveyors of popular culture, particularly the film industry, were wary of such explanations. Even before the puritanical Production Code of 1934, in its relatively few "fallen woman" films Hollywood preferred sensational melodrama to facts. It served up such fare as *Faithless* (1932), in which the loyal wife takes to the streets for money to help cure her ailing husband, and *Safe in Hell* (1931) and *Panama Flo* (1932), scenarios of prostitutes who lament their lost loves against steamily tropical backdrops. In *Blonde Venus* (1932), an improbably lush Marlene Dietrich turns to soliciting to support her little son, whom she has kidnapped from the husband who tried to separate her from the child. In an equally farfetched film plot, the ethereally beautiful Greta Garbo of *Susan Lenox, Her Fall and Rise* (1933), swallowed up in an almost unrecognizable Hollywoodization of the Progressive David Graham Phillips's muckraking 1917 opus, follows a man to the ends of the earth to atone for her stint in the very trade to which he had driven her in the first place. When the film industry did recognize the prostitute as a victim of the Depression, its notice was oblique at best.[51] In what was for Hollywood the daringly naturalistic *Dead End* (1937), a hard-bitten gangster discovers in a harsh reunion scene with his venereally diseased girlfriend that she has turned prostitute in his absence. Normally, however, Hollywood preferred to disguise her as a gangster's moll (*Public Enemy*, 1931), an out-of-funds party girl (a miscast Myrna Loy in *Penthouse,* 1933), or a dance hostess (Bette Davis in *Marked Woman,* 1937). Always, despite her past immorality and present punishment (by the film's end, she either atones arduously or dies young), she longs to be a helpmeet to the man she loves, to seek, if not find, redemption through altruism. Still, despite the reluctance to locate the prostitute in the economic desperation of the Depression Era, Hollywood made it clear that whether she rose above her sin or was paid its biblical wages, "no woman could perform work functions not directly related to sex."[52]

On the surface, the prostitute of the "Bottom Dogs" novel was a compromise between the fact-finding of the journalists (itself not devoid of sentimentality) and the unreality and sex stereotyping of the film industry. One of a cast of characters on the emotional-economic edge, this feminine equivalent of the small-time gangster—or, in her most sordid incarnations, the jailbird transient—she is ubiquitous. In imagining her, the novels are often faithful to facts of the commercialized sex trade. The Neptune Beach prostitutes in the Brooklyn denizen Daniel Fuchs's *Low Company* (1937), whether resigned to their trade or anxious to ply it, eke out a living in the small, furtive apartments that had replaced the flashy bordello phased out by the vice raids of two decades before. Algren, who was a venereal disease control worker in Chicago under the WPA, gives a similar veracity to the methods of Norah Egan. A cut below Fuchs's women, she emerges from her seedy hotel to pick up customers, conceals evidence of illness from them, and reacts with a knowing cynicism to their flattery and their insults. This does not mean that Algren and his colleagues labeled every woman involved in the sex world a prostitute. In his short story "Within the City," produced for Jack Conroy's radical midwestern journal *Anvil* in 1935, Algren bears out the contention of the eminent University of Chicago sociologist Walter Reckless that the burlesque girl or taxi dancer could remain in her trade without resorting to prostitution. It was an observation Edward Newhouse's *You Can't Sleep Here* (1934) made as well in reference to New York City strippers. Nor are women who profit from the earnings of prostitutes inevitably harridans. Edward Dahlberg's Lizzie Lewis supports her son Lorry by dressing the hair of the local brothel dwellers. Though worlds away from Ma Joad, she is not demonized. It is her casual mothering, not her manner of earning a living, that seems to propel Lorry to a vagrant's life; his ambivalence about his mother is at the core of the book.[53] For the most part, however, the female landscape of Dahlberg, Algren, and their contemporaries bears out the observations of "Boxcar" Bertha Thompson in her 1937 hobo autobiography, *Sister of the Road*. On street or in freight car, women routinely exchanged sex for food or money.

When, in *Waiting for Nothing*, Acel Stecker comments without conviction that it is the "smart" (94) women who turn to prostitution, the narrative is merely using 1930s diction to recycle Jacob Riis's view of working girls of New York driven to the streetwalker's trade: such women should prefer "death to dishonor."[54] In the full story of Norah Egan, Algren fleshes out this late Victorian article of faith. *Somebody in Boots* was reduced by Jack Conroy—who still managed to praise it in *New Masses* as a "terrific indictment of capitalistic society"—to "a story of . . . cheap criminals, bums, whores, perverts, jailbirds, and scum of the earth."[55] But it is more than that. For the story of the small-town Texan Cass McKay, a man who takes to riding the rails, is also one of a criminally inclined youth. Forever drifting, he nevertheless craves some love, some stability, without being able to articulate the need. His crowning misfortune is to seek it in the person of Norah, who offers him affection and even a form of love but abandons him to survive on her own.

Even in her early days with Cass, Norah is a pathetic creature. Despite some realistic elements culled from his WPA stint, Algren (as Conroy did with his harlot's progress tale of Helen) relies on a subliterary tradition rather than proletarian observation. In her fall to the street, Norah is the spiritual descendant of those starving but virtuous sewing girls of mid-Victorian penny weeklies. "The Slave of the Needle" (1850) was one prototypical British title, sanitized for American audiences in once-popular stories like T. S. Arthur's *The Seamstress* (1843) and Wirt Sikes's *One Poor Girl: The Story of Thousands* (1869) and fin-de-siècle seamstress-to-streetwalker fiction like Edgar Fawcett's *The Evil That Men Do* (1889) and Crane's more notable *Maggie*. Algren writes as if W. I. Thomas had never produced *The Unadjusted Girl* (1923) or the social hygienists had never conducted a survey of women arrested for soliciting. Rather, Algren's Norah fills out the formulaic mold of her innocent but fallen literary predecessors. He completely ignores prostitutes' sexual impulses, much less the possibility that their sadomasochistic recklessness is born of childhood incest or, in alternative interpretations, the absence of constructive communal values during adolescence, and that, last but not least, perhaps they yearn for better things. All these post-Freudian theories of prostitution had been available to social psychologists and artists alike from the 1910s.[56]

It is true that Algren tries to give an American Writers' Congress gloss to Norah's virtue betrayed melodrama, reshaping the old poverty determinism plot to social protest needs in much the same way as did his fellow leftist Mike Gold—before the antivice *Jews Without Money*—in the 1928 *New Masses* story "Love on a Garbage Dump."[57] There, muting the tradition of the original *Masses* magazine, in which John Reed had published vignettes glorifying the prostitute and viewing her as the supreme survivor, Gold defended one Concha's "right to ask for a dollar" for sex with a fellow worker "if she needed it" ("Dump," 185) to round out her meager pay. Gold rationalized her sexual barter by contrasting the legitimacy of her life to the parasitism of the "lazy, useless" rich woman "who forced Concha so low"—enforcing one law for the rich and another for the poor. Later in the tale, referring to "Communist[s] marching to the barricades" (185), he envisions a world in which the working class would be set free and the Conchas would not have to sell themselves. A similar sentiment informs Algren's tale of Norah Egan's decline from earning $7.50 a week to $4.00 for the same work, to washing windows for 35 cents to burlesque dancer to—his earlier bow to Walter Reckless notwithstanding—a street woman. Algren makes it clear that, cut off from decent garment trade work, Norah and her working sisters everywhere are unable to find jobs that are not sex-related. In the wreckage of industrial capitalism, she has nothing to sell but herself.

But if he pays lip service to the view that in the capitalist marketplace Norah has only herself to vend, he castigates the woman he desexualized in her prelapsarian days when those days are gone. As in Anderson, Kromer, and others, Algren's embittered emphasis on her survival skills implies that in her drive for an economic foothold, woman survives at man's expense. And that becomes a powerful charge against her when men inhabit the flophouses and form the breadlines this kind of novel describes so minutely. Algren first works out this idea in a minor prostitute character, Signe, who is judged more than reported on. She has "a spoiled mouth and a waspish air, a bloodless face above a sleazy green dress" (167). Predictably, given so damning a description, she takes the hayseed Cass for his money, as does Norah Egan after her. Norah picks him up to roll him and stays as his paid companion, to run out on him before and after his stint in prison.

Norah's second desertion of Cass, which brings the narrative to a close, does not prompt the literary equivalent of a Gallic shrug the reader expects in a scenario of such psychological aimlessness and emotional anomie. Rather, in a confused attempt at ennobling Cass, however worthless he has appeared throughout the narrative (among other foul deeds, he participated in a hobo gang rape of a black woman), Algren reveals that the young man had been able to love someone—Norah—and that her departure throws him back to the emotional nihilism of the transient. On the surface a sacrifice of sorts—she is sick and does not want to infect him—her running out on him is really, Algren insists, a business decision; she will continue to ply the trade rather than risk economic uncertainty with Cass. In refusing Cass the spiritual mothering he craves, she has sold her soul as well.

Algren bolsters his indictment of woman's sex work by tirades about the city of Chicago, which he twice calls a "whore" (219, 237). He compares Standard Oil and Chrysler to corrupt customers who degrade the body of the city and likens the World's Fair, which was then luring visitors and cash to the town, to a prostitute selling fake excitement. Like her city a worker turned whore, Norah has undergone the negative transformation central to the "Bottom Dogs" subgenre; she has traded joblessness for a desperate corruption.

Despite a surface verisimilitude, Algren's tolerance for the prostitute's "work" is complicated by opposite impulses. Placed within the context of male economic anxiety, this chastising vision of female sexual waywardness indicts women as flawed comforters, failed spiritual rescuers. It is one that the strike novel, a proletarian form depicting more respectable wage earners, extends to the so-called disreputable woman as well.

Many 1930s strike novels by men as well as women concentrated on industries in which women were minorities or absent entirely and thus omitted woman's role in industrial militance. But like a few isolated writers and the male Gastonia novelists (all of whom are examined in chapter 5, contrasting them with female novelists of such woman-fueled uprisings as that 1929 North Carolina textile strike), it is no accident that the few masculine practitioners of the strike novel who did place women at the work site recounted ineffective labor protest. One such narrative is *The Land of Plenty* (1934), Robert Cantwell's carefully crafted novel of an uprising in a West Coast wood factory, praised for its fidelity to the workingman's speech patterns and simmering resentments.[58] Although he is largely forgotten today, in his time Cantwell earned the admiration of the severe *New Republic* reviewer Mary McCarthy, who proclaimed him the "only proletarian novelist with a literary style."[59]

Nor does Cantwell erase the widening feminine participation in strike and trade union movements (noted in chapter 1). Instead, his account of the short-lived strike includes women on the picket lines who endure police clubbings. And he points out that they picket with good reason. Their wages are even less adequate than the men's and they are treated just as callously, their pride in their work eroded by an unscrupulous management and the condescension of the white-collar girls who work in the factory office.

As the narrative opens, the power has failed in the factory, and Hagen, the electrician, after rightly blaming the venal company foreman, has been fired, setting in motion events that inspire the male workers to a sit-down. Ellen Turner, the principal female character in *Land of Plenty*, her sexuality temporarily muted by the demands of her work—her hair is covered with sawdust, her eyes are haggard—fears Hagen's fate. She and her sickly sister Marie have been threatened that day with reprisals for imaginary infractions. Like Johnny Hagen, the factory-hand protagonist and son of the cast-out electrician, with whom she is thrown into contact during the strike, she has known rage at the overwork, the pay cuts, the dangerous work site. To these are added her woman's grievances as well.

In touching on them, Cantwell, using observations culled from his own years in a Washington State plywood factory, offers the beginnings of a feminist analysis. Ellen's male co-workers routinely mix nativism with sexism to taunt the "little Polack[s]" (232) (the Turner name had orginally been Dombroski), call them "a bunch of chippies" (113), and reflect how easily "they could have made" (271) a girl like Marie. To drive the point

home that Ellen and Marie are oppressed as women and workers, Cantwell includes a scene anterior to the strike in which one of the workers—
notably, though, a college boy who deems himself superior to the herd—
tries to rape Marie. She comes to this attempt fresh from a backstreet
abortion—the result of an affair with an unstable factory hand—whose
debilitating effects she covered up for fear of being fired. And Cantwell
defends Ellen, Marie, and their women colleagues by portraying them,
despite their on- and off-the-job harassment from men, as reliable, even
"adroit" (69) workers.

Such feminine steadiness is called into question at the end of the novel.
The night before the strike erupts into a confrontation with the police
massed outside, Ellen and Johnny, alone in a portion of the darkened factory, make love on the floor. Cantwell constructs the scene in such a way
that the woman who had chided Johnny and his lumber mill mates for
mistreating women now bears out Johnny's earlier reflections about her
sluttishness. "All of his life he had known about the Turner girls. . . .
Even in grade school he had known about them" (115). But by this time,
Johnny's impulse toward Ellen is not a contemptuous one. On the eve of
labor violence, much like Cass McKay in search of Norah Egan, he looks
to her for comfort. But though Cass has no redeeming interests, Johnny
does. The lovemaking scene occurs in a section entitled "The Education
of a Worker," and it is clear that Johnny's initiation is both sexual and
political. Ellen's promiscuity thus plays on the stereotype of "easy" working women the novel had questioned and symbolizes the constricted role
available to women in male strikes. Cantwell almost transforms Ellen's
giving of her body into a commemoration of the strike. Instead, in an
unsuccessful attempt to reconcile Ellen's labor and gender identities, he
endows the scene with confused and contradictory meanings. Ellen is
both worker and unpaid prostitute, political activist and willing sexual
sacrifice.

As the novel closes, Johnny, invigorated by a feminine workplace sexuality in which carnality and self-sacrifice are mixed, is newly poised for
action. But the strike is soon violently put down and he never engages in
it, his immobility emblematic of the abortive nature of the uprising itself.
It is Ellen who is beaten by a policeman, not Johnny. She is still offering
up her body to the cause, though in a different way—further evidence that
the men's protest has gone awry. What is a bow to women's historical part

in strikes is, more significantly, a portent of at least this strike's failure. Certainly Johnny's is a thwarted militance. He makes no move to enter the labor fray with Ellen, and as he joins two other workers seeking refuge from the police, he learns that his own father has been shot, a martyr to an abandoned protest. In this dispiriting—or at best in-medias-res— conclusion, the strike is lost because its aims are dissipated in ineffectual feminine heroics and a masculine inability to seize the moment.

If Cantwell reduces the politically engaged female wage earner to a nurturing harlot and sometime strike victim, in *The Chute* (1937) Albert Halper, another of the few male novelists to place women at the site of labor exploitation, sees her as an unreconstructed prisoner of sexual cravings.[60] Halper makes a closer connection between an abortive strike and the distracting presence of women. His lengthy book, one of a series of four about workers exhausted by technology and routine, draws on his experiences on the lowest rung of the mail-order business, in which he had worked as a young man. In *The Chute,* men and women alike live at the pleasure of the huge conveyor that runs from floor to floor and receives packages from all departments, a "terrifying force that shapes and dominates the lives of all who work at Golden Rule Mail Order Company."[61] A few silent women attend the meetings at which a union is planned, and at the company some of them listen to shop-floor news about an incipient job action. But their true agenda is apolitical.

Halper slightingly terms the segregated area where they all work the "chicken yard," and with reason. As the largely masculine discontent with company spies, cutbacks, and Draconian efficiency experts mounts, the women wrappers—seemingly the more experienced in their packing work, the more "hardened" (188) in other ways as well—make the work floor a sexual hothouse. The nubile, aptly named Eve, a seasoned worker, eyes any man she finds attractive and engages in catfights with her co-worker Helen over the attentions of one handsome newcomer. Mrs. Shumway, the jilted mistress of a middle manager, redoubles her attempts to lure him to her bed. And even the chaste young Italian girl who has just been hired fixates on marriage, oblivious to the groundswell of masculine labor discontent around her. To the problem of women's too-palpable presence in the male work world, their dissipation of masculine energies that would be better directed to fighting management chicanery, Halper provides a Ma Joad solution. His immigrant mothers, Steinbeck's family bulwark transplanted to ethnic Chicago, hover over their tired worker sons, cook special foods, go without nourishment so that their boys may eat, and sacrifice without measure. His equally devoted sisters save their meager salaries to send their factory-bound brothers to college someday, more interested in these young men's job problems than in their own sweatshop exploitation or romantic and marital prospects. In imagining such paragons, Halper attempted to redeem women from the carnality that other writers had invoked to characterize the more typical sirens of the mail-order work floor. Constructing work as a feminine character flaw, he joined writers from Gold through Cantwell in the credo that there were too many workplace Eves and not enough mothers at home.

African-American Sons and Variations on the Mother Theme

If the white social protest novelists created a composite vision of work as a moral no-woman's land, their black male counterparts had far less difficulty with the issues raised by black women in the labor world. For one thing, as a Women's Bureau bulletin on "the Negro woman worker" pointed out in the late 1930s, that tradition had been established before the Civil War, when a female slave's ability to work governed her market value.[62] After the war, black women continued to fill the financial gap created by the low earnings of black men, who did not need the Depression to be consigned to unskilled jobs with the lowest earnings and least possibility of advancement. By 1930, one out of every six women, or two million of the eleven million feminine labor force, was a black wage earner (Brown, 1). Black married women worked five times as often as equally impoverished foreign-born wives.[63]

Against that background, even as early as the artistic and literary flowering of the 1920s, the Harlem Renaissance, Claude McKay in *Home to Harlem* (1928) and Wallace Thurman in *The Blacker the Berry* (1929) exposed what Langston Hughes's biographer Arnold Rampersad called "the daily humiliations of black men and women."[64] In chronicling pre-Depression Harlem, McKay and Thurman gave an interpretation of working-class difficulties that highlighted how women, in these novels not subject to joblessness but wage earners in a range of jobs from cook to saloon singer to teacher in a black school, suffered from more than relegation to the jobs that white women did not want. Whether McKay's scrub maids and saloon singers or Thurman's college-educated Indiana emigrants, these women may have steady employment, but they collaborate in their emotional and economic exploitation by their men. Playing on the idea of the promiscuous black woman, neither writer denies the association of Harlem women's work and waywardness, but each places it in a context that renders it far less negative than white (or black) women's wage earning is depicted in white authors' 1930s texts. To be sure, McKay's Jake and Zeddy and Thurman's Alva and his disreputable drinking buddies are given the offer to be, or are engaged in, "living sweet" (*Home,* 87) on sexually willing Harlem women's earnings. Yet the point is that the arrangement, though neither Zeddy nor Jake is aware of it, demeans men and women alike. Even if, like the longshoreman Jake, these men do unskilled work themselves, they internalize white society's vision of their supposed inferiority and work out their anger in part through manipulating the myriad women who people these texts, ever willing to support them. In both novels, the mere attention to the variety of urban jobs women fill—as maids, cooks, restaurant help, beauty shop attendants, sales clerks, lower-rung entertainers, and willing denizens of the informal apartment brothel known as the "buffet flat"—is something new. But the deeper interest is that, in the after-hours world of the Harlem dance palace and cheap rooming house, these women, in a frenzied search for men they can respect, remake their lovers into a species of sweatshop boss and permit the men to earmark their pay for flashy clothes and dates with other women. Even the "little ginned-up negresses" who, among other jobs, engage in sex for hire, lament when their lovers are "not interested in [their] earnings" (*Home,* 109, 114). Men and women alike in these two books, without families or estranged from them, lacking strong moral controls or vocational futures, seem gripped by a desperate hedonism that caused the two books to be misunderstood as condemnations of the race. In fact, they are angry explorations of the forces that produced Harlem's rootless psyche.[65] Particularly in scenes where Thurman's well-educated heroine is shunned as too dark by black employment agencies ("our Negro business men have a definite type of girl in mind and will not hire any other" [*Blacker,* 86]), the novels illuminate the psychological effects of discrimination on black working women in other ways as well.

Yet their most trenchant perception was that black women would not achieve dignity until, like their men, they could overcome the negative image of blacks that both sexes played out in gender relations.

McKay and Thurman initiated a discussion that Langston Hughes, who admired both men, relocated in the pre–World War I Midwest, outside the northern cities to which, both before and after the war, blacks migrated in search of better jobs.[66] By so doing, he not only placed the relationship between the jobless or inequitably employed male and the overworked female in the context of the black family; he also honored black women's work in a way that McKay and Thurman did not. Partly autobiographical, his retrospective novel *Not Without Laughter* (1930), like his poignant poems "Song of a Negro Wash-Woman" (1925), "The Negro Mother" (1926), and "Mother to Son" (1931), draws on his Kansas-Missouri boyhood as the son of a domestic.[67]

One of Hughes's important achievements was to cast a cold eye on the exploitation of black women in segregated America without denying their labor the dignity it deserved. These women are not drones or ciphers, although the conditions of their lives as maids, waitresses, laundresses, and cannery women conspire to make them so. In a section called "Work," his young protagonist, Sandy, experiences the humiliation of seeing his mother, Anjee, unjustly treated by a southern white employer only to walk by her side after her lengthy day and watch her greet neighbors asking how she is with "Right smart, I thank yuh!" (65). To that early vignette are joined scenes of Sandy's grandmother, Hager Williams, in her frenetic, slavelike home laundry work, her kitchen like a caldron, and of his lively young aunt, Harriett, who surveys her extensive menial work history and disgustedly sums up local female labor conditions (male work is scarce, and men like Sandy's itinerant railroadman father halfheartedly seek work elsewhere) as "thirteen hours a day in tomato season . . . nine cents an hour and five overtime after ten hours" (75). Though in the linkage of women's work and sexuality that seems endemic to male writings, her work activities include paid encounters at the local hotel, Harriett, too, is a maternal figure. In what proves a wise career decision, she runs off with a circus and later finds the work as a blues singer that, she declares at the novel's end, will send her nephew for more schooling. Rather than condemn Harriett's situational morality, as might a Steinbeck or a Conroy, Hughes wrote of her in his 1940 autobiography: "That night when Harriett ran away to join the carnival was more than I could stand. I knew I would miss her."[68]

If Sandy's three mother figures range in attitude toward their work lives from Christian acceptance to dignified anger to enraged resentment culminating in flight, as sexual beings they are equally diverse. Hager's old-time religion abhors "sin." Anjee practices a passionate monogamy. Harriett's sexuality is expressed in promiscuity, sometimes for hire, sometimes for love. The larger point is that whether their sexuality is repressed, channeled into marriage, or flaunted for the world to see, these women's wages, not their morals, are the bedrock of the family. In this they mirror their real-life counterparts, the more than 20 percent of woman-headed black families and countless husband-absent ones that fared as well as those with male heads (Greenberg, 197).

Interestingly, the New Masses, to which Hughes, an intellectually committed party adherent, had contributed some early fiction, interpreted his novel as traditional proletarian fiction, chiding it only for an overemphasis on blacks rather than the entire working class and for an insufficient revolutionary agenda.[69] In reality, the novel's references to male work are secondary, and not solely because the women, who will take the lowest wages, are more actively employed. There is a deeper sense that whatever the ego deflations endured by black men, most of the family's tensions stem from the literal and emotional transience of Sandy's father, Jimboy, who is too feckless to be the family head. What is as important as the analysis of wandering black fathers, however, is that, because he viewed his subjects in the round, Hughes broke down the oppositions between earth mothers and streetwalkers so central to proletarian and social novels alike. He fuses women and (aside from a brief reference to Harriett's past cannery work) the nonindustrial workplace. In any event, his women stand in favorable contrast to the saintly—or controlling—matriarchs and workplace sluts of white protest writers.

After the broad sympathies of Hughes, it is a shock to turn to Richard Wright, another party adherent and New Masses contributor. His finest novel cannot be fitted into a tight proletarian slot. In this it is unlike his depressing Lawd Today, a day in the life of a permanently disgruntled black postal clerk who hates breadwinning and domestic women alike, completed in 1937 but not published until 1963. His Native Son (1940), like the

Steinbeck novel rewarded with best-sellerdom for its ability to dissect and then transcend its immediate subject (and no doubt for its murder plot as well), locates a "Bottom Dogs" protagonist in the context of inexorable environmental tyranny in a naturalistic manner reminiscent of Dreiser.[70] As in Hughes, there is no mother-worker split, but the Damoclean sword of black unemployment that hangs over a woman-headed family, whose gender tensions are dangerously disruptive. To the reader, Mrs. Thomas is a flawed but loving figure. To Bigger, she mirrors the oppressions of the larger society: exhorting, chastening, and demeaning him in the name of moral guidance. Comments Robert Felgar, Bigger Thomas's mother "oppresses him when she insists on . . . defining his 'manhood.'"[71] To her, that means a dead-end service job with white employers, a masculine version of what she has done all her life and, now on relief, what she is frightened that she will not be able to continue. Fearful, resentful, and ashamed of her, Wright's rage-filled protagonist gives his own version of the black job market. "You shine shoes, sweep streets; anything. . . . You don't make enough to live on. You don't know when you going to get fired. Pretty soon you get so you can't hope for nothing" (326). Such sentiments bespeak a larger resentment of the discriminatory white world. It erupts one evening early in his employ at the home of the pluto-cratic Dalton family, with whom, at his mother's urging, he has taken a job as chauffeur. In his fear at being found in the daughter's bedroom, to which he has carried her after a drunken evening out spent trying to "convert" Bigger to her incongruously Communist beliefs, Bigger suf-focates her and disposes of her body in a gruesome fashion. In a second act of extreme violence against women, he murders his girlfriend Bessie Mears to prevent her from informing on him. In the relentless logic of the narrative, he is quickly jailed, convicted, and left to await his execution.

Bigger's hatred of Mary Dalton is in large part a projection of his ab-horrence of white privilege; his hatred of black women, who are typified by the two domestics, his mother and Bessie, is a projection of rage at his own passivity: "He hated his mother for that way of hers which was like Bessie's" (226). Save as objects of Bigger's anger and sometime guilt, the two women do not figure prominently in the narrative; in tandem with their resigned response to their lives even before the violence Big-ger unleashes, their secondary status has prompted some feminist critics to call them "mindless," "childlike," and "at the bottom of the scale of human intelligence." [72] Others, perceiving their wordless resignation as an alternative to black male violence, have more accurately seen them as the repository of values and the human desire for something, however minimal, as a reward for hard work. [73] Part of that humanity is evidenced in the way Bessie, though fearful that Bigger has committed a crime and justly terrified he will punish or implicate her, tries to express her creed. In a poignant speech, she speaks too for what Bigger, in his act of violence, has in a way tried to erase, the paid female servitude of those like herself and Mrs. Thomas: "All I do is work, work like a dog! From morning to night. I ain't got no happiness. I ain't never had none. I ain't got nothing and you do this to me. After how good I been to you. Now you just spoil my whole life. . . . I ain't done nothing for this to come to me! I just work! . . . I just work. I'm black and I work and don't bother anybody" (170).

Lacking the courage and minimal opportunities of the working women in the works by McKay, Thurman, and Hughes, Bessie Mears is a born victim, unable to choose men who will not injure her, unable to assert her worth. Reliant on alcohol, without a religious anchor or much of a conscience (she has aided Bigger in thieving from her ungenerous employers), she is an end-of-the-road version of Harriett, Anjee, and even Bigger's mother. And Mrs. Thomas is Hughes's lawgiving matriarch Hager Williams adrift in a city world that undermines her economic and ethical authority. Though she rightly fears the family's fragmentation (she tells Bigger, correctly, that he will end on the gallows), her inability to inculcate her streetwise eldest son with her turn-the-other-cheek morality reinforces Wright's theme of willessness, his view that blacks are victims of an entrapping poverty that explains, if it does not excuse, the acts of violence of those like Bigger Thomas.

Central to the novels of Hughes and Wright about the black man's experience in a racist workplace, both rural and urban, is the sympathetically portrayed maternal figure, whether or not her effect on her male relative is redemptive. In comparing the era's radical chroniclers of the black labor experience with their white counterparts, we find the mother less one-dimensional, in part because hers is the wage-earning role that was historically allotted to black matriarchs. Too, these writers imagine the self-supporting black woman, though hemmed in by masochistic ties to unstable lovers, as a sympathetic figure, perhaps because she is customarily imprisoned in domestic work and is no competitor for men's jobs.

(Unfortunately, these authors did not do similar justice to white women, who are routinely stereotyped as emblems of privilege.[74]) Furthermore, as if all black women's work were an extension of their family role, Hughes and Wright neglected the significant minority of black women in manufacturing and garment trade work, some of whom spearheaded all-women strikes.[75] When women's wage earning was not linked to the family, as in the works of the pre-Depression authors McKay and Thurman, the self-supporting Harlem women were far more taken up by their emotional difficulties than their labor ones. And one of the few black writers to ring changes on the conventional strike novel, William Attaway, in his historical novel *Blood on the Forge* (1941), did so at women's expense. They occupy their familiar positions as black mothers waiting down South or as camp-following immigrant prostitutes in the Pennsylvania steel towns. The mother/whore split remains.

Back to the Home: Men's Texts

In his memoir *Starting Out in the Thirties* (1962), the venerable critic Alfred Kazin reflects that the typical writers of his time, Steinbeck, Farrell, Cantwell, Dahlberg, Fuchs, Roth, Algren, and Wright, brought the authority of workers to their writing and "understandably flourished their experience, their hard knocks, their life on the road, their days on the picket line and in the hiring hall."[76] Kazin makes much of the farm, mill, factory, low-level clerical, and assorted manual jobs on which these authors drew for their art. And it is certainly true that their novels, whether social or proletarian, whether, like *Grapes of Wrath, Studs Lonigan,* and *Native Son,* they snared the Book-of-the-Month Club's commercially useful accolade or were as unread as *Bottom Dogs* and *Somebody in Boots,* filled their pages with extended descriptions of male labor.

But Kazin's inventory, to which Gold, Conroy, Hughes, and Halper should certainly be added, scants the subject of the next chapter, female authors, and the feminine "proletarian" experience, whether envisioned by men or women. So, too, did the writers he finds so representative of "the [literary] age of the plebes" (12). They so minimized and truncated breadwinning womanhood that only proletarian men learned from workplace oppression; women, imprisoned in their sexuality, did not. When they did locate woman outside what they deemed her rightful mothering sphere, they projected the shop-floor prurience onto her best exemplified in *The Chute*: "The girls, most of them between the ages of sixteen and nineteen, were . . . warm-blooded and lively fillies, bursting with youth," some of them even fond of "pushing [their] pointy breasts . . . into the back[s]" of men (28). Even if, for the sake of argument, there were some women who bore out these bizarrely erotic observations, like all of the authors lauded by Kazin, Halper painted the workplace as an arena in which the brash, sex-crazed, or husband-hungry woman improperly acts out impulses better channeled into home as vocation. An intruder on the labor scene, she is, to use Dorothy Dinnerstein's expression, a "carnal scapegoat," blasted for deflecting the male energies needed for a new political day.[77]

For the male social protest writers, there were no migrant mothers in field work or urban industry, no female Tom Joads leaving the domestic space to walk the land or enter the hiring halls of nation and city. There were only ideal and failed mother figures. When, as in Gold, the idealized mother actually crossed the gender line and became the breadwinner, at her workplace she was defused and depicted only as a source of advice and compassion, not one whose earnings might emasculate the men of the family. For even the good wife, if untamed by lawgiving men, might degenerate into the unregulated woman, threatening to castrate and destroy. Interestingly, though this nightmare of feminine power is rehearsed in Daniel Fuchs's trilogy of teeming ethnic Brooklyn, *Summer in Williamsburg* (1934), his harpy-matriarchs and aspiring matriarch-girlfriends are without paying jobs (or have jobs sketched, and dismissed, in half a sentence). Nags, shrews, and worse, they join Farrell's Mrs. Lonigan in their true occupation: the spiritual murder of their men.

Erasing the woman at work, social novelists like Farrell and Steinbeck still anticipated the era's proletarian novelists either by lamenting the unholy family created by this suffocating mother or alluding to nondomestic womanhood as sexually wayward. Proletarian "conversion" fiction took the harlot image further and conflated such feminine sexual waywardness, and even prostitution, with all of woman's breadwinning work. So did "Bottom Dogs" fiction. Although there was some attempt there—and even more in strike novels—to legitimize women's economic needs, it foundered in a distrust of female carnality.

Partial exceptions occurred in works of black male writers: alive to the injustices of race in a way that white authors were not, their maternal characters are well-intentioned wage earners, neither saints nor monsters, humanized, indeed victimized worker-mothers or self-sustaining female breadwinners. But there, too, as in late 1920s precursors Thurman and McKay, working women were tied to their family roles or to aberrant emotional relations with men who reduced them to convenient sexual objects.

With such hostile, ambivalent, or otherwise constricted analyses of female work in domestic service, agriculture, and manufacturing, it is no wonder that radical male texts conveyed the same message as the era's back-to-the-home apologists: to turn from mothering was to be dangerously oversexed and, paradoxically, quintessentially unwomanly. To such a message a trio of women writers, Tillie Olsen, Meridel Le Sueur, and Agnes Smedley, framed powerful responses. In reinventing the maternal figure, though not without their own conflicts regarding the mother-worker split, these women moved toward a verisimilitude absent in men's texts.

Chapter Three

FEMININE SOCIAL PROTEST FICTION AND THE MOTHER-BURDEN

Marion Post Wolcott, *A Woman Migrant Packinghouse Worker and Her Eldest Child Preparing Dinner,* Belle Glade, Florida, 1939. Library of Congress.

Suddenly [Mazie] would see before her a monster thing with blind eyes and shaking
body . . . a woman with her mother's face grown gaunter, holding a skeleton
baby whose stomach was pushed out like a ball.
—Tillie Olsen, *Yonnondio* (1934–37; pub. 1971)

The women were often left alone, the men gone. . . . Migrating, lost, silent, drunk
father[s]. . . . My grandmother raised her own children, my mother hers, and I mine.
—Meridel Le Sueur, *Crusaders* (1955)

To induce my mother to stop beating me I . . . would say yes, I had lied and was sorry,
and then she would whip me for having withheld the admission so long.
"I have but one child who is stubborn and a liar, and that is Marie,"
she would tell strangers or neighbors.
—Agnes Smedley, *Daughter of Earth* (1929; abr. ed., 1935)

L inking his work as a factory hand, hauler, and road paver to the
rest of the manly toil described in his novel *The Disinherited,* Jack
Conroy reminisced years later about "all those jobs I worked on
or observed."[1] Another young author of the 1930s committed to labor
themes, John Steinbeck, while a student at Stanford, rejected the largesse
of his well-off parents and paid for that education by manual work. He
never finished his degree, but by the time he published *The Grapes of
Wrath,* he had fully matriculated in Conroy's school of hard knocks. Like
Conroy, Mike Gold, Richard Wright, and their numerous male contemporaries, Tom Joad's creator skillfully drew on his labor-class experiences
for literary material.

But for every Steinbeck, whose writings caught the popular imagination without deviating from working-class subject matter, there were
countless social protest writers who could not live on their work as sometime laborers or unemployed writers. Although others stared hunger in
the face or were lucky enough to find a place on a WPA writers' project,
it was not unusual for them to live on women's earnings. This state of affairs was sardonically described by Alfred Kazin: "The old neighborhood
poets . . . had got themselves married to girls older than themselves, with
good jobs."[2] In between jobs while completing his novel of masculine
labor, Conroy had to depend on his wife's pay for a time, and even a not-

yet-famous Steinbeck relied on his spouse's unpaid typing skills and small salary.[3]

Yet when it came to acknowledging the woman breadwinner, much less the worker-wife or mother, the insights of life rarely infiltrated men's art. Even those male protest writers who did not share the unemployment plight of their colleagues—or of their roaming protagonists—routinely extolled the home-front Ma Joad for knowing her place, shuddered at a companionate model of family earnings, scanted the single working mother, and looked askance at the self-supporting solo woman.

In contrast to the proselytizing for motherhood that informed the male protest genre, a trio of female journalist-novelists paid homage to the working-class woman by disrupting the earth mother myth of their (predominantly) masculine colleagues. To be sure, other radical women's texts, and a few men's, offered feminine characters whose political circumstances defied the idealized mothering of *The Disinherited* or *The Grapes of Wrath*. Such protagonists symbolized new combinations of married—and single—wage earning, particularly in fictionalized accounts of the Gastonia textile uprising. But Tillie Olsen, Meridel Le Sueur, and Agnes Smedley, none of whose novels, significantly, appeared in completed form in the 1930s, merit separate scrutiny. Unlike the Gastonia writers, they did not seek inspiration in an isolated historical event in which for a brief time women combined family, work, and social activism. Nor, in further contrast to the Gastonia school, did they attempt to reconcile the woman on the barricades with a motherly ideal. Instead, virtually alone among 1930s devotees of the literary left (Olsen and Le Sueur were in the Communist Party, Smedley sympathetic to its views), they endowed their burdened mothers with a psychological or a revisionary mythic dimension absent in most masculine portraits. Permitting such women to voice the myriad complaints a Ma Joad never entertains, the trio envisioned maternal figures whose roles are defined—and often flawed—by poverty, spousal brutality, desertion, and unassisted child rearing, not to mention their own scarred psyches.

As practitioners of social protest fiction, Olsen, Le Sueur, and Smedley produced an amalgam of "Bottom Dogs" and conversion fiction, casting the daughters of their fictional mothers, like the Tom Joads in men's fiction, as poised for political action. But in an attempt to psychoanalyze or reinvent as matriarchal the hard-luck blue-collar family, they centered their narrations on the female working-class subject in a "revis[ion] of the classic proletarian novel." [4] And they did so through attention to the troubling emotional baggage the proletarian daughter, trapped by and fearful of replicating her mother's life, must carry, or, in a more optimistic scenario, by examining her commitment to a manless extended family of underclass women. In any case, unlike the sons of Ma Joad, these fictive daughters neither stride off without looking back to the family, succumb to the damage wrought by their monstrous mothers, nor drift aimlessly as economic losers raging at and longing for mother surrogates. In Olsen's apprentice warm-ups for an unfinished 1934–37 manuscript of *Yonnondio*, in Le Sueur's short fiction, later collected in *Salute to Spring* (1940), her published sections of *The Girl* (1939–45) and related short fiction, and in Smedley's *Daughter of Earth*, Conroy's widowed home laundress Mrs. Donovan, Ma Joad, and Gold's tireless Katie character are drastically rewritten.

The Three: Some Left-Literary Biography

Olsen, Le Sueur, and Smedley carved reputations both for their reportorial dissections of labor strife under capitalism and their clear-eyed contributions to the growing body of proletarian fiction. Their work appeared in the same leftist journals as did that of Mike Gold, James T. Farrell, Erskine Caldwell, and Nelson Algren.[5] Most of the opening chapter of *Yonnondio*, for example, was first published in the *Partisan Review*, to which Le Sueur, dubbed by Conroy in later years one of the two "deans of proletarian literature" (Thompson, 168)—he offered himself as the other one—contributed fiction with titles like the 1935 piece "Tonight Is Part of the Struggle." And though his claim that she published all parts of *The Girl* in the *Anvil*, Conroy's John Reed Club outgrowth, was exaggerated, between that journal and *New Masses*, several segments on her favorite subject, the female down-and-outer of the Midwest, saw print. As early as 1927 parts of Smedley's proletarian bildungsroman *Daughter of Earth* had also appeared in *New Masses*. That journal was also a ready conduit for her Chinese dispatches, most notably those on the new revolutionary woman factory worker. Smedley also sent back accounts of Chinese "red" activities—including those of women intellectuals, students, and peasants—to the *New Republic*, to which Olsen contributed her equally impassioned accounts, including one of her arrest in connection with the 1934 San Francisco maritime strike.

However prolific and well-known both as fact-gathering contributors to liberal and radical-minded journals and as writers of social protest novels Olsen, Le Sueur, and Smedley were, their literary output was abbreviated. The reasons were diverse. In the late 1930s, Olsen had all but completed half of the manuscript of *Yonnondio* when organizing and motherhood deflected her energies. Le Sueur's 1935 *Anvil* sketch of a male worker discovering solidarity, "Alone in Chicago," was advertised on the cover above a linoleum cut of manly workers at a forge, but her book-length celebration of a male-excluding feminine collective, *The Girl,* could not find a publisher. Smedley did bring out her fiery novel of feminine political awareness, but when it was reissued in the mid-1930s, the editor cut away the inflammatory last third. Despite the differences in their publishing histories, the difficulty all of these literary daughters of the Depression had in being heard suggests that even in radical circles their vision of working-class womanhood was too troubling.

What *was* published was their "acceptable" proletarian literature, although both Le Sueur and Smedley were reprimanded in *New Masses* circles for defeatism and bitterness.[6] Le Sueur's "I'm Going, I Said" (1940), for instance, fit that category. But some of her other fictive vignettes, dubbed negative, such as "Salvation Home" (1939), were probably considered too involved in women's issues, for there were myriad proletarian novels far more defeatist. It was one thing to critique capitalism by demonstrating what Paula Rabinowitz terms the "prison of working-class womanhood."[7] It was quite another to treat the male breadwinner's home itself as an oppressive feminine work or living place. Even more daring was to cast the daughters as oppressed by the mother, with a psychic usurpation ever in danger of punishing the girl child, as did Olsen and Smedley, or to suggest that girlhood oppression would not occur in a matriarchal household, as did Le Sueur. Locating the ills of a pinched proletarian upbringing in the male-headed family, these women add a disturbing dimension to the earth mother myth, one that they themselves, in their allegiance to a class analysis of oppression, could not fully acknowledge.

Neither adulatory nor denigrating, Olsen, Le Sueur, and Smedley, informed by a leftist orientation and by what Constance Coiner terms a "prescient but latent consciousness" of feminism, illuminated the difficulties of leftist mother worship.[8] By so doing, they gave new identities to the proletarian mother and her worker-daughter, so often distorted by male texts. Before examining these women's revisioning of the woman as embittered—or abandoned—toiler for the proletarian family, however, it is important to analyze how that rare 1930s forum for an exploration of women's exploitation, party literature, addressed the issue of women's work at home.

The Communist Party and Women's Work

At a time when magazines like *Good Housekeeping,* its title, like its content, propaganda for a sentimentalized domesticity, extolled woman's home function, U.S. Communists offered an opposing vision. Articles appeared in party organs that deplored housework, perceived particularly as a poor woman's burden under capitalism. Although by the late 1930s, in a Popular Front attempt to broaden their appeal to the American masses, CP thinkers softened their position, in the first half of the decade they echoed Lenin's view of the drudgery of the capitalist hausfrau. To many, she was the "slave of a slave," a "drudge" chained to "bourgeois-imposed conditions of life," which would be overcome "as part of the basic proletarian struggle."[9] They regularly invoked the Soviet model, in which many forms of maternal protection, particularly workplace day care and cooperative housekeeping, were believed to herald American women's emancipation from the rigors of unassisted mothering. The party Women's Commission head Margaret Cowl wrote that in the Soviet Union one finds "state protection of the interests of mother and child."[10] (Notably absent from American leftists' paean to Soviet enlightenment, however, was praise for the availability of birth control, much less abortion, legal in the Soviet Union until 1936.[11]) Under the auspices of the commission, party adherents joined non-Communist groups such as the Women's Trade Union League in advocating a Women's Charter, which called for protective legislation for women, including working mothers.[12]

If the majority of theoreticians were adamant that any improvement in housewives' lot under capitalism would slow the process of change, there was an attempt to cast the housewife as a domestic heroine for enduring her lot patiently while directing her energies, as *Working Woman* exhorted in June 1933, to "fight with the . . . workers for immediate relief [and] unemployment insurance," or as the *Daily Worker* urged a year later, to join "the husband . . . in the class struggle."[13] The *Communist* reminded its readers that a Detroit housewife, Mary Zuk, was elected in 1936 "on a people's ticket to protest high prices," with the full support of the United Auto Workers (Cowl, 552). With models such as these in place to carry out party policy to "win the women" (Cowl, 551) and shore up the image of the housewife's importance, such writers ignored the fact that theory did not separate housework from the women who performed it or that housewives were undervalued. The effort was to convert the homemaker into a part-time activist spearheading antieviction protests, unemployment councils, grass-roots rent strikes, and mothers' drives against the high price of milk, implying that her work lay in providing a "We Help Them Strike" force on the picket line.[14]

Disturbed that the image of the housewife-drudge and the emphasis on freeing her devalued what she did in her "bondage," a minority struggled to defend housework as true work, locating women's domesticity as "workshops in the form of 'homes' where these women toil."[15] Here the focus, unpopular in party circles, was on the housewife as economically productive because "a woman caring for her husband who worked in a Firestone factory was as much a part of the production of automobiles as he was" (Dixler, 132).

In the main, however, fiction by male (and some female) authors cast woman's domestic chores as a necessary sacrifice until the Soviet model of maternal protection could be put in place in America. Whether they were party adherents or more loosely allied to the radical movement, such writers judged the housewife, always a secondary character, by how well or poorly she represented what the firebrand Elizabeth Gurley Flynn in *New Masses* called the idea that every housewife was a heroine.[16] Texts such as Edward Newhouse's strike novel *This Is Your Day* (1937), therefore, preached of the good Communist housewife, a bourgeoise with a radical overlay who sees her housekeeping and her party involvement as twinned duties.[17] Mrs. Darvas, the freethinker as homemaker, lovingly rises early to wake up her family, including her Young Communist League (YCL) daughter's live-in lover ("Alma and Gene were sound sleepers, and Mrs. Darvas felt safe in bending over to kiss her daughter . . . [who] turned slowly toward Gene and placed her hand on his shoulder" [39]), before she bustles about serving them, her husband, and her grown sons their first meal of the day. To bring home, so to speak, the message of the party housewife, Newhouse adds that, much as she wishes to mend her slipcovers, the welcome chore must wait until she finishes "the cushion that had been promised to the International Labor Defense bazaar" (46).

Although the novel is rare enough in devoting three full pages to home-front duties, from emptying trash to cleaning bedrooms, all of which this good comrade cheerfully takes on, this picture of a sexually tolerant version of Ma Joad, with a roof over her head, glosses over the child-bearing and homemaking difficulties of many a worker's wife. So does Meridel Le Sueur's fellow *Anvil* contributor Helen Coppell. In her 1933 short story "Out of the Hole," in which Mary, the labor wife, is cast as a stereotyped patient Griselda, she regards her militant-striker husband "hopefully" with "her trusting gray eyes" as "she put a plate of boiled potatoes before him." [18]

If both Mrs. Darvas and Mary are the good housekeepers lauded regularly in the pages of *Woman Today,* the woman's magazine counterpart of the *Daily Worker* ("the United Women's Councils of New York support the strike of the International Baker's Union," read a June 1933 headline), their zealous enjoyment of family and home care seems atypical (even of the more savvy readership of the party's periodicals). Other texts were more forthright about the toll taken by such a life. Larry Donovan's Aunt Jessie in *The Disinherited,* once a pretty girl, is prematurely aged and broken by the sheer weight of it. But, true to the heroic housewife mold, she tends rather than complains. As such, she is the antithesis of the slovenly or unruly proletarian wife in James Steele's ponderous 1935 book *Conveyor,* who undermines the labor movement by selfish concern for her own lot. As Cantwell's 1934 wood factory novel *Land of Plenty* makes clear, men must complain to raise labor consciousness; long-suffering mothers and factory wives must listen and be silent.

Whether distantly sympathetic to these stoics of the kitchen, sternly reminding the proletarian wife and mother to do her job well and sometimes casting it as an extension of her party duty, male and more doctrinaire female writers reflected the dominant thinking on the matter in leftist circles. For the most part, though, the heroic housewife functioned as literary shorthand in a narrative reluctant to take time from chronicling labor pains that had nothing to do with childbirth.

Tillie Olsen and, even more aggressively, Agnes Smedley questioned the role of the heroine housewife by portraying her as psychically scarred, angrily despondent. Meridel Le Sueur offered the manless mother as an alternative heroine and suggested that working-class maternity was at its best in the absence of a feckless male provider. Though offering no program for freeing women from home and mother work, Olsen dramatized through Anna Holbrook how much "productive" labor such roles involved. *Yonnondio* anticipated party maverick Mary Inman's plaint in *In Woman's Defense* (1940) that the housewife toils in her own "workshop" (147) and that to "do hard toil, and useful work, yet be branded as dependent . . . labeled 'supported,' nothing in the world is as galling as this" (146). If, as Deborah Rosenfelt observes, Olsen was "finally unable . . . to suggest a systemic solution," Le Sueur and Smedley, despite their divergence on the "romance" of mothering, came closer.[19] Le Sueur, ever the mother's advocate, implicitly advanced an argument for paid maternity, particularly for the single mothers whom state and federal bureaus of child welfare had dubbed "risky" well before the Great Depression.[20] She focused on the needs of destitute and, often, sexually active women whom, in her view, the social service system unfairly labeled unfit, refusing them child care payments, even sterilizing them after consigning their babies to foster care. In her plea for maternal justice, her *New Masses* and *Anvil* fiction deplored the institutional settings, philanthropic or punitive, in which women waited out their pregnancies and the substandard living quarters in which they pooled their resources and raised the children the system had not snatched from them. Smedley may well have responded with distaste to Le Sueur's ode to solo motherhood, but she, too, argued for mothers' right to refuse to be mothers. Her protagonist, the embittered child of an equally bitter mother, *Daughter of Earth*'s Marie Rogers is denied birth control and suffers through dangerous abortions. Through her fictive alter ego, Smedley mounted a challenge to the radical Left. Her message was clear enough: be as active in supporting contraception for poor women as in espousing maternal insurance and exhorting housewives to "man" the consumer boycott barricades.

To an extent that two of the three, CP members Olsen and Le Sueur, did not themselves acknowledge, the trio "subvert[ed] restrictive elements with a leftist subculture" (Coiner, 165). And they did so in a variety of ways, including focusing on mother-daughter rather than on the mother-son relationship so dear to Steinbeck, Conroy, and Farrell and establishing a true scrutiny of mother work. These two departures led them to a third: departure from the idealized magna mater of the male proletarians. These artistic decisions, evidenced in Olsen's and Smedley's scenarios of confused and misdirected rage and in Le Sueur's of an empowered community of abandoned mothers, produced fiction on the casualties of mothering, the costs of forced maternity, even in the proletarian holy family.

Yonnondio and Mother Prisons

Like Meridel Le Sueur and Agnes Smedley, both of whom, when they had fallen into neglect decades after the Depression, she resurrected in her celebrated 1962 *Silences* essays on forgotten women writers, Tillie Olsen rooted her fiction of labor frustration and angry men, of overwork and battered women, in a novelistic form combining the "Bottom Dogs" and strike subgenres. Writing within a naturalistic mode that wove a pessimism about working-class change with an optimism about the resilience of the human spirit, she offered in *Yonnondio* a vision of the hard-luck Holbrook family's life. Set in the 1920s, it is also a bleak exploration of Olsen's 1930s—first in a Wyoming coal-mining town, then on a disastrous Dakota farm, and finally amid the satanic conditions of an urban Midwest, possibly in an Omaha slaughterhouse. In the recovered, still unfinished original manuscript, eight chapters piece together what, in Olsen's 1970s phrase, the "long ago young writer"[21] had published only as excerpts in the 1930s. Toward the end of the manuscript, the packinghouse workers merely comment that their work under "Beedo" (the dreaded Bedaux speed-up system of the 1920s) is "hell" (114). But there is no evidence of the move to overturn it. Furthermore, although in one of the projected endings (not part of the 1971 published novel), Jim Holbrook does lead a strike, he is blacklisted, hardly the ringing ending that so often provided closure in other strike fictions.

In another projected version, Anna dies from a self-induced abortion; in others, Jim is an increasingly desperate father of four, a wife-beater and an opponent of working wives. He either abandons his family or is of so little spiritual help that Anna Holbrook kills herself. In a final variant, his eldest son, Will, reacting to the fragmentation of the Holbrook family, becomes a hobo like Algren's Cass McKay.[22]

Again like Le Sueur, who was a chronicler and WPA teacher of the female unemployed manufacturing and sales workers of St. Paul, and like Smedley, who held degrading jobs as hired help and sweatshop worker, Olsen was a veteran of the slaughterhouse, the food-processing factory, and the hash house. She well knew the paid work of the woman laborer.[23] Her notes for *Yonnondio* list the lower rates of pay women received for meatpacking jobs such as eardrum cutter and head-splitter, jobs that in the novel itself are matter-of-factly dubbed those "men will not take."[24]

But the most hopeless job site in *Yonnondio* is another place men will not work, the home front, where Olsen explores a more troubling form of labor exploitation. Those commentators who contend that the stay-at-home Anna has the satisfaction of being needed while Jim, frustrated by his out-to-work day, "only needs" (Pearlman and Werlock, 51), scant the fact that Jim, no stranger to the camaraderie of the neighborhood barroom, can escape both the 106 degree factory and Anna's kitchen. His wife, in contrast, as she cooks the family meals, puts up preserves, possibly to sell, and does other people's laundry in stifling conditions, is the imprisoned caretaker. Jim at least can imagine a strike or another job; Anna cannot plan for herself and can do so only in a vague way for her children because she exists in an anguished present. Applying the male focus on paid work to the laborer's own home, Olsen analyzes Anna's house as an unending workplace. She has the worst of both worlds: unassisted child tending combined with home laundering, a thankless occupation easily categorized, with her industrial piecework at home, as "bottom-of-the-barrel wage earning."[25]

Almost a decade after *Jews Without Money* had extolled the efficiency with which the mother, Katie, tackled the home, Mike Gold, in a rare acknowledgment of the desperation working-class housewives might experience, commented that men "would get too morbid to live under such a regime" (qtd. Dixler, 129). He brushed over further discussion with the familiar period conclusion that these women were heroic. Olsen's contribution, however, whether she herself acknowledged it as such, is to not reinforce the heroine ideal but to enter the mother's consciousness, and the moment she does that, regardless of her avowed intention to chronicle what a recent reviewer called "the great weight poor women carry," she particularizes Anna.[26] In so doing, Olsen undercuts the familiar Steinbeck/Conroy generalizations about overburdened proletarian motherhood. Not all working-class mothers have mental breakdowns or, "bitter and brutal" (6) like Anna Holbrook, beat their children until, like her daughter Mazie, they are "degraded" (32). The tranquil, stolid Mrs. Kryckski, an equally put-upon factory wife and mother who comforts Anna, is textual proof that mothering brings out the latent emotional instability of some women, not all. Of course, Anna's bouts with the beginnings of mental illness are exacerbated, and her energies scattered, by the pressures of caretaking, by a physically and sexually abusive marriage, too many children, and no money or support save from the occasional kind neighbor or brusque doctor.

Despite the novel's urgent attempt to locate Anna's spiritual illness in her taxing existence, a deeper truth emerges. In what psychologists term the mother's unconscious expectations of her child, Anna tyrannizes over Mazie.[27] Coercing, both subtly and not so subtly, a child barely eight years old into a mother role by the unfinished novel's close, Anna in effect robs Mazie of her childhood. It is there that Olsen offers an insight about some of the daughter-experienced tensions that she herself seemed unwilling to acknowledge, an insight born possibly of her relation with her own mother, Ida Lerner, who deployed the young Tillie as a mother surrogate to a large brood of children. If so, not surprisingly, it was an unwelcome insight and one that Olsen consciously evaded in her autobiographical fiction from the 1930s and later. Whether in *Yonnondio* or later works such as "I Stand Here Ironing" (1956) and "Tell Me a Riddle" (1961), the trope of the mother, a backward-looking character whose young maternal years were the 1930s and who cannot "distinguish her desire for the child from that imposed on her," occasions the authorial impulse to explain the distant mother, to account for her remoteness.[28]

Olsen strenuously resisted the idea that a mother could psychologically damage her children. In one particularly candid interview, she noted: "It is irrelevant to talk of a core of Self when circumstances do not sustain its expression or development, when life has tampered with it and harmed it."[29] But her stories belie her sentiments. In her later works "Tell Me a Riddle" and "I Stand Here Ironing," grown daughters of Depression Era mothers seem incomplete or troubled. In *Yonnondio,* Mazie's problems are even more severe.

To be sure, Olsen deliberately locates the Holbrooks' collective unhappiness in the oppressions of poverty and to a large degree withholds blame from the parents for the deprivations their children constantly experience. Modern critics, ignoring D. H. Lawrence's sage advice to trust the tale rather than the teller, make much of this exculpation, although few go so far as to reinvent Anna so that she becomes one who "always presses back through singing, loving her children, and affirming what she believes is right" (Staub, 137). Not only is this an overly generous assessment; it is a transformation of Anna into Ma Joad that excises her self-absorption, bursts of rage at her children, and breakdown following a miscarriage that is as psychological as it is physical. But most interpreters, even if they do not revise Olsen's Anna this way, implicitly lend credence to this extreme view when they erase the tensions (tensions recapitulated in "I Stand Here Ironing") between scrutinizing the psychically flawed mother and locating her within a class analysis. They respond more to Olsen's didacticism than to the characters she actually portrays. The fashionable argument is that in "another writer's hands a mother who has exiled or excluded her daughter during her formative years might be seen as a reprehensible figure" (Pearlman and Werlock, 60). But supposedly "this is not Tillie Olsen's point" in *Yonnondio* or in her other works in which the mother is remote, distracted, verging at times on, or entering into, madness. Why not? Such tensions have as much to do with the individual character of Anna as they do with her maritally oppressed status.

Olsen particularly admired two proletarian women in fiction. One was the creation of her contemporary Jack Conroy, whom she knew from gatherings like the American Writers' Congress (he later recalled she attended in a Young Communist League uniform [Thompson, 153]) and whose novel appeared while she was working on *Yonnondio*. The other was the protagonist of Rebecca Harding Davis's 1861 mill worker tale, "Life in the Iron Mills." Disparate as were the works in which they appear, Davis's Deborah Wolfe, a hunchback creature with a "spaniel's" devotion to her oppressed menfolk, patiently endures.[30] So does Conroy's Mrs. Donovan, who is one of the "Spartan women of the mining camps" (53). When, newly widowed, her children ruin the laundry she must now do to eke out a living, her only thought is to soothe them: "I don't want to see your spirit crushed too soon. There's little enough fun for a lad in a coal camp" (69). But Anna Holbrook is not like this: she is on the edge, not poised for forgiving, and often forces the child on whom she depends the most, Mazie, into a placating posture. Mazie Holbrook experiences true mothering all too fleetingly in the novel, a feeling of security in being loved only, ironically, when her mother has gone into a reverie and is absently stroking Mazie's hair.

Relegated by critics to, at best, a few sentences in a recent study, there is thus an obscured dimension to the Anna–Mazie relation. More than the other children whom Anna also routinely subjects to meanness born of frustration with her lot, Mazie is her "mother's victim" (Pearlman and Werlock, 32). Yet the novel—billed as "about struggle, not 'selfhood' " (Pearlman and Werlock, 44)—contains ample evidence not only of maternal rejection under pressure of poverty but what is probably worse: the mother's psychic usurpation of the daughter's identity, which goes beyond "punish[ing] their children with the violence of their own despair." [31]

In its unfinished form, *Yonnondio* remains Anna's book rather than Mazie's, in part because Mazie's self-definition is so connected to that of the good daughter.[32] But a selection called "The Iron Throat," appearing in *Partisan Review* in 1934, contained hints of Mazie's urgent need to please a pair of unhappy, wretchedly distracted parents—a mother with a "tired and grimy voice," a father in "an evil mood." [33] Significantly, the answers to Mazie's search for ways to gain their interest is revealed in a key speech to her father at the end of the *Partisan Review* piece. As if to restore domestic order, Mazie offers herself up to placate the furies of both parents: "Pop, I can make the bacon when I stand up on the box, and I can wash the baby, honest. Pop, Momma sez I'm gonna get a edjication [too]" (9). Read one way, Mazie joins all of the edgy, aspiring children of working-class parents. Read another way, and placed in the context of *Yonnondio* (it is in the first half of the initial chapter), the speech acquires a far different meaning. Mazie's selfhood is predicated on her efforts to garner parental—especially maternal—love by offering herself up to her unhappy parents. In service to this futile task, she must ceaselessly stave off her very real fear of rejection by Jim and Anna, who, absorbed in their own difficulties, lack the psychic energy to see her as a person. Thus her constant feeling of "horror," of a "sense of evil," an "undefined pain, filling her heart" (7).

Mazie's characteristic state is fear. Viewed in this light, her precocious intelligence, evidenced by her constant questioning, is an offering to gain parental love and approval. In the chapters that follow, however, it is her mother alone who defines her daughter's life goal, an "edjication" (3), and whose own traumas and disasters dominate the girl's awareness. Responding to Anna's injunction to do well in school, Mazie clearly internalizes the message, as much in frightened compliance as out of a desire to learn. Indeed, in developing Mazie's often supplicating relation with this unstable and controlling figure, *Yonnondio,* whether consciously or not, supplies disturbing evidence of maternal numbness, an insensitivity that psychologists find central to childhood difficulties in developing a secure identity.[34] Interestingly, from what scanty biographical evidence exists on Ida Lerner, Olsen's mother, Anna, like Ida, turned her little girl into an agent of herself (Duncan, 210), constantly directing her to take care of the others, to do chores better left to an older child, and in short, to be an extension of Anna (Ida?) herself. Neither in interviews nor in published reminiscences has Olsen reproached her mother, but her fiction from *Yonnondio* onward certainly features mothers who, however guilt-ridden or embittered, merited it.

The most compelling evidence that Mazie Holbrook, in striving to placate, to please, confuses her identity with her mother's comes from the little girl herself. Despite the stirrings of selfhood in her precocious curiosity about the world, she begins to fuse her identity with Anna's. When, in psychic flight from an arduous miscarriage, Anna begins to break down, Mazie has a "remote dream look in [her] eyes as if she were not there at all" (67). Later in the narrative, Anna's baby Bess is born, and Mazie feels the pains (88–89). Most interpreters scant the view of the modern commentator Michael Staub that Mazie's characteristic retreat into a fantasy realm in times of stress is a "movement toward madness" (134). Yet there is certainly an element of disconnectedness in her dealings with the world, one observed as well in Depression case studies of families in which the disturbed mother had to be removed from the family. Social workers routinely observed that an awareness of the mother's mental illness "lurk[ed] ominously in the background of [the children's] consciousness," causing fear, repression, and an agonized sensitivity to the world, all reminiscent of Mazie Holbrook.[35] Modern observers have rounded out the picture of the distressed response to a failed mother by remarking on children's tendency to idealize the woman who has served them so badly. Often this response includes, in effect, constructing a "false self" (Winnicott, passim), the placating product of parental expectations.[36] Despite a projected suicide in the unfinished manuscript, Anna's mental problems may not be as severe as in the cases of prepsychotic mothers cited above. Still, in her often contradictory agenda for Mazie (education as escape, endless home chores as compliance) and, to a lesser extent, her younger children, she fits the profile of women who regard their children as "possession[s] for which one has a particular goal" (Miller, 75).

Although Jim Holbrook's violent nature does much to disturb the little girl's sense of security, there are a number of striking passages about Mazie's response to her mother's inconsistencies that evidence a traumatized reaction to a disorganizing mother. Many times the little girl is so frightened that she becomes disembodied, a vessel for Anna, who is herself a confused but threatening amalgam of exhortation, moral instruction, and chore-giving. In these episodes, Anna all but forgets that Mazie is her daughter, perceiving the child instead as an extension of her own mounting anxiety about the growing household chaos. Ordering Mazie to tend to one of the male children, Anna confusedly reflects, "Such a mess. . . . I never asked her: Is that Ben or is it Will is wettin the bed again? Yes, get things back to regular" (87). The ambiguity about "her" reinforces Anna's disjointed thinking to produce a sense that Mazie is not a daughter but a part of Anna's troubled consciousness. When at other times, Anna is remote, writhing in the pain of labor or a beating—or a rape—by her husband, Mazie is still an extension of her mother's emotions. There are no boundaries between self and (m)other. Thus, filled with Anna's pain, Mazie's habitual fear—on one level, a fear of loss of self, on another, of imagined reprisals—escalates. Suspending sympathy for the mother, Olsen often pulls the reader into the daughter's fear as, ceding to her mother's urgency, she abandons her own identity: "Mazie, a voice came shrill, you see that tub of diapers? Git to that tub of diapers. Yes, Ma. You will recite, Mazie. A hushed voice, faltering, that was she" (58).

In one key scene, not long before Anna gives birth to another child, Mazie experiences a kind of waking nightmare in which she beholds the image of a monster with her mother's face holding a skeleton child. The picture fills Mazie's consciousness, as if commanding her to worship the terrifying parent and the newest baby. Far more than a scenario of rivalry with an unborn sibling, though there is an element of that, Mazie's is a scene of obedience to a terrifying mother force. Confronted with her own projection of the monstrous in Anna's nature, a terrified Mazie convinces herself it is "useless to resist" (59).

Other narrative devices reinforce the unhealthy fusion with the mother prompted by what one critic terms Mazie's "ill-defined sense of self" (Staub, 133). There are repeated and abrupt shifts from Anna's to Mazie's mind, so that it is sometimes difficult for the reader to know to whom "her" and "she" refers (68). Many are the swift movements from Mazie to Anna to Mazie's internalizing of Anna's dislocated mental state. To cite but one example, after Anna's miscarriage, Mazie shakes her mother and begs, "Wake up" (74); there is an abrupt shift to Anna's pained rousing and, as if without interruption or transition, a swift narrative movement back to Mazie, so much united with Anna that "her head [is] under the bedclothes, trying to stifle the fear and horror" (75).

Commentators who see no mother-daughter fusion, only a novel with more than one narrator and thus an attempt at a collective voice, explain such passages as a subversion of standard narrative strategy (Coiner, 178). Certainly elsewhere in the novel the crosscuttings from Jim's work-tired mind to Anna's worn-out mind to Mazie's ever-responsive mind do reveal Olsen's literary experimentation with giving voice to a composite labor-class community, in factory and kitchen and child's space. But in other ways, ways that Olsen herself never acknowledged, the passage above is another kind of subversion entirely, a critique of the era's maternity myth. Anna's "madwoman" sections should not be looked at only as indictments of poor medical care, an ignorant husband, and an oppressive society, though all these elements bear some responsibility. Knowingly or not, an oppressed Anna exacts her own revenge on the completely powerless, choosing her oldest daughter as her chief victim. Thus Mazie, so devoted to her mother, is numbed not only by poverty but by the energies drained in what psychologists term the effort "not to betray" her inadequate, demanding mother (Miller, 69).

Olsen's preoccupation with distant mothers and damaged blue-collar daughters is evident even in her apprentice work. Two manuscript versions of a short story composed in her girlhood, "Not You I Weep For," feature a character alternately called Nena and Fuzzie and her thwarting mother.[37] In this early work, though, Nena/Fuzzie's mother is a ridiculer who does not comprehend her daughter's aspirations for an aesthetic life. When Nena tries to compose poetry, her mother bellows. "Downstairs

[the] mother began cursing one of the children. Hard, raucous, the words marched up the stairs, 'dirty little brat; I oughta skin ya alive. . . .' At the sound [the girl's] radiant words faltered, leapt up again, sank into desperate silence; the luminous glow from [her] face vanished." And later: " 'I've taken enough crap offa you today, Neen,' came up the stairs. 'Thought you was going to put papers on the kitchen floor; now Eddie's tracked it up so it looks like a privy. You come right down and mop again' " (Berg 2, 9). Like her mother, whose emotional cruelty, as in *Yonnondio,* is explained away by a hard life—seven children and her husband a "bitter enem[y]"— (Berg 1, 1), Nena/Fuzzie is subject to other withering forces. Aspiring to an artistic career, she flounders in a poor job and, like her creator, has a disappointing affair with a man at her factory, a debilitating abortion, and a lung illness (Pearlman and Werlock, 14). Olsen, of course, rallied, survived it all, and soon found meaning in the Young Communist League and labor agitation. Nena has no such future. With so obstructive a mother, however overburdened, neither the artist nor the woman in Nena can bloom. Her thwarted life snuffed out in the fashion of a Katherine Mansfield heroine—increasingly in love with solitude and death, she courts it on a wintry night—the girl dies, young and unfulfilled.[38]

Despite its social protest focus, *Yonnondio,* like Olsen's tyro writings, also gives abundant evidence of maternal thwarting and of constricted daughterhood. In the way of fearful children, Mazie is the good daughter, malleable, acquiescent, identifying with the aggressor to ward her off. And, to my mind, Mazie's very fear suggests a subversion that Olsen may not have been aware of: an indictment of Anna Holbrook not because she delights in controlling, like Farrell's ominous Mrs. Lonigan, but because she becomes a mother without the emotional or financial resources to undertake the task.

Olsen's male contemporary Farrell lamented Studs Lonigan's inability to oppose his mother's will; Algren sympathetically cast the drifter Cass McKay as the motherless orphan; and Steinbeck and Conroy described the cherished children for whom the Ma Joads and Mrs. Donovans sacrificed so much. Olsen envisioned an alternative family story for the proletarian child. As *Yonnondio* ends, Mazie's selfhood seems thoroughly grounded in meeting impossible maternal demands to fuse rather than, as Olsen projected for the never-finished manuscript, in becoming a person in her own right, a writer who presumably embraces activism (Pearlman and

Werlock, 52). Olsen's creation seems headed only for continued passivity and emotional strife.

Whether Olsen realized it or not, the pall of sadness over her text is just what the novel struggles to deny: psychological damage, spiritual poverty. Her commitment to a class analysis notwithstanding, what makes *Yonnondio* a richer experience than the finished works of her male colleagues is that, like its British precursor *Sons and Lovers* (and, for that matter, another Lawrence study of a childhood mother obsession, "The Rocking Horse Winner"), it demonstrates that class alone cannot account for family hardship and certainly not for maternal pathology. If Olsen is too good a comrade to acknowledge the mother's responsibility for wounding her daughter, she is too good an artist not to dramatize it.

Le Sueur's Alternative: Manless Motherhood

In contrast to Olsen's revision of her era's maternal ideology, fellow party devotee Meridel Le Sueur offered no fictionalized lament for the trials of her mother's life or her own. Only ten years into the new century, her mother, Marian, a suffragist, educated and strong, took her children and departed from a loveless marriage. She clearly had far more options than had homebound, Yiddish-speaking Ida Lerner, tied to housework and seven children. With the help of her own WCTU-devoted mother, Marian ran an efficient household for Meridel and her brothers before marrying the Socialist lawyer Arthur Le Sueur shortly before World War I. Unlike Tillie Lerner before her labor organizing and reportorial days and her subsequent common-law (later legalized) marriage to fellow CP activist Jack Olsen, Meridel's girlhood was neither sickly nor reined in by child tending and factory work. She even had some Hollywood silent film successes before turning her back on such frivolity and embracing left-wing authorship. She joined the party in the late 1920s and by the early 1930s was a divorced mother of two girls and at her midwestern literary peak.[39]

The economy of scarcity depicted in her fiction and her reports on female strikers, factory, store, and domestic service workers, women relief recipients, and unwed mothers never extended to the spiritual. Furthermore, Le Sueur's mothers never punish their children for their miseries; her daughters, if let down by their fathers, at least find mothering somewhere. "My grandmother raised her own children, my mother hers, and

I mine," she wrote in a memoir, a description of generations of maternal self-sufficiency that informed much of her writing.[40] In a variant of the Freud statement, Le Sueur was the success-fated woman beloved of her mother. Thus when she came to mothering, she took up the task sans husband with seeming ease; Yasha Robinoff, a dedicated labor organizer, was at best a shadowy family figure, apparently unenthusiastic about fatherhood, and she soon divorced him (Yount, 33). Neither in life nor in art did she seem concerned with the perils of the maternal.

Le Sueur's artistic celebration of the solo mother who had no nostalgia for or much memory of a marital past was a form of rebellion against Ma Joadism. In its opposition to the earth mother as mainstay of a patriarchal family, her revision of proletarian literary tradition was as radical as Olsen's. Relocating motherhood outside blue-collar male terrain, Le Sueur also subverted her leftist masculine colleagues' mother myth. She is most commonly described as the muse of hard-luck midwestern women who form a support system, a sororal network of the disfranchised. But an analysis of her short fiction, including the sections from *The Girl* published during the 1930s, reveals something else as well.

Here was an indictment of the male state, personified by what Le Sueur perceived as a morally intrusive social service bureaucracy that offered moralistic judgments of unwed mothers (and their promiscuous women friends), forbade some women to mother by confiscating their newborns, or callously permitted mothers and children alike to fall through the cracks of a rule-ridden relief system. She extolled mothers whose parenting role the state tried to usurp, often successfully ("Sequel to Love," 1935, "Salvation Home," 1939). And she praised women who raised children without men in communities or extended families of mothering women ("I'm Going, I Said," 1940, "The Dead in Steel," 1935), sometimes deserted through widowhood ("The Laundress," 1927), though more often through male frailty ("Annunciation," 1935).

Modern commentators resurrecting Le Sueur wax poetic, as she so often does herself, on the theme of motherhood as transformation, of woman completed by pregnancy.[41] Particularly in works the party criticized as too feminine, Le Sueur may well have created her own "mythic Mother" (Gelfant, 183), "an elemental female . . . containing all, creating all" (Yount, 93, 92). But by separating women from the heterosexual world, Le Sueur also indicted men, including, by implication, politically radical men. In much of her oeuvre, men lack the strength to work both in the world and in the family and have given over parenting to women. Her 1920s fiction and 1930s reporting describe the problem of the male laborer whose energies are taken up and frequently depleted by killing toil; her more famous fiction of the 1930s invokes a manless solution. Another way of putting it: in vignettes such as "They Follow Us Girls," the good Communist deplored the situation of the female unemployed. In pieces such as "Annunciation" she blames the times for causing men to desert their pregnant, unemployed wives. The good feminist knew otherwise. Whatever the vagaries of men, her women do not leave their babies.

Her fiction sidestepped the dilemma of calling on male comrades to be better fathers by lauding the female comrade as single mother. Like Olsen, Le Sueur was split between an analysis of class and male oppression, and there are two voices in her work. Her fiction alternates between an "official" party voice and an "unofficial" critique of masculine conduct on the home front (Coiner, 169). But whereas Olsen's men, unconvincingly defended as prisoners of circumstance, stay, if only, like Jim Holbrook, to act out their anger, Le Sueur's leave. As absent fathers, they have not simply ratified the sexual division of labor but have disappeared from the family landscape as if they had never inhabited it. Even the few mothers in her work who do have marital pasts are alone: widows of steel workers, aging laundresses, and others chained to domestic work. Though survivors, they seem no better off and, in some cases, worse off than the women in Le Sueur's supportive St. Paul Hoovervilles, her close-knit communities of the feminine downtrodden.

Interestingly, though, particularly for a party sympathizer committed to depicting the spectrum of lone female worker-activists, Le Sueur's fiction after the late 1920s ceases to feature, much less tackle the problem of, the breadwinning mother, unwed or solo, married to a striking or workless man. Her editors rebuked the so-called negativism of her 1932 *New Masses* sketch "Women on the Breadlines," with its vivid catalog of the callousness of employment agencies and of the agonies of women too proud to stand on breadlines who were starving alone in bedrooms. But in their very decision to publish her sketch (a decision echoed in the *Anvil* publication in 1939 of "Sure Honey!", a fragment of *The Girl* that focuses on her hard-luck lover, Butch), the left-wing literati recognized her kinship with the Chicago down-and-out school of proletarian fiction. Le Sueur, after all, warmly praised Conroy, Farrell, and Algren in her 1935 talk to the American Writers' Congress.[42] Though negatively received by the male *New Masses* editors who printed it, her piece of the year before, "I Was Marching," was half-fiction, half-reporting. In it women factory workers, joined by zealous members of the ladies' auxiliary, supported the 1934 Minneapolis teamsters strike, presumably setting aside their own problems as laborers, teamsters' wives, or mothers of workingmen's children.[43]

Indeed, underneath Le Sueur's evangelical call to merge "with a million hands, movements, [and] faces" ("I Was Marching," 165) is the message that women are at their best as reserve troops in labor skirmishes. A passage near the end of the sketch—"men died from that day's shooting," "men lined up to give them blood transfusions," and "Black Friday men called the murderous day" (164)—reiteratively suggests that men teach women to be militant. The female narrator's initial awareness of gender difference—she begins the piece acutely aware of males on picket duty and females in soup kitchens—vanishes by the end of the rousing piece as she is drawn by three militant women marchers into a vast parade. She and her new sister marchers merely follow a vast male movement. Unlike the vocal mother who graces the end of Olsen's "The Strike," "a pregnant woman . . . her face a flame" [*sic*] in anger at police shootings during the San Francisco general strike,[44] Le Sueur's mother figure appears only briefly to utter a warning to the narrator: "If you have any children . . . you better not go [marching]" (163).

The mother as potential activist does figure in "Women Are Hungry," in a section called "Old and Young Mothers," but as a member of a defeated community and one without a radical political consciousness. More in line with party doctrine is the attempt to make a "straightforward . . . political point" about a collective effort, men and women united, in the story "Tonight Is Part of the Struggle."[45] But ironically, as in much of Le Sueur's party-line fiction, women once again learn to recognize their communal identity as students of men's protest meetings. Furthermore, though the women are invited to come down to march to demand security for workers, the sketch clearly separates male and female forms of productivity; men produce in the factory, women in the belly, reflects the pregnant wife of a striking laborer, a vision the story does nothing to contradict.

Only in the 1940 *New Masses* piece "I'm Going, I Said," another section of *The Girl,* are party and feminist concerns briefly integrated. The young protagonist (earlier left, in the longer manuscript, by her gangster boyfriend Butch, whom she had promised to abort their child) faces single motherhood by ignoring the stay-at-home warning issued by a frightened woman in "I Was Marching." Inspired by Amelia, a devoted party worker, who urges her to join the workers, the unnamed Girl presumably learns that women can strike *and* be motherly. But as Linda Ray Pratt points out, "the character of Amelia, the communist organizer from the Workers' Alliance, [is] a rather clumsy and undramatic intrusion" (262) into a community composed solely of women grappling with the trials of joblessness and hungry children. The political currents of the day are forgotten as this community extends its mothering to a dying prostitute, Clara, and closes ranks to care for the babies and old women the relief system has no use for. As the title of the sketch suggests, the Girl, leaving her own newborn child in this sororal trust, must join the fight on a political front, presumably with male colleagues. But Le Sueur seems unable to resolve the contradictions between her protagonist's commitment to feminine and masculine causes.

In other 1930s stories, collected in the 1940 *Salute to Spring,* Le Sueur abandons the problematic resolution of genderless solidarity on the barricades and returns to her initial vision of a universe of needy women, disfranchised but solid, and thus moves toward recasting the party ideology of the maternal comrade wife. She is at her most inventive when she transforms the single mother, routinely pictured in male protest fiction as overwhelmed by the unnatural and unwanted role of sole support, into a self-sufficient provider. Le Sueur's knowledge of her mother, Marian, who fled a didactic preacher husband to raise her children alone, and her own observations of poor women when she worked in St. Paul at the Workers' Alliance and on the Minnesota WPA (Yount 32, 33) produced images of feminine self-reliance from which Steinbeck's timid Rose of Sharon, bereft of her unstable husband, Connie, might have profited.

Steinbeck's *Grapes of Wrath* restores what to him is the rightness of things when Rose of Sharon, miscarrying in part from the shock of her husband's desertion, is accidentally freed from bringing up a child outside a traditional family. Similar "resolution" stories occur in the male proletarian novels most concerned with desperate maternity, the "Bottom

Dogs" form. There the Rose of Sharon figure becomes the wandering mother, bereft of Joad ties and tormented by the memory of her baby. But she, too, cannot be permitted to mother: in Tom Kromer's morose 1935 on-the-road novel *Waiting for Nothing,* she abandons her two-week-old baby on a park bench so that a policeman can find it and the state can rear it, rightly convinced that hard times have impaired her maternal abilities.[46] In a variant, the crazed young woman at the heart of the title of Ashley Buck's 1940 *Anvil* contribution, "Now He Is Safe," carries that conviction to what seems to her a logical conclusion. She drowns her starving child, unable to bear the idea that she cannot be a mother and cannot find sustenance for him.[47]

Reversing the ideology that mothers under pressure become mad-women, Le Sueur revisits the desertion scenario, even playing daringly on the idea of the Virgin Mary as divinely unneeding of a husband in "Annunciation," written in 1935 and republished in her collected stories five years later.[48] The story explores the pregnant narrator's conviction that, her husband, Karl, out of work and unreliable and the marriage disintegrating, what was happening to her as a woman was "some kind of loveliness" (87). The less support he lends her—by narrative's end he decamps entirely—the more she feels connected to the life growing within her. Eventually, she even views those who pity her deserted state as not "alive" (97). There is no desperation but a transcendence culminating in a remarkable closing paragraph that celebrates mothering as part of the cycle of nature: "Before I came into [my] room I went out and saw a pear tree standing motionless, its leaves curled in the dark, its radiating body falling darkly, like a stream far below into the earth" (97). As the tree metaphor suggests, when a Kromer or Buck protagonist, faced with no food for her unborn child and no husband to provide it, might well sink into madness, the narrator emerges strengthened, centered, nourishing her child and herself, a tree of life indeed.

In these and other stories, Le Sueur skirts the issue of mind-numbing, unremunerated housework, for her characters either abandon or cease to keep a home in which a man expects such wifely services. And she romanticizes the underside of mother work, the care of impoverished homes and fatherless children. Yet there is no ambiguity in her conviction that single motherhood is the alternative to Ma Joadism—or is the birth of a new Ma Joad, self-born, self-referential, distinctly manless.

Le Sueur's central subject was young mothers, not their daughters grown to womanhood. Yet in "Biography of My Daughter," a rare but important story of the proletarian daughter as working girl that appeared in the 1935 *American Mercury,* the title character perishes, not surprisingly, for want of a supportive women's community and of a militant spirit.[49] The narrator and another firebrand character, Marie ("they should do with workers like with horses," she notes sardonically, "make glue of 'em, when they wear 'em out" [102]), act as chorus. They wish they could have mothered the sickly Rhoda; now, with her biological mother, they can only visit her at a sanitarium, her health fatally weakened by overwork. Her mother, a defeated figure, has followed the traditional path of wifely deference in a male-headed family. In the familiar Le Sueur scenario, she has been let down by her husband, an unemployed clerk who nevertheless identifies with the middle class and apparently refuses to become angered with the economic system that has tossed him out. Significantly, he does not come to see Rhoda, and the mother visits with the two fiery women who often preach feminine resistance to unrewarded labor. When the mother learns that her daughter has died, she is sorrowfully puzzled that all of Rhoda's hard work—a brief time at college, sixteen-hour days as a servant to afford it—have not rescued her.

Rhoda's parent is another of the squelched bourgeois women with their dead-end lives and subordinate spirits whom Le Sueur limned so eloquently in pieces like her 1931 story "Corn Village." Less concerned with economics than anomie, that melancholy story indicts the emotional sterility of small-town Kansas. But "Biography" turns the spiritually moribund midwestern wife of the earlier tale into a bewildered lower-middle-class woman who misguidedly trusts a capitalist economy that fails her husband and kills her daughter by overwork. The narrator and Marie, the tale intones, might have nurtured and given life to Rhoda. They would have taught her to fight the owners who exploited her, to march, to stay alive. "She was not my daughter," ends the piece, "but she might have been and my daughters may be lying dead like that. What happened to her must stop happening" (110). As in earlier stories of women who stay within a father-headed family, "The Laundress" and "The Dead in Steel," feminine fidelity to a system depending on male economic power (even if that power has not benefited a long-dead or out-of-work husband) has produced only maternal loneliness and defeat.

On one level, "Biography" is clearly another CP call to arms, whatever one's gender. But like much of Le Sueur's more interesting fiction, looked at more closely it contains a message on failed motherhood. As with Olsen's Mazie Holbrook and Nena, the tragedy of the betrayed proletarian girl is rooted in the working-class family. For whatever his wage-earning potential, the father is no spiritual breadwinner and the mother, though neither bitter nor crazed (only Le Sueur's bourgeoises have those failings), is not up to the life-giving task.

Rejecting the male Left's pervasive, sentimentalized homage to a woman without needs of her own, Le Sueur and Olsen illustrated how the working-class mother, caught in a net of endless family obligations, left her daughter her legacy of pain. But as party loyalists elevating collectivism over individualism and unwilling to transform feminist insight into dissent, they ultimately retreated from the implications of their revisionist position. Agnes Smedley, a third important woman radical who recreated the mother myth, did not.

Smedley: Motherhood Revised

Daughter of Earth, published in 1929 and reissued in shortened form at the height of the Depression six years later, also addresses the burdens of and mistakes made by working-class mothers.[50] Unlike Olsen and Le Sueur, however, both personally and politically Smedley cast a cold eye on motherhood, even in a future socialist state. When her early marriage was failing, she chose abortion over childbearing. Both at home and, throughout the 1930s, abroad, she campaigned for birth control, not a central concern of the other two women's texts. Before and during the Depression, when Olsen and Le Sueur were covering American labor unrest, Smedley waged her battle for class justice outside the United States, first in Germany and India, then in revolutionary China. On her brief visits home, although she engaged in ideological skirmishes with left-wing men, she was less dependent on their good opinion than were Le Sueur and Olsen, who worked closely with male party functionaries. Most important, except in some propagandistic pieces to further the cause of the Chinese revolution, Smedley's fiction and reporting repudiated the mother-daughter bond. Though she acknowledged the emotional cost of this repudiation, her daughter figures wage a battle for separateness that Olsen's and Le Sueur's do not.[51]

Daughter of Earth, following Smedley's pre-China life fairly closely, charts Marie Rogers's formative years on a joyless northern Missouri farm and in squalid Trinidad, Colorado, mining camps; her succession of low-level teaching, sweatshop, office, typing, and stenographic jobs from New Mexico to New York City; her search for education in California, growth as a radical journalist, and stint as a night student at New York University; and her failed marriage and impassioned involvement in the cause of Indian independence, including a second marriage to one of its fervent advocates. The original novel catalogs Agnes/Marie's emotional and political ties to Indian revolutionaries; the abridged one omits the lengthy Indian section. In both versions, however, the deepest imperatives of the protagonist's life, as of Smedley's own, were to overcome the imprisoning conditions of the mother's existence and, in so doing, shed the negative self-image that parent had imposed on her. For Smedley created in Mrs. Rogers a maternal figure who, despite her ability to pierce through her own suffering to show concern for her daughter's future, is at once more manipulative and insidious than any in Olsen's or Le Sueur's works.

. Smedley recorded her quest for a spiritual foremother in a remarkable series of *New York Call* articles on women prisoners whom she met when she was jailed for pro-Indian agitation in the early 1920s. In her novel, however, the mother figure is so wanting that, building on whatever was positive in her identification with her own more charismatic father, the quest is for male role models who will inspire her with manly strength. "For I was my father's daughter!" (15), Marie proclaims early on, as if to anchor herself. The father, though, with his frequent absences, philandering, bouts of drunkenness, and low opinion of all women, his daughter included, provides a limited model at best. His callous conduct following her mother's death only shores up the young woman's decision to exile herself from family. Without a maternal model, Marie decides to identify with men in their imagined freedom but is unable to liberate herself by doing so. Only when, in the uncut version of the novel, she finds in an older Indian nationalist some comradely affection does she discover spiritual peace, though, again, in the face of prejudice from other male activists in the independence movement.

Unlike Olsen and Le Sueur, Smedley, though favoring some party positions, particularly those of the German Communists on birth control and the Chinese on class revolution, was critical of the CPUSA for its "simplistic glorification of the working class as full of selfless idealism" (MacKinnon and MacKinnon, 121). "Because of this," she later remembered, "I was often attacked. . . . One American . . . Communist long delighted in dubbing me a Smedleyite."[52] Such rebelliousness may have given her the freedom to offer a proletarian mother whose anger borders on the sadistic and whose vagaries cannot be explained by class oppression. In any event, *Daughter of Earth* offers a negative appraisal of the mother figure to which Smedley held fast, even in her post-Depression vignettes of Chinese orphans in *Battle Hymn of China* (1943), whom she presented as far better off in the army than with any mother, birth or adoptive.

In the early sections of *Daughter of Earth* about the protagonist's formative period in rural Missouri and the Rockefeller-owned mining camps, Smedley amplifies her warning to the Communists about idealizing the proletariat by depicting two dangerous mother figures. The protagonist Marie's Aunt Mary was a thinly veiled version of Smedley's own aunt/grandmother. This strange kinship was created when Smedley's maternal grandfather married her father's elder sister, Mary. So demonic a figure was she that, years after writing *Daughter of Earth,* Smedley seemed unable to exorcise her, describing her, though not without admiration, as one who would have been burned as a witch in earlier days (*Battle Hymn,* 4). Certainly in the novel this Mary is an arch-manipulator, scenting in Marie's precocious intelligence a challenge to her family hegemony (her own husband feared her). Such a woman gave Marie only mocking "laughter which left deep wounds" (20), the identical phrase Smedley used to describe her own Aunt Mary in a letter she wrote to a friend a few years before the novel appeared (qtd. MacKinnon and MacKinnon, 95).

Marie's mother has a more complicated autobiographical basis; the Mrs. Rogers character incorporates aspects of Smedley's own mother but is crueler and, in a complex Oedipal triangle, more determined to engage in rivalry with her daughter for the husband's attention. Smedley's own mother, who took in laundry and boarders and died of exhaustion at thirty-eight, when her daughter was only sixteen, by Smedley's own account was "hard-working, gentle, and devout" (*Battle Hymn,* 4). Such a characterization does not fit Mrs. Rogers; in that literary creation Smedley may well have been exploring long suppressed guilty or negative feelings about her mother and ridding herself of them by creating a mother more worthy of scorn. In the same letter to a friend in which she described her hostile Aunt Mary, she also wrote that she had always harbored "contempt" for her mother for lacking both the "imagination" and strength of a man (qtd. MacKinnon and MacKinnon, 95). But there is nothing to indicate that Mrs. Smedley was a power-hungry child beater.

The daughter/artist thus reinvents a pitiable maternal figure as one who singled out the most imaginative of her children for the "tough little switch that cut [Marie] like a knife." Deviations from maternal rule earn the threat that she would "stomp [Marie] into the ground" (11). If on one level this parent successfully urges education on the unformed child, projecting her own unfulfilled desires, ironically that same intellectual ambition makes Marie more useful to her father, who notices his daughter's "edjication" (104), even though he still depends on his wife for record-keeping and family accounts. But before that, the mother has savagely punished the girl, thwarted the burgeoning artist, and canceled out what seemed an overactive imagination, beating Marie for saying the animals and trees spoke to her. Public humiliations follow private ones, as Mrs. Rogers tells the neighbors that she has one flawed daughter, the "liar" Marie (12). Not surprisingly, the girl recalls, the only time she was in her mother's arms she initiated the embrace—on Mrs. Rogers's deathbed (136).

If Marie's mother is a victimizer, distant, angry, inspiring matrophobia more than compassion, in this she is unlike the prostitute aunt, Helen, whom, Smedley observes, "no man dared mistreat" because she "was pledged to obey no man" (142). The character is only loosely based on Smedley's Aunt Tillie, who was more in the mold of Theodore Dreiser's Sister Carrie than Stephen Crane's streetwalking Maggie. Smedley may well have transformed Tillie to buttress her objection to male proletarian writers' yoking of work and feminine waywardness. Helen's professional prostitution certainly radicalizes the novel's declaration that her job, producing autonomy, is preferable to that of the traditional mother, who has no income and no identity outside the family. Helen, too, is a far cry from, for instance, Nelson Algren's pathetic Norah in *Somebody in Boots,* who sacrifices any human relationship to her livelihood as a Chicago street prostitute. Ironically, Helen's immoral work permits her to mother: her concern for her sister's children and ability to generate steady money save the family in the face of the father's emotional and physical absence and his inadequacy as a provider. (Langston Hughes's *Not Without Laughter* offers a similar scenario in the story of the promiscuous Harriett, who at novel's end provides her nephew's education money; but by then she is a saloon singer, not a prostitute. The Smedley character remains in the trade longer, is more defiant about it, and stands up to her sister's enraged husband by reminding him she is a better provider.)

As Marie recognizes later in the narrative, Helen's life can quickly turn to bondage. Her youth and customers gone, she is reduced to work in a cigar factory, almost as enslaved, suggests the narrator, as the birth mother of a poor family (142, 189). Marie, the autonomous worker-daughter, must look to herself for a good mother. And so she does, finding herself first through the mode of the autodidact and then in pride as a self-supporting journalist committed to revolutionary politics. By the end of both versions of the novel, she considers her own life proof that "a woman who made her own living, and would always do so, could be as independent as men" (189).

In the saga of Marie Rogers, selfhood is not only battling the limitations of the mother's life but also choosing the rebel's identity rather than the good daughter's. Again the parallels to Smedley's own life are telling. Recalling her psychic struggles, she wrote, "I resented my mother's suffering and refused to follow in her footsteps" and "live the life of a cabbage I would not" (*Battle Hymn,* 7, 11). It is all the more interesting that in the novel offered to mid-Depression audiences, the editor Malcolm Cowley tamed the rebellious battler and excised the lengthy final portion of *Daughter.* In it, she begins to come into her own as a revolutionary, zealously harboring (and sleeping with) Indian nationalists and being arrested for treasonous activity. Despite Alfred Kazin's retrospective assertion that Cowley nurtured any writer for whom " 'revolution' was now the new stage of development" (16), the *New Republic* editor's response to Smedley was conflicted at best. In both his preface to the revised edition and his recollections of Smedley written much later, he revealed a revulsion, personified in his description of this "coal miner's daughter's [lack of] urbanity" and of her large eyes that "bulge[d] and glint[ed] with [anticapitalist] hatred."[53] All of this was certainly a strange reproach to a seasoned reporter whose plentiful China dispatches, many printed in his *New Republic,* were urbane enough.

If her novel, censored or not, makes clear the empowerment that the mode of lonely rebellion—against family, state, and masculine radicals' expectations of a less vocal woman comrade—gives her alter ego Marie, a few years before the unrevised *Daughter* appeared Smedley herself was engaged in a search for feminine role models who would heal the lingering wounds of childhood. Although after she left Colorado she came to feel posthumous pity for her mother, like Marie she included the long-dead woman in her resolve to "forget I had a family at all" (*Daughter*, 143). Her relationships with other women were never to be easy. She had a good mother of sorts for a short time in an ambivalent stab at psycho-analysis with Dr. Elizabeth Naef, a therapist Smedley saw in Berlin in the mid-1920s. But she briefly found unlikely feminine inspiration in four women she encountered when, like Marie, she was imprisoned during World War I for espionage. She had kept anti-British Indian correspondence, codes, and foreign addresses and been charged with a violation of the U.S. Neutrality Law for her associations with Indian nationalists opposed to British rule (*Battle Hymn*, 8–9). Accused of being an agent for the Indian Nationalist Party, she was also charged with violating an anti-birth-control law because copies of Margaret Sanger's *Family Limitation* (1914) pamphlet were found in her possession and thus earned six months in the New York City prison aptly named the Tombs. The resulting four "Cell Mates" pieces won her "the respect and future support of liberal editors at the *Nation* and the *New Republic*" (MacKinnon and MacKinnon, 65).[54] Their appearance in the February and March 1920 Sunday supplements of the Socialist *New York Call*, on whose staff Smedley worked with Margaret Sanger before being arrested and subsequently voyaged with to Germany and China, launched her as a significant journalist.

Two of the cellmates profiled in the *Call* articles, a prostitute and a forger, seem queer candidates for surrogate mothering. It was fashionable in radical circles to follow John Reed's example in the pre–World War I journal *Masses* and depict female sexual outcasts as heroic, which Smedley does in "Cell Mates." But as well, with a minimum of romanticizing, she demonstrates how, along with a suffragist and a revolutionary, two other women Tombs prisoners, the two social misfits exhibited qualities that the mother figure in *Daughter of Earth*—and, apparently, Smedley's own mother—lacks: a fierce survival instinct combined with a benevolent attitude toward Smedley herself.

Smedley received from her first cell friend, the over-the-hill Irish prostitute Nell, a primer in prison high-spiritedness: "No one could be depressed for long with Nellie present" ("No. 1," 2). With unwavering vitality, Nellie cheered Agnes on, made light of their incarceration, and browbeat the disapproving matrons. More important, in the words of critic Judith A. Scheffler, the older woman "respects [a] spirit that cannot be imprisoned."[55] From her second cellmate, the forger May, who "constituted herself my guardian," Agnes was tipped off that spies might be sent in to incriminate her ("No. 2," 2).

If she learned courage and wariness from the prostitute and thief, she found spiritual sustenance in the lives of two political crusaders. One was "Cell Mate No. 3," Mollie Steimer, a revolutionary and follower of Emma Goldman who told Smedley to hope for the day the prisons would be overflowing with workers so that the world would wake up ("No. 3," 2). Steimer, jailed for distributing leaflets opposing American intervention in the Russian civil war, faced fifteen years in prison. The fourth, the British suffragist and birth control advocate Kitty Marion, had been forcibly fed more than two hundred times in Holloway Prison for her voting agitation ("No. 4," 2). Marion was in the Tombs for a month for giving a birth control pamphlet to a spy for the repressive Anthony Comstock's Society for the Suppression of Vice. Impressing her less vocal fellow advocate, Smedley, she invariably greeted the censorious matrons with, "Three cheers for birth control" (2). Steimer and Marion, well known in their political day, like the women Smedley would soon profile in her dispatches from China, found absolute self-definition through involvement in activism. More than simply alter egos, these women provided an example of committed courage foreign to any woman in *Daughter of Earth* but Marie herself.

Interestingly, though, the novel's representation of Smedley's 1920s prison experience erases the courageous four. In it, the jailed streetwalker, no hard-nosed Nellie, is weak and pathetic. Smedley's other three cellmates are omitted in favor of assorted female victims: diseased unwed mothers, hapless thieves, rich shoplifters who get off without a sentence. It is as if Marie has taken on the identities of the *Call* cellmates herself. A less flattering interpretation is that, in what Smedley called the conflict between her "bitter feminism" and her "contempt for women as a sex" (qtd. MacKinnon and MacKinnon, 91), she needed to reassert that she was self-mothering and thus self-born.

The good mother theme emerges again, in revised form, in Smedley's vignettes of women in revolutionary China. These sketches build on the new facts of peasant uprisings that include women, the entry of women into heavy industries like mining, and the weakening of traditional family structures in the face of war and revolution. These portraits, to be sure, skirt the child-rearing issue. They focus on women whose children are grown. The new Chinese mothers need not abandon their families, for history has propelled their sons and daughters into the army. Smedley produced these portraits at a time when Olsen and Le Sueur were covering the labor upheavals in San Francisco and Minneapolis in which women, though mostly in auxiliaries, marched and helped the strikers. The Chinese women, in contrast, are often fierce combatants and in various ways transcend the confines of mothering. In "The Women Take a Hand," which draws on Smedley's experiences with guerrillas in southern China in 1938, once-traditional women—venerable mothers with many grown children—naturally become crusaders. "They never just sat and listened while their menfolk dispensed wisdom; they took part in conversations, conducted propaganda about almost everything on earth, went to mass meetings." [56] Despite surface resemblances to the conduct of American CP women leading consumer boycotts or rallying around their men, Chinese women, given the history of their country, are groundbreakers indeed.

Smedley lived on and off in Shanghai from 1929 to 1936 and was in China by late 1928, when the Kuomintang of Chiang Kai-shek conducted a terror campaign against the "Reds" and "liberals," and in the early 1930s she traveled with the Chinese Red Army as one of the first reporters to visit Communist leaders Mao Tse-tung and Chou En-lai. [57] Despite extensive battlefront reporting, she managed to give much time to feminine subjects. Notable is the mother of "Shan-fei, Communist," a fictive sketch that reads like reportage, published in *New Masses* in 1933. Though reared in the world of foot binding, this mother flouts the tradition by unbinding her daughter's feet, breaking the girl's engagement to a rich man's son, and lauding her part in a student strike at the local school, thus launching her daughter's revolutionary career and incurring the wrath of the local authorities. The mother of Shan-fei would not have stood for the degradations endured by Marie Rogers's mother, who was schooled in bitter resignation, and she would never have shown jealousy of her child's success. Nor would she placate the local powers, as does Mrs. Rogers, who serves an exploitative mine owner a meal, only to weep and take to her bed when he turns around and cheats her family of her husband's rightful wages. A similar defiance animates the subjects of the 1934 "Women Agricultural Workers," who form revolutionary committees, have unbound feet, and proclaim, "We can walk and work like men!"[58] Perhaps the most impressive are those portrayed in "Silk Workers" (1933) in the Shuntek region of the South, whose factory-spinning work grants them the economic independence to reject marriage and mothering, devise a women's work culture that extends after hours, and laugh at unsubstantiated charges that they are lesbians. This vision also characterizes Smedley's 1930 *New Republic* praise of the new generation of educated women of Mukden. "Their hair cut short, their hands in their pockets, their feet big and their minds free . . . free of gait and manner, self-confident and proud," they are worlds away from the old-style nonrevolutionary women, worn out by childbearing and "still half-slaves."[59] If taken in their totality Smedley's portraits lack a coherent vision of child rearing in the new China, particularly among the peasant poor, they do present old women who urge liberation on their grown daughters and young ones in no hurry to curtail that liberty by choosing motherhood.

It is ironic that Smedley found a rejection of age-old socialization in so tradition-bound a country as China, while in Popular Front America her left-wing colleagues were extolling the heroic housewife whose permitted revolutionary activities did not extend to questioning that role. A further irony is that when, fairly late in life, Smedley did consider mothering—in 1940 she tried to adopt a Chinese boy who had been her aide in her travels with the Red Army—she turned the event into a vindication both of her earlier refusal to enter the maternal arena and of her belief that children who choose their "parents" fare better. In her telling of it in *Battle Hymn of China,* the child needed no mother but the Chinese army, which would give him—or, presumably, her—the moral principles and emotional support necessary for the new citizen in a postrevolutionary state (463–75). If, as Paul Lauter argues, *Battle Hymn* is a sequel to *Daughter of Earth* ("Afterword," *Daughter,* 409), in the later book Smedley substitutes herself for her own mother as one untrammeled by subordinating marriage or the old forms of maternity. Yet she still rejected the maternal idea just as she had in *Daughter* fifteen years before.

From her novelistic portrait of the hostile mother to her vignettes on

Chinese women who threw off or in some way altered a maternal role that limited their autonomy, Smedley offered the era's most subversive response to the mother as family bulwark. It is all the more significant that her lengthy novel was produced before the hardening of Depression Era thinking on feminine roles. Unlike Olsen's and Le Sueur's fragmented 1930s writings, Smedley's rejected the nurturing ideal outright. She shared their desire to revise their masculine literary colleagues' version of the proletarian family. But for both political and personal reasons, the creators of *Yonnondio* and *The Girl* ultimately sympathized as much with the mother's burden as the daughter's. Despite a distant pity for the mother figure, Smedley, who preached a gospel of mother-defying self-nurturance, demonstrated no such sympathy.

"A Shame to Have Children Then": Reconstructed Mothers

Even a limited sampling of interviews with mothers of the 1930s, breadwinners or not, reveals little outrage at the maternal burden or longings for a manless community to help overcome it.[60] And in the same interviews and other oral histories, daughters of these mothers, old women reminiscing about Depression life, showed retrospective empathy with their ailing or overworked mothers, a lack of resentment at being given chores when young, and an appreciation of the maternal wish for educated and thus upwardly mobile children.[61] These daughters repeatedly gave the impression that their mothers, including those who worked, sometimes to support the jobless male as well as the children, carved out pragmatic solutions to the problems of motherhood.

But Olsen, Smedley, and Le Sueur spoke for these mothers and daughters too, for their hidden sorrows and unacknowledged resistances, fleetingly evidenced as well in the candor of a New York City garment trade worker who admitted, "It was a shame to have children then."[62] In the trio's composite revisioning of the male social protest authors' mother myth, the home, far from a family preserve, is an arena of daughterly trauma or, alternatively, a woman's community. Diverting attention from the Tom Joads to the Mazie Holbrooks, the three women, particularly Olsen and Smedley, focused on a labor-class daughter impeded by her psychic inheritance and bitter maternal legacy.

Creating all-too-human characters, the three writers also entered the consciousness of the mother who left that legacy. It is true that in Le Sueur, a new, enlightened mother, profiting from the errors of those who lacked the courage to rebel, is free from the need to placate male society and can raise a daughter not bound by a husband's or father's constraints. But the implication is that if motherhood can flourish, it is only in a mythic country of underclass women, a vision undercut by Le Sueur's own alternative fiction on the undernurtured daughter. In Olsen and Smedley, no maternal utopia exists. The mother stifles because she is stifled, at once casualty and victimizer of her Depression Era family. Olsen's girls flounder there; Smedley's overcome.

Differences aside, in their reconstruction of mothering in the 1930s, Tillie Olsen, Meridel Le Sueur, and Agnes Smedley were responding in part to their own mothers, who were either weakened or, in Le Sueur's case, strengthened by marital difficulties, and recapitulated in the events of their lives as economically dependent, newly divorced, or mistreated wives the lives of many 1930s women. In so doing, these authors vented complex resentments at the impersonal society and the rigidly patriarchal family structure that preempted true nurturing or transformed the mother figure into the family head, alone making a virtue of necessity. As female revisions of male ideology, their fictions challenged the distinction between male wage earner and housewife, between men's and women's paid labor, between domestic drudgery and labors of love, between the oppressed and the oppressing mother. True, Olsen and Le Sueur subordinated the discussion of female wage earning to an analysis of the maternal burden, and Smedley renounced the mother idea to concentrate on her alter ego's search for autonomy. But all three, in revising Depression Era motherhood, questioned the cultural acceptance of "mythic ideals impossible to achieve on the level of social formation" (Kaplan, 3). They asked nothing less than that the idealizing veil be removed from the novels and short stories of family life, whether such fiction was published with the blessings of the left or serialized in *Good Housekeeping*. It remained for the novels of other imaginers, oppositional and mainstream, male and female, to refashion the breadwinning woman who was not struggling with the mother's duties or the daughter's restrictions.

Chapter Four

LOVE'S WAGES: WOMEN, WORK, FICTION, AND ROMANCE

Vincent La Gambina, *The Life Cafeteria,* 1936.
Museum of the City of New York.

Nothing else mattered but . . . [him]. . . . Before his wishes, all things went down.
—Fannie Hurst, *Back Street* (1931)

[She realized] she had made up mushy daydreams about a man instead of learning how
to be really useful to the union. Men didn't act that way.
—Leane Zugsmith, *A Time to Remember* (1936)

Oppression masks . . . many aliases, and when applied to women,
one of these masks is called love.
—Mary Inman, *In Woman's Defense* (1940)

As part of their effort to define a new proletarian community, the novelists of the day, debating how and whether the feminine working class should comfort embattled manhood, addressed the nature of womanhood itself. A minority, such as the three authors discussed in the last chapter and those discussed in chapter 5, challenged the dominant vision of woman as nurturer in the home and workplace. If, with exceptions like Agnes Smedley or Mary Heaton Vorse (*Strike!*, 1930), the challenge was muted or ambivalent, the women dissenters were still irritated by the prevailing view, even in radical quarters, that, baldly stated, man is rational, woman emotional. Indeed, many male authors, despite their allegiance to social protest, implicitly approved Lord Byron's famous assertion in *Don Juan* that "Man's love is of man's life a thing apart / 'Tis woman's whole existence." The former Young Communist League and sometime Socialist Murray Kempton explained that even politically involved women of the 1930s led "lives . . . controlled by love."[1] If "lovers [appeared in their lives] . . . too late or not at all," they inevitably "died inside" (217).

Lovers or Comrades: Definitions of Womanhood

Undoubtedly the iconoclastic Agnes Smedley would have chafed at such thinking, echoed in Maxwell Bodenheim's 1934 *New Masses* poem "To a Revolutionary Girl." Only woman was subject to "illogical / Disturbance of . . . mind"; her sex alone "like[d] romance" and its ideologically frivolous trappings.[2] Smedley would have been just as offended by the passion-struck heroine of John Steinbeck's 1937 short story "Chrysanthemums."[3] In it, a self-reliant farm wife is enraptured by the attentions of a traveling salesman out to con her. A willing dupe, the rural woman is reduced to crouching at his feet, like a dog. Smedley's fictive embodiment Marie Rogers, in contrast, struggles to liberate herself from a series of demeaning affairs with fellow revolutionaries. At novel's end she declares, in desperation, "I hate love!"[4]

Like the more agit-prop heroines of the day, Marie refashions herself by rejecting any love relationship in which she finds herself dependent. She places her own future hopes in companionate relations between the sexes. Yet the fact that Marie's strong-minded creator had herself been embroiled in love affairs that she needed to exorcise (by psychotherapy as well as writing) was telling enough. Smedley and her sister authors Olsen and Le Sueur, however much they lamented their labor-class protagonists' mistreatment by men, never repudiated the centrality for women of the love relationship, especially in its heterosexual romantic form.[5] It is true that the three joined those party adherents who constructed plots in which feminine romanticism was transformed into political camaraderie.[6] Their sympathetic portrayals of deserted mothers and jilted workers echoed the male radical cry for women to put aside personal desires in the fight for a common cause. It was an argument that the period's Kollontai-style appeals for female sexual liberation only helped to strengthen.

If the feminine appeal for freedom was never popular in masculine quarters, comradeship still remained ideologically superior to romantic or marital love, perhaps because what Kempton called the "Comrade Woman" embraced a multitude of home-front and picket-line duties and became with her sisters the "housekeepers of the movement" (213). But, whether in the early 1930s or in the later Popular Front period, many in the official or vaguely affiliated Left, in the anticonservative ranks, or simply on the economic margins associated the impetus to marry with a suspect feminine agenda. Again to quote Maxwell Bodenheim: "But you are a girl. Your problem [the need for romance] cannot be denied" (8).

One *New Masses* story read like a cautionary tale to women contemplating such a plan. Moe and Esther, he a shipping clerk, she a factory worker, meet one weekend at Coney Island, soon go to City Hall to get married, and spend a passionate seven days, on borrowed money, at a Manhattan hotel. By week's end they recognize that they cannot remain married. Their earnings are needed by their large and needy tenement families. Weighed down by the dread of how "worried and busted up about things" they would soon become, they realize the honeymoon is over.[7] When they part at the subway, he to Brooklyn, she to the Bronx, the implication is that Esther will have the more difficult time. At least by so abrupt a termination Esther avoids the fate of Clifford Odets's discontented wife in the well-known 1935 drama *Waiting for Lefty*. Her illusions crushed, her husband out of work, she taunts him that their dreams of roses and waterfalls have not materialized.

As we shall observe, an otherwise divergent group of 1930s writers, male and female, leftist and status quo, white and black, questioned the wisdom of romance, much less wedlock, in so tumultuous a time. They held the woman in love up to scrutiny, not as an alternative to the ideal or flawed mother figures of the writers discussed in the second and third chapters but as an attempt to comprehend the emotionally hungry female breadwinner. In one way or another, these analysts of womanhood all refigured work as the favored antithesis of love. In this they were joined by some of the era's most visible women breadwinners: on the "labor stage" and at "workers' universities."

No Time for Love: "I Am a Woman Worker"

The feminine rejection of romance was given a seal of approval in *Pins and Needles,* a 1937 labor revue put on under the auspices of the ILGWU's Education Department, complete with garment workers (drawing the same pay they did in the trades) as the cast. Dedicated to the by-then-muted philosophy of the communistic Labor Stage—a true Workers' Theater— the musical takes a satiric look at political parties and policies at home and abroad.[8] It also includes a particularly popular tune, "Why Sing of Stars Above!", or "Sing Me a Song of Social Significance." In it, the women take center stage to discourage their marriage-minded suitors. Reversing stereotype, they take a dim view of men's wooing and love talk when there are strikes to be won and millions trapped on breadlines. In any case, they wish not for a suitor but for a job and a meal. Although in another ditty the women acknowledge that a companionate marriage helps further every garment worker's union goals, the lyrics also disavow romantic— and its likely sequel, familial—womanhood.

In their offstage lives, the women, who, according to the *New York Times* drama critic Brooks Atkinson, so feistily sang Harold Rome's clever tunes, were, like the male cast members, ILGWU dressmakers, cutters, and pressers.[9] In becoming actors (they temporarily left their jobs to take the play to Broadway and even to the Roosevelt White House), women and men alike took advantage of one of their forward-looking union's Education Department initiatives, which was meant, like other activities, to engage workers in celebrating and studying the labor movement. But there was an added learning component for these and other women who involved themselves in programs ranging from dramatic performances to discussion groups. The education director Fannia Cohn, concerned that women take charge of their economic future, exhorted her female worker-students to abandon "romantic delusions."[10] Whether they remained single or juggled work and family building, Cohn urged, they had to prepare to be "in the industry to stay" (1203). To that end, some took college courses at their union's Workers' University. There they discussed political and economic questions, penned experience-centered compositions and speeches, and learned the rudiments of theory-based labor organizing. Others enrolled in the workers' colleges (the radical Brookwood in upstate New York and Commonwealth College in Arkansas) and summer schools solely for women workers (the more moderate Bryn Mawr, Barnard, University of Wisconsin, and, for their counterparts in the rural textile trade, the Southern Summer School for Women Workers).[11] All were places where typically extensive feminine "industrial histor[ies]" were carefully tabulated, students' reasons for entering and leaving, enduring or disliking various jobs scrutinized by facilitator-teachers, and women's labor careers after "graduation" followed proudly.[12] More important, the autobiographies working women attendees left behind, some excerpted in Women's Bureau bulletins, others published in period "scrapbooks," reveal how they discovered their labor-class voices. As they wrote about their working lives, they were implicitly questioning the still entrenched belief that female trade unionists were husband hunters just visiting the workplace.

Only a few thousand women at most attended these relatively short-lived workers' colleges and summer schools, but those who did sounded nothing like the man- or family-focused characters in much of the fiction examined thus far. Instead, these amateur narrators breathed life—and hope—into the silent work group dismissively alluded to at the end of *Jews Without Money,* those "little Jewish and Italian girls . . . [who] dripped with sweat . . . haggard, as though in pain."[13] In contrast to Gold's superficial treatment of the feminine laborscape, the hundred or so essays in *I Am a Woman Worker,* published in 1936 by the Affiliated Schools for Workers, an agency that coordinated workers' education with the aid of New Deal grant money, read like a handbook of the feminine workplace.[14] It is as if Gold's narrative voice has been replaced by those of the not-so-little factory girls he noted only in passing in his hurry to address the sweat and pain of men at labor.

Though each is brief, only a page or two long, most of the *Woman Worker* narratives reflect the expertise and understanding born of a decade or more of feminine labor experience. The product of class assignments in various workers' schools of the day, the pieces chronicle lives spent in the dailiness of textile, candy wrapping, tobacco, bean picking, restaurant, department store, waitressing, or similarly taxing "women's work." Simply written but alive with detail and conviction, all the sketches are eloquent testimony to what the author of "One Day of Labor" calls the "demanding, driving, compelling nature" of the factory (25). They testify to an array of womanly survival tactics, including warning one another of an approaching foreman, expressing concern for co-workers, and urging a walkout when one of the group is mistreated. Many essays address the job-site injuries to lungs, hands, skin, and back that frequently resulted from polluted or dangerous workplaces, speedups and stretch-outs, whether in rural southern mill or northern urban sweatshop. Others carefully catalog the mean-spirited wages, particularly for piecework, that employers in woman-filled shops knew the market—and the women—would bear. And still other essays, reaching for sisterhood, commiserate with the plight of unemployed women jailed or laid off for unionizing or for facing down an unscrupulous employer. In producing such workplace autobiographies, the women mapped out their own labor territory. Intelligent explications of the inequities, ennuis, turf wars, and triumphs of their days on the job, the pieces are attempts to invoke a standard of industrial fairness against which the work these women did could be measured.

Men, when they do appear, range from intractable bosses to remote co-workers with better-paying jobs to, more occasionally, fellow strikers.

But, probably because of their relegation to gender-segregated fields, the women received little aid from the male-run umbrella unions. In any case, the masculine presence in their texts, whether at work site or in job action, is not strong. Moreover, as Lillian Robinson, one of the few to illuminate the collection for modern readers, points out, equally scant are selections "where women workers are shown discussing their boyfriends and husbands, how being married affects their role in the labor force, or how the [traditional] 'feminine' image . . . conflicts with the identity they must develop to survive on the job." [15] By such omissions, the women implicitly reject the widespread trade union perception of them as subordinate workers. In fact, in the work-focused world of the collection, the narrators seem to feel no need to identify themselves as women at all. They are workers, first and foremost. Paradoxically, by articulating their concerns as women who work, these eyewitness labor historians both include and transcend a focus on women's oppression. For in the seriousness of purpose that characterizes all of the essays, class imperceptibly replaces gender; "women's work," with its supportive implications, ceases to be a descriptor. [16]

What distinguishes the *Woman Worker* collection from period ideology about the marriage-hunting working girl is its reflection of the determined attempt, spearheaded in the late 1920s by those like the workers' education advocate and New Deal luminary Hilda Smith, to counter that stereotype. [17] As early as 1927, Smith described what leisure time meant at the all-woman Bryn Mawr Summer School. "The two schools [Barnard and Bryn Mawr] had meals together, danced together . . . and discussed the relative merits of each school during a very happy week which made us realize anew that we were a part of a movement larger than any one school." [18] In a similar fashion, the *Woman Worker* essays convey a vision of feminine self-interest that minimizes or excludes the pursuit of personal satisfaction outside of the workplace. Indeed, the essays erase the real-life heterosexual socializing, recounted in *The Autobiography of an American Communist* (1977), which led the YCLer and working girl Regina Karasick (later Peggy Dennis) into the common-law arms of the rising party star Eugene Dennis. There are no job-site or union hall romances in *Woman Worker,* whether culminating in wedlock, a common-law union, a brief affair, or an abrupt jilting. No sooner does the title character of "A Romantic Realist," for instance, engage in a fantasy about the man who will wear the ties she produces than she brings herself back to earth—"no time for rhapsodies"—by reminding herself of her new cut in salary (29).

Of course, the women chosen to attend the workers' colleges, particularly the noncoeducational summer ones, would have been similarly serious-minded, probably more so than many of their workplace sisters who were uninterested in schools and trade unions. Nevertheless, the exclusion from their essays of all but a few satiric references to. flirtations with men, to the excitement of the male presence during or after the workday, or to fantasies about marriage suggests what one analyst of today's woman-filled textile industry calls the unresolved tension between "sisterhood and strength and the picture-book romance."[19] After all, from the turn-of-the-century sweatshop to the modern-day factory the "clear passion for engagements" (Westwood, 108) and for "a world of romance and sexuality" (101) has been a fixture of the friendships expressed on the shop floor as in covert resistance to the "imposition of work discipline and management controls" (96). It is difficult to believe that even the creators of "I Got a Job in a Union Tobacco Factory" or "My First Experience in Jail" would not have witnessed or participated in such a workplace culture. The work talk of *Woman Worker,* therefore, seems as much the result, in Fannia Cohn's words, of the group's guided education in developing a "working-class psychology" (1204) as a reflection of their job-site interests.

What somewhat artificially emerges, then, as a vision of feminine self-interest, for all its ideological power, seems opposed to the overriding importance of social life as a workroom subject identified by historians of women's work culture (Tentler, 72). Such a determined exclusion, furthermore, points to an unresolved difficulty in conceptualizing workplace womanhood.

The era's fiction both inherited and explored this difficulty. But how does fiction by male and female authors acknowledge the tension between 1930s women's romantic and work preoccupations? Are their heroines less concerned, like those *Pins and Needles* singers, with romance than with a job and a meal? Conversely, if texts acknowledge the romantic worker in quest of an emotional life, is it at the expense of her life as a wage earner?

To find representative voices of female industrial work in 1930s fiction in texts that make sense of the female worker craving both an emotional and a workplace life, we turn to one group that crossed genre lines to form what the critic of American popular culture John Cawelti labels "anti-romantic romances."[20]

Romantic Femininity in the Antiromantic Novel

Whether best-seller awash in pathos, strike novel, or black female bildungsroman, all used romantic femininity as a framing device. It became a way of understanding the working-class woman who is neither (or not yet) the all-giving mother nor, her seemingly inevitable alternative, particularly in such tough economic times, the self-absorbed harlot. All such novels reverse or condemn the popular fictional form embodied in confession magazines and pulp novels for encouraging working women in job-site daydreams. Though respecting woman's workplace "gossip," all portray the hazards of a concern with romance rather than with economic realities. In so doing, they are among the few to pay serious literary attention to the assumptions about love and marriage many women brought to the workplace, even if these writers found such assumptions oppressive to the women who clung to them.

Most, particularly those under the socially conscious rubric, were not read by the female labor-class audience they were trying to warn, though a few were commercial successes.[21] They were misunderstood as lachrymose celebrations of the woman who lives for love or party-line indictments of a capitalist state that did not permit the worker's wife, any more than the worker himself, to marry and prosper.[22] Nevertheless, such studies of female self-devaluation through romanticism and laments for the starry-eyed worker's wife whose dreams fizzle out joined the period's bildungsromans of romance-obsessed shopgirls turned strikers, variants skeptical of such plotting, or celebrations of the black southern woman who, though eschewing politics, can take love where she finds it. All hold romantic womanhood up to a 1930s mirror. Whether sentiment, social protest, or folkloric female quest narrative, all caution women against economic and psychic dependency alike.

Of that small but diverse group whose novels and stories addressed romantic womanhood, it is logical to begin with an author known well before (and even after) the 1930s as the "sob sister of American fiction," Fannie Hurst.[23] A careful rereading reveals that she sent her vast female readership a message quite critical of the love-struck woman. In Hurst, as in texts by Catharine Brody, Edward Newhouse, Leane Zugsmith, and Hurst's onetime protégé Zora Neale Hurston, all of which took up the theme of women at waged labor, economic passivity, not a broken romance, is the true emotional danger.

Hurst: Back Street as Breadline

In her day Fannie Hurst was as maligned by critics as she was popular with, and prosperous because of, a wide (and white) female following,[24] though she seemed to be blamed for luring the proletarian (and for that matter, bourgeois) woman away from the social protest subgenre. Among her fans were already the countless labor-class readers buying escape fiction such as the sin-suffer-repent stories filling *True Story, Real Love,* and *Dream World* and their counterparts in the day's film magazines.[25] (*Back Street* [1931] and *Imitation of Life* [1933] found their way into film versions in the 1930s and remakes afterward.) By 1925 her stories of female suffering—pre-, extra-, and marital itself—from the parlors (*Every Soul Hath Its Song,* 1916) to the shop floors (*Just Around the Corner,* 1914) to the servants' galleys of America (*Lummox,* 1923) had made her one of the highest-paid writers in the country. She was an integral part of a privileged group that included Edna Ferber, Ellen Glasgow, Sinclair Lewis, and Scott Fitzgerald.[26] Hurst thus joined a stable of writers whose positions in the literary world were far more lucrative, and whose reputations were more secure, than those of the struggling leftists whom *New Masses* would soon publish. And there was no better proof of Hurst's luminary status even before the Depression set in than that the moneymaking *Cosmopolitan,* long known as a family-oriented magazine with a literary emphasis (it serialized *Back Street* in 1930), was already paying her $5,000 per story in the 1920s (Shaughnessy, 32; *Anatomy,* 242).

When *Back Street* appeared in book form two years after the Crash, playing on the twinned Hurst idées fixes of feminine romantic devotion and suffering, it was an immediate best-seller. All the important taste-making journals, *New Republic* included, paid grudging attention to it. They uniformly lamented her trademark sentimentality, bad taste, and stereotyping but felt compelled to praise her narrative skills. A few reviewers even noted that her newest book transcended the tearjerker in its psychological verisimilitude.[27] The *Nation* found the story "absorbing"; the *New Republic,* though lukewarm, linked Hurst to Dreiser's *Jennie Gerhardt* in her defense of a working-class woman's decision to become a wealthy man's mistress.[28] What no one, not even her avid feminine readership, seemed to realize was *Back Street*'s coded warning to women workers in the Depression on the wages of love; the novel as a parable of the dangers of female passivity.

Instead, given the dominant perception of Hurst's novels and stories as better-than-average potboilers, her tale of Ray Schmidt, a kindhearted but lightly promiscuous clothing store clerk-buyer who quits a good job to be kept for a lifetime of shabbiness and emotional exploitation by Walter Saxel, a narcissistic (and married) banker, was widely reduced to a woman's weeper. Reviewers accepted the power of popular literature in the Hurstian vein to elicit audience identification with the suffering heroine. But they misread the cautionary message at the novel's core as, braving the social ostracism leveled at the "other woman," the foolhardy Ray loves, in their opinion, not wisely but too well.

One of a long line of Hurst's love slaves, Ray is, the argument went, a post-1920s "liberated woman" update of that eternally sentimental type, a fixture of American popular fiction since Mrs. Rowson's seduction novel *Charlotte Temple* (1791). Hurst herself was simply carrying on the long tradition begun by Samuel Richardson's *Clarissa* (1748) in what one student of popular culture has dubbed the "feminine equivalent of the adventure story" (Cawelti, 41). In Rowson, as in Richardson, a woman gives all for love, suffers, sacrifices, is betrayed, and dies. All Hurst had done was merge the eighteenth-century novel of sensibility (Clarissa is forever registering her impressions of the villainous Lovelace) with the late nineteenth-century working girl's romance perfected by Laura Jean Libbey—with the sexual knowingness of the 1920s flapper tale added for spiciness. Ray Schmidt combines the vulnerability of a sentiment-driven leisure-class heroine with the shopgirl's desire for marital rescue by a merchant prince. If in the Libbey romances the protagonist holds out for a wedding, as one of the more perceptive reviews pointed out, poor Ray turns herself into the "true wife" denied the benefit of wedlock. She sacrifices, supports, plays a graceful second fiddle, and, above all, stays on (*Nation,* 1931, 195).

In the 1930s Fannie Hurst was far from celebrating anything about Ray Schmidt's decision. In her public utterances she excoriated the woman able to work who let a man support her. She even elided the distinction between wife and kept woman in a 1934 speech to a professional women's group. There she argued that three forces prevented women from holding decent jobs: the Depression, the new fascist ideology of keeping women as kitchen slaves, and, most of all, the "languid psychology of the hordes of women who still observe the twenty-four-hour-a-day working hours of the industry of gold-digging" for economic security.[29] She had supported the year-long Passaic textile strike of the mid-1920s, in which women figured prominently as organizers, picketers, and arrestees. By the early 1930s she was writing Mrs. Roosevelt to urge that women servants be organized (*Anatomy,* 304). Continuing her efforts to support women wage earners, three years after *Back Street* was published she appeared on a radio show sponsored by the ILGWU with union president David Dubinsky, AFL head Bill Green, the organizer Rose Schneiderman, and Labor Secretary Frances Perkins to rally support for better work conditions for women and men in the hard-hit garment trades.[30] Although there is no evidence that she saw *Pins and Needles,* she would have applauded its female singers.

As an aspiring writer in post–World War I New York City, she was a fascinated participant-observer of the "daily grind of people who work with their hands and feet" (*Anatomy,* 178). She had been a factory hand, a waitress at Child's, and a salesgirl in Macy's bargain basement (Burke, 442). In a similar research spirit, she attended sessions of prostitutes' arraignments at the night court, where she was disturbed "by the nightly haul of women off the streets, the men going unchallenged" (*Anatomy,* 178); exculpating the man who pays the woman for sex would resurface in veiled form in *Back Street.* Such concern had similarly infused her 1920s servant saga *Lummox,* with its careful delineation of cleaning women's scanty wages, as well as the unfeeling employment agencies and extractive employers who handled them. (No less an activist for working-class change than Leon Trotsky liked the book very much, Hurst later recounted proudly.) As if already a captive of the next decade's economic troubles, the woman at the center of *Lummox* never aspires at all. A permanent member of the servant class (even the "happy" ending finds her married to a widower glad to find a compliant wife-servant for his many children), Bertha knows only social prejudice against "thieving" immigrants, dirty work, long hours, and cast-off clothes. Yet even her creator, who places the tale at the turn of the century but infuses it with a 1920s viewpoint, finds Bertha partly culpable for her inability to imagine a better life. In spite of her compassion for the overworked Bertha's fatigue at the end of a seventeen-hour day begun with stoking the coal range at 6:00 A.M. and climaxed by placing a silver pitcher of water by the master's bedside, the woman's oxlike passivity, "a trait," stressed one biographer, Hurst "deplored," makes her a collaborator in her exploitation.[31] To Hurst, speaking in the optimistic 1920s, when single women's work outside the home was becoming more accepted, "woman's place" was "where she [could] get the most out of life" (qtd. Frederick, 361). It is a place poor Bertha never tries to find.

Back Street comes out of a different time, when women's job options were constricted, as Hurst well knew because throughout the Depression, she "continued to walk among the apple vendors, the soup lines" (*Anatomy,* 303) and to visit the night court. True, she set the tale of Ray's young womanhood well before the Depression, and by novel's end, at the onset of the 1930s, Ray is living shoddily in Europe, grubbing out an existence at the gambling tables of Aix-les-Bains. Though leading a hand-to-mouth existence, she is far from the exigencies of the American moment. On the surface Ray's tale seems antihistorical because she is impelled by self-destructive forces that differ little from those of Hurst's lovelorn types twenty years before. Looking deeper, one sees that *Back Street* imbues a 1920s theme—workplace mobility as a woman's right— with 1930s overtones. A small businessman's daughter who helps her father in his Cincinnati dress trimmings store, Ray comes out of a typically midwestern milieu that enables her to work and develop a skill. A stylish girl, she has a reputation for flirtatiousness bordering on the wayward with traveling salesmen visiting the store. But she enjoys a wary acceptance in the community and even receives a marriage offer, which she promptly turns down, from a drab local businessman. For she whom Hurst calls "the astute Miss Schmidt" has a place in the semiprofessional world of rising saleswomen rather than in Bertha the lummox's servant depths.

Though not fearful of unemployment in the way characteristic of those interviewed by the Women's Bureau or those observed by Hurst herself as she walked in the tenement districts of New York, Ray begins her work life as her father's counter clerk and could presumably do such work in her Ohio town indefinitely. Ray, however, persuades herself that life is not worth anything without the attentions of Walter Saxel, a man beyond her social and marital reach. In her more lucid moments Ray acknowledges that her image of Walter is a glorification. His origins are not much grander than her own, and he has risen in the world by a combination of charm and good luck. Although on the edge of her awareness hovers the realization that her own self-minimizing stands in her way, Ray plods on, all but deifying Walter when he rejects her to marry a respectably ornamental woman who will aid his social aspirations.

When Walter marries, Ray, echoing many women readers of the book, views work without romance as a poor but inevitable alternative. She takes a job in New York, where in the early 1900s jobs were still plentiful. Almost involuntarily, she begins to take hold of her job life. Compared with the unskilled woman wage earner at the turn of the century, or even thirty years later, Ray is doing very well. She earns $20 per week to the $4 or $5 of Dreiser's turn-of-the-century Sister Carrie (not to mention the little more than $10 per week, and often less, of many female factory hands and sales personnel the very year *Back Street* appeared). She begins to develop a buyer's expertise and in New York earns more, though not enough to live well. She minimizes her work value and her business skills because she has had a romantic reversal, what she calls a "crash" (114) (an interesting buzzword for a 1930s audience). In so doing, she devalues herself completely, as Hurst reiterates. Meeting Walter by chance some years later, Ray reinvests the man (who has risen from bank clerk to officer in the years between his marriage and their reunion in New York) with the aura of a worldly success she can never attain by her own efforts. Though the chief feature of her work existence is its monotony, not its sweatshop conditions, Ray transforms Walter into a version of the workplace savior and begins a psychic downward trajectory. She quits her job to be his mistress, in a rear apartment, decidedly off Central Park West.

Hers is no mere kept woman's life, as it turns out, but a career as alternate wife. Ray underscores her wifely role when defending her liaison to a skeptical relative (287). She certainly gives Walter wifely job advice and, ever the helpmeet, rather improbably does market research for him ("I love looking up data for you, Walter" [177]). She listens to all of his worries, worries he conceals from his own wife, who sounds like the real mistress. Another fact revealing that the liabilities of the wife's role have accrued to Ray, not its benefits, is her management of his second household on a very tight budget; she lives more like a working man's mate than a capitalist's fancy woman. Although Walter obviously could choose either to give her more or allow her to have a job, like men in far less lucrative positions he strengthens his claim to manhood by controlling Ray's money and assuages his (minimal) guilt at the adultery as well. All in all, he keeps her very meanly so that she is constantly scrimping to keep the household in good trim. Putting up a luxurious front, serving him elegant food, she must secretly do part-time piecework, china painting sold to the neighbors, to make ends meet.

The author rescues her narrative from the woman's magazine bathos that threatens to engulf it. Rather than drown the book in what one recent critic, confusing teller and tale, calls the "code [that] women . . . exist for the good of men" (Shaughnessy, 49), Hurst delineates the corrosive mental dependency that is the by-product of Ray's man-centered thinking. In a variant of a familiar 1930s scenario, Ray, fearful of hurting her mate's pride, refuses to fend for herself when he has forbidden it. Though Walter is no working stiff, the situation in which she finds herself at one point in the novel ironically reminds one of that of the fearful 1930s spouse. Her man, like Ray's, does give her enough to live on and will not permit her to upstage him by finding work. Midway through the novel, with Walter off on vacation, Ray imagines he has forgotten to leave her money to live and, unable to "defy" him by getting a job, she walks the city, hungrier and hungrier. Ready to starve rather than take a step of which he would disapprove, she is rescued only by an eleventh-hour discovery of the money he had left for her. In a metaphor for the economic mill he puts her through, it had slipped out of sight by accident.

If the economic fruits of living for love are scanty, the psychological ones are even worse. By closing herself off from wage-earning work, Ray has created a private Great Depression for herself in which she is fearful of how to make ends meet and incapable of finding even clandestine jobs to bring in added income. She lives in a mental back street, in that drab world of psychic dependency unwittingly shared by the many 1930s women far worse off than herself.[32] And in her last years, after the Depression has begun and Walter has died, leaving her nothing in his will (even his son, who disapproved of the liaison, is both shocked at how little his father kept her on during his lifetime and disturbed by this posthumous injustice), Ray's economic privations catch up with her emotional ones. Now she, too, tramps the streets looking for work, not as a buyer, in her deskilled state, but as a cashier or a low-level saleswoman, work she cannot secure. Though but in middle age, she is already a "gaunt oldish tragedy" (417).

Worse is to come. Though she has enough to make it to Aix-les-Bains to survive from the gambling tables, she spends her days there "scuttling" (481) from casinos for handouts to her wretched room sans plumbing; psychologically, she has become a bag lady. At novel's end, she is unrecognizable as the self-sufficient Cincinnati business girl who could fend for herself. In shedding her former self-reliance, Ray in effect is completely dehumanized: deluded, unclean, repulsive. Her life comes to a nightmarish conclusion that even women thrown out of jobs by the Depression would have pitied.

Ray is an extreme case of the problems feminist psychoanalyst Jessica Benjamin described in *The Bonds of Love* (1988), a study of the links between the feminine construction of romantic love and the corollary desire for subordination. Although Benjamin refuses Freud's definition of the very "hallmark of the feminine" as "woman's renunciation of sexual agency and her acceptance of object status" (87), she concurs with his formulation of woman "adoring the man who possesses" what she lacks. It is "a love," reasons Benjamin, "in which the woman submits to and adores an other who is what she cannot be" (86), a psychic problem but one "largely the work of culture" (90). Like many women before and after her, Ray had entered a love relationship to "acquire vicariously something [she] has not got within [herself]." Her "sexuality is bound up with the fantasy of submission to an ideal male figure" (89). Her misfortune is to have chosen one whose narcissism is untempered by charity. In contrast to the strength Margaret Mitchell's Scarlett O'Hara, left to run a starving plantation while her idealized lover is off to war, may have found by keeping the romantic lamp lit, Ray's debilitation increases the more her supposed "great love" prospers in the world, as if he grows at her expense. The reason is clear enough. Scarlett, unconsciously or not, uses romantic sacrifice only as a rationale for taking control of circumstances as well as the lives of others. Ray, fleeing self-proclamation, can live only by extinguishing her identity in the name of love.

Back Street's glaring psychological dimension, surprisingly little remarked then or now, reinforces rather than denies its revelation of the moods, desires, and anxieties of the time and society it depicts. On one level, this best-seller plays to the period's feminine fear of being tied to a male breadwinner (or employer) who starves and enslaves. Emotionally, financially, and professionally, Ray is as far from being a member of the *Pins and Needles* cast or student in the Bryn Mawr Summer School as she can be. Because her lover is her employer, love brings starvation. Give up your economic freedom for a man, the book reveals, whether for money or love, and you may end up a sister to the Bottom Dogs welfare seekers of Meridel Le Sueur and Tom Kromer.

Viewed another way, Ray, whose true fall is from self-supporting worker to obsessed romantic hanger-on, personifies Hurst's own fears writ large. By her own admission, she experienced a terror of what would happen to her if she ever relinquished control, if she ever experienced a "lessen[ed] . . . capacity for creative work" (Frederick, 360). In her autobiography, she records how "apprehensive" (*Anatomy,* 302) she felt as her success grew. It was as if her good fortune would disappear and she, too, would be inhabiting a rear apartment, staying in all day on the chance that the telephone, an extension of a man, would ring. Neither professionally nor personally did Hurst allow the specter of such dominance. After wedding the musician Jacques Danielson in 1915, a marriage she kept secret for the first five years, she decreed that they live separately and spend only three nights a week together.[33] As the benefactor-employer of Zora Neale Hurston in the mid-1920s, "at times she treated Hurston as a friend" but at other times distanced herself from friendship and treated her "as a personal maid" (Wilentz, 28). And she crafted a public persona of tireless strength; even by the mid-1950s, she revealed in a *New Yorker* piece dubbed "Powerhouse," Hurst was still maintaining a "killing pace": five hours of sleep and a predawn rising.[34] No wonder that the woman who gave birth to the passive Ray Schmidt needed to destroy her.

Brody: Starved for Love and Money

Although the period's (and Hurst's own) worst fears are realized in the destitute woman conclusion, because *Back Street* ends with the coming of the Depression, Ray Schmidt, having lived in her own version of pinched circumstances with the tight-fisted Walter, comes to grips with the anxieties of real economic hardship only at the end of a romantically delusive life. Molly, the semiskilled factory woman at the core of Catharine Brody's novel *Nobody Starves* (1932) (the product of Brody's incognito workplace investigations as a *New York World* correspondent), lacks Ray's knowledge as a seasoned buyer. Ray had a sizable savings account, at least before she became a kept woman. Molly has never been as fortunate. On strike at a midwestern pottery works in the years leading up to the Depression, she is sacked only for demanding that her pay not be cut. Molly has never been a stranger to privation, even before an ill-starred liaison, in her case marriage to an unstable workman. But like Sister Carrie before her, she sees her weekly pay quickly disappear as she pays board to her scroungingly dependent relatives and hoards for a new winter coat.

Brody, a onetime office worker and another of the numerous *New Masses* contributors who used their novels to make political points, had already produced fiction of what might be called unreconstructed womanhood, most notably *Babe Evanson* (1928), about a drab New York stenographer. Though lacking the economic urgency of *Nobody Starves,* the eponymous novel shares with Hurst's work an indictment of the working woman who finds no sustaining values. Babe's emotional life revolves around moviegoing, makeup (what Mary Inman would soon pinion as the "feverish emphasis on beauty for women" [72]), and fantasies of rescue. So alienated from her stenographic job that she often arrives hours late (clearly this was a pre–Depression text), she invests her love affairs with a miraculous antidote to anomie. As in Hurst, men are constructed to fill an identity void. Women realize, all too late, that the emptiness remains long after the bride has become a wife. At novel's close, however, Babe has yet to come to this realization. She pursues the obscure masculine object of desire and remains heedless of the fact that among her friends and family, "none of them knew why they had married their husbands."[35]

In *Nobody Starves,* Brody widened her scope from the fairly well-paid business girl of *Back Street* and her own previous novel to the labor-class woman in manufacturing. The type represented the still over three-quarters of American working women who remained outside unions and their increasingly militant concerns (Woloch, 449). In what will prove her undoing, the focus of Molly's dreams of upward mobility, circumscribed by her economic privations, is transformed from what she can achieve by her efforts at work to her prospects for marriage. Whereas Hurst's Ray gives up any attempt at joining a working woman's culture for a backstreet exile, Molly shares in that "explosive sociability of the factory" (Tentler, 67) that modern historians of women's work have charted from the turn of the century onward. She explores with her chatty work group that preoccupation with what Dreiser succinctly termed "clothes and men." [36] "Who's your man, now?" (38), she and her friends chorus to one another during and after hours. Trousseaux, breakups, the occasional divorce, movie dates, kisses—the stuff of flight from the meager pay and tedious assembly line—fill Molly's waking thoughts. For her and her workmates, love is an antidote to despair but not a solution because what passes for hardheaded pragmatism about limited prospects can prove to be quite other.

As one who advocated alternative ways that working women could take hold of their lives, Brody imposes on Molly's near-obsession with wedlock a critique shared by many left-sympathizing novelists and social critics, most notably Ruth McKenney and Mary Inman. As if analyzing Molly's devotion to the movie theater, in the important 1940 essay "Women Are Human Beings," McKenney criticized the seductive effect of mass culture. She deplored the "immense body of propaganda for the dream world of romantic love," silly stories in which "Greta Garbo either dies for love or gives up an important job for ditto." "Everywhere the [working] girl turns . . . she is faced with that four-letter word writ in flaming colors: L-O-V-E." [37] Inman concurred, citing the cultural deluge of "sentimental effusions" (73) and woman's "economic dependence upon a personal relationship . . . [which make] a revolt against this overemphasis of her love life difficult" (73).

In Brody's reading, Molly, displacing her inarticulate longings onto approved cultural fantasies, is not so much moving toward what she believes as being unable to find anything more substantial to believe in. Nor, in the brief courtship scenes, does it seem that Molly is impelled by romance. She experiences, without realizing it, a marriage-centered, diffused maternal impulse that encompasses both her suitor Bill and her future children by him. Their so-called great moment is worth quoting at length:

She stood tremulous, tense. If this was the moment, then everything would be decided. If not. . . . He said nothing but kissed her. It was not a sudden kiss to Molly, though it came without warning. . . .

"Aw, Molly, come on out [to Detroit] when I get work. Then we'll get married and. . . ."

There, the words were out. They had kissed before but these new kisses were ready to give much that he desired. She made no objections to furiously searching hands and only looked around once or twice to see that no one was coming. She smiled at him, a cherishing, clement smile, just the least bit amused, infinitely and unconsciously pitying and cherishing what it pities. She would smile in just that way at her children, at the rapt, solemn greed of their hushed faces that inhaled the milk of her breasts.[38]

Had Molly realized it, this scene clearly subverts the woman's romance she sees on the screen. Still, just as Ray would have gone to see the 1932 film version of *Back Street* for escape, not warning, so would Molly, taking Bill with her. When she and Bill move to Detroit in search of a better life via the vast auto industry, the only movie analogue would be the struggling couple in King Vidor's *Our Daily Bread* (1936). As the industry reels from cutbacks and labor unrest, Molly and Bill feel no impetus to join striking communities of workers; far from it. Both approve Bill's decision to invest at the company-tied bank (which later fails), plan to own a house, and look to their earning power as a couple as a bulwark against the growing financial uncertainty outside. Would-be miniature capitalists, they believe in the system that was about to come crashing down around them. As they lose hold of full-time, then part-time, employment and sink into debt and impending dispossession, love sours fast. Soon enough Molly joins all of the other married women, and not a few of the hardened single ones, in a disillusionment encapsulated in one woman's comment: "All this love stuff just kills me" (195). For Molly, these words will prove particularly prophetic.

What begins as a leftist novel naturalistically placing the imperiled working-class marriage in the context of the national crisis—the quarrels, the growing tension, the pinched economies—rapidly turns into a sequel to an earlier naturalist work, Frank Norris's 1899 *McTeague*.[39] The once-fastidious Molly falls to a Trinaesque slovenliness and depression of spirit. The once-polite Bill turns to blows and insults to ward off half-understood feelings of inadequacy. The dissolution of families may have been a popular theme in leftist fiction, but husbandly personality disintegration—from wooer to wife abuser—was not. If Brody's relentless portrait romance, never very heartfelt, turns to weary alienation on the woman's part, what happens to Molly may be a political tragedy but it is also a personal one. As her marriage disintegrates in bitterness and recriminations better leveled at the economic situation, she becomes "a cold gray fact herself" (260). Reduced to a human being simply trying to survive, she has no emotional time for a lover or husband. There is "no energy left with which to pick him up and dust him off and send him out" (263). She is further punished, however, for the death of love when Bill's disillusionment with his jobless existence finds expression in resentment of, then murderous hatred for, his wife. Blaming Molly for his troubles, he blows her brains out with a shotgun and calmly takes a walk in the park—if not exactly at peace, at least released from intolerable anger.

Brody sensationalized the domestic strains documented in period studies of working-class marriages, particularly of what one survey of another manufacturing city, Chicago, charted in interviews with wives of jobless men. The masculine tendency was to quarrel with wives when there was "nowhere to go" because there was no work (Bauman and Coode, 77). Possibly also inspired by some actual tabloid stories of the time, her novel caught popular attention and did better than most Bottom Dogs fiction. *Nobody Starves* went through two printings, receiving respectful attention from the middlebrow and liberal journals. Interpreted as a story of "what the depression means to people on a really ragged edge," it was likened to *Main Street* for its "unsentimental scrutiny" of an ill-assorted marriage.[40]

What went sadly unremarked was that the woman worker was at its core. Though she recaptures in the waning stages of her marriage the premarital impetus of her tile factory days to "save herself" (263), she is a casualty of male rage.

Newhouse and Zugsmith: Love as Trivia

Though not encouraging in the era's women wage earners a paranoia about prospective husbands, Brody does take *Back Street*'s cautionary message even further. *Nobody Starves* is a darker tale of the perils of femi-

nine psychic dependence in the murky name of a love that first compro-
mises liberty and then snuffs out life itself. Edward Newhouse, journalist,
City College dropout, itinerant factory hand, and sometime resident of a
Hooverville, which provided the raw materials for his well-received 1934
You Can't Sleep Here, would have probably commented that despite the
murder of one worker by another, his fellow leftist Brody did not take the
novel far enough.[41] That is, only when the male-centeredness of women is
channeled into useful (though subordinate) female political fervor would
tragedies such as this stop happening. This rapid transformation forms the
subplot of the sequel, *This Is Your Day* (1937), which continues the saga of
Gene Marsay begun in the 1934 work. He is a newspaperman who loses
his job, takes to pilfering milk bottles and bakery rolls, spends his days
in the New York Public Library, and winds up organizing the denizens of
a Queens Hooverville. Through Gene, his Hooverville period over and
now a party organizer, Newhouse proves that Gene's malleable new YCL
wife, Alma, can conquer her own irrelevance by limiting her romantic
outpourings to those of supportive party wife. She participates in, but
never goes beyond, her husband's politics.

But it is in the earlier novel, a party-flavored critique of lovelorn
femininity worthy of Murray Kempton and Maxwell Bodenheim, that,
through Gene, Newhouse exposes feminine romanticism as a chimera.
Furthermore, by allying such apparently gender-linked foolishness to the
affluence of the bourgeois (and gainfully employed) woman, Newhouse
transforms an unthinkingly apolitical feminine loyalty to a lover into an
affront to all working-class manhood. The earlier chapters are reminiscent of the talented "forgotten man"-meets-insistent-rich-girl plotting of
the screwball comedy *My Man Godfrey* (1936): Gene has the cumbersome
devotion of the well-off Eileen. Her clumsy generosity hardly inspires its
return. All she earns is his resentment. "[I] hadn't done a thing to keep
[her]," he reflects. "If she had been less splendid she might have insisted
on setting up together and then I would have been driven to crawl for
a job."[42]

Probably to Newhouse's sardonic amusement, Hollywood might have
been intrigued by the romantic elements in his plot. Many are the references to Eileen's unwavering fidelity as her reluctant lover, unable to
afford the price of a meal, dines with Eileen and her similarly well-heeled
friends. He leaves them to prowl around for a place to sleep that night

and then spends the next morning aiding hotel workers on the picket line. Such subjects, despite a brief Warner Brothers vogue for (nonstriking) workers in film, were, of course, far less appealing to the movie moguls than any comic fare starring William Powell and Carole Lombard.[43]

Nor would Hollywood have cared much for the gloss that Gene, suppressing the tender feelings that he fears will unman him, puts on his relations with Eileen. "Brother Marsay," he tells himself, "[you are a] down but not outer, you need a lay, need it bad, need it bad" (141). Rather than specialize in literary close-ups of the two principals, who long to unite but are separated by Gene's manly pride, in the world of the novel Eileen's romantic absorption is out of step with history, or as Paula Rabinowitz would have it, the book's concern not with the "history of hunger" but with the "history of desire" (41) is an affront. One of the more astute reviews rightly found Eileen's presence in the book "extraneous."[44] Still, she is a familiar character in radical fiction. She is that collegiate daughter of privilege, taken perhaps too seriously by Lauren Gilfillan in the fictionalized autobiography, *I Went to Pit College* (1934), who falls for the excitement and the politics of a man outside her class—for a while at least. Or, presented more attractively in novels by the observant Josephine Herbst or the acidulous Tess Slesinger, she is a woman of liberal or radical sympathies whose solidarity with the workers hardens as she sees her own professional life eroded by the Depression. But in male leftists' novels, *You Can't Sleep Here* chief among them, the cossetted bourgeoise is obliviousness itself. She is unable to realize the iniquities of the system that has made her prosperous and is certainly unwilling to give up her easy life (no Hooverville for Eileen!) to join the struggle to subvert it. And there is no doubt that, her philosophical conventionality the badge of her inability to be the comrade wife of Newhouse's later novel, as Mrs. Gene Marsay Eileen would only siphon off masculine energies better devoted to organizing. Significantly, we know little of Eileen's own paid work—at some vaguely defined white-collar job—because she so wishes to live for love. The novel leaves her little with which to construct that life.

Ironically, having skewered Eileen's longings as antirevolutionary, the novel holds back from conferring political activism on the many working-class women for whom romanticism was a luxury. Not only is male poverty the focus. The book also reflects an apparent conviction that when women thrust themselves into strike politics, as does the minor character Carmen, a Puerto Rican hotel worker who acts suggestively toward Gene, they become wantons. In the familiar way of many male (and some female) social protest authors unable to confront or create the all-too-real rebel girl, Newhouse conflates Carmen's political and sexual urgencies. Her picket-line talk with Gene, who has dropped by to support the strike, sounds like a solicitation. In Newhouse's fictive world, the woman who espouses activism but lusts for sex is no more palatable than the one who sighs for love. She is just easier to jilt.

The problem of misguided feminine emotionalism in an era of widespread social dislocation was one that writers as diverse as the sentiment-drenched Fannie Hurst and the more forward-looking Catharine Brody delineated intelligently. But they joined Newhouse, who at best made gestures toward a redirection of his women characters, in an inability to infuse their plotting with such a revisioning. The leftist journalist Leane Zugsmith, a member of the League of Women Shoppers, a kind of left-wing Consumers' League, tried a more forceful approach to the problem. In the once fairly well-known *A Time to Remember* (1936), set in a New York City department store about to erupt in a strike, three portraits reverse that of the Hurstian love slave.[45] Zugsmith reinvents Ray Schmidt, Newhouse's Eileen, and Brody's Molly as evolving rather than static characters. She charts the positive effect on two salesclerks, Doni Roberts and Aline Weinman, of a dawning militance. And she contrasts their growth with the downward trajectory of Myrtle Matthews, a store worker's jealous wife whose insecurities about his fidelity quickly propel her to suicide.

By the Depression, sales, once billed as a career path and pictured as late as 1929 as a complacent feminine work world (Donovan, *Saleslady*, passim), had, at least for nonimmigrant women, lost the luster of its vocational appeal, as even an overage Ray Schmidt finds when she seeks a job after Walter's demise. Some 1930s saleswomen did "fare better than their male co-workers," but only because they were cheaper to hire and easier to control; they also held the lowest-paid jobs such as packers.[46] Such women's relative job security must also be placed in the context of wage cutbacks, poor rehire prospects (Bauman and Coode, 44), and managements determined, as in the Zugsmith novel, to keep unions and collective bargaining out. Still, compared to her counterparts in the industrial and restaurant trades, the saleswoman was hardly associated with labor militance, although in 1935, the year before *A Time to Remember,* Zugsmith—with Newhouse and others identified by the sympathetic *Daily Worker* as writers in "aid [of the] Orhbach Strike" ("Writers," 3)—interviewed that store's employees about their long fight against constant layoffs and wretched hours. (Reginald Marsh commemorated their battle in his painting *End of the Fourteenth Street Crosstown Line,* in which, amid the chaos of subway construction, pickets carry signs reading "Don't Buy at Ohrbach's.") The strike, which ended in a victory for labor, was the prototype for her novel, though Zugsmith might also have found copy in the protests against Macy's and Gimbel's in the early 1930s.

Nevertheless, with some urban exceptions involving a few hundred workers at most, the retail store was not a likely arena for the strike tale. Because hers is, in Walter Rideout's term, a "conversion" novel, Zugsmith's choice of setting would seem peculiar were it not that the store world was an ideal venue in which to reverse the literary associations with saleswomen that Hurst's Ray Schmidt certainly could not.[47] From O. Henry onward, the fictional shopgirl's "life's ambition," as he wrote in his famous 1906 story "The Trimmed Lamp," had been "the drawing of a matrimonial prize."[48] Dreiser gave the aspiration poignant resonance more than two decades later in the pathetic Roberta of *An American Tragedy* (1925). So did Hurst. While expanding on O. Henry and Dreiser, she could not sever her own characters from an unhealthy reliance on men's opinions of them.

Zugsmith clearly has a different agenda. At the novel's opening, the pathetic Doni Roberts, clearly Ray Schmidt's spiritual cousin, masochistically calls up a man who has rejected her; Aline Weinman, a well-bred Eileen type pelted by the unrealistic social expectations of her declining middle-class family, is guilt-ridden over her social failures, including her inability to marry right. By mid-novel, caught up in the collective anger at management's high-handed treatment of store personnel, Doni and Aline are women reborn. Making common cause with the other already politicized male and female store clerks, they develop confidence in themselves as people and, in the now-fashionable phrase, are empowered—at least to a point. For, curiously, Zugsmith feels impelled to reward Doni and Aline with the prospect of romantic involvements with Matt (now free of the clinging Myrtle) and his union ally Bert, men who spearheaded the store strike. Read another way, this finale may be the "let me call you comrade" brand of romance envisioned by the lively *Pins and Needles* singers. But, interestingly, the minor female characters Ettie and Maxine, who coauthored the finally successful collective bargaining that wins the strike (and in an imaginary sequel to the novel, might have questioned the sexual division of labor still operating in the stores) are not so "rewarded." Although it is difficult to pinpoint authorial attitude, the intertwining for Doni and Aline of strike victory and department store relationship does little to contradict a male union leader's assertion: "Girls had a lot to learn [about strikes] and even when they'd learned it, there would always be a lot of biological machinery holding them back" (151).

A Time to Remember was one of the few feminine social protest novels popular with both the *New York Times Book Review* and the Left-sponsored Book Union (Rideout, 235). It would be pleasant to believe that its popularity stemmed from its clever reversal of what both considered hackneyed romantic plotting. Zugsmith's dictum that when women shed retarding obsessions, they can enter into a truly egalitarian love relationship is tantalizing. Yet this is the same author who saw no minimization of women in Newhouse, whom she knew personally and praised lavishly for the "bite, insight, and substance" of his 1930s novels.[49] Given this attitude, a more trenchant reason for her own novel's "cross-cultural" appeal to bourgeois and CPer is that her women are portrayed only in relation to men, even if those men are as much teachers of realpolitik as potential husbands.

Thus the pair of burgeoning romantic comradeships providing closure to the novel skirt what Elsa Dixler terms the "balance of power" in those relationships (95). True, Doni trades in her light reading for John Strachey's *Coming Struggle for Power* (1933) and proclaims in tones that would baffle Ray Schmidt, "I'll never be like what I was" (344). But she has a bureau photo of the handsome Matt on the picket line, suggesting that she may be trading one form of romanticism for another. Aline is similar, if more independent-minded, conflating political tutelage with a possible love interest. If Zugsmith's message is that a working woman must shed psychic dependency to become a force for political change, she herself seems curiously unwilling to shed the trappings of the literary shopgirl of old.

Hurston: Romance as Antiromance

Interestingly, it was a writer associated not with the white industrial wage earner of the northern cities but with the black folk heritage, Zora Neale Hurston, who most lucidly explored the period's feminine inner life. She was neither a journalist-novelist of leftist allegiances nor a Fannie Hurst stalking best-sellerdom. Yet her work sold better than that of Brody and Newhouse, and she was the best-known black woman writer of her day.[50] More important, she was the "only Harlem Renaissance writer raised in the rural folk traditions that several sought to tap."[51] For a time she was a protégé of Hurst, for whom she worked from 1925 to 1927 as a secretary and chauffeur while she attended Barnard College. Hurston admired her manipulative employer's craft, even fulsomely terming her a "great artist."[52]

In Hurston's novel of woman's loving, *Their Eyes Were Watching God* (1937), there is a plot of "three marriages, the first of which brings [the heroine] safety, the second wealth and prestige, and the third love," with a women's magazine ring, even a Hurstian one.[53] And the heroine's aspirations are not so different from those of Hurst's Ray Schmidt. But the Hurston novel bears only tangential and superficial relation to *Back Street*. Although in many public utterances she minimized racial differences and claimed in her autobiography that her interest was to "make a man or a woman do such-and-so, regardless of color" (*Dust Tracks,* 151), her true concern was not the dependent white but the reflective black woman. Ray Schmidt does not know who she is; Janie Crawford ardently wants to find out. Both search for self-definition in heterosexual romance, but only Hurston's Janie, appreciated where Ray is exploited, carves out some autonomy in so doing.

Their Eyes Were Watching God bypasses the social protest mode, a choice that earned Hurston Richard Wright's scornful charge that she continued "in the tradition . . . [of] the minstrel technique," the singing and dancing Negro.[54] To the less hostile, she used the traditions of black folk culture and the unique angle of vision she brought to them to create "mythic realism . . . within a lyrical black idiom" (Gates, 261).[55] Building on the folklore researches she conducted in the South and in Jamaica and Haiti in the decade before writing the novel, first as a student of the eminent Columbia University anthropologist Franz Boas in 1927, she refashioned the historical Eatonville into a linguistic Arcadia where talking on the porch and swapping anecdotes of prowess takes on a life of its own. In her capable hands, those cursorily depicted by Jack Conroy as members of an oppressed, virtually wordless group take control of the narrative. Their interchanges are the spirit of the novel. Their tall tales, imaginative taunts, and reflections on the chief figures of the town, Janie and her second husband, Mayor Starks, among them, fill the literary void left by white proletarian authors. Such a coming of age through language describes the protagonist particularly well. Janie Crawford's recounting of her three marriages frames the novel and evidences Hurston's ability to transform the Hurstian romance into a more authentic quest for feminine self-development.

In this regard, it is no accident that the protagonist of *Their Eyes Were Watching God* is liberated from the menial black women's tasks to which Hurston herself was no stranger. She grew up in the early years of the century in a family of shifting fortunes in Eatonville, Florida, the first all-black incorporated village in the nation. She knew that the townswomen worked outside for whites as domestics (just as she was aware that the men answered to "the bossman"), though *Their Eyes,* set in an Eatonville she artistically transformed, makes the briefest of allusions to these ironclad realities. Certainly Hurston's life after Eatonville furthered her understanding of black female labor. During her years of study at Howard Prep in the closing years of World War I and then at Howard University from 1919 to 1924, she worked at jobs ranging from maid to manicurist. Still, at least to judge by her autobiographical summary of all this work as "uninteresting," she "just was not the type" (*Dust Tracks,* 91). Although she resented being patronized at times, she could turn a menial job into a writer's laboratory, dwelling on the range of human types she encountered in it (*Dust Tracks,* 112–20). But she never had to endure the degradation of the black female factory hands described in *Nobody Starves.* Brody's Molly, given the better work usually allocated to whites, barely notices the "Negro" scrubwomen at her auto plant who hover over a barrel of hot suds, in the "witchlike, pulled-up rags that their jobs made necessary" (6).

Hurston's protagonist exists outside of the harsh world of black female unemployment that was so emblematic of the black South of the 1930s. Though Eatonville was badly hit by the Depression, neither Hurston's novel nor Janie's life gives evidence of it, as Hurston biographer Robert Hemenway observes (221). The author sets the novel in the period of her early life in the Florida town. Yet Hurston could not have been unaware that by the decade of the 1930s black female joblessness had risen enormously, even in rural Florida. As many as 50 percent of black women wage earners were out of work in some southern states, compared with 25 percent of white women. Those who were employed, usually at food-processing, meatpacking, and service jobs that whites rejected, earned pittances such as $6.50 per week in a 1930 Atlanta laundry for a twelve-hour workday.[56] No such women dominate *Their Eyes Were Watching God*. Only a minor character, Janie's confidante Phoeby, a field hand, even comes close.

In the years preceding the novel, again more as observer than participant, Hurston was at least marginally aware of the hard facts of Harlem women's work. Yet in her portrait of a woman elevated through passive wedlock from the worker class, she made no comparison to the rare black urban wage earners, such as the dress pressers of New York City's Local 60, who broke out of the servant role in a more active way. Missing as well from *Their Eyes* are the vocal city militants, the New York City, Chicago, and St. Louis laundry workers who are a far cry from the hapless Delia Jones of Hurston's "Sweat" (1926). Particularly within the United Laundry Workers, an affiliate of the Amalgamated Clothing Workers, black as well as white women agitated for better pay.[57] (Even the IGLWU, frequently accused of racist practices, sent black women delegates to a Harlem labor assembly, a federation of African-American trade unionists in New York dedicated to unionizing black workers.[58]) Nor does Hurston take any notice of the admittedly small numbers of other empowered black working women, from the scanty number in the Harlem "branch" of the party to those sent to Federal Emergency Relief Administration educational training camps for the unemployed.[59]

In all ways, Hurston's art avoided the unionist strivings, "class confrontations of the Northern cities," and budding militance characterizing at least some of the southern women who came north, as one woman put it, to "answer the insults of 'white only'" (*Black and Red*) in the age of Scottsboro.[60] Lacking such an oppositional consciousness, Hurston's Janie passively marries a series of men who ably support her. (With the money from her second husband, she can, if she wishes, keep her third, younger one.) Far from inheriting her family's legacy of the black woman's labor-intensive lot, Hurston's relatively well-off heroine balks at hard rural "woman's work." Her dissatisfaction quickly inspires her to leave her first spouse, an exacting farmer, for a union with the shrewdly entrepreneurial Joe Starks.

Her prospects differ in another way from those of the woman in a more realistic 1940 piece by a largely forgotten black writer, Ramona Lowe. Lowe's affecting short story, "The Woman in the Window," appeared in the important Harlem journal *Opportunity: A Journal of Negro Life,* to which Hurston had herself contributed in the 1920s. True, Janie's work-weary grandmother, who grooms her for a financially secure (and loveless) marriage, is all too aware that the "nigger woman is de mule uh de world" (14). But the old woman is referring to marital as much as workplace exploitation. In any event, her Janie completely escapes the sad fate of Lowe's heroine. That job-seeking character, a desperate single mother who unwillingly transports a racist stereotype of black woman-hood north, is displayed in a downtown department store window in a southern mammy costume, cooking flapjacks for white amusement.

Hurston gave brief literary attention to black women's "legacy of degradation" (Hemenway, 236) in her unjustly neglected 1926 story "Sweat."[61] It is a strange tale of the twinned oppression familiar to so many black women. At its core are the burdens of underpaid laundry work (a theme explored in her onetime friend Langston Hughes's *Not Without Laughter* a few years later) and a shiftless, philandering husband. The man is ever a threat to churchgoing Delia Jones's peace of mind. Hurston dubs him Sykes (shades of Dickens's bully Bill Sikes in *Oliver Twist*) and fashions him into a figure of energetic hatred. Always ready to beat or desert Delia, he finally attempts to kill her by planting a snake in her laundry basket. In an ending marked by poetic if not legal justice, she leaves the snake where its fangs will sink into Sykes's own flesh and listens, unmoved, to his dying pleas for her aid.

In one of her many confusing disavowals of a racial perspective that aroused such ire in the era's leading African-American authors, Hurston remarked, "I do not belong to the sobbing school of Negrohood who hold that nature somehow had given them a lowdown dirty deal" (qtd. Hemenway, 11). Even her naturalistic "Sweat" embodies in embryonic form the theme of feminine liberation through self-assertion. But "Sweat" also reveals that, contrary to her many public pronouncements, Hurston could explore the ills of black womanhood. Particularly in *Their Eyes Were Watching God,* however, her treatment differed greatly from that of Richard Wright in *Native Son*'s depiction of pathetic Bessie Mears, bullied by white employer and black lover alike. Janie's resentments of her first two husbands and their high-handed behavior are real enough, particularly when she realizes she is a marital employee in her husband's life. Whether in his fancy home or his prospering general store, he will not let her speak, much less make decisions. She is directed to "look on herself as the bell-cow [with] the other women . . . the gang" (39). Her prosperity, though not a Bessie Mears–like maid's existence, is the price of her confinement.

Hurston believed that to deal with the romantic longings of black women, whether they aspired to Janie's economic security or, like Bessie, could not imagine it, required a framework other than the hostile northern workplace of *Native Son* or the joyless rural one experienced by the unhappily wed laundress of "Sweat." She found it in the emotional journey of Janie, who, born illegitimate and lovely, ingenuously waits on the eve of her marriage to a man for whom she has no passion "for love to begin" (21). The wait will be a lengthy one.

Many critics conceptualize the novel as a romantic search, a quest for self fulfilled in freely chosen love.[62] As Janie experiences successive disillusionments, first with the rather sepulchral Logan Killicks and more slowly with the relentlessly commanding Joe Starks, she hardens in her resolve to find "a meaningful love without loss of self-esteem" (Smith, 109). Her eventual empowerment arrives not in spite of or in triumph over love. For when, after the death of Starks, and nearing middle age herself, Janie meets young Vergible "Tea Cake" Woods, she achieves a confidence in her ability to own her life. She can finally reject her long-dead grandmother's strictures and decide on a mate who, despite his failings, allows her to explore her needs and wishes. With his freewheeling habits, his gambling, and his occasional violence toward her, Tea Cake hardly merits Janie's perception that "he was a gift from God" (102). But there is nothing of Hurst's spiritually enslaving Walter Saxel in him.

The message Hurston carried to a black female worker audience was completely at odds with that of a Wright or a Claude McKay. In her hands, the feminine love quest, without discarding the sensuality those male authors often saw as promiscuity, has a transcendent dignity, even if the man chosen for a mate does not. Nor does woman's loving preclude freely chosen work. Janie resents the hardships of her first marriage and the glorified clerking role of her second. Yet, leaving Eatonville for a time to work in the bean and cane fields of the Everglades, she works by Tea Cake's side. In the egalitarian milieu necessitated by migrant labor, her tasks are not subordinate to his.

But if there is a fulfilling love, the very nature of the migrant's role precludes a corresponding fulfillment in work. Janie, in fact, deskills herself. She forsakes her recently acquired entrepreneurial experience in running the general store that was left her by Starks. She joins the Georgia sharecroppers and Bahamans who, beginning in the 1920s and well past the Depression, flocked in winter to the Everglades as (racially segregated) agricultural wage earners.[63] They composed a "rural proletariat" that alternated between family farm and waged work (Jones, *Dispossessed,* 158). As if to palliate her vocational descent, Janie's migrant life with Tea Cake is idealized. Instead of the seven to eight dollars a day that Hurston claims for her bean-picking labors (147), in the 1930s Janie would have received for her backbreaking work three dollars daily (Jones, *Dispossessed,* 69). This was the return to the chief black "woman's industry" that her grandmother feared and southern black women had to endure before the work propelled them into Florida coastal food-processing plants and tobacco-stemming in Virginia and North Carolina.[64] Hurston does acknowledge that the "hordes of workers" surrounding the lovers are "ugly from ignorance and broken from being poor" (125). But this admission only serves to heighten the uniqueness of the couple's joyous relationship amid the overworked migrants. Her love for Tea Cake makes his urging that she "come git uh job uh work out dere lak de rest uh de women" (127) pleasurable. It puts a romantic gloss on the days in the fields—and nights in the many "jook joints" that offered alcoholic escape from the rigors of the Florida workday.

In the Everglades section, Janie is liberated from the disapproval of her townsfolk on her third marriage, and the love relation with Tea Cake blossoms. As the heat and glare provide a sensual atmosphere, she accepts Tea Cake's view of the supposed difficulties associated with store work: "Clerkin' in dat store wuz hard, but heah, we ain't got nothin' tuh do but our work and come home and love" (127). Janie's real-life sisters would have been less enthusiastic, for such hand-to-mouth wage earning—at the mercy, again, of white bosses—was not likely to provide self-discovery or empowerment.

These truths Hurston herself obliquely recognizes in the jarring ending of the tale. The marriage could slough off individual pressures such as Tea Cake's youth, his unpredictable ways, his infidelities, his occasional violence. But it cannot withstand the weight of circumstances, particularly the humiliating white racism that commandeers Tea Cake for menial cleanup work when a hurricane strikes the Everglades. This unjust edict sets in motion the tragic circumstances that destroy him. Forced to stay behind as a cleanup worker, he is bitten by a rabid dog; driven to a murderous rage by the bite; and killed by Janie in self-protection. Tried and acquitted by a white jury scrutinizing every aspect of her life, Janie returns home to tell the tale. Love has finally fed her spirit, but Starks's legacy keeps her alive. The latter is a perception that Janie scants but that Hurston, who during the 1920s and 1930s scrambled for fellowships and patronage to be able to write, did not. At narrative's end, Janie is thankful to Tea Cake, who remains alive in her memory.

Her closing insight is in distinct contrast to Hurston's self-perception as a writer, a preference for work over love that led her quickly to end two initially passionate marriages, the second of which, notably, was the inspiration for the Janie–Tea Cake one (*Dust Tracks*, 188–89). The voice of her autobiography may occasionally sound like Janie's, graced as *Dust Tracks* is with assertions about how necessary love was to her. Note especially a chapter called "Love": "[It] may be a sleepy, creeping thing with some others, but it is a mighty awakening thing with me. I feel the jar, and I know it from my head on down" (181). Nevertheless, she clearly sacrificed it to an unattached life as a professional artist.

What Hurston was able to achieve in *Their Eyes Were Watching God* was considerable. Outside mainstream as well as both white and black leftist literary tradition, she avoided the demeaning stereotypes of mindless (or criminal) black exuberance that marred white authors' works like the onetime party man Maxwell Bodenheim's *Naked on Roller Skates* (1930). At the center of her art is a belief in the emotional fulfillment of black women that implicitly challenged the defeatism of Richard Wright encoded in Bessie Mears. Because Hurston largely excluded the problems of racism and female vocation, she endowed her love-struck protagonist with the meaningful identity that writers from Fannie Hurst to Leane Zugsmith either found futile or transformed into comradeship with a male political tutor.[65]

Still, *Their Eyes Were Watching God* is "something less than a primer of romanticized love" (Walker, 521). At novel's finish, a romantic woman must kill her own lover/husband to go on living. Given the intensity of Janie's bond to Tea Cake, the final message is ambiguous. But it is perhaps no coincidence that Hurston used this method of resolving an unsuccessful marriage consistently in "Sweat" and other stories in the early Depression years.[66] In a curious way, she joins the other period foes of the romance mode.

Love's Wages, Women Workers

Two decades after the Depression, Simone de Beauvoir argued that "love represents in its most touching form the curse that lies heavily upon woman confined in the feminine universe, woman mutilated, insufficient unto herself."[67] The 1930s audience had no difficulty agreeing that men were more prone to romanticism than women. But with the widespread cultural and literary emphasis on feminine supportiveness, it was not fashionable to explore the implications of that idea or, those like Mary Inman apart, to anticipate de Beauvoir's controversial statement. In their own way and for reasons often at odds with de Beauvoir's assertion, however, a small but significant group of 1930s novels did challenge the woman's romance novel and pave the way for her feminism.

For reasons ranging from a Hurstian dedication to plots embodying the female love/work split to left-wing ambivalence about feminine political militance to a refusal to place (black) womanhood squarely in a labor-class context, these writers did not liberate wage-earning womanhood from the thinking that de Beauvoir, and Inman before her, found so oppressive. Yet from Hurst to Hurston, they did hold lovelorn womanhood up to a Depression Era scrutiny. They dramatized the soul- and potentially life-destroying effects of feminine love slavery in a time when economic desperation knew little gender difference. Even when, in the iconoclastic Hurston novel, there is an alternative vision of the woman liberated through love, the (financially solvent) heroine finds her deepest strength after her lover dies, accidentally, at her own hands. It was a troubling message, particularly given that Hurston's less affluent minor women characters never find romantic liberation.

Whether rejecting the female romantic outright, attempting to weave a new romance of the workplace, or granting woman a great but transitory love, this group critique both of feminine romanticism and of the structures of popular melodrama kept woman in the emotional rather than the economic world. Like the many other social protest authors who purveyed images of saintly or flawed mothering (or whoring), these anti-romancers, whether male or female, still saw the woman wage earner in relational terms: woman first, worker second, she is a 1930s update of Lord Byron's reductive formulation. From Hurst to Zugsmith, when woman achieves emotional redirection, it is her man who undertakes it. In female authors, that redirection—a potential love affair with the strike organizer—retains a romantic overlay. In male authors, working women are so apolitical or sluttish that there is little hope for their reformation at anyone's hands.

This preoccupation with transforming the romantic female into the hardheaded worker, or with the perils of her remaining "the overpainted little shopgirl" on the prowl for love (Salpeter, 612), rang changes on the Depression's familiar antipathy to wage-earning womanhood. Even Hurston's focus on self-development revealed an evasion of the realities of female survival, particularly for the black woman, who, outside the charmed circle of an all-black south Florida village, all too often experienced job discrimination.

The 1930s serious fictional treatments of feminine romanticism performed a literary service, if only to rescue the emotionally hungry working woman from her period's literary neglect.[68] But like the era's more numerous male and female novels of saintly or hard-pressed motherhood (or parallel versions of wantonness), such fiction did not resolve the issue of whether womanly emotionalism precluded activism. It remained for novelists chronicling strikes of nationwide importance to make a more daring literary contribution to the debate on working-class femininity. Would the strife-torn streets outside the Loray Mill in the six key novels of the Gastonia School be the setting where feminine energies were not channeled into the roles of mother, whore, or slave of love?

Chapter Five

THE RISING OF THE MILL WOMEN: GASTONIA AND ITS LITERATURE

Two women textile workers struggling with National Guardsmen during the Gastonia textile strike, April 1929. Archives of Labor and Urban Affairs, Wayne State University.

"[The mill] took my youth, it took my babies. It took my man. One thing it couldn't
take—that's my fightin' spirit."
—Dorothy Myra Page, *Gathering Storm: A Story of the Black Belt* (1932)

"I just want my chance."
—Fielding Burke, *Call Home the Heart* (1932)

Down here men still ruled life,—no matter how poor a man might be, he still was
the head of his household and kept his dignity. He didn't like to see
his natural place usurped by little girls.
—Mary Heaton Vorse, *Strike!* (1930)

The Depression hit early on in the Piedmont South, those remote mill towns of Tennessee and the Carolinas where much of the textile industry was concentrated.[1] By 1930 the bank and movie theater of Le Clay, North Carolina, had disappeared.[2] The local mill hands were more likely to spend their little extra cash on a rare cinema visit than on building a bank account. But both closings provided added proof that the textile town's characteristically "[un]educated, economically insecure, and socially isolated individuals" (Newman, 205) were increasingly denied the benefits of their toil. Indeed, in Le Clay, as in many mill villages throughout the textile South, people had long suffered the negative effects of local mill owners' paternalistic control of town government, education, health, housing, and even religious worship—a situation only exacerbated in the mid-1920s by cutbacks and stretch-outs.[3]

Similar injustices existed more than one hundred miles to the west, in Gastonia, North Carolina. But that strike-torn town would achieve national prominence in the spring of 1929 and inspire a half-dozen pro-labor novels by those such as the labor journalist Mary Heaton Vorse, the textile-labor reformer Grace Lumpkin, and Sherwood Anderson of *Winesburg, Ohio* (1919) fame. In Gastonia, the Manville-Jenckes Company, the proprietor of Loray Mill, had implemented a series of wage reductions and rising production quotas that caused increased hardship in the "mill hill" workforce.[4] Thus it was not unusual that a few months before the Great Crash, workers there joined those in Elizabethton, Tennessee, and Marion, South Carolina, among other venues, to strike an industry ripe for it. What *was* surprising was that this series of violent, nonimmigrant protests inspired militance in women as well as men. In both a region and an industry that traditionally squelched its few male unionists, the passivity of the mill women who formed the large lower stratum of the workforce had generally been a given.[5]

By the early years of the Depression, textile work customarily drew in armies of women; nationwide, they made up 40 percent of such laborers.[6] Although the number of those labeled by the 1920 census as "gainfully employed women" was significantly lower in the South than in other parts of the country, and only 10 percent of North Carolina's feminine wage earners were in manufacturing compared to over 30 percent in agriculture, those who did paid nonfarm labor were as likely to be found in textiles as in other southern industries.[7] One study of 1920s mill women found that more than one-third had been working on and off in the cotton mills for fifteen years or more (Lahne, 105). And in North Carolina, in the decade before the Depression females in textiles constituted over 60 percent of women who worked in any industry.[8]

Though more privileged southerners upheld the ideology of work as unwomanly, poor white women had been recruited for the mills since the first waves of rural émigrés settled in company villages in the 1880s. The numbers of both men and women working in the mills increased in the industrializing South before and after World War I. The very size of the company housing was increased by the growing number of hands, including the mother of the house, going out to work. By the early 1920s more than one-quarter of female breadwinners were also mothers, a figure that would double by 1930 (Lahne, 104).[9] "Wherever the . . . owners had a choice," comments one historian of the southern mill, "they preferred women . . . to men" (Lahne, 103). When child labor laws began to be enacted, at least for children under fourteen, all women, perceived as "a tractable work force with nimble fingers" (Newman, 205), became even more desirable.

When in April 1929, angered by the reduced circumstances of their lives, they took up the strike cudgel, Gastonia women were not only fighting for their family economy. They were protesting the substandard conditions they worked under; that snatched them and later their young teenaged children from school to employ them as child labor; that made them susceptible to pellagra, which sprang from their malnutrition and attacked the brain and body functions; and that, because of the mill's refusal to let them off of night work, robbed them of time to tend to their children.[10] Mothers or not, women were required to work the night shift, for no southern textile state, including North Carolina, prohibited it. (Comparatively munificent South Carolina allowed women to leave at 10:00 P.M.) Day or night, the shift was ten or eleven hours (Anderson, *Women's Place*, 8). Their wages were "universally low" (6) and were declining well before the Crash, although pay envelopes in firebrand 1929 Gastonia were not among the skimpiest in the South. One woman in the Poinsett mill of South Carolina received $3.50 for forty-seven hours of labor.[11] But whether it was a pay envelope that wretched, or the more typical $9 or $12, at best $15 a week, woman's wage labor, far from "pin money," often provided the needed second or even sole income for her kin.[12] All themes from pellagra to poor wages would be emphasized, to varying degrees, by female Gastonia novelists Mary Heaton Vorse's *Strike!* (1930), Grace Lumpkin's *To Make My Bread* (1932), Dorothy Myra Page's *The Gathering Storm: A Story of the Black Belt* (1932), and Fielding Burke's (Olive Tilford Dargan) *Call Home the Heart* (1932), as well as male authors Sherwood Anderson in *Beyond Desire* (1932) and William Rollins in *The Shadow Before* (1934).[13] But in this newly militant labor community, where women fueled the textile trade but men dominated in every way, how would these writers portray whose strike it really was? Answers reside, first, in the history of the events themselves.

Gastonia as Erasable Female Labor History

Women of Italian, Irish, and Polish extraction had participated fully in larger, earlier, nonsouthern textile strikes, notably in Lawrence (1912, 1916, 1919, and 1922), and New Bedford, Massachusetts (1928), and in New Jersey's Passaic (1913, 1926) and Paterson (1913, 1924) strikes.[14] But in a state known as the leading textile center of the South, Gastonia, the largest town in Gaston County, was home to more than forty mills, the largest number of spindles in the state. Save for the simultaneous strike at the Bemberg and Glantzoff mills and a few isolated southern precedents in 1919 and 1921, for both the South and for native-born textile women, Gastonia, quite apart from the unusual amount of publicity it generated, was new.

This is not to say that Gastonia was solely a women's strike, nor even one that, like Elizabethton, began in the female workrooms of the factory. In May 1929, months before the Elizabethton strike ended, like Gastonia, in defeat, "the spirit of protest had jumped the Blue Ridge and spread through the Carolinas" to involve thousands of male as well as female workers in thirteen different mills, including Gastonia (Hall, *Family*, 214). In Gastonia, on the morning of 1 April 1929, eighteen hundred of the Manville-Jenckes's Loray Mill's more than two thousand workers left their jobs.[15] The walkout was to protest the firing of a handful of men and, depending on the account, one or two women, who were trying to unionize the plant.[16] The Communist Party played an important part in the ill-fated April walkout, but homegrown resentment of Manville-Jenckes's high-handedness was real enough. The workers who planned the initial walkout were far more militant than Fred Beal from the Communist-affiliated National Textile Workers Union, who balked at the first call for a strike.[17] As mill hands met and picketed, there burst out a strike of such militancy that the party, which had largely ignored the labor-class South, directed increasing attention—and, eventually, twenty-three Communist organizers—to it (Draper, 15).

Wishing to see in the historically unorganized poor whites of Gastonia what an 1 April *Daily Worker* headline termed the "first open struggle of enslaved mill workers under real union leadership," the party had planted seeds for the walkout as early as mid-March, when Beal returned to the South after reconnoitering during the winter to build a secret union structure. From then until his arrest in June with other northern party leaders and Gastonia strikers, the party oversaw every aspect of the mill revolt, from protesting evictions, to creating a headquarters and relief station, to relocating strikers in a tent colony, to engineering marches. The CP legal arm, the International Labor Defense, defended the leadership during two trials, and the party apparatus supported the strike, though often more with press releases than with funds, from its inception to its unsuccessful termination five months later.[18] And party-orchestrated responses to detentions of local strike leaders, particularly to the June arrests of the strike inner circle on murder conspiracy charges, took on international proportions.[19]

To aid in the effort, the *Daily Worker* frequently ran exaggerated columns on the progress of the strikers. At a time when the *New York Times* restricted its coverage of Gastonia women strikers to blurbs about northern women organizers, occasional mentions of a local female striker arrested with a group of men, or disapproving references to the women protesters, the *Worker* mentioned women among those arrested for striking or featured them prominently in front-page photographs as they did battle with "deputy-thug[s]."[20] The paper also called attention to women's role in the relief effort, particularly that of Violet Page, also known as Violet Jones, a striker who came north to appeal for aid and recount horror stories of female life in the mills. (Either won over or intimidated by mill owners, as the strike waned she greatly disappointed the leadership by returning to work as a scab.[21]) Letters and poems from mill girls whose lives were stunted by the work also appeared on the front page of the *Worker*. Despite the good comrade message such publicity disseminated, however, women were rarely mentioned in day-by-day coverage in the crucial months of the strike. Photos of mass demonstrations outside the Loray Mill depicted crowds of men, conveying the party message that women were junior partners in a male effort.[22]

Despite the quasi-egalitarian radical-press coverage, it has been forgotten that Gastonia was a strike that began when unionist women as well as men were fired.[23] Gastonia leader Fred Beal's account of the strike locates women's presence from its inception—at rallies to decide whether to strike, at early meetings during the heady first days, as organizers imported from the North. In his autobiography, *Proletarian Journey* (1937), he dubs Ella May Wiggins "the minstrel of the strike" (159) and praises other local women, including Gladys Wallace and Ruby McMahon, who are otherwise lost to women's history (148). But Beal basically perceived Gastonia as a male enterprise.[24]

Although feminist labor historians remind readers of the female Gastonia, the majority of commentators, following the lead of males writing in the years directly after the strike, erase women's participation, save for, a half-sentence on Ella May Wiggins, who, in their presentation, was the strike's only female hero.[25] In a sense, the women of Gastonia, immersed in a culture of compliance that was fed by family and church, colluded in their self-erasure. They imported from their rural backgrounds the conviction that there was men's work and women's work, even though, both on the family farm and at the loom, women did many men's jobs. (In fact, the ability to "work like men" [qtd. Hall, *Family,* 18] and still meet childbearing responsibilities was a twinned source of pride.) Yet Matilda Robbins, an Industrial Workers of the World (IWW) organizer in the unsuccessful 1914 Greenville, South Carolina, strike and a Socialist veteran of textile strikes in both Lawrence and New Bedford, Massachusetts, was appalled by the southern woman's plight.[26] In a recollection prompted by 1914 events in Greenville and another failed strike there in 1929, she described mill wives as "the slaves of slave husbands."[27] She pointed out that in the mill family economy, after supper the men's tasks were finished but the women were chained to the endless tasks of housekeeping unrelieved by any timesaving conveniences ("Notebook," 5).

On strike, whether in 1914 or 1929, these women demanded nothing that spoke to women's very real concerns such as sexual harassment in the mills, child and prenatal care, and teenage children's labor. Nor, Wiggins excepted, did the Gastonia female ranks contain budding women's advocates who might lobby for them at a later stage of the strike. Though Wiggins "dealt with men in ways that allowed males to save face," she was also more independent than most of the women who were at the heart of the Gastonia uprising.[28] Wiggins was not the only woman connected with the Gastonia rebellion who had gone outside the region to better her understanding. Joining female mill hands from Elizabethton and Marion, where more single women worked in the mills, a few Gastonia women attended the Southern Summer School for Workers in the late 1920s to take advantage of education programs for workers.[29] One homegrown strike leader's wife whose husband was arrested with Beal, Bertha Hendrix, even published a restrospective account of the 1929 protest when she attended the school almost a decade later.[30] These occasional sorties into the world of labor education, however, did not generate a woman's agenda at Gastonia. Wiggins may have argued for her place on the fledgling, Beal-created National Textile Workers Union's executive committee, as would, though without success, female auto workers facing down the masculinist United Auto Workers during a 1937 convention.[31]

From all accounts, Wiggins, the northern NTWU organizer Vera Weisbord, and the other Communist women never put forth a platform that directed attention to mill women's difficulties as breadwinning mothers. They may have encountered the dilemma that had plagued two generations of female organizers, "how to advance the status of women within a workers' organization without undermining . . . class solidarity."[32] A month before the Gastonia strike began, Weisbord published articles in

Equal Justice and another party–trade union journal, *Labor Unity,* urging that unions encourage women's participation and pay more attention to working women's interests. Amy Schechter also wrote for *Equal Justice* and *Labor Unity.* But not one of them was an adherent of any alternatives to the male-centered policies of the NTWU. Such alternatives, though short-lived, had been much discussed in northern Women's Trade Union League circles in the 1910–11 shirtwaist strike days (Glenn, 228–30) and by an all-woman local founded years before the Loray strike (236). A transient movement toward separatism had even been carried out sporadically by late nineteenth-century Massachusetts shoe workers, by Jewish, Polish, and Italian garment tradeswomen in Chicago and other cities in the late 1910s, and by IWW domestic workers in 1917. Twenty years later, Mexican coastal cannery workers seemed to be motivated as much by what the historian Mary Blewett has termed striking women's "shared identity as females" as by a desire for better conditions for male and female workers.[33]

At Gastonia, despite a bevy of women organizers, there was no such shared consciousness. The teenaged Sophie Melvin, who helped look after the strikers' children; Amy Schechter, in charge of relief efforts; Vera Weisbord, the rallier of the women (and common-law wife of Albert Weisbord, national secretary of the NTWU); and NTWU vice-president Ellen Dawson, also in Gastonia (like the Weisbords, a veteran of the New Bedford textile strike the year before) were all under orders to advance the strike, not the status of women.

Nor in the South's racial climate did the white female rank and file recognize the allied plight of black mill women. Less than 1 percent of Loray's workforce was black (Foner, 234), and like the black men, women were spatially segregated and consigned to underpaid, menial cleanup jobs. As did their men, poor white women, remarked one historian of working-class race relations, believed in "the need to distance themselves from any suggestion of social equality with black people."[34] In this context, Ella May Wiggins "attempted the unthinkable" (Garrison, *Vorse,* 223) in the black neighborhood outside the mill village where she lived. She tried to persuade black workers to sign union cards. She had no more success than northern NTWU organizer Vera Weisbord, who visited the town's black women. Hunched over ragpicking work, they would not talk to her (Hall, *Family,* 227; Weisbord, 208–9).

Uncritical of the caste system that gave them nominal superiority to blacks and opposed to working alongside them, much less unionizing them, poor white women thus collaborated in black women's oppression. (In one Gastonia novel, a mill mother acts out that role. Glad that she can get good help so cheaply, she hires a black co-worker's daughter to mind her children while she is at the mill [Lumpkin, 321].) Along with the men, real-life Loray women resisted the efforts of the party's northern organizers, including black ones, to integrate the strike. Little progress was made in converting the men of the local committee to take in blacks although there were some male gestures in that direction (Draper, 23; O. Hall, "Negro's Experience," 4). Although black men were experimentally permitted to attend a union meeting at nearby Bessemer City, in a wired-off section (Foner, 234), there is no record of women of either race participating.

Gastonia's white female strikers did not discover, much less articulate, a desire for self-definition, pursue individual aspirations, or aspire to a cross-race sisterhood. But precisely because it was a strike in which, though excluding disfranchised blacks, white women could marshal their energies on behalf of the working class, Gastonia appealed powerfully to more doctrinaire, non-Smedleyan exponents of proletarian realism, including the four established female radical writers in question. Their novels fit the flourishing fiction of left-wing thought, for, as Elsa Dixler points out, like heroines of the Communist periodical fiction of the time, the typical Gastonia protagonist "did not seem interested in . . . 'being somebody yourself.' "[35]

Gastonia women, newly drawn to trade unionism, lacked that altruistic dedication to an abstract "movement"—what one early garment trade striker in New York City called the "holy cause"—but within the historical and ideological constraints enumerated above they were indefatigable battlers nonetheless.[36] In the period fiction honoring them, what was the feminine mythology of the great Gastonia strike? Was there a female equivalent of what Sylvia Jenkins Cook, the most perceptive critic of Gastonia fiction, called the "effort to weld a new imaginative hero from doctrine, fact, and fiction" (87)? If so, did the Gastonia female striker counter the sexualization of working women evident in Steinbeck, Conroy, and lesser lights? How much relation did portraits in Gastonia novels have to the real-life Ella May Wiggins, local leader and balladeer, whose unsolved murder symbolized the defeat of the strikers? Were the mill women in revolt merely a backdrop for the legend of Ella May? And was that legend only an extension of Ma Joadism?

Gastonia Defended, Gastonia Rearranged

In the early 1900s, old-moneyed Marie Van Vorst produced a novel based on her time spent incognito at a Columbia, South Carolina, textile plant much like the Loray Mill.[37] She had set out some markers: the oppression of the woman-filled work site, the misery of substandard housing, the work-sickened children, all themes elaborated on from a more radical perspective by novelists from Page to Vorse.[38] But, equally afraid of mill women's sexuality and their political awareness, Van Vorst had not approached, much less solved, a depiction of their revolt in the conservative South.[39] In taking up this task, the earliest of the Gastonia novels, Veteran Amalgamated Clothing Workers' organizer and labor journalist Mary Heaton Vorse's *Strike!*, establishes the rhetoric of the labor protest that Page, Lumpkin, and Burke would follow as well.[40] In Vorse's account, frustration at cutbacks and anger that mill owners forbade the left-wing, party-affiliated National Textile Workers Union fuel a secret meeting, a strike vote, and a mass walkout at an important local mill. As the strike spreads to other mills and northern organizers lead local people in setting up a strike headquarters and relief station, the company evicts tenants from company-owned housing. Soon masked men break down the facility, a tent colony is erected in revolt, and more violence ensues as antiscab picketers, women among them, clash with and are arrested by police and militia. A wave of terror ensues in which dubious deputies storm the tent city and the local police chief (in real life, Chief O. F. Aderholt) is killed. The northern leaders and a few southern ones are arrested and tried twice—the first ending in a mistrial. Before the second trial, in which all of the male strike leaders are sentenced to stiff prison terms, a pro-union rally is sabotaged, proof of the local financiers' power. Further weakening morale, Ella May Wiggins, the activist balladeer of the "Mill Mother's Lament," is shot dead in an open truck carrying a score of union members by someone in a mob who fired into a group of strikers, probably a mill owners' thug. She becomes the martyr of the failed Gastonia.

In the works of Vorse and her female colleagues, as in novels by Sherwood Anderson and William Rollins, many divergences occur from the actual, though not most of the crucial, events of the strike. I will say more later in the chapter about the license taken with the real-life Ella May. Suffice it to say here that Vorse, who renamed her Mamie Lewes, slightly alters the event that memorialized her by locating her murder, more dramatically, at the center of a union rally, not en route to it. Lumpkin endows her Ella surrogate, Bonnie Calhoun, with many of Wiggins's principal traits but, trying for a more hopeful finale than the events admitted, omits the killing and sends Bonnie off to a workers' convention outside the South at novel's end. Page, with a similar motive, has two Ella Mays: the character in her own right and the apprentice-heroine Marge Crenshaw, who mounts the platform after Wiggins at meetings and carries on after Wiggins's death. Burke, the female Gastonia novelist most conflicted about womanly activism, splits Ella off into several characters, though she is most evident in the homesick grass-roots speaker-organizer Ishma Hensley, who abandons Gastonia before the strike is squelched.

In equally deliberate rearrangements of historical events, Vorse kills off the Beal character (who in real life fled to Russia while out on bail), thereby shifting the focus on martyrdom to him. Lumpkin refashions the Wiggins funeral. Dramatized with a pomp it never possessed in reality, it coincides with the time the indicted strikers are out on bail, as if to create a sense of movement solidarity. Page, in a similarly propagandistic vein, puts a more positive gloss on what was, like so many textile strikes, a stymied attempt by omitting the arrest and trial of the Beal contingent. In a more ambiguous ending, Burke omits the trials and the Wiggins assassination and sends the protagonist home to the mountains before the strike unravels.

But whether strictly or loosely following the events, all four, in contrast to the masculine imaginers of the strike, transform the backward handful of worn-out women pictured by Van Vorst into a corps of women participating eagerly in the revolt of the mill workers. Integral to the rhetoric of Gastonia was the scene or series of scenes dramatizing such feistiness. "It was under way now," wrote Vorse of a picket scene, "more girls and women than men" (93). Fierce resistance inspired descriptions of those like the alternately scratching and cajoling Mrs. (Ma) Gilfillin, "a tiny brown wisp of fury" (141), in Vorse's *Strike!* "Never you mind. We'll be bailed out by tomorrow, 'n back on the picket line," choruses Page's woman striker (*Gathering Storm,* 321).

The steeliness of feminine resistance suggested in the fiction was evident in several confrontations in the early weeks of the strike—particularly on 4 April, when the National Guard was sent to protect scabs and prevent picketing on mill property, on 10 April, when there were cracks in the picket lines, and on 22 April, when strikers marching to the mill clashed with the police. Vorse, Lumpkin, Page, and Burke, replicating these realities, envision an ensemble effort in which groups of women taunt the "laws," cry encouragement to one another, and urge the scabs not to "go against [their] own" (Lumpkin, 348). In *Call Home the Heart,* "when Anna Jenkins objected to being pushed roughly along by a soldier, and he ignored her objection, she struck him over the head with a stick, and rebelled so vigorously that three brother soldiers were called up to help take her to jail. Anna was the mother of four children" (318). This incident, like many in the female Gastonia novels, actually occurred to one Bertha Tompkins (discussed by Weisbord, 177–78). In *Strike!* the older mill women who join the sassy young girls and younger matrons on picket lines and in crowded jail cells replicate what the organizer Vera Weisbord remembered: "Brown as leather, thin as witches," Old Mrs. Whenck and Ma Gilfillin, possibly modeled on Mrs. McGinnis and Mrs. Totherow, "ran among the men and urged them on" (93).

But there was one aspect of the militant woman's Gastonia, the NTWU fraternization policy that encouraged women protesters to flirt with the National Guard (Pope, 258), that made female novelists uneasy. Even though the high-spirited picket who plays coquette to win over the enemy bore little resemblance to the Van Vorstian stereotype of the sluttish working girl bound for no good end, in Page's novel it is the older women who taunt the Guardsmen, "Boy, why you come here?" (293). Lumpkin is equally uncomfortable with the association of promiscuity and militance that often accompanied female participation in 1930s protests and informed radical male writers from Steinbeck to Cantwell, and it is also her mill matriarchs, not the young girls, who implement the policy. Burke makes only oblique reference to the policy, and Vorse suggests it was divisive, driving one more wedge between female and male organizers. Whatever their reluctant awareness of the policy, the female Gastonia novelists repudiated the sexualized working woman so familiar to readers of Steinbeck, Cantwell, and Halper.[41] The comment by Sylvia Jenkins Cook, one of the most perceptive to analyze these women authors, that Burke's work exhibits "very little interest" in sexuality "as an aspect of feminist revolt," applies to them all. For "when sexuality is discussed at all, it is viewed as yet another threat . . . to communal goals of organization and class struggle" (124). In Page's *Gathering Storm,* young Marge reflects, sex is "a forbidden, evil thing, that got you in the corner, and cursed you with extra mouths to feed" (102). Again: "Marge knew about the carryins-on in the field beyond the mill . . . the scandals of babies without fathers, of . . . city boys taking mill girls for rides" (93). The frank sexuality of one mill woman, Lucy Martin, becomes in that novel a sure sign of promiscuity; in another, *To Make My Bread,* the wayward Minnie Hawkins compounds her sin by spying for the company. In *Call Home the Heart,* the married heroine runs off with another man, but, in a Tess-like defense, she seeks economic freedom, not a lustful union. Far from acknowledging female sexuality, the novels err in the other direction, creating no climate for protest of the moral policing of mill women that occurred in southern towns like Le Clay, where women were forbidden by the mill superintendent to smoke on their porches or wear shorts in public, much less be pregnant out of wedlock (Newman, 212). In Elizabethton, women were forbidden to wear makeup (Hall, "Disorderly Women," 364). These rules were even more unfair in that sexual harassment by the mill foreman, who even required newly hired women to sleep with him, was known in the Loray Mill and probably elsewhere as well (Weisbord, 196).

Gastonia women writers rebut the familiar period accusations of wage-earning women's censurable conduct in another way. Their mill women see no contradiction between being strikers and mothers. "Come on, women, we're walkin' out for more food for our chillen," proclaims Page's Marge Crenshaw (*Gathering Storm,* 280). But these mother/strikers soon take on an ideological sameness. A faceless group poised for the assault on the National Guard, the mothers are rarely individuated. It is only with the Ella May Wiggins character or, in a variant, a similarly mythic figure, that the four female novelists crystallize women's central contribution to the strike: through Ella May paid homage (Vorse/Lumpkin), doubled (Page), or replaced (Burke). The centrality of her character points to both the strengths and weaknesses of portraiture in the female Gastonia School. To these individual novelists' responses to her we now turn.

Vorse: Gender as Involvement

Mary Heaton Vorse's *Strike!* is an ambitious novel, chronicling how the years of resentment felt by mill men and women alike burst out in a strike orchestrated by the party import Fer Deane (Fred Beal) but in large part carried out by a curious array of feminine strikers, or, as Sinclair Lewis wrote in reviewing the book for the *Nation* in 1930, "the mountain women who have been enticed to the mills, and who join the union only when they discover that the bossmen . . . are condemning them to starvation."[42] Period reviewers who found the material powerful but fragmented (*New Republic* and *New York Times* reviewers, though positive about the novel, alluded to "structural weaknesses") as well as those who overlooked Ella May Wiggins's role in the narrative unwittingly pointed to its strategic problem: how to do justice to both the male and female Gastonia.[43]

More than any other Gastonia novelist, Vorse attempts to meld men's and women's experiences of the strike, male strategists and female rank and file. Arriving in Gastonia on assignment for *Harper's*, she chose as her teller a male journalist, who sticks close to Fer Deane to tell the strike story. At the same time, the women, in the words of a northern female leader, were "pluckier than the men" (11). Vorse constantly shifts attention to Mamie Lewes (Ella May Wiggins) and a supporting cast of case-hardened old women, young-old mothers, single girls, and women CP organizers ranging in personality from doctrinaire to compassionate. All carry out the picketing, and many fraternize with the National Guard, taunt the scabs, and scuffle with the police, who usually succeed in arresting them. The opening scenes set the rhythm of the novel. The narrative begins in medias res, in the third week of the strike (when Vorse herself arrived in Gastonia), with a speech at strike headquarters by Fer Deane. There follows a scene in which not-yet-prominent Mamie, the woman in and of the crowd, has heard Fer's speech and is later asked by him to join the union. (The real Wiggins was a member well before the Gastonia events.) Again and again, men exhort and women follow. In a series of scenes, appearing at thirty-page intervals (and sometimes more often), in which, with names like Ma Gilfillan and Mis' Whenck, Mrs. Totherow, Mis' West, old Mrs. Holly, and girlish Della King, they bear out Mamie's rebuke to an antiunion scab who has called her unmotherly: "Ef I kin leave 'em [the children] to work I kin leave 'em to picket" (35). Although the naming serves to type rather than individuate, the women, from the aging "brown [i.e., weathered] women" to the "kids of the picket" (39), appear to be custodians of the strike effort, carrying out Fer Deane's directives zealously while the men balk at his injunction to leave their rifles at home. Much, too, is made of the brutality experienced by women strikers (as in the actual strike), whether in the form of evictions of pregnant and ill women from company housing or of police violence against woman-headed families.

As in all four of the women's Gastonia fictions, the Wiggins character or her surrogate plays the unofficial spokeswoman for the wage-earning mill mother, who is incensed by the new stretch-out and ready to challenge the powers that be. But she is more muse than firebrand, more universally significant than gender-symbolic, so that when she sings her "Mill Mother's Lament," "it was the history of every one there put to song" (53). To cement her identification with the mill proletariat, Vorse stresses Mamie's simplicity, not her oratorical skills. All of this distances her from the real-life Ella, who formed part of Beal's executive committee and won his praise as one of the best of the southern union leaders (Beal, 148). Vorse instead reified the portrayals circulated at the time by the union. She glosses over the real Wiggins, who was no pious widow but an independent woman who took back her maiden name and had a child by her "cousin" Charlie Shope after her husband disappeared (Hall, *Family*, 227).

Still, gender dictates involvement, much as it did in the events themselves. In Vorse, female energies are released in singing and keeping the strike circle unbroken; Mamie Lewes sings at rallies but after Fer Deane or Dewey Bryson has spoken at them. (In the actual strike, Beal himself often led in singing the "Internationale.") Vorse's Gastonia men mount the soapbox, plan strategy, react to mill owners' moves, and defend against strike headquarters, then tent colony raids, violent incursions by the deputized thugs of the "Committee of One Hundred." Things come to a head when, as occurred at Gastonia in early June, two months after the strike had begun, the local police chief is murdered in a vigilante-style raid (some claim by his own men). The men are detained for trial, but—

countering actual happenings—the few women organizers are eventually let go. The male unionist is the centerpiece in Vorse's account of the trial. In the interest of artistic economy, she omits the fact that there were two September trials, one in which women organizers, including Vera Weisbord, with whom Vorse had roomed for a time while covering Gastonia, the relief worker Amy Schecter, and young Sophie Melvin were tried along with the men. (That legal proceeding, as Vorse well knew, ended in a mistrial. In the second trial, following the release of the women, the men received stiff prison terms.) Before attention shifts to the impending trial, Mamie is killed at a rally. The spirit goes out of the strike, much as it did in actuality.

But in Vorse's imagining, the men are again central. In the closing pages of the novel, borrowing from events at strike-torn Marion, South Carolina, Fer and a series of fictional strike leaders are killed, *their* funerals—not Mamie's (Ella's was a quiet affair)—providing the sad coda to the novel. Vorse's novel, because it is attentive to actual events, suggests the dilemma of imagining women's role at Gastonia. On one hand, the novel upholds the centrality of the male role in the strike by pointing out that women strikers deferred to male ones and by replicating their experiences as southern mill women, wives, sisters, and daughters. On the other hand, *Strike!* contains a subplot pointing to the gender tensions released by the Loray walkout, tensions covered over in party press releases and ignored by the mainstream press and subsequent period histories. As Vorse points out, male strikers had to be placated constantly, for they objected to women leading the picket lines, or, in one of Fer Deane's less noble moments, refused to come on the line at all for fear of danger. *Strike!* also includes the gender struggle Vorse observed among the imported strike leaders. Irma Rankin takes sharp issue with Fer over strategy and fraternization policy. And Mamie's very success at merging with the male leadership may well be attributable to her dealing with them in a way that poses no challenge to their hegemony.

Vorse emphasizes Mamie's role as a mill mother less than do any of the other novelists, approaching, but not stressing, the idea that in real life Wiggins was "a woman alone. . . . It was *she* who must buy for her children; it was *her* wages that were too low" (Hall, *Family*, 227). Vorse alludes to the real Wiggins's companionate relationship with Charlie Shope in a brief scene with a male striker, Dewey Bryson. Nevertheless, wary of tarnishing the Wiggins legend, Vorse does not reveal, any more than do the other female Gastonia novelists, that Ella was living with the man, who in a sop to propriety she called her "cousin"; she claimed that he helped care for her children while she aided the strike.

The truth was that Shope was her lover. She had already borne him one child and was pregnant with another at the time of her murder (Frederickson, "Heroines," 90). In union circles it was felt that this relationship would counter her image as a mill mother if during the strike Wiggins "had to deal with charges of immorality." But after her murder, probably at the hands of Loray Mill scabs, who were arrested but acquitted of the crime, mill owners circulated the rumor that she had been shot by an irate boyfriend.[44] In any case, as part of the sanitizing impulse, Vorse's Shope stand-in, Dewey, is a starstruck visitor to Mamie Lewes's cabin, and, in contrast to the Wiggins-Shope alliance, his idealizing tendency informs their encounter: "She seemed to him the spirit of everything he was fighting for" (183). He moves to embrace her, but sexuality is quickly squelched. Mamie, always with her sights on the strike, says they have no time for romance. She reasserts the importance of the archetypal mill mother. That women's problems as working women were completely submerged in a dedication to the cause is an issue Vorse leaves alone.

Following the actual Gastonia chronology—Ella May did not live to see the end of the strike—Vorse kills Mamie off before the questions her true life raised about militant mill women's departures from the all-mothering—or pious, hard-hit widow—role could be addressed. Like Mother Jones and Lucy Randolph Mason, to name two noted examples, who came to womanly prominence in the southern labor movement, Wiggins was shrewd enough to defer to male leaders. But had she attempted what Alice Kessler-Harris has called the "task of reconciling class and feminist issues" ("Organizing," 15), she might have experienced tensions felt by generations of northern female trade unionists when an entrenched masculine hierarchy excluded them from real power or failed fully to support their efforts to organize women workers. Furthermore, the author's gestures toward demythifying but ultimate refusal to do so does little to center the novel on the rank-and-file women for whom Wiggins spoke. Nor does she more than glance at the tensions roused by the female partner in a southern strike. Despite a Vorse biographer's claim that the novel "focus[ed] on women's courage and strength" (Garrison, *Strike!,* xvi), it suggests that men and women experienced a parallel awakening by labor leaders. Vorse was aware of gendered bickering among party leaders— "Beal [was] depressed by the failure of Dawson, Buch [Weisbord] and others to acknowledge his leadership role" (Garrison, *Vorse,* 220). But her novel upholds the (male) narrator, who forms a friendship with the central character, Fer Deane/Fred Beal. Although it could certainly be argued that Fred Beal created the strike more than Ella May Wiggins did, it seems odd that Vorse, who spent a good deal of time among the women of the tent colony, should adopt a male angle of vision and scant such feminine subject matter. Garrison argues that such an angle legitimized the material (*Strike!,* xv). Nevertheless, it also distanced the book from the female Gastonia. Undoubtedly, as a good journalist she was trying to balance the male and female Gastonia, but she chose a strange way of doing it, for she sacrificed the unofficial female history to the official male one.

Lumpkin: Migrant Mother to the Podium

In *To Make My Bread,* North Carolina–born Grace Lumpkin, whose fiction, some of it appearing in *New Masses,* often addressed the southern poor, also attempts to meld the male and female experience of the strike by what Sylvia Jenkins Cook calls "dual heroes" (113). Bonnie/Ella May has a brother, John, a mill worker who at first seems interested only in becoming a foreman but undergoes a conversion that triggers Bonnie's own. Lumpkin's Bonnie is so dedicated to a communal culture, to family, that it is only in the last fifty pages that, haltingly, looking to her mentor in militance, her brother, and a local organizer, she emerges, in the set piece favored by all but Burke, to take the podium and sing the Wiggins song. Lumpkin, like Vorse, relies on the Wiggins legend and a cast of faceless supporting characters (or stereotyped ones?) to symbolize the female involvement in Gastonia. But as in *Strike!,* male energies open and close the narrative. Grafting the legend onto the fictive tale of Bonnie Calhoun, Lumpkin gives her heroine an independent, moonshiner grandfather, and, when that patriarch dies, a wage-earning, widowed mother and aunt who are strong by default. Although they learn by doing that the mill grinds them down, it is not until the next generation (her son John) that, as they finally learn, the message is to "fight hard, like the men" (335).

There is very little in the opening sections of *To Make My Bread* to indicate that Bonnie is the Ella May figure. Up to the time of the strike, her life experiences are prefigured by those of her mother and aunt, who also discover that the workroom of the mill is no haven from rural impoverishment. As if the women's individual discoveries lead to the larger truth of the Gastonia strike, much of the novel traces the hegira of Bonnie's poor white family from hill to mill-town poverty. It follows the uncertain fortunes of the heroine, who, like Ella May, marries a man unable to support the family; the sorrows of her mother, Emma, who comes down with the dreaded pellagra; and the struggles of her aunt to combine child raising and mill days. If the women either weaken or become radicalized, so, too, do the men. The aging patriarch, Grandpap, cannot withstand his uselessness in a mill economy; Bonnie's husband becomes debilitated and dies. But Bonnie's brother John organizes a union and helps teach Bonnie the way to political truth. Under such tutelage, her resistance to the mill owner's authority soon becomes spirited. She is jailed; she tries to prevent bad feeling against black scabs by persuading a black woman not to take a striker's job; and, of course, on the day of her death she addresses a rally. But at crucial moments such as when she tries to win over the blacks, either she invokes male experience or, in a rearrangement of the historical actuality, the focus quickly shifts to the male-propelled events of the strike.

In the lengthy final section of the novel, Bonnie sheds her passive identity as a mill mother enmeshed in family trouble. Deserted by her husband, she becomes the "singing woman," who, in Mary Heaton Vorse's flattering *New Republic* review of the Lumpkin novel, "cheers on the strikers and is at last murdered by thugs." Bonnie's conversion, however, builds on her earlier persona. She simply widens her arena of sacrifice beyond her family circle to the strike itself.[45] Certainly Lumpkin's Ella May is not as independent as Vorse's. Like her doomed mother, Bonnie is born to be martyred. But she falls in a battle that the novel suggests men can survive to keep waging but women cannot. By novel's end, as one reviewer of the book pointed out, Bonnie's brother looks to a fellow organizer for hope. "I was feeling," John says, "as if everything was finished." "No," said the other. "This is just the beginning" (384).[46]

Although there are some female picket-line scenes, even more than in Vorse, it is the experience of martyrdom that defines the female Gastonia.

Much of the narrative is taken up with the tragedy of Bonnie's mother, Emma, who comes to the mill with hopes of supporting her large brood, exhausts herself, and comes down with pellagra, which robs her of the ability to reason. Shorn of this maternal role model, the novel's Ella May figure does little that is not the result of male mentoring. Even more than Vorse's Mamie, Lumpkin's Bonnie is an acceptable labor militant for 1930s audiences: the good mother as trade unionist. Instructive in this regard is Bonnie's philosophy of the strike rally. It is touched with the language of religious revivalism (as the Gastonia meetings often were): "She felt a loving care toward all the people and a gratefulness to them for having come out, for seeing that this was the best thing to do" (344). In the requisite scene where Bonnie mounts the podium to sing her ballad, Lumpkin stresses the artlessness of her nature, her fear at public appearances, and her appeal to the women to understand that "I couldn't do for my children any more than you women on the money we get" (345). Adhering to the Gastonia rhetoric in which Wiggins is the prominent woman, Lumpkin then offers Bonnie as Lange's migrant madonna on a speaker's platform, the novel's second politically correct militant mother.

Page: Mill Mother as Good Comrade

Dorothy Myra Page brought to her fictionalized Gastonia a propagandist's Communism and her varied experiences as an Amalgamated Clothing Workers activist, a Norfolk textile mill organizer, the author of *Southern Cotton Mills and Labor* (1929), and a left-wing journalist on all such subjects.[47] Whether in spite or because of her labor writer's vita, she infused *Gathering Storm* with more optimism about female militance than either Vorse or Lumpkin by employing a pair of Ella May figures. One is the Wiggins of approved legend, the other her fictional protégé, the Communism-imbibing protagonist Marge Crenshaw, who comes to hope at novel's close that Riverton (Gastonia) would eventually resemble the utopian Soviet Union, "folks like her running the factories, folks like her making the laws" (372). To bolster the message that if one Gastonia woman is murdered, another rises to take her leadership place, the novel locates both Ella May and Marge in a protest tradition that encompasses Old Marge, a prime mover in a textile strike of the 1890s; Ella Ramsay, a veteran of the Concord, North Carolina, strike of 1921; and, in the closing pages, the brave new Communist woman of the Soviet Council of Moscow, a "red-cheeked girl, now her sister" (368), whom Marge admires at a party conference well outside the South. A mill mother destined for the Trade Union Educational League instead of a union buster's bullet, Marge graduates from tending Ella May's children and listening at her feet to becoming part of the strikers' inner circle and their female representative at party-led conventions attended, in Page's expansive vision, by those culled from the workers of the world.

Page paves the female way to the "Corey Mill" strike and beyond with a narrative history of a mill-town family of rural origin. As in Lumpkin, fathers and husbands prove sickly or improvident; once more the women earn the family's bread because no one else will. But by shifting her heroine's work venue from one southern mill town to another, Page widens her scope to encompass the unrest following the end of World War I and the mill workers' disappointment at the halfway measures of the AFL's United Textile Workers leadership. Well before she mounts the Gastonia speaker's platform after Ella May, Marge Crenshaw comes to realize that she and her kind have "been sheep long enough" (186).

During her young womanhood, Marge remains in the South to make that insight active, while her brother Tom undergoes a parallel realization. His, however, is an on-the-road education that includes Passaic steel mill strikes, an IWW membership, marriage to a Russian Jewess active since the 1910 shirtwaist strike, a party affiliation, and comradeship with a black stockyards veteran and labor organizer, whom he brings home to help implement party doctrine at Gastonia. When Tom returns to the textile town that is for him the crucible for the southern labor movement, he does so as a composite of Fred Beal, on whom he is modeled, and the Gastonia men who led the 1 April walkout. Tom's appearance inspires his sister to immediate action, as, turning off the power in the mill (Page's borrowing from events in the Elizabethton, Tennessee, strike), she leads the women out. She is prominent among those arrested on the picket line, which she departs with a ringing "We'll be bailed out by tomorrow, 'n back on the . . . line" (321). Swayed by, or drenched in, Tom's newfound Marxism, she, too, joins the party. And (again Page borrows from nearby strikes) she aids in Tom's biracial strike plans, applauding his faith in black organizers at interracial meetings in which she marches with the black cleaning women who, in Page's new southern fantasy, can meet her on terms of casual equality.

All of this visibility notwithstanding, to be true to Gastonia rhetoric, Ella May and her songstress's persona must for a time overshadow Marge. But to ensure the passing of the torch, Page has Marge gain Ella's trust by the sororal act of caring for the Wiggins children, and Ella promotes her from political apprentice to soapbox equal. Soon after, in Page's further reinventions of strike events, Marge acts as a composite of Vera Weisbord and the other women organizers; she is arrested, with Tom/Fred Beal, for the murder of Chief Aderholt. In this fictionalizing of the Gastonia leadership (no southern women were arrested), Marge is freed by a mistrial in time to be present at the crucifixion, a horrified witness to the unavenged murder of Ella May. Her centrality as both defendant and eyewitness enables the character to be colored by and yet develop beyond the confines of the Wiggins martyrdom. Now a committed political heroine, unlike her equivalents in Vorse and Lumpkin, she is dedicated, but not sacrificed, to the cause.

The final section of the novel sees both a passing of the feminine torch and comradeship with a masculine role model. Tom Crenshaw, unlike the real-life Beal, who was convicted of murder and fled to Russia, remains free to press on with his family's political education. He introduces Marge to labor internationalism not by fleeing the country but simply by journeying outside the South. When Marge accompanies him to Cleveland to the Trade Union Educational League meeting, an actual event that boasted the attendance of Rose Wortis and Ann Burlak and at which women were 10 percent of the delegates (Foner, 263), she trades the "Mill Mother's Lament" for the "Internationale." What lies ahead is marriage to the movement à la Clara Weatherwax's good comrade Mary, who "walks almost like a man" and finds no clash between her service to the movement and her feminine home roles after work.[48] Too, her belief that "it's kind of good to know that no matter what happens to any of us in the movement, somebody goes right on where you left off" (Weatherwax, 98) could have been uttered by the newly converted Marge as well. Gazing raptly at a Russian woman whose work and childbearing problems have been solved by Soviet social engineering, Marge could fit into a faction meeting anywhere from Ohio to the Lower East Side.

But Marge's departure from Gastonia and her roots raises questions about her potential return there. For the very problems that prompted Marge and the mill mothers she represented to strike become far less urgent than membership in an international movement. Marge's new internationalism may enlighten her, may magically resolve her own conflict between class and gender, but it also removes her from the life of the southern woman on strike. Furthermore, Page's argument that the two interests are identical does not solve the problem of who Marge would be were she to return home. For if she was too powerful to meet Ella May's fate, she was also too powerful to remain a local mill woman. That is, *Gathering Storm,* for all its doctrinaire treatment of the Gastonia women activists it also extolls, points to some important ideological problems with them. Marge is left alive, not to be Ella May redivivus but to form part of a new society of men and women modeling themselves on comradely Soviets. No less than in the other Gastonia novels, the South is a problematic place in which to be an educated woman militant. Page offers, however unwittingly, only two solutions: relocation or death.

Burke: The Valkyrie's Fate

Call Home the Heart, Fielding Burke's response to the female militant in general and the Ella May Wiggins legend in particular, is even more ambiguous. Burke, though better known as a North Carolina woman of letters, was an avid reader of the *Daily Worker,* a self-styled "vivid red" evaluating the significance of Gastonia.[49] A large final section of her book is clearly an account of the middle months of the Gastonia strike. The novel was praised by the *New Republic* when it appeared in 1932 as "topically interesting . . . for what it reveals of . . . labor conditions like those at Gastonia" and by Robert Cantwell in the *Nation* as "class-conscious fiction."[50] And the Ella May stand-in, Ishma Hensley, is, like her model, a mountain woman come to town for loom work who has shed one feckless husband to stay with a more sympathetic man. Again like Wiggins, Ishma "converts" to Communism to understand the strike and earns the respect of the mill mothers, first for her desire to help better their lot and then as a key organizer in the local strike hierarchy. To a sheriff's deputy carrying out evictions from company housing, she proclaims, "No man needs this sort of a job" (322). Stung by her logic, he forestalls the eviction. Kidnapped (a frequent ploy by vigilantes seeking to suppress labor), she is threatened with death by a sheriff's gang, as was the real-life Ella May. But she displays a Wiggins-like defiance—and lives on.

Ishma promises to outdo Ella May as a mythic figure. From the novel's inception, she is a down-home Valkyrie. If by night she runs the thread-bare family home because her complaining female relatives cannot, by day she plows and plants the fields her shiftless brother-in-law neglects. Fearful of marriage as a drain on her formidable strength and a curb on her liberty, she fights her love for the feckless town musician, Britt Hensley, as long as she can. She falls in love with him after all, they marry (on her earnings from field work), and she succumbs to the local wisdom that "a gal she must carry" (63). Disillusioned and pregnant, Ishma flees a husband who lacks her energies and ambitions. As she waits for the unwanted baby, she settles in Winbury (Gastonia) with the artisan Rad Bailey until she can find a way to be free. In this relatively affluent time with him, she plays mill-town angel of mercy to the loom mothers. The child's early death accidentally propels her to the mill as a worker and, after leaving her second mate, paradoxically provides her the liberation she has always craved. She begins to read political theory, meets a woman active in the famed but largely failed 1921 Concord, North Carolina, strike, and joins the strikers to educate herself further in the rights of labor.

Her Gastonia activities aside, Ishma resembles a textile Tess of the D'Urbervilles. Beautiful, sensitive, and sexually unorthodox, she is offered as morally superior to her family and her accusers (the mountain preacher drums the adulteress out of his church). Burke fiercely defends her heroine's marital defection as a legitimate search for fulfillment in a repressive culture. And, unlike the fate of Thomas Hardy's heroine, Ishma's sexual liaison does not lead to a mother's responsibilities. Her child conveniently dies, and soon Ishma's life conforms to what Vera Weisbord and Dorothy Ray Healey, among other professional organizers, called the prerequisite of female militance: the rejection of childbearing (Weisbord, 166).[51] Never enthusiastic about motherhood, Ishma is determined not to be bound by it again. "I don't want to tie up, and have children, and get helpless again, when there's so much to do," she boldly tells her common-law husband (267). That is just the beginning. Constricted by a second "husband" who wishes to tie her down, she engineers his falling in love with their young boarder, presses them to marry, and leaves for the strike lines.

In reaching for more than the limited freedom Wiggins actually secured, Ishma becomes a woman who must be defused. In a crucial scene in mid-strike, the boldness Burke's protagonist displays is more resonant of Emma Goldman and Elizabeth Gurley Flynn than Ella May. In fact,

Ishma's powerfulness is too much for the novel to sustain. In Burke's en-
hancement of Gastonia events, the Loray strikers admit blacks to meetings
and accept them as union members (315), but even the male leadership
would quail at Ishma's plan to save a black organizer, Butch Wells, who
is about to be lynched by vigilantes. In a mythically self-empowering
scene (the real-life black organizer, Otto Hall, was rescued by a group of
Gastonia strikers), Ishma tracks the culprits to an abandoned place. She
threatens to shoot herself to give the appearance, she tells them, that she
has chosen death over rape by them, a ploy she has quickly devised to
force them to let the black man go free. Playing as it does on a Margaret
Mitchell model of southern ideology, this creaky plot device is bolstered
by Ishma's: she has told a union friend whom to arrest if she is indeed
found dead. A confused Rad shows up but only appears to save Ishma.
It is her threat that saves the day. She gathers up the beaten-up Wells and
exits, with Rad in tow. When he reproaches her for the danger she has
courted in the name of the strike, Ishma, her trial by fire having only
strengthened her, replies in the language of heroes. "I've got a hard life
ahead of me—a rough life. I didn't get killed tonight, but the next time
it may be different. Better get off here, Rad, and I'll turn toward Butch's
house" (381).

But just when Burke's Valkyrie has defended two disinherited southern
groups, blacks by her rescue and women by playing the savior, without
male leaders' imprimatur, Burke and her heroine recoil from the action.
The novel's strategy of empowerment soon disintegrates, and with it
the coming of age of the female militant herself. Having returned the
wounded Butch to his community and surrounded by the grateful women
of his house, Ishma momentarily moves to a larger understanding of her
own actions. She even acknowledges a cross-race sisterhood. "She loved
those black and bronze women with their big, tender eyes" (382). But
when Butch's illiterate wife, "very fat and very black," tries to validate that
sorority and moves to embrace her with cries of "Sistah! sistah!" (383),
the meaning of what Ishma has done fills her with such "uncontrollable
revulsion" (383) that she rains blows on the hapless woman.

On one level, faced with the possibility of true bonding, Ishma is re-
claiming the racism that she and other white leaders had articulated at
various points in the narrative. On another level, however, her violent
act transcends her visceral denial of solidarity with black workers. It is
nothing less than a denial of the Ella May in herself and of the chance

for truly revolutionary political power, however idealistic her notion of interracial unity might be.

Moreover, at the very point in the novel when she might have assumed a more crucial role in the strike, Ishma, cowed by her own daring, becomes the frightened woman she never was. She reverts to the safety of domesticity, to the security of gender subordination. With the strike at its height, she returns to Britt Hensley with vague plans for a farm that will take in the refugee children of the Loray strikers, a return to the home front that caused Burke, her heroine "drained" by Gastonia, to acknowledge that Ishma was less subversive than she had planned.[52] In the mythology of female Gastonia, having dared to outdo the legendary Ella May, Ishma's atonement is to erase herself from the strike landscape. The Wiggins legend remains unchallenged.

The Female Gastonia School: A Summary

What a Burke explicator called the "strategic problems" (Shannon, 442) in presenting the southern strike heroine faced Vorse, Lumpkin, and Page as well. Ishma's longings for a self-definition not linked to the maternal role made manifest what was latent in the other novelists' Ella May figures. For none of these authors did the mill mother's right to strike confer what Ishma so ardently coveted, the right to be free from an irksome marriage and from the ties of mothering. In all four authors, quick martyrdom, removal to the liberal North, or renunciation of ambition were not true solutions. Rather, transcending southern women's limited experience of trade unionism, their imagined Ella May, or, in a variant, a mill woman transiently imbued with her militant spirit, amalgamates the dual realities of many Gastonia women's lives: maternity and mill exploitation. The result is either a depersonalized Wiggins or a more vibrant character who initially outdoes the Wiggins of legend only to leave the strike stage for her mountain home and lawful husband. Though under attack for her "immorality" by the local pro–mill owners' press, the actual Wiggins was a credible strike figure, able to lead a self-delineated personal life without loss of caste. But, much like the party press of the era, Vorse, Lumpkin, and Page reinvented her; and Burke, though offering another unorthodox woman, limned a journey of self-discovery, not political empowerment, in which her alternative female militant ends, so to speak, where she began. The point is that whether their Ella May is idealized or replaced, all four writers were driven to repress the aspects of Wiggins at odds with an ideologically acceptable Depression Era feminine militant, in the South or elsewhere.

If the real Ella May was censored for her own good, so, too, were the nameless Gastonia women who formed some of the protest cadres. Modern critics remind us that the "purpose of proletarian fiction was to reinforce class identity rather than idiosyncratic personality."[53] So as neither to weaken the ideological force of a female Gastonia poised for class revolt nor to challenge their traditional gender roles, departures from acceptable mill mothering are rarely touched on in Gastonia fiction. When they are, as in Vorse, there is often a sense of unnaturalness, as in a scene in which a near-idiot husband—the only man who would take on women's work?—looks after the children while his wife strikes. But that minimization of role reversal, like the exclusion of other Gastonia women's divergence from type, is not without cost. Those observing striking workers in another industry that draws women, the West Coast cannery, have remarked on "the distinctive personalities among those present" at strike meetings.[54] More differentiation of the feminine protesters might have produced a more forceful statement about the mill personalities drawn to the strike.

The women novelists' reliance on the Wiggins legend skirted potentially troubling questions about whether the interests of Gastonia women, particularly the single women denied access to "men's" jobs in the mill, coincided with those of the males who planned the strike. The women of Gastonia, at least from historical accounts, showed no disposition toward gender separatism; their primary definitions of themselves were cast in terms of family. Still, some of them, with what Vorse glancingly terms their "jauntily swinging skirts and their lip-sticks" (39), mirrored the irreverent and sexually defiant women of the 1929 Elizabethton, Tennessee, strike, women who, according to historian Jacqueline Dowd Hall, sought work out of "adventurousness" ("Disorderly," 362), who "no longer looked to their mothers' lives as patterns of their own" (371) and led "unconventional private lives" (374).

Nor was the Elizabethton model an isolated one. As early as 1913, some of Atlanta's mill girls welcomed sexual pursuit from men, experimented sexually, and even engaged in sexual bartering for treats and gifts.[55] Although Vorse largely avoids imagining such women, she leaves the suggestion that before the events of Gastonia harnessed their sexual energies for political ends, such young women must have experienced the sense of freedom that wage earning can bring. This was so even if, like the young women boarders touched on in passing by Fielding Burke, under the Manville-Jenckes speedup "all a girl [could] make [was] her board and clo's" (39).[56] Yet the single young women who carried out the strike committee's fraternization policy certainly seemed to welcome the transient release from their workaday and kinship roles to engage in sexual guerrilla tactics.

As we can see, the southern mill worker's maternal altruism did not have universal application. Moreover, Gastonia women may not have brought away with them enduring lessons about union organizing or the injustice of woman's double burden. But the female novelist might have taken the opportunity to tease out strands of personal ambition, whether it took a sexual or vocational form. Only Burke makes gestures toward addressing the themes of emotional and vocational fulfillment and then recants, packing her heroine home to wifely duty. That all four novelists passed up the opportunity to explore similar ideas, whether in the name of workers' solidarity or not, is suggestive.

Too, from Vorse through Page, mill women's prestrike work culture—how they spelled each other, what they talked about, what mill rules most bothered them, and to what extent work produced a self-esteem that supplemented or in some cases overshadowed family involvement—is given short shrift in the texts, as if such concerns would divert attention from the male Gastonia. Women's complaints about their treatment in comparison with that of male employees, voiced in reminiscences recently published, are similarly missing. Instead, by focusing on the class oppression of the southern mill worker, *Strike!* and the other novels imagine a genderless commitment to labor protest. They scanted a reality that was inconsistent with the solidarity theme: that, as "an elaborate hierarchy of male employees controlled the large unskilled female workplace," in the mill women did not advance (Frederickson, "I know," 161). In recollections of mills like Loray, women said they knew that "if we had demanded to be supervisors or anything like that, we would have been laughed out of there" (qtd. Byerly, 76). This is an awareness apparently denied those like Page's Marge Crenshaw, who, before the events leading to the strike, greets the prospect of her brother John's promotion to foreman with a placid acceptance of the rightness of things. In Cannon Mills at Kannapolis, North Carolina, remembered one woman, "they put in them new winding machines, I asked them to learn me how to work em and they did. If I'd been a man no telling how far I'd a-gone."[57]

Nor is there much on relations between CP women and mill ones, an angle that also might have individuated the strikers. Considering that CP women were imported early in the strike, led tent colony preparations, and were duly arrested after the police chief's murder, they might have inspired a certain response—even resentment—among the women who followed their activities. Weisbord herself recorded prison conversations with other women arrested on the picket line in which the local women told her about their sense of inferiority (196). If they did not inspire the reverent attitude evident in letters written by turn-of-the-century sweat-shop workers to the well-educated professionals of the Women's Trade Union League (Eisenstein, 152–60), Melvin, Schecter, and Weisbord, all sophisticated theorists who had published in the party presses, must have prompted some reaction after their arrival on the scene.

In sum, the feminine literary emphasis on the iron strength of the poor white woman ("We *gotta* keep on. Somehow." [*Gathering Storm,* 227]) erases as much as it reveals. It is not that Gastonia's female rank and file represented New Womanhood. There was far less of a sense of personal and political empowerment than in the Uprising of the 20,000 or the 1936–37 Flint sit-down strike, however transitory that sense of new possibility proved for the women involved in those strikes. But there is a push in Gastonia fiction to limn feminine solidarity via the Ma Joad model. The creation of the fiercely determined woman striker founders because of the ideological baggage these novels had to carry. Leftist fiction turned the revolt-minded mill woman into a female militant palatable to the dominant culture.

If women novelists, who put the migrant mother on the picket line and denied, though overzealously, the Van Vorst/Erskine Caldwell stereotype of the promiscuous southern mill hand, what did the male novelists do with the female rank and file of Gastonia and with the figure of Ella May Wiggins? The answers lie in Sherwood Anderson's Molly Seabright and William Rollins's Mickey Bonner.

Male Writers' Gastonia

By the time he had taken notes on Gastonia, covered the strike at Elizabethton, "crowded with girls" (527), for the *Nation,* and supported a third strike, at Danville, Virginia, in 1931, Sherwood Anderson was lending his name to CP involvement in labor resistance. A faded luminary of American letters, he had been heralded, some years before, for *Winesburg, Ohio,* in which he explored the "starved side of American small town life."[58] In his apolitical midwestern Winesburg, unlike in the Langdon of his Gastonia novel *Beyond Desire,* the inarticulate residents, groping for personal meaning, are denied salvation, not, as in the mill-town South, a decent living. They are, in any case, unaware of the solution implied in a 1930s *New Masses* symposium, "How I Came to Communism," in which Anderson himself would participate.[59] Still, his 1932 textile strike novel is in many ways a rural, proletarian *Winesburg.* It contains a lengthy section, "Mill Girls," that probes these women's thwarted longings and fears of sexual initiation and intensity. Only later in the novel do these silent girls, so long prisoners of frustrated interiority, become "singing women" (*Desire,* 272), inspired by Ella May to chant of solidarity. As if to sharpen the group focus, Wiggins herself is martyred offstage while this mass of newly politicized women lives on to face jail time and reprisals. But the difficulty of revising the novel's initial—and more resonant— vision of mill women remains.

By its very length and preoccupation with their romantic sexuality, "Mill Girls" suggests that the kind of woman who mistakes Anderson's ineffectual wanderer-protagonist, Red Oliver, for a Fred Beal is seeking not political but personal liberation through fantasies projected onto any man who sparks her imagination. It is true that, in the words of Alfred Kazin, Anderson "implored men [and women] to live frankly and fully by their own need of liberation" and against the "constraints of . . . modern commercial and industrial life."[60] And it is equally true that Anderson was an apt student of "laborers' rooming houses" ("Anderson on Winesburg," 13), of job-site banter, and of female camaraderie. He was thus a faithful recorder of lives often bound up with minutiae—the snacks favored on breaks at the mill, the gossipy confidences shared in leisure moments, and even the benevolent envy of the northern organizers sent to inspire them to militance—overlooked in the high seriousness of a Vorse or a Lumpkin.

Nor was Anderson's agenda less ambitious than theirs. In envisioning Gastonia, he sought to reconcile the frustrations of emotionally and economically muzzled female mill hands with the possibilities unleashed by their transformation into strikers, who, in his uncertain vision, would somehow harness the "magnificent," "disconcerting" power of the machines that held them in thrall ("Elizabethton," 526). But neither in his novel, a pastiche of events in Gastonia (Beal, the tent colony, the raids, the Wiggins-like activism, the trial) and the other southern strikes he witnessed, nor in his corollary writings on the mill such as *Perhaps Women* (1931), does Anderson reconcile the contradictions between his characters' dreamlike fixations, their curiously unreflective interior monologues, and the "betterment of the working classes—especially working women" ("Elizabethton," 526). Thus the confrontation between pickets and police that results in the accidental martyrdom of Red Oliver and the murder of Wiggins herself, glancingly noted earlier in the narrative, seem a weak scaffolding for a plot concerned with individual longings not beyond desire but synonymous with it.

To his credit, Anderson sketches in a mill world in which a quartet, indeed, a network, of representative women, whether single or married, moves through pre-Gastonia days responding not only to the brutalities of the loom day but to what social historian Kathy Peiss called the promise that "cheap amusements" increasingly held for working women's lives in the twentieth century.[61] Both at toil and after hours, Anderson's Doris, Grace, Nell, and Fanny, their names plucked more from working girls' romances than from the nomenclature of the South, prize the activities of "an emergent consumer culture" (Peiss, 72), Coca-Colas and Milky Ways and movies that "made [their] nerves tingle" (*Desire,* 82). *Beyond Desire* even includes a fairground scene at a poor southern version of Coney Island's Luna Park, in which the women cement their friendships and act out at the gambling and ferris wheels fantasies of being released from the "mill-bound world" (81) that constrains them.

Unlike the female Gastonia writers, bent on exorcising the allegations of a Marie Van Vorst, Anderson does not demonize the feminine sexuality for which mill work serves as a crucible. Both lured and frightened by men's interest, particularly in the heat of the work site, his lower-class women imagine outlets for longings fired by the very proximity of their co-workers. Longings also envelop the novel's vapid bourgeoises; ironically, it is the proper Ethel Long who—in an experimental spirit—seduces Red Oliver, not the yearning, married Doris, who observes him longingly. But the implication is that Doris and her kind are more involved in their bodies than are the Langdon middle classes. Andersonian dreamers, they are prisoners of urges no less vital for being half-understood.

As in other masculine portraits of working-class womanhood from Stephen Crane to John Steinbeck, sexuality makes an object of the women who possess it.

> Nell said, "We work from cansee to can'tsee. They got us. They got the bee on us. They know it. They got us hogtied. We work from cansee to can'tsee." Nell was tall, swaggering, profane. Her breasts weren't big, like Doris'—almost too big—or like Fanny's or too little, just nothing, a flat place, like a man, like Grace's. They were just right, not too big or not too little. (*Desire*, 95)

In Anderson's Gastonia, what begins as sociological reporting ends in authorial self-titillation. Certainly Nell's angry realizations of her group's work-site life as she proclaims, "We're only machines ourselves" (95), are deflected by Anderson's prurient woman-as-sex-machine. As in his survey of the mill strike at Elizabethton, where a recognition of working women's oppression ends at their "lovely little" bodies, so much "nicer" than those of middle-class women (527), Anderson resurrects the sexually available woman of the people.

As their sexuality is rechanneled into workplace outrage—"There was a little flame of anger always in Doris" (73)—what began as Anderson's sexualization becomes their own identity, best personified by a character with promiscuous literary antecedents, Molly Seabright. A woman with a checkered past who works in a nearby mill, she is glimpsed most often in the rural setting associated with Henry Fielding's ever-wayward Molly Seagrim of *Tom Jones* fame. Indeed, the sight of Red Oliver—the middle-class protagonist seeking to join the proletariat—generates in this descendant of Fielding's lusty wench that combination of ambition and sexual excitement the original Molly felt for her "gentleman." But the 1930s factory Molly, aware of class exploitation, also sees Red as a savior figure, here to give the strike definition.

Women's very carnal knowledge, however, seems intertwined with a corresponding political ignorance, an inability to retain the hard truths of their work lives. Molly Seabright, who hears men talk of past union battles, when she tries to give reasons for these protests, "didn't know" (276). The same is true of the crowd of women who pile onto the trucks headed for rallies, fight with scabs outside the mill, and sing political songs. Of them Anderson remarks, "There couldn't have been a chance on earth that the women on the truck knew for themselves what communism was, what communism demanded, what the communists were fighting for" (272). On one level a reference to the myriad meetings and lectures at which Beal and his colleagues "enlightened" Gastonia strikers, on another the comment resonates with Anderson's deeper vision of the female Gastonia. Even though some of the workers did undergo an ideological conversion, Anderson's women are incapable of thinking toward a militant end, unable to comprehend the basic issues in the strike. Mill women's assumed ignorance, then, is the handmaiden of their sexual knowingness. (His subsequent quasi-strike novel, which includes textile strike scenes, *Kit Brandon* [1936], shows the coin's opposite side. The sole woman organizer pays for her political understanding with a broad-shouldered manliness and a complete lack of femininity.) Imprisoned as much in Anderson's dichotomy—men yearn to know, women to feel—as in the self-preoccupation indigenous to all of his characters, Gastonia females are largely reduced to camp followers.

William Rollins's *The Shadow Before,* by contrast, has virtually no female Gastonia. As in Anderson, its center is occupied by a confused male protagonist, in this case Harry Baumann, a mill owner's son pursuing radical involvement who loses his life in the course of a strike propelled, as was Gastonia, by party imports. For another, the Rollins book is modeled as much on the 1928 New Bedford textile strike (which featured vocal Portuguese and Irish immigrant women) as on the southern one the following year. Gastonia events pepper the narrative, but the sole woman firebrand to be highlighted, the mill worker and organizer Mickey Bonner, gives no evidence that her creator, who covered the trials of Beal and the other male organizers, observed southern females. Mickey's persona, vulgar, streetwise, drawn to liaisons with men who can show her the town, is pure northern, urban self-reliance. Her switch to party thinking does much to alter her spiritedness but does nothing to ally her with a southern labor-class persona. At the novel's close, the strike largely defeated, she decides to name her coming child, whose illegitimacy she makes no effort to conceal, after Lenin.

Her wish to devote herself to the expected child places yet another feminine activist in the 1930s mother slot. It also distances Mickey from the New Bedford strike orator-strategist Elizabeth Donnelly, on whom she is partly modeled (Foner, 218). Ellen Dawson and Vera Weisbord were also visible at New Bedford. They were among the women arrested at Gastonia on trumped-up murder charges, but despite their dual potential as strike fireballs, in the Rollins work they are mute.

Not surprisingly, this scattering of female political energies did not prevent an enthusiastic reception for the book.[62] That Rollins was the least reliant of the six Gastonia authors on the strike itself may have entered into his decision to use experimental techniques. Shifting from interior monologue to news headlines evidence to impassioned dialogues between key characters, the novel distinguishes itself by its ability simultaneously to render ideology and break literary ground. Yet as the last period attempt to do justice to blue-collar southern women, it comes up short.

Rollins and Anderson share with the period's female authors the difficulty of creating a female Gastonia without, in their view, weakening the working-class statement the strike was to have made. More than their male colleagues, the female creators of Gastonia fiction attempted mother/worker/activist portraits. But, true to an ideological agenda of gender solidarity, their strategy was to subordinate the faceless feminine rank and file to the more dramatic Ella May, transformed into a figure of maternal legend rather than the self-sufficient unionist she was. For the male writers, Ella May did not signify. If men, they implied, could not personify the focused organizer of the determined rank and file, they could serve as symbols of failed promise. And in a universe of mill-working men in turmoil, though Anderson acknowledged feminine inner lives, neither he nor Rollins could legitimize women's strike motives. Both fell back on the stereotype rejected by the women writers: the sexually experienced mill girl, avid for men, not politics.

Visible but Invisible: Whose Strike Was It?

In Gastonia fiction, as in the strike itself, women are visible but invisible. Shunted to the margins of the "main" narrative, the history of a male strike, bereft of the attention they merit, the heroines of Gastonia share the literary fate of their striking sisters throughout the nation. By the 1930s, garment making, for example, was to New York State what textiles were to the South; dressmakers constituted the largest group of workers in the needle trades. Two decades before, in an era of immense curiosity about the controversial new working woman, the woman-fueled Uprising of the 20,000 and the great New York shirtwaist strike of 1909–10 produced a host of novels.[63] The great dress strikes of 1932, 1933, and 1936, all of which engaged more numbers than the 1910 strike, stirred no such interest. As Walter Rideout points out, a masculinized industry like lumber was more likely to seize public attention.[64] In rare exceptions, such as department store novels, as noted in chapter 4, a strike plot doubled as a romance one.

In contrast to Ella May Wiggins, the Jewish émigrés and their first-generation daughters who contributed so mightily to the 1930s garment trade strikes represented a far less acceptable image of the woman striker. Weaned on a tradition of protest and unapologetic about personal economic survival, they may have threatened to divert interest from what one author routinely described as the "men who made the unions."[65] Their very submergence in a male mass validated the historian Sharon Strom's assertion that "women workers needed to challenge women's place to organize effectively in the thirties."[66] They could, as in the 1930s garment trades, "struggle collectively on occasion" (379), but they could not undo the fixed perception that women might be workers, "but men led the strikes" (Dixler, 124).

The 1929 strike at Elizabethton, Tennessee, was even more of a case in point. "So here were these girls organizing," marveled Sherwood Anderson, "and the movement grew like wild-fire. The men came in" ("Elizabethton," 526). Like so many textile strikes of the time, it was squelched, but not before the "girls," by dint of secret union meetings, defiance of state police, and inspiring male workers to join them, had spontaneously provided a protest example. A spirited southern walkout that preceded Gastonia, Elizabethton prompted no school of fiction. It was not even listed in the encyclopedia *Labor Conflict in the United States* (1990), though it was the first in the famous wave of strikes in the southern textile industry in 1929 and originated in what Mary Frederickson called "women responding collectively to the treatment of an individual worker and adding to the original grievance broader workplace issues affecting all of the workers in the community" ("I know," 164). For any 1930s novelist, the story had potential: events moved from the demotion of a woman worker who organized the workers in her section to five thousand workers out and two large rayon plants shut down. But neither in the novel nor in the press did it generate the attention Gastonia did.[67] The NTWU passed it by, and its support from the AFL-backed United Textile Workers (UTW) was lukewarm (Foner, 230).

Such journalistic and literary silence suggested that the Tennessee walkout had not generated a culturally acceptable female labor legend. For, far more than at Gastonia, Elizabethton's strikers, many of them young, single, and self-supporting, represented "new figure[s] [on] the New South stage . . . white working-class wom[e]n who saw no contradiction between fighting the mill boss and charting new sexual terrain" (Hall, "Private," 71). Women with names like Trixie Perry and Texas Bill adopted a provocative stance both on the picket line and in the courtroom. Perry took no trouble to conceal her sexual past and illegitimate children (by several men); Bill dressed (and cross-dressed) flamboyantly. Both incurred the displeasure of their own local organizers, who, feeling the women had carried the fraternization policy too far, tried to send them home (Hall, "Disorderly," 375). Nor were these two the only Elizabethton "flappers" to view sexuality as both an end in itself and a weapon in the unionizing struggle. Yet their conduct does much to suggest why Elizabethton has been forgotten by labor historians, who have adopted the view that a "woman, usually a younger woman, could be a striker, acting alone, as an individual, or with a group of her own." But she was merely "young and impetuous . . . wild and disconnected from normal society" (Frederickson, "Heroines," 104).

In the era's stereotyping of southern labor union women, and to a large degree of northern ones as well, if women were older or dead, they were heroic. These were ideas rehearsed in the Gastonia fiction, to be sure. But aside from Mary Heaton Vorse's glancing reference to "Cactus Kate," a flirtatious picketer clearly borrowed from the Elizabethton strike, such fiction without a maternal slant could provide only a limited rhetoric of female militance. Nor did the Great Textile Strike of 1934, a massive but ultimately ineffective nationwide protest that spread to thousands of mills, and in which women of the working South again participated vocally, inspire novels in praise of such action. The mill women's literary moment had passed.

Only in the depiction of Ella May Wiggins was there sustained literary attention to the female militant. But Vorse did not individuate her beyond the known facts of her martyrdom; Page and Lumpkin sanctified her; Burke defused any possible alternative to her. So, too, in a different way, did Anderson and Rollins, who bypassed the mill mother of Gastonia in favor of the sexually available working women. None of the Gastonia novelists suggested that a woman could, as the real Wiggins did, see in the union a chance to develop her talents and escape the confines of the workaday world. Better educated than most mill women in her time and region, Wiggins served as secretary for the union and joined a delegation sent to Washington to lobby for the workers' cause (Hall, *Family,* 227). It is understandable that this Ella May is omitted from ideological fiction about a strike directed—even co-opted?—by men. In the world of the novels, her assassination does not so much cut short a life as give birth to an acceptable heroine.

In the novels of the Loray Mill walkout, as in the fiction that imagines other key strikes of the era, women remain cadre and protest helpmeets. However strong their belief in the right to combat mill conditions, women's own dual consciousness as nurturers and wage earners controls their public image and, from the available evidence, seems to define their private selves to a large extent as well. To the Left-literary community bent on popularizing Gastonia, women were "supporting players" (Hall, "Private," 271) on the labor stage. The enduring lesson of the North Carolina textile strike and of the fiction that recounted and reinvented it was that the militant female proletariat was nowhere in sight.

Chapter Six

WITH APOLOGIES FOR COMPETENCE: WOMEN, PROFESSION, TALES OF CONFLICT

Raphael Soyer's study in white-collar alienation, *Office Girls,* 1936.
Whitney Museum of American Art (Purchase 36.149).

The thought that nothing could stop her from finishing the work she had promised
calmed her. . . . She reached toward [her husband], patting him with her hand as if he
were her child and she could take away his sorrows and soothe him to sleep.
—Josephine Herbst, *Rope of Gold* (1939)

These strange days, when women were out in the world, on their own, they seemed
temporarily to have got ahead, to be going still farther while men, surprised, exhausted
in the fight, sat down with open mouth in a stopping-place in the road.
—Tess Slesinger, *The Unpossessed* (1934)

"I like power. . . . I do! I do not want to spend my life paying grocery bills! . . ." [Her
ex-suitor responded,] "You're a little too big for me. I have a career of my own.
And if I married you, I'd simply become your valet."
—Sinclair Lewis, *Ann Vickers* (1933)

I n the pinched 1930s, educated women, unlike their labor-class sisters
in the mills, factories, fields, and canneries, were particularly fortunate to possess high school or college diplomas, much less graduate
degrees. Constituting under 15 percent of the nation's eleven million
working women, they filled the ambiguously broad census categories
of "Professional, Technical, and Kindred Workers" (including teachers,
nurses, physicians, and lawyers) and "Managers, Officials, and Propri-
etors." [1] But whether their vocational talents were those of senior clerks
or medical doctors, they joined their blue-collar counterparts as targets
of disapproval in the 1930s. Business magazines were particularly wary
of the ambitious woman and explicitly or implicitly censured her interest in a career other than marriage. [2] More positive journals ran columns
lauding women's entry into fields other than those traditionally open to
them, social work and education. [3] Some even proclaimed that "every year
the percentage of women department store executives is increasing—and
particularly for college women," though it was assumed that feminine job
aspirants would not attempt to enter any profession perceived as the prov-
ince of men. [4] Thus articles in the *Ladies' Home Journal* could envision for
the "50,000 college girls and 350,000 high school girls ready for graduation" gender-appropriate openings in, among other fields, merchandising,
copywriting, book reviewing, and catering. [5]

Yet whether they suspected women's professional aspirations or more subtly circumscribed them, such articles could not erase the fact that out-of-work college graduates were now competing for the very jobs that, in earlier decades, their education had enabled them to escape. At least those who could not remain in positions for which they had prepared had access to the better clerical and decently paid sales jobs—the sergeants' ranks of a three-million-member army of female foot soldiers billed as semiprofessionals—that traded a loss of status for an income superior to the wages of blue-collar time serving.[6] In the cynically titled "Jobs in the Sky" (1935), Tess Slesinger's Miss Paley, twenty years a teacher, a women's profession that lost ground in the 1930s to men, accepts with gratitude a bookselling post, another arena in which her learning counted. The less conventional Comrade Ruthie Fisher in the Slesinger novel *The Unpossessed* (1934) pragmatically supports herself and dreams of revolution by taking dictation at a representative $22 a week, a bountiful salary compared to a Gastonia mill woman's or a female reliefer's dole.[7]

What for some was a pragmatic compromise seemed a "dreary job" to others.[8] In *The Company She Keeps* (1942), Mary McCarthy's autobiographical Vassar girl with diploma in hand, the aspiring writer Margaret Sargent takes a stenographer's job, for which she admits she is less qualified than a business school graduate, with a singular lack of enthusiasm. In real life, with competition for stenographic jobs so intense, Margaret's apathy was not without risk. Aware of the newly constricted vocational climate, deans at a number of women's colleges urged graduates not to try to find work, a suggestion underscored by Labor Secretary Frances Perkins.[9] By 1934 it took over a year for the average white female college graduate to find work, and the higher the expectation of job-site fulfillment, as was the case with the Barnard class of 1932, the more likely the letdown. Only one-third of the Barnard graduates found jobs that hard year (Hymowitz and Weissman, 307). For the graduates of black colleges—or, for instance, the twelve young African-Americans in the Radcliffe class of 1935—professional jobs were both harder to attain and lower paid (Brown, 12–13).[10] The percentage of all women in the professions fell from 14.2 in 1930 to 12.3 a decade later, a reality that modern historians variously interpret as status loss or holding-their-own tenacity.[11] Whatever the interpretation, it is clear that the deprivations of the Depression affected educated women, whether they were in work for which they had trained, underemployed in dead-end but well-paid clerical or sales jobs, trapped in more menial work, or jobless altogether.[12]

This constricted marketplace had little use for the ideology of the New Woman, a term that surfaced at the turn of the century to denote the middle-class, often collegiate women who were forming the advance guard of those who sought a public role.[13] In fact, the careers of some New Deal women, most notably Perkins, first took shape in what Mary Ryan calls the era of "social housekeeping."[14] But in the postsuffrage era of the 1920s, New Womanhood, always a loose concept, became a terrain of conflicting definitions: self-involved careerist, flapper, Bohemian, or a variant type, the nighttime rebel, still bent on a daytime vocation. Her feminism at best diluted, the New Woman would soon suffer further retrenchment.

The New Woman, Revised

By the Depression what remained was a revised New Woman, popularly defined everywhere from *Saturday Evening Post* stories in which female professionals stepped down to court social approval to the *New York Times Magazine* ("The College Girl Puts Marriage First").[15] What was left of the New Woman's legacy was a largely premarital pursuit of economic security that often precluded "the collective demands of feminist political reform in favor of an individualized feminism" (Todd, xxvii). Fictions of married professionals often chastised the women, featuring their apologies to their husbands for having better jobs or, as in the avidly read James M. Cain's noirish novel *Career in C Major* (1936), providing jeremiads about castrating careerists.[16] One Cain villainess taunts: "You can't get work. . . . But something has to be done. If you can't earn a living, then I'll have to" (8). But her angry husband tells her off: "You're only trying to make a bum out of me, and I'm not going to buy it" (9). For the politically conservative, unaligned, or simply apathetic women of the 1930s, the fantasy of vocational success was more likely to be embodied in Christopher Morley's alertly entrepreneurial Kitty Foyle or, in Civil War dress, the resourcefully ruthless Scarlett O'Hara, than the self-lacerating wife of a leftist luftmensch at the core of Slesinger's *Unpossessed*.[17] While countering Cain's misogyny, the fiction of Tess Slesinger and Josephine Herbst provided a briefly married heroine who is less insulting but whose professional aspirations are more muted. A titular leftist, the Herbst-Slesinger woman longs, at least in principle, for social justice.

A writer with even more ambiguous leftist loyalties, the recently rediscovered Rachel Maddux, in one rare short story "The Little Woman" (written ca. 1935; published 1992), offers a professional woman who emits a fierce "no!" at those who seek to diminish her.[18] She is scornful of her barroom companions, who can only oppose "the illiteracy of their employers" (232) by slipping into drink, and of the fact that she is often only a few dollars away from poverty. She is proud of her small room over a garage, of her ability to ride out the storm, and, the narrative voice implies, of her own wit and intelligence. "There isn't a soul I'd let inhibit me" (238), she trumpets. Her proclamation has as much to do with independence as sexual liberty, particularly when she breaks with her self-absorbed left-wing lover.

In Maddux's rejection of altruism, her women, educated, alert, and defiant, reject any attempt to objectify them or place them on the period's familiar maternal/sexual axis. Responding to her time and place, Maddux chronicles the dents in feminine pride, but her heroine responds with anger at unworthy work. The Maddux protagonist even sheds jobs when too fed up with them: "I'd move someplace, quit work and be alone until my money ran out" ("Little Woman" in *The Way,* 234). "For as long as the check lasted I was going to live the way I wanted to live" (235). Her heroine is out of step with leftist and mainstream culture alike. Satirical about the "familiar lullaby" (232) of 1930s radicalism, she rejects all creeds. Scornful of the semiprofessional work that pays her rent, she is far more able to articulate this discontent than a Catharine Brody autoworker heroine or a Gastonia School mill woman.

But Maddux's defiant personae remained unavailable to 1930s audiences. "The Little Woman," for all its importance, did not appear in print until recently. To what extent did the era's published authors of female professionalism take a leaf from Maddux? Did they temper her literary self-proclamation with culturally approved humility, guilt, or maternal impulses, particularly in the face of male professional joblessness? How far did any of them, especially leftist novelists such as Tess Slesinger and Josephine Herbst, who successfully doubled as journalists, go in creating fictive alter egos, careerist women who contest the repressive stereotyping characteristic of novels about blue-collar women? And how did "apolitical" or antileftist writers like Margaret Mitchell, Christopher Morley, and Sinclair Lewis, whose immensely popular writing often earned the scorn of the Left, at once empower and repress the great women whose stories they plied for avid mass consumption?[19]

In addressing these issues, it would be well to consider two real-life career successes of the 1930s: Frances Perkins and Dorothy Thompson. Both helped inspire *Ann Vickers* (1933), the Lewis novel that, to judge by its large readership, apparently told the culture what it wished to hear about female achievement.[20] The two women's appearance in a best-seller aside, they were, respectively, the most visible female New Dealer and the period's foremost woman journalist. How did they combat—and internalize—the conflict of 1930s women professionals between the "passivity expected" of women and the "assertiveness demanded" by workplace duties?[21]

Frances Perkins and Social Mothering

In her early fifties when she became *the* female professional woman of the Roosevelt cabinet, Frances Perkins was the product, like so many women in the New Deal political arena, of a female Progressive social welfare milieu that espoused a social feminism—women altruistically committed to social service—to meet the ills of industrial society. Growing out of the professionalization of female philanthropy initiated in the previous century, this movement, influenced by such women as Jane Addams and Lillian Wald, cloaked a "drive to power" in the "empathetic and unaggressive woman" still culturally required, even in the Progressive Era culture.[22] As the labor secretary, Perkins of necessity modified the turn-of-the century New Woman's Hull House credo that only a community of women reformers, extending the mothering role to society's needy, adopt what Jill Conway terms the role of the "professional expert" or "social engineer" (168).[23] Yet as a middle-class woman "in a public position that was supposedly reserved for working-class men" (Wandersee, "I'd Rather," 7), she continued to espouse a philosophy of government that issued from the belief that "the middle-class reformers did more for the working class than did the unions" (Wandersee, "I'd Rather," 12). There were inevitable differences between her approach to reform in her early days as a Consumers' League investigator and member of the New

York State Factory Safety Commission and her far more prestigious post in the Roosevelt cabinet. A new revisionism about her political acumen, her diplomatic effectiveness with organized labor, and her role in settling crucial strikes like the San Francisco dock strike of 1934, may reveal a far more assertive and "masculine" Perkins than hitherto acknowledged.

Still, it is indisputable that Perkins, who never used her married name, whose husband was absent from her inauguration (a chronic emotional invalid, he stayed out of the public eye for his own mental good as much as his wife's), early on in her career donned the mantle of the social mother—and its inevitable cultural associations with the "old maid." She manipulated it with a certain success in her dealings with an otherwise male cabinet and a public that preferred a career woman not to be threatening. Perkins was thus not so much balancing career and marriage as overhauling what the 1920s called the "Lady in Lavender," that intelligent spinster of settlement house, college, and schoolroom, for government service.[24] Rare indeed was the media allusion to her real-life motherhood—she had a college-age daughter by 1933—though the few such allusions always carried the implied criticism that Perkins's true identity should have been the mother's, not the puissant labor secretary's. In the main, however, most journalistic references to her could make sense of Perkins and her "man-sized job" only by turning her into a cabinet-level Jane Addams.[25] Although she told an interviewer she had no intention of being a "schoolteacher to Congress," Perkins created a personal style that *Business Week* typically defined as that of "a pleasant little schoolma'am."[26] Quite dowdy, she kept what some head shots of the 1930s reveal to be a strong, noble face (Bernstein, photo section) looking determinedly grandmotherly by shunning makeup. Her clothes, as one period wit put it, "look[ed] as though they had been designed by the Bureau of Standards" (Bernstein, 14). All in all, her self-presentation provided the nation reassurance that, far from being a sexual threat, or even what she was, the mother/wife of a shadow husband, she was the New Deal's aging vestal virgin.

From most accounts, her social style in Washington, like her management style as secretary, was "conciliatory" (Wandersee, "I'd Rather," 16). If anything, with her upper-crust Boston accent and pleasant manner, she capitalized on her (willed?) ability not to appear "domineering."[27] Perkins was never in FDR's inner circle of advisers (Ware, *Beyond,* 191), but she accepted her exclusion. She was never invited to cabinet members' all-male social functions. And she even acquiesced sans protest to being seated with the cabinet wives at other events (Woloch, 456, 425). Though accused at times of abrasiveness, she generally adopted a strategy of tactfulness, self-effacement, and matronliness, age-old tools of the mothering woman.[28]

Perkins was like many of the other women instrumental in the New Deal—the Democratic National Committee Women's Division head, Molly Dewson, born in 1874; the Workers' Education director, Hilda Smith, born in 1889; the WPA Women's and Professional Division administrator, Ellen Woodward, born in 1887, Mary Anderson of the Women's Bureau, born in 1873—a woman who looked her age. She was what one historian has termed the "hardy and celibate spinster," "the kind of woman who could devote herself wholeheartedly to a career" (Stricker, 3), a devotion that, in a sense, exculpated her from wielding the power she actually did. Some feminist historians, rejecting the ignorance of realpolitik implied by the Perkins-as-spinster model, now dispute the extent to which she actually placated the masculine establishment. Susan Ware has argued that the labor secretary used both her status and the network of women in the New Deal to advance the postsuffrage status of women. Yet it is clear that Perkins's efforts to place women in positions of obvious power, much like her attempts to wield it herself, were carried out very much behind the scenes (*Beyond,* 176, 190; Wandersee, "I'd Rather," 9n).

In any case, the purpose here is not to analyze the political effectiveness of Perkins and important New Deal women such as Dewson but the image crafted for public consumption. Photographs of Perkins and her female allies suggest a persona, if anything, rather similar to the business "nun" portrayed in *Fortune*'s 1935 survey of women in the office world. Amid a gallery of "competent, agreeable, thirty-odd-year-old, intelligently dressed wom[e]n" (55)—"amenable," "obedient," and "making the office a more pleasant, peaceful, and homelike place"—the only woman in a fairly secure and powerful position, "Miss Mary Orr," is sixty-five, bespectacled, and serenely dowdy. Like Perkins, Orr by her very appearance was excused for being "the first woman . . . elected to" the board of a large corporation, in her case Remington Rand. Reassuringly, too, the role of sole support of needy relatives (for Orr, a widowed mother and a nephew, for Perkins, a mentally ill husband who filled a dependent's role) cast both as spinsters/careerists by necessity, even if the truth about Perkins was otherwise.

Dorothy Thompson: Vocation as Rebuttal?

If Perkins's message to ambitious women in politics or business was that they could be more than Miss Orr, that shrewdness could prevail, her customary nonassertiveness, ironically, underscored the message of the era's advice manuals to women preparing for business careers. Cautioned one self-styled 1930s guru, "The woman who has been coarsened or hard boiled by her business contacts is seriously handicapped in the winning of a mate. The qualities she has acquired repel men." [29] Ellen Wiley Todd has found that even career guidebooks, far from embracing solo career climbs, underscored the ideology of woman's place on a male-managed office team (308), what *Fortune*'s mid-1930s advice to women in business termed "making the office a more pleasant, peaceful, and homelike place" (55). Although they paid lip service to equal access to opportunities, period guides reinforced the idea that womanly compliance was admirable, implying the willingness to be exploited with which Tess Slesinger took issue in her irony-drenched 1935 story "The Mousetrap." [30] Clearly Perkins was not the anonymously submissive office wife of guidebook exhortation or Slesinger's satire. But by dressing modestly, behaving supportively, and possibly, as her critics charged, ignoring the needs of women for jobs above subsistence level (Woloch, 456), she too modified assertive femininity so as not to "repel" the men of the Roosevelt cabinet.

The schoolmarm or nun of business was not the decade's only permissible model for achievement, as the career of the stylish foreign correspondent Dorothy Thompson flamboyantly demonstrated. Whether interviewing Adolf Hitler in 1931 for Fannie Hurst's romance venue, *Cosmopolitan,* or lecturing throughout the country on world affairs, she was far more the Hurstian elegant than the Perkins-like wallflower. She would achieve her great success with her syndicated column "On the Record" for the *New York Herald Tribune* in the late 1930s, a time when, though the woman reporter was visible in Hollywood films (Stricker, 6), her real-life sisters were making fewer gains than in earlier decades. Thompson, however, was breaking the boundaries between the male and female worlds without incurring the wrath of the fourth-estate estab-lishment.[31] Although some marveled at the ability of this statuesque and strong-minded "blue-eyed tornado" (Harriman, 29) to maintain her at-tractiveness while she did man's work, she was the butt of misogynist satire in the Tracy-Hepburn film *Woman of the Year* (1942). But if in it a "globe-trotting foreign correspondent, plainly modeled . . . on Thomp-son . . . is cut down to size" (Kurth, 340), the notoriety that prompted the film suggested that her place in a man's realm was secure.

Still, in her apparent rebuttal of the social mother as career persona, Thompson was aware of conflicts regarding woman's role, although she saw room for feminine professionalism in few lives other than her own. Sounding the Perkins note of social mothering, she wrote that woman's business was "to take care of human values," but it had an even nar-rower meaning for Thompson than social welfare work.[32] As the darling of the women's club lecture circuit, she urged other women to stay home and be mothers (Marzolf, 55), sounding the late Victorian argument that woman's mission was to "make a new world" and produce "stronger, freer, more co-operative human beings" (qtd. Kurth, 212). Such a mis-sion, furthermore, could be understood only in the context of a marriage in which men recognized their wives' "nurturing, brooding qualities" (Thompson, "Is America," 60).

Even if much of this theory was produced for the feminine magazine audiences who read her advice pieces, it was a domestic model her let-ters to her husband, 1930 Nobel Prize winner Sinclair Lewis, impatient at her globetrotting, would also espouse. But theory aside, domesticity was a way of life she herself could never sustain. During the 1930s she surrounded her young son Michael with a bevy of playmates and kindly servants. Yet she was absent from home on journalistic assignments—though not without guilt—for much of the time. Though torn by the contradictory pulls of domesticity and independence, in moments of can-dor she acknowledged that, as one of her interviewers remarked, she found conventional women "tedious" (Alexander, 11).

Thompson publicly rewrote her own absent motherhood by associating herself with the mothers of America and writing a *Ladies' Home Journal* col-umn, "It's a Woman's World"—ironically in response to a Tess Slesinger attack on the woman-centered trivia published by the *Journal*.[33] In her rebuttal of Slesinger, the famed journalist deftly defended the American woman for not involving herself in world problems "that one cannot possibly solve." She was apparently oblivious to the irony that she was giving this soothing advice "on the ocean, en route to the Balkans" ("It's," 25) to cover political developments there. Deliberately associating (and ingratiating) herself with her home-loving audience, she also included motherly advice to her son. Yet, quite apart from using a public forum for a letter home, there was an unreal quality to a mother who would advise her son not to "treat trees as though you were a Nazi and the trees a political opponent" (25).

Adding to Thompson's inability to sustain a more traditional maternal role was her uneasy bisexuality, evidenced by an intermittent affair with a Budapest baroness that was carefully hidden from public scrutiny but that suggested, even more than her "Woman's World" column, a strong ambivalence about heterosexual homemaking.[34] Sinclair Lewis professed to tolerate Thompson's European trysts. But he took revenge in *Ann Vickers,* in which, sanitizing Thompson's own sexual preferences, the title character is the chaste object of unwanted kisses from a lesbian roommate. (Less kind to Thompson's real-life amour, the baroness, the woman becomes in the novel's version a mannishly lesbian department store executive with a suitably "unfeminine" item on her vita, a doctorate.) In any case, whether as political pundit or sexual experimenter, Thompson eschewed the compliance urged on women professionals from quarters as diverse as the FDR cabinet and the pages of white-collar job manuals. Yet, taunted by the press, by Hollywood, and by Lewis himself, she did not escape censure for failing in the wife/mother role to which she paid lip service but never adopted.

In sum, Frances Perkins balanced conformity with professional renown by updating presuffrage, spinsterish New Womanhood and its idée fixe, vocational altruism. Dorothy Thompson, equally famed, combined a self-assertive, postsuffrage vocational individualism with the private remorse of a career woman unable to satisfy family demands. In the rather scanty fiction of Depression Era professionalism, the constrictions of both the Perkins and Thompson modes shape the heroines who are caught between—or rebel against—motherly self-abnegation and self-advancing careerism. As if responding to the flaws inherent in both images of the female professional, they experience frustration, guilt, or "unfeminine" triumph. In any event, the limited choices symbolized by the labor secretary and the international newswoman inform fiction as different as Sinclair Lewis's great woman tale; Christopher Morley's glossy and Margaret Mitchell's veiled executive stories; and even the novels of Tess Slesinger and Josephine Herbst, whose left-leaning heroines seem, on the surface, removed from New Deal, journalistic, or business power.

In Whose Steps?: Slesinger and Herbst

Slesinger, born in 1906, and Herbst, born in 1892 (but claiming 1897), belonged to that second and third generation of college graduates who, like their predecessors of the 1890s, "stressed the importance of jobs and exulted in their own economic independence" (Wandersee, *Women's Work,* 95). A teenaged Slesinger, enrolled at Columbia in 1925, and a late-blooming Herbst, graduating from the University of California at Berkeley in 1918, were no doubt aware of talented achievers such as Freda Kirchwey. A member of the Barnard class of 1915, Kirchwey married the next year but kept her own name and became a "role model for a new life-style of career and marriage" (Showalter, 5).[35] A onetime suffragist, supporter of labor, and (shades of Lewis's title character Ann Vickers) prison administrator, she became managing editor of the *Nation* in 1922. It was a position that a fledgling Slesinger, writing book reviews for the *New York Post* (Biagi, 225), and Herbst, stagnating in an editorial position with a pulp magazine by the late 1920s, might well have envied.[36]

In *The Unpossessed* and *Rope of Gold,* the two novelists, married more or less in Kirchwey's emancipated manner but divorced by the mid-1930s, built on their own difficulties in finding any job, much less Freda Kirchwey's, commensurate with their abilities.[37] Their heroines, even more embroiled than their creators in the battle for vocation, bear out Herbst's contention that what set women free was not postsuffrage liberty but a good job ("Year," 73)—provided one could be found.

Recent interpreters, revising this Herbst-Slesinger credo, focus on the authors' political beliefs. According to their reading, protagonists Margaret Flinders and Victoria Chance are women in search of work that is politically meaningful, that is, associated with leftism, and yet consonant with their need for personal independence.[38] Echoing this interpretation, other commentators label Slesinger and Herbst contributors to a radical tradition of revolutionary fiction, casting the two women's on-the-job heroines as intellectuals rather than working professionals.[39]

For a time Slesinger was a satellite of the Jewish-leftist *Menorah Journal* circle, the product of her marriage in 1928 to Herbert Solow, the assistant editor. *The Unpossessed* provides an unforgiving satire on the sexism of that group, unleashing her anger at the obsessively talk-filled political discussions of her novel's roman à clef Bruno Leonard circle.[40] Unlike Herbst's, Slesinger's signature is as absent from the famous 1935 *New Masses* call for an American Writers' Congress to celebrate "the revolutionary spirit" as is her name from Daniel Aaron's *Writers on the Left* (1961).[41] And, again in contrast to Herbst, her fiction is omitted from Rideout's classic survey *The Radical Novel in the United States* (1956).[42] For a year or so following her divorce from Solow in 1933, while publishing fiction on women-filled white-collar work, she did sharpen her political commitment through support of the striking leftist Office Workers' Union. But if sporadically involved in political activity, she also "abandoned the intense dogmatic left-wing loyalty that characterized her former husband" when she quit the marriage (Biagi, 226). Rejecting the tunnel-vision intensity of his *Menorah Journal* and en route to a good Hollywood screenwriter's job, she used the *New Republic* not as an Agnes Smedley or a Tillie Olsen might but to vent her annoyance at what she described as the parochialism of the *Ladies' Home Journal* reader uninterested in the issues of the day ("Women," 126). Furthermore, evidencing in some *New Masses* pieces the political concern she found so absent in this bourgeois womanhood, Slesinger nevertheless cultivated her literary fortunes in the wide-circulation *Story, Scribner's, Vanity Fair,* and *Redbook,* middlebrow publishing venues that Mike Gold would hardly have approved.[43]

Herbst was a more committed leftist, though always skeptical of the party's manipulativeness and dogma.[44] A stalwart of gatherings such as the 1930 meeting of the International Union of Revolutionary Writers (in Kharkov!), she offered a journalistic variant on Dorothy Thompson's Hitler coverage by using her solid Communist ties to cover anti-Nazi activity in 1935 Germany.[45] In the mid-1930s she had produced many pieces that, in contrast to Slesinger's Mencken-like castigation of women's magazine readers, preached to quite different Americans, those already converted to radical truths. By the time of *Rope of Gold,* she had reported enthusiastically on a revolutionary soviet in Cuba, farmers' revolts near her Iowa hometown, and—along with her like-minded colleague Mary Heaton Vorse—auto strikes in "sit-down" city, Detroit (Garrison, 272, 280). To bolster her critique of the passive bourgeois families from which her fictive protagonists Victoria Wendel and Jonathan Chance rebel, she wove all of that reportage into her novel.

Yet, like Slesinger, Herbst paid serious attention to the rebellious daughters of the middle class seeking renewal through work, whether socially responsible or not. As both authors well knew, the representative professional woman of the 1930s scorned, avoided, or was simply oblivious to the Left. Although their fiction has not been seen as an assessment of this feminine type, it nevertheless integrates into its discussion of leftist-intellectual duty and comradely wifehood the quest for profession.[46] Slesinger's Margaret Flinders, with her marginally white-collar career, and Herbst's Victoria Chance, who hopes to break into byline journalism, feel underemployed, struggle to find a professional footing, and are as pulled by guilt at a spouse's inadequate work situation as by the call of politics—none of these peculiarly leftist plights. Moreover, the Slesinger-Herbst husband, no doubt like many real-life mates, on the Left or not, is an unequal opportunity employer, for his personal obsessions and ineffective politics render him demanding, brooding, and guilt-provoking.

Well before marriage, Slesinger and Herbst joined other vocation-seeking women and took lesser jobs in department store and lower-rung journalistic work. They were justice-minded mavericks. Yet they soon parted company with the unwed and materialistic single girl, en route to her new job of bourgeois wedlock, praised in the columns of the *Ladies' Home Journal*. Their novels' emphasis on vocation issued in large part from their disillusionment with their own late-1920s marriages, whose flaws they largely perceived as the end result of the "free love" era described in Slesinger's own cynically retrospective "Memoirs of an Ex-Flapper" (1934).

By the early years of the Depression, both women had replaced the 1920s companionate Bohemianism and its 1930s successor, dependable comradeship, with a desire for literary and journalistic territory. To universalize their protagonists, they transformed these characters into less talented, more average versions of themselves. In so doing, they combined a feminine critique of the male Left with a 1930s update of the New Woman novel. Their frustrated heroines, trapped in leftist wedlock and mainstream job quest alike, are victimized by both, emancipated by neither. Moreover, by these women's very inability to follow the path of Perkins-like self-sacrifice or Thompsonian self-advancement, they point out the strictures of each model.

The Unpossessed and Rope of Gold: Perils of Success

When Slesinger's marriage dissolved, with it went her wavering allegiance to the coterie she pinioned in her semiautobiographical *Unpossessed* as those who "play at making revolutions for a band of workers [they have] never seen" (331). Like her one novel, Slesinger's stories issued from a New York period before her transition to Hollywood scriptwriting. Two of her most famous tales deal with the lower rungs of white-collardom. "Jobs in the Sky" concerns salespeople in the genteel book and stationery department, many of them destined for layoffs after the Christmas rush; "The Mousetrap" with receptionists, stenographers, and other clerical staff in a strike-torn office.

To be sure, both stories imply that these women should, in the words of one labor historian, question the myth of the community of interest between themselves and management.[47] Slesinger's shrinking females vaguely realize that they serve at their employers' pleasure. They are thus, at least in the terms of proletarian fiction, poised for class awareness. Yet, resenting exploitation without any idea how to remedy it, they are a long way from class consciousness. Nor does Slesinger castigate them for this. Her more urgent concern is with the internalized shame of the woman who is dismissed from her job rather than the political importance of her shedding such psychic shackles. Slesinger's scrutiny of the Depression (and depressed) female psyche goes beyond the formulaic proletarian novel to examine the emotional costs of feminine compliance—not a theme popular with most leftist authors.

As in her shorter fiction, the woes of *The Unpossessed*'s protagonist as a white-collar girl—Margaret Flinders puts in long hours as a secretary to a demanding business manager—are far more psychological than class-based. Well-bred and married to a leftist intellectual who resents his similarly quasi-professional employment conditions, Margaret is dissatisfied with a boss "to whose hell she responded all day, in whose aura she lived all day" (10), a job that seems part of a larger unhappiness with her life prospects. In her day job, the ardently pro-capitalist Mr. Worthington squeezes out of her all the rote typing skills of which she is capable. By night her involvement with Miles Flinders, who alternately compels her sympathy for his uninteresting work and urges her to socialize with his useless radical clique, is a job just as draining.

The satire in *The Unpossessed,* with its self-absorbed radical husbands, some philanderers, others ineffectual brooders, and both treating wives or mistresses as mothers while they mouth sexual egalitarianism, could only have been produced by an insider. Well before the novel appeared, Slesinger had concluded that the radical sexual and economic doctrines supposed to liberate the feminine spirit oppressed women on the (leftist) marriage front. The cleverness with which she presented her argument provided her a wider success than that achieved by the orthodox male proletarian novel to which her argument so often applied. Books by male leftist authors created a flurry of partisan interest but then passed on, whereas her novel went through four printings and a British edition.[48]

Reviewers quickly picked up on her ability to satirize the "shopworn big talk, inverted feelings . . . that pass[ed], among the second-rate intelligentsia, for the state of being alive."[49] They skewered Miles Flinders, whose wife undergoes an abortion because, cloaking selfishness in ideology, he wills her to do it. And anticipating modern feminist views of the novel, period critics saw Miles's fiat against Margaret becoming a mother in a corrupted world as further evidence of the "empty rationalizing" that prevents her from finding maternal fulfillment.[50] Why, after all, wrote male reviewers, should Margaret deny "her birthright for a mess of masculine pottage"? (Matthews, 52).[51]

Neither period male nor modern female interpreters treat *The Unpossessed* as a commentary on the decline of the professional woman in the postfeminist 1930s. Yet Slesinger herself, far more defiant than any of her novel's quartet of women characters, used that quartet to shape the novel into such a commentary. These women, educated, skilled, and floundering, are clearly made miserable by a halfhearted obedience to their husbands' or lovers' creeds. Slesinger ridicules Margaret's belief that she would "gladly spend her life on her hands and knees plucking the stone up out of [her husband's] path" (42). Equally absurd and husband-coddling is naive Norah Blake. Like Margaret, Norah makes more money than her husband, a decent salary by factory women's standards, but gives it over to her philandering mate, Jeffrey, for whom she goes home after work and knits a sweater while he trysts with the muddleheaded and lovelorn "Comrade Ruthie." A vastly different character, the flapperish Elizabeth, is a talented artist who paints, without conviction, murals of workers for foolish cocktail parties given by wealthy, neurotic hostesses (to which she wears Poiret gowns), but she discounts her abilities and fragments her purpose in an "endless chain" of "drinks and unloved lovers" (128).

Margaret and Elizabeth are the novel's most compelling examples of women abandoning vocation lest it lead to mannishness, whether Perkins-like asexuality or, a more vivid fear, Thompsonian usurpation of the male role. Witness Margaret's rueful denunciation of egalitarian goals, as if she has reached them and found them insufficient. "We are sterile; we are too horribly girlish for our age, too mannish (with our cigarettes, our jobs, our drying lips) for our sex. . . . O Economic-Independence Votes-for-Women Sex-Equality! You've [given us] a cigarette; a pencil in our hair" (93). This world-weariness, echoing the worn-out Elizabeth's, invokes a disillusionment with New Womanly hopes for fulfillment that neither woman has a right to proclaim. For both wrongly locate their failed relationships with unstable men in their own postcollegiate vocationalism. Indeed, Margaret's conviction that she has sold her womanliness for business work is paralleled by Elizabeth's, who abdicates her art and emancipation through work to "live . . . in a frame of men's reactions" (310) in a latter-day flapperism with her lover of the moment.

If the novel's message to Elizabeth is to abandon the frenetic sensuality that is a nonmaternal dead end, the novel's message to the child-craving Margaret is to refashion herself as well. Margaret's vision, though, is even fuzzier than Elizabeth's, a lack of clarity enhanced by her fixation on pregnancy and her acceptance of the novel's masculine trumpeters of women as literal or figurative nurturers. Convinced that despite overwork by Mr. Worthington, she has nothing in common with the working class, she has no use for the Office Workers' Union. Nor is she attracted to the kind of Business and Professional Women's Club that in upward mobility novels of the 1920s such as Ruth Suckow's *Cora* help the title character gain poise and plan a promotion strategy. Allied to neither clerical workers nor upwardly mobile executive secretaries, she engages in breast-beating for going out to work at all. Because her preoccupation with motherhood is her "solution" to the problem of balancing marriage and career, she entraps herself; she simply cannot see that the terms of the argument are not marriage versus career so much as how she has allowed herself to be devalued in both.

In her shorter pieces, Slesinger parceled out conflicting ideas in pairs of white-collar characters, as in "Jobs in the Sky" and "The Mousetrap," so that if one woman bends to a store or office manager's whims, the other is defiant. In her novel, Slesinger uses a similar device. Margaret and Elizabeth variously represent the feminine impulse to comfort and the pain of a talent wasted, the fear of wounding the male ego and the rebellion against commitment. By overhauling familiar categories within the proletarian novel to cast Margaret as mother and Elizabeth as sexual rebel, the novel splits those who, like Margaret, "would . . . purge [her man] with her comfort" (12) and the sexually defiant type with a more subversive vision of men. Margaret is aware that her husband, almost like Perkins's behind-the-scenes invalid spouse, is compelling her to cloak her ambitions, to cast everything she does as for the good of others. Nevertheless, it is Elizabeth who proclaims the insights Margaret dares not entertain—that in a time of masculine job insecurity, the woman is often the strong one. "Somebody's got to have the guts" (287), she remarks. Savoring her skills as an artist, Elizabeth moves toward a model of feminine achievement. But the Thompson model is no sooner invoked then she retreats before her own astonishing candor about "weak men" (284) to brood about an elusive lover and become in her own eyes a woman again.

If, in a familiar feminine trajectory, Margaret has more guilt and less boldness than Elizabeth, it is Elizabeth who might have taught Margaret and convinced herself to remain bold. But, satirical rather than documentary, the novel never unifies these perceptions in the person of the working professional. Shirley Biagi has called *The Unpossessed* Slesinger's act of separation from her earlier life (229). After it, she was free to carve a popular rather than a politically correct career, to update the New Woman without requiring her to be a Communist. Of course, the dilemmas imprisoning Margaret and Elizabeth were more culturally representative than Slesinger's own self-liberating career choices. If, in the world of her novel, no woman successfully takes the cultural lead provided by a Perkins or a Thompson, it is because neither model resolves the contradiction between emotional attachment and workplace (or political) commitment. As we shall see, such contradictions bedevil Herbst and her heroines as well, though in a different way.

In *Rope of Gold,* as Herbst's Victoria Chance moves from a leftist wife-appendage to become her own person, she comes closer to winning, though at great marital cost, the sexual-political power struggle that Margaret Flinders, weakly consenting to an abortion and a lackluster job, clearly loses. By novel's end, Victoria has penned or gathered data for articles on farmers' movements in the drought-afflicted Midwest and, in a Cuba gripped in 1935 by a general strike, ferreted out interviews with important protest leaders. If she has "achieved a new relationship to her work" (Rabinowitz, *Labor,* 162), it is one in which political and personal goals coalesce. Although a male colleague's machinations prevent her from receiving the byline that Herbst had won for "Realengo 18" (her 1935 *New Masses* reports on Cuba's revolutionary collective, defending its land against Fulgencio Batista and the sugar companies), Victoria realizes that her ability to report on proletarian politics may well point to a future both morally defensible and professionally fulfilling.[52] When last viewed, though crushed by her erring husband's affair with another woman, she makes a vow to all strikers—"I won't forget them"—and, perhaps more important, to herself. "I have myself. . . . No one can take that from me" (406).

With these pledges, Herbst's budding labor journalist becomes the first woman among the rough-hewn Chances and stuffy Wendels to depart from male-centeredness. She separates from the sporadically pioneer-strong but always self-subordinating female generations watching from offstage as the Chance and Wendel men go off to war, found businesses, or, in Depression times, fail in them.[53] Raised to accept, as did her mother, that "men often enough thought that they alone were human, that little girls were quiet eggs waiting for the great moment" (46), Victoria is also formed by the ambitions of a mother who, from economic need, quit college and became a seamstress, determined that her college-educated daughter put to use the training she herself never completed. But as the novel opens, nothing of Victoria's premarital past as a white-collar worker and supporter of radical causes—touched on in Herbst's earlier novel, *Pity Is Not Enough* (1933)—is mentioned, as if in marrying she had erased her own history. Instead, her mother's contradictory messages inform Victoria's self-conception. She has gone on forays as a journalist and written articles on the plight of hard-hit farmers. But she still presents herself as someone whose job is to be an adjunct to her husband, Jonathan. She begins her hegira toward personhood only when she expresses gratitude to Jonathan for allowing her to "share his joy" (171) when he cements his ideological commitment as an organizer for the party. Such questionable gratitude further propels her to a Slesinger heroine's confusion of husband with child, made only more intense by a miscarriage so that, in the familiar maternal rhetoric of the era's social protest novel, Victoria sees her husband "as if he were a little boy and she must protect him" (199).

Unlike Margaret, however, whose unwanted abortion results in an angrily passive resentment, Victoria, responding to her miscarriage, musters a resolve to erase her pain. She even stills her new fear of losing her child-husband to a party-fed political involvement that, all too often, signaled that he was "the only needed one" (88) of the pair. Meaningful work, not marital dependency, she concludes, can bolster her sense of self, much as it does his.

Pragmatic where Margaret is not, Victoria faces facts, redirects her energies, moves to the city, and goes out to professional work. Ironically, the decision quickly prompts her rueful observation that, for all his dedication to proletarian economic freedom, Jonathan "seemed never to have got anything for himself" (161). Soon her research job in New York and after-hours language lessons prepare the way for an economic future. And the novel implicitly applauds her plans in the story of a secondary character, the rural wife Stella Regan, who gives up her dreams of entering the business world to marry a hard-luck widower with children, only to merge her identity in wanting what he wanted.

Yet, as in *The Unpossessed,* vocation threatens to bring on the fate of the Perkins-like spinster, trading family for selfless—and loveless—emancipation. Too late, Victoria realizes that her husband likes "women who yield" (332) and has even taken up with one named Leslie Day to suggest her timeliness in his life. Victoria's own efforts to find and keep urban work have outdistanced Jonathan's minimal organizing successes among near-bankrupt Pennsylvania farmers. The marriage over, she perceives its decline as her fault and is last glimpsed both remorseful and en route to a true career.

Herbst had rehearsed this emotionally Pyrrhic job victory before in her autobiographical short story "The Enemy," published in 1936 in the *Partisan Review.* In it her title character, another journalist on assignment, reflects sadly that "she had made her own way and making her own way had taken her" from her husband, a conviction the story neither refutes nor defends.[54] So, too, in *Rope of Gold.* Whether Victoria's sorrows are self-made or thrust upon her, well rid of Jonathan or a victim of his hostility to female professionalism, is no clearer than her next career step. At novel's end, the firing of Lester Tolman, the emotional bully (and one in search of "some nice motherly woman" [307]) with whom she had covered the Cuba strike, suggests only contradictory possibilities. Because it was Tolman who had, in between his rejected sexual advances, manipulated her into giving him the byline, his abbreviated career could imply a kind of feminist justice. But because his left-leaning politics displeased his *New York Post* employers enough to dismiss him, his fate could foretell a similarly bleak job future for her.

In any case, Victoria's unfinished story is one of the novel's many inconclusive, interlocking stories. There is the subplot of her sister Nancy Radford, a tradition-minded wife and mother sans professional skills who vows to go down with the sinking bourgeois ship of her jobless husband. Another concerns Steve Carson, a rural radical who finds his bildungsroman way to the 1937 Detroit sit-down strike, leaving his pregnant wife home struggling on the farm. As with Victoria, the truncated quality of these other lives underscores the novel's message that ambition is dwarfed—and families fragmented—by crucial historical events at home and abroad. Various sections of the novel forecast the rise of repression in Germany, Italy, and Spain. Others consider the uncertainty of labor victory. Yet in a counterversion of the proletarian novel, a category whose rigidity would always irritate Herbst, the final segment, located in medias res as Carson scales a wall to join the auto industry strikers, is as ambiguous about collective success as earlier sections are about individual triumph.

Rabinowitz remarks that Victoria drops out of the narrative just at the point when, liberated from an alternately cloying and rejecting mate, strikes swirling about her, she is about to "enter history" (162). But given the adroitness with which Herbst's protagonist manages to fuse her workplace and political worlds, an alternate interpretation is that, in the landscape of strife and political uncertainty inhabited by her heroine, Herbst can find no place for Victoria's success at combining ambition and social conscience. However much Herbst rejected period critics' complaints that she had not written an orthodox social protest novel, presumably because the female intellectual Victoria Chance is a more important character than the male working stiff Steve Carson, the novel ultimately could neither applaud nor integrate feminine professionalism.[55] Herbst herself may have longed, as Walter Rideout claims, for the classless society that made irrelevant the very middle class whose disintegration she chronicled ("Forgotten," 35). But there was another Herbst as well, one who knew that her artistic responsibility to define, and her personal one to live out, feminine independence took precedence over self-effacing party wifedom or the wider culture's version of such feminine subordination. Herbst moved toward creating in her alter ego Victoria Chance a realistic career woman for the 1930s, neither a Valkyrie-like Thompson nor a self-abnegating Perkins. The irony was that, having carved out an alternative New Woman, vocationally dedicated yet physically passionate, individually ambitious yet politically committed, willing to balance the search for work with the struggle for marital approval, Herbst had no novel in which to place her.

Ambivalent about their heroines' movement toward professionalism, the few leftist literary discussions of New Womanhood foundered when they could not resolve contradictions between the political and the personal. Yet there were other period authors, worlds away from and scornful of proletarians and leftists—remarks a Lewis mouthpiece in *It Can't Happen Here* (1935), "I'm tired of apologizing for not having a dirty neck!" —who did produce fables of feminine vocational triumph.[56] Their determined title characters are women who bypass soul-searching social consciousness, much to the applause of a middlebrow audience avid for any success story in a dispiriting time—provided, as the best-selling formula decreed, that feminine ambition did not ensure marital fulfillment. Tenacious in their job-created prosperity, Christopher Morley's Kitty Foyle and Sinclair Lewis's Ann Vickers were vastly popular with the same audiences that, a decade before (when Morley began his novel and Lewis was about to court the inspiration for his, Dorothy Thompson), looked to a Ruth Suckow or an Edna Ferber to delineate the financial and emotional pleasures bought with a businesswoman's salary. And though the Morley and Lewis heroines' rapid nine-to-five ascension and busy emotional life (unimpeded by a self-involved husband) offer as much fantasy as inspiration, Kitty Foyle and Ann Vickers do symbolize women's entry into two of the rare growth fields for 1930s women: cosmetics and social work. Disparate as are the two professions and the fictional women who enter them, they represent the balance of self-propelling ambition and altruistic empathy that Slesinger or Herbst had not enacted. Yet, given the persistent national animus toward female jobholders, particularly well-paid ones, would this New Woman's mainstream imaginers resolve the problems plaguing her more political sisters? And, if so, would the label "unfeminine" still be her reward for achievement?

Sexy Professionals

It was in 1939 that Herbstian womanhood, fleeing middle-class stagnation through a reportorial allegiance to the proletariat, helped earn *Rope of Gold* plentiful, if mixed, reviews, but sales of only a few thousand copies. In the same year, Christopher Darlington Morley, Rhodes scholar and former editor of the *Ladies' Home Journal,* was in the exact middle of a fortunate career grounded in the belief that the bourgeoisie, far from declining, was alive and well and buying what he wrote.[57] When his *Kitty Foyle* (1941) appeared, Morley had been successfully courting middle-class, middlebrow readers for some time, through his reign as a Book-of-the-Month Club judge (a Sinclair Lewis work made the list the year after Morley began, but not one proletarian novel made the list in the 1930s), his longtime column for the *Saturday Review of Literature,* and his authorship of numerous works featuring bookish males like himself.[58]

Kitty Foyle proved a racier bid for this audience. Because of the heroine's office romance with the mainline Philadelphian Wyn Strafford and her subsequent, if valiant, abortion—Wyn, whose reputation would suffer, "must never know"—it was banned in Italy and Ireland (Wallach and Bracher, 67).[59] Perhaps for the same reason, it enjoyed top-ten sales in the United States. Its sexual content apart, it was Morley's literary compromise with the hard facts of the Great Depression. In a form of novelistic noblesse oblige, he departed from his "country-gentleman" (Rubin, 135) fascination with belles lettres to tell what one disapproving critic referred to en passant as a "story of a girl of the lower middle class."[60] For more enthusiastic reviewers, Kitty's private life was of less concern than her workplace representativeness. She was less the errant female than the struggling white-collar girl who by then was one of every three New York City working women: "You've seen Kitty Foyle on a Fifth Avenue bus, you've seen her behind a counter, you've seen her taking dictation, you've seen her giving dictation, you've seen her in cafeterias at noon."[61] In his own publicity campaign for the novel, Morley further downplayed Kitty's extramarital sexuality. He immodestly compared his book to *The Grapes of Wrath,* which had appeared the same year. He even claimed to give "a voice" to "mutes," those overworked white-collar girls who were "sharecroppers in the Dust Bowl of business" (qtd. Wallach and Bracher, 69).

Despite his fantasy, that is not the story Morley tells. The novel hardly reduces Kitty to a daughter of the people. Working in a well-paid position at the Philadelphia magazine where she begins the affair with Strafford, she is proud to be the only one who does not join a union. In a time when the out-of-work "business girl" was writing pleading letters to Perkins and FDR, Morley nevertheless views Kitty's decision as pragmatic.[62] For her tenure in low-level sales and clerical work is so brief that, as she remarks with complacency, "I never had to take the Depression seriously" because "the . . . line [I was selling] was moving so fast. Matter of fact bad times make good sales talk" (307).

If Morley's Dust Bowl remark was an allusion to Kitty's pre-1929 job trials, even there, despite a vernacular style, a no-frills candor, and a girlhood in a neighborhood near "freight trains and coal yards and factories and the smell of tanneries" (16), the only obstacle in Kitty's path to New Womanhood is a busted love affair. Like her father, a management-devoted night watchman and onetime groundskeeper for the rich, Kitty prizes individualism over strikes, property over solidarity. Actuated by a lively self-interest, when her father's illness and subsequent death cut short her college career, she enrolls in a business school, does a stint in sales, and, by 1930, has worked for two years at a fair salary. Enmeshed in a cross-class romance with the vacillating Strafford, on the rebound she changes jobs, cities, and careers, happening onto the cosmetics trade.

Mary Ryan has included the 1930s in the "Cosmetic Age" (299); Kitty's choice of career is a shrewd one. The elegant Fifth Avenue salon of Helena Rubinstein, dubbed by *Life* magazine "the world's most successful businesswoman,"[63] opened in the depths of the Depression to do on a grander scale what Kitty, apt at the makeup trade herself, vernacularly summed up as "making dames look like they don't really" (272). As Rubinstein and Morley's heroine well knew, 1930s women who succeeded in business were more likely to do so in the upper reaches of the cosmetics trade than in most other areas because, despite small overall increases in the number of women managers, prejudice and discrimination continued to hold back most aspiring female executives in other industries (Ware, *Holding,* 75–76). At the height of the Depression, Kitty's yearly salary of $3,000, two to three times the earnings of the majority of high school teachers (Lewis's Ann Vickers would make an even more impressive $5,000), was not impossible in an era when *Fortune* found the office workers it profiled routinely spending a sizable portion of their salary on cosmetics ("Women," passim). By 1941, three-quarters of all American women were using them ("Rubinstein," 642). Throughout the decade, American housewives were bombarded with makeup advertisements, and even the *Daily Worker* outgrowth, *Working Woman,* had a section on beauty tips. Never out of work after her ascension to the cosmetics world, Kitty breathes life into the encouraging statistic that a 1930s woman earning what she did had only a one in ten chance of unemployment (Ware, *Holding,* 71).

Far from limning a white-collar Okie, through his eponymous heroine Morley appeared to center his story on attacking the era's prejudices against businesswomen on the rise. Her affair with her blueblood boss, whose interest in her prompts a guilty but insincere marriage offer, marks Kitty in the same way as her seductive blue-collar counterparts examined in chapter 2. In the words of the *Fortune* magazine pundits, this bad seed of white-collardom had rejected the suitable if time-limited premarital role of office wife or its longer-lived variant, the nun of business, for "passion-in-industry" (55). Succumbing to intimacy in a workplace where, as the art historian Ellen Todd has phrased it, she knows that, despite her efficient air, she is on "visual display for men" (182), Kitty was an amalgamation of the lusty, inviting secretaries and salesgirls of Reginald Marsh's paintings and the confident, poised ones of Isabel Bishop. Dorothy Thompson, commenting on what she, too, saw as the prevalence of office romances, might have explained Kitty's office style and subsequent romance as ways of "making some sense" to herself of monotonous work ("America," 60). Yet Kitty's very sexual availability calls up the stereotyped Gal Friday, who had been the subject of misogynistic diatribes about the "sorceress at her machine, tapping the celluloid keys" since the early 1900s.[64] By refusing her lover's halfhearted marriage bid she departs from the type whose eyes are fixed on an economic mobility won by sexual allure, not secretarial acumen. But as the woman who turns the sexless office wife into the office mistress, Kitty clearly rejects as well that ultra-efficient, Perkinsian Miss Orr praised by *Fortune* magazine. In Morley's imagining, Kitty could move on and up because she was neither fixated on altruism nor locked into a role as a Hester Prynne of the 1930s. She is certainly an advance on an earlier character who is a bit of both, the long-suffering Minnie Hutzler (hustler?) in Morley's 1932 novel *Human Being*. Kept in the shadows by her married employer, Minnie melds a backstreet sexual role with her devoted and somewhat underpaid usefulness as his executive secretary. In Morley's revision of this fallen woman plot, Kitty, unlike the aging Minnie, faces facts and stops battling her vacillating lover's snobbery about wedding her. She procures an abortion with dispatch (though not without sorrow) and proceeds to create a new job life. Soon she parlays a shrewd head for style and fashion trends into a series of ascensions. Though burdened by regret, she moves toward a more triumphant if less introspective self-definition than that discovered by period heroines seeking political truth but constricted by the ideology of the reliable comrade.

There is, nevertheless, an unintended consequence of Kitty's rejection of the sexy mistress and Perkinsian secretary alike for the Thompsonian model of career promise, and it gives the lie to Morley's claim of sympathy for feminine job seekers. After hours, Kitty Foyle borders dangerously on the torch-carrier. Constant references to her great passion legitimize the affair, which drags out until Wyn's proper marriage to a socialite. (Even Thompson herself sounded obsessively sorrowful when her marriage to a rejecting Lewis was dissolving [Sheean, 298–301]). But rather than call up the fleetingly Thompsonian or the enduringly Hurstian love slave, Morley treads the path of his Progressive Era predecessor David Graham Phillips. Another patrician claiming to speak for feminine independence, Phillips created a series of quasi–New Woman novels in which assertive and sexually emancipated careerists anticipate Kitty Foyle. They are certainly compelling romantic alternatives to the effete society wives "kept" by their capitalist husbands or even, as in Phillips's *A Woman Ventures*, keeping their own husbands in the background while ascending their career ladders. Although these women symbolize new cultural alternatives to what Phillips argued was female parasitism in marriage and socialized ineptitude at the workplace, by novel's end, like the feisty Kitty, all are settled with or still looking for the man to master them. Kitty, who finishes up nicely in the clothing trade, most resembles Phillips's dress-shop entrepreneur Juliet Raeburn in *Old Wives for New* (1908), who alternately proclaims womanly ambition and longs for the commanding male who will rescue her from it.

As with Phillips's characters, Morley's sexy professional woman, though financially successful, restricts herself to the more feminized business fields and is never a threat to capitalist male dominance. But there is an important difference between the two authors. Phillips's Juliet Raeburn, who finally exchanges business for the business of affluent marriage, comes from the genteelly impoverished middle class. However alluring and independent an aspirant to gentility Kitty may be, her lover Wyn and her creator slot her as the kind of lower-middle-class woman who makes the perfect mistress. With her vernacular style, pragmatic intelligence, fine body, and job of her own, and posing no danger of scandal, she is Hurst's Ray Schmidt with emotional stability. Even in the novel's deus ex machina finale (meant to shore up Kitty's reputation for her bourgeois readership), as she contemplates marriage to a Jew whose religion she (and Morley) finds an embarrassment, he suggests that she is tainted by her class origins. How else to understand his pronouncement in a letter to a friend that she is "an agreeable bitch" (qtd. Wallach and Bracher, 69–70)?

In *Kitty Foyle*'s ahistorical neverland, the Depression intrudes as an abstraction that none of the novel's characters need experience. The New Woman seeks a profession by default because she cannot meet the requirements of the class-bound society personified by her blueblood lover. If to an extent Morley questions the masculine literary proletarians' ever-promiscuous wage earner, Kitty's depiction nonetheless embodies the era's contradictory inclinations to empower and degrade professional womanhood. As in Slesinger and Herbst, the opposition between sexual and emotional intimacy and vocational self-development remains; feminine independence is still contingent. Again, the Thompson model proves too assertive and the Perkins one too selflessly asexual.

Slesinger and Herbst chose not to endow their heroines with their own professional advancement; Morley built up, then dismissed, the New

Woman by tarring her with the brush of past promiscuity. In contrast, Sinclair Lewis's focus is the great woman who makes no apologies for her competence, a character who provoked his most ambivalent praise.

Great Womanhood: Ann Vickers

Paying homage of sorts to Frances Perkins and his wife, Dorothy Thompson, two models he acknowledged in a letter to Thompson herself (Kurth, 212), Lewis anchors feminine professionalism in *Ann Vickers* (1933) in a fusion of the two women's public lives. His title character pursues public service with a driving ambition realized through claiming the male terrain of prison reform. A sociologist and the warden of a "model" house of correction, she has a better mind (and career) than her first and second lovers and, in between these romances, her ineffective husband. In all ways she transcends the thwarted Carol Kennicott of *Main Street* (1920) and even the modestly successful entrepreneur Una Golden of *The Job* (1917), who succumbs to unimaginativeness and marries her boss.

Though a disappointment to H. L. Mencken and Malcolm Cowley at the *New Republic, Ann Vickers* garnered critical approval both at home and abroad, was a best-seller for two years, and appeared simultaneously in thirteen languages.[65] Some critics, apparently convinced the book was a celebration of Ann, euphemized her steamy love life as part and parcel of the new "emancipated" womanhood. Others, finding the old satirical Lewis at work again, noted the wide array of subjects he tackles so satirically: women's suffrage, Communist zeal, Babbittry and boosterism, Greenwich Village–style free love.[66] Whatever the critics' reading—and both sides were partly correct—like Morley, the author had obviously achieved a succès de scandale with the sexual content of the novel. Ann, too, has an abortion, but, doing Kitty one better, she also has a social life, including Village bisexuals, a number of extramarital affairs, and a child out of wedlock with a married lover. If the novel's sensational content helped pull in a wide audience, it also played to the public's interest in famous women, both in the New Deal and in the famous author's own marital life.[67] To underscore the timeliness of the Vickers character, Lewis limns a chorus of newly empowered—and mannish—career women who are Ann's personal and professional acquaintances: doctors, real estate brokers, chemists, labor organizers. All of them help define a new world of feminine achievement. Because Lewis sold more than one hundred thousand copies to Herbst's and Slesinger's few thousand each, it may be too much to argue that Ann and her circle, preaching survivalist strong-mindedness without guilt, provide a more marketable plot than the breast-beating of leftist New Womanhood. But Lewis was certainly anchoring Ann in an individualist philosophy that appealed to audiences suspicious of what one recent critic has called the political writer's penchant for the authoritarian novel, a form that at least loosely includes the Slesingers and Herbsts.[68]

Ann Vickers was the period's most detailed chronicle of a brilliant career. Ann's bedroom vicissitudes have little effect on her public life. If anything, the more unorthodox her love life—at one point she returns to live with her estranged husband, illegitimate child in hand, while her lover is in prison—the more rapid her rise in her profession. To limn that professional history, Lewis draws on the prejournalistic phase of Thompson's career and, more extensively, on Perkins's early professional years. A youthful college graduate, Ann works enthusiastically for suffrage, as Thompson did from 1914 to 1917. Just as Thompson took a publicity job with a New York State women's suffrage association (Boyer, 683), Ann becomes a mainstay of the New York headquarters, later moving to Ohio for a stint at "incessant" suffrage rallies (*Ann*, 115). Like Perkins (Bernstein, 12), she takes a graduate degree in sociology from Columbia University and is an intimate of those who run a settlement house—for Perkins, Greenwich House (Wandersee, "I'd Rather," 9), for Ann, the Corlears Hook Settlement in Lower New York. By 1916 Ann is part of a committee investigating conditions in the garment and textile trades (Lewis, *Ann,* 156); five years before, Perkins had reported on the aftermath of the 1911 Triangle Factory fire, and, one year after the imaginary Ann, she worked on the New York State Factory Safety Commission.

Ann's career resembles Perkins's far more than Thompson's. Her arena is vocational training in women's reformatories, not Thompsonian scoops on the rise of Hitler, even though, after an undercover stint as a prison matron, Ann publishes a quasi-journalistic study of brutal jail conditions in the South. A Perkins-like public professional, Ann is exposed to self-absorbed millionaire women philanthropists, for whom she works as an aide; manipulative slum-born women prisoners, whom she deals with in reformatories; and political infighters among her jealous subordinates, who try, unsuccessfully, to steal her job as director of the Stuyvesant Industrial Home for Women. But there were more than factual reasons to draw, and then embroider, on the life of Perkins, the "professional social worker" (*Ann,* 535), whom Thompson herself ceased to be well before the American entry into World War I. Lewis gave proof that Perkins's non-threatening careerism represented all that Thompson could not achieve. He subtly taunted his wife for her anti-Perkins persona in a *Pictorial Review* article on career women that appeared, with her companion piece, a few years before *Ann Vickers.* He made the point that Perkins, an "extremely good wife and mother"—more so than the globe-trotting Mrs. Lewis— proved that some women pursued careers without a "loss of femininity" ("America," 54).

By 1933 Lewis's hostility to his wife's "greater notoriety and distressing independence" (*Ann,* 441) was evident in more than polite magazine pieces. In *It Can't Happen Here* (1935), written shortly after *Ann Vickers,* Barbara Melosh charted a plot encoding masculine anxiety about "men rendered ineffectual by women."[69] Lewis gave abundant proof in his personal correspondence that he feared Thompson was outdistancing him. He puts into the mouth of Ann's unimpressive husband his own crack to his spouse, "Being married to you is like sleeping with the Taxation Problem!" (440). And he peppers the novel with thinly veiled anecdotes of the marital tensions that continued to simmer the year he published the novel. He even ascribes to Ann what one Thompson biographer called the "now-you-see-me, now-you-don't" philosophy of wedlock (Kurth, 165), the equivalent in her public life being a boldly unapologetic assertiveness in decision making. Despite her social service affiliation, Ann's style is confrontational, not conciliatory; she is a reformer, but with her eyes always on the main chance. In a kind of neurotic dialogue, the novel marvels at what Lewis defines as Ann's New Womanly feminism, though there is not much evidence of it once she takes on prison reform.

In any case, Lewis keeps up a constant stream of praise for Ann's roster of accomplishments, incorporating his own suspiciously unctuous public manner toward his wife. He takes his revenge in familiar jibes about his heroine's sexuality. In fact, his ambivalent attitude toward the woman of exceptional ability results in a protagonist endlessly in search of a sexual philosophy. At various points in the novel, she vows lifelong chastity, flirts with lesbianism, is frigid, near-promiscuous, wifely, or poised for marital, then extramarital, maternity. Her ultimate "solution," proclaiming that a "working woman has a right to her child and her lover" (469), suggests not Lewis's philosophical approbation but his inability to come to a consistent position on the female professional.

By novel's end, Lewis finds a refuge from such ambiguity in the castration metaphor. The more Ann triumphs, the more she undermines the men around her. In the novel's improbable last scene, she installs her once-virile lover, a former judge who has been in prison for corruption, in the proverbial cottage longed for as a wedding gift for the June bride. But no man's salary provided this nest; Ann's once-powerful judge is financially and spiritually bankrupt, and it is her money that has purchased the property. The breadwinner and dominance roles he once played are now reversed. In a telling picture of Lewis's greatest fears, the male tends the love child, cooks, and offers to check the statistics for Dr. Vickers's recent article in the *Journal of Economics* (562).

However much this nightmare of lost male control resonated for men in the period, the fantasy propelling most of the narrative has nothing to do with the rise of New Deal Era womanhood. What in another novelist's hands might have been a final comment on jobless men and job-stealing women in Lewis is quite other. Throughout the novel, as in Morley, there is no true admission of the Depression's negative effects on work. *Ann Vickers* occasionally sops up the fads and phrases of the 1930s but little else. Lewis even sounds like a parody of Herbert Hoover when he refers approvingly in passing to "a new, taut, lean spirit creeping into the swollen land" (497). And his great woman, though an enlightened penologist, a prison superintendent, and someone with a decided bias against business, is absolutely pro-capital and completely bored by discussions of economics and politics. Furthermore, she has a horror of "radicals" and sees no relationship between prison reform and labor conditions.

Women's prison reform had peaked as a field just at the time Ann supposedly makes her greatest success in it. The gains she is able to produce occurred ten years before, during a time when the reformatory movement achieved the goal of removing women prisoners from male environments and control.[70] Rather than research the job stagnation of the 1930s, Lewis had dipped into the usable past, using a New Woman social service story like Elia Peattie's *The Precipice* (1914). In it, the pre-Perkinsian heroine, modeled on the Child Welfare Bureau's Julia Lathrop, achieves increasing status in the social welfare world while more or less dictating her own marital and romantic agenda.

By writing himself and Thompson into the novel, Lewis attempted to throw off the insecurities about feminine achievement for which not even his status as the first American to win the Nobel Prize consoled him. His twofold reincarnation in the novel is as Ann's husband, the Babbitt-like bumbler, and her lover, the has-been. Thompson fares little better: as Ann, she is a woman whose vocation diminishes husband, lover, and, by implication, all men. The autobiographical tensions in *Ann Vickers* thus point to the larger problems of the era's professional women: the constant need for a defensive posture and a disillusionment with the work/love balancing act and, in some cases, with heterosexual love itself. Part of the savagery of Lewis's attack on female careerism is evident in his creation of a protagonist who never apologizes for the emotional damage she supposedly causes. But in real life, Dorothy Thompson seemed truly divided by her contradictory roles and greatly upset by Lewis's rage at her inability to reconcile them. Although she inspired his portrait of the great woman, she never overcame his resentment that she was Dorothy Thompson, not Frances Perkins.

Final Solutions: Scarlett O'Hara and Profession

Three years after Lewis's commercially popular novel might have taught Slesinger and Herbst that, packaged satirically and spicily enough, the feminine vocation plot could snare a large readership, another writer cleverly harnessed an even more lucrative form. It was the *Anthony Adverse* (1933) type of escape novel, not a male fantasy of the Napoleonic Era but a fable of feminine monetary survival in the South during and just after Reconstruction. Taken less seriously by critics but more widely read than *Ann Vickers*, Margaret Mitchell's *Gone with the Wind* (1936) was the lengthy product of a sometime Smith College student and conflicted southern belle who had tried to break into the male newsrooms of Atlanta.[71] But her journalist's life was largely lived on the *Atlanta Journal*'s Woman's Page and Sunday edition and she found few among that city's well-off women to approve woman's economic independence, marital or otherwise. Her early story "Matrimonial Bonds" (1926), in part a reaction against a husband and culture dictating completely separate gender roles for women and men, advocated educated women's "labor, independence, and integrity" (Pyron, "Southern," 212) and echoed many of the veiled New Womanly romances she penned while writing *GWTW*. But it was only when she offered a woman who, having taken on the masculine role while the men are on the battlefront, prefers to retain that role upon their return, that she both expressed the longings for liberation from southern constraint and censored those longings by punishing her own brainchild, Scarlett O'Hara.

Mitchell had preceded her sister journalists Josephine Herbst and Herbst's fictive Mrs. Sidney to Havana, visiting it in the mid-1920s. She journeyed there not in the name of leftist reportage but of rejection of Atlanta's elitist stuffiness—only to flee home with the ironic complaint that Cuban men had no chivalry (Pyron, "Southern," 196). From then on, Mitchell was consumed by the reverent reconstruction of the very chivalric code that constrained her own life as a newswoman and against which her Scarlett would rebel. Despite her Atlanta salon and reputation as a literary hostess, the semi-invalid Mitchell was in reality a latter-day version of Victorian "sensation novelists" like M. E. Braddon and Mrs. Henry Wood, who liberated their amoral heroines because they could not defy society themselves.[72]

Mitchell, never emancipated on racial or class matters, saw in the success of her book the fruits of a decade devoted to an ode to Georgia during the Civil War and Reconstruction. The public, less nostalgic over the plantation culture than fascinated by a good yarn, bought over one million copies in the first six months of 1936. *GWTW* even garnered the Pulitzer Prize the next year.[73] During this time, Mitchell claimed dismay at the parallel acclaim for its centerpiece, a creature of pure will, Scarlett O'Hara, a plantation belle forced to take care of an extended family impoverished by Yankee depredations. In a period of what historian Alice Kessler-Harris terms one of "unprecedented discussion of who was and was not entitled to work" ("Gender," 38), *Gone with the Wind,* despite its author's claim that the sweet-voiced child-woman Melanie Wilkes was a paragon, heroinized Scarlett as a woman who prospers financially and psychically from the dislocations in separate sphere ideology created by the Civil War and its aftermath.

While the Scarlett of the first half of the novel, as Marion J. Morton remarks, meets the 1930s litmus test for working wives in that there is no one else to rally her family when the men are off at war, by the second half she has traded survival for ambition.[74] The novel reasserted both the grudging period acceptance of woman thrust into the "provider role" ("Gender," 40) and its boundless disapproval of married women working, much less running their own businesses. Condemning the ruthless Scarlett for the very qualities that initially enable her to save her family's lives, it in reality offered nothing less than an allegory of 1930s professionalism in an economically war-torn landscape. Under its fancy-dress cover, it was the most influential attempt of the period to meld old and new womanhood.

As is well known, the novel is not only rich in details reflecting the mind of the wartime and postbellum South but provides a male alter ego for Scarlett in the hard-driving and mercurial Rhett Butler, who pursues and later marries her. But the heart of the tale is Scarlett herself, for the bulk of the narrative a woman surrounded by febrile and failing men. Her flirtatious girlhood—Mitchell began writing the novel in the flapperish 1920s—ill prepares her for the South's first great depression, the War Between the States. Early in the novel, she earns her self-reliance spurs by inventive if subsistence-level farming of the impoverished family plantation. Like many of her Depression counterparts, she soon finds that men are either absent, ineffective, or invalids, all needing a feminine lead, an experience that both embitters and strengthens her. As a war widow, she is shrewd enough to realize that despite hard-won agricultural skills, she must find a new marital identity—the wife helping in the husband's business—if she is to undertake the managerial role she craves. When she weds her sister's aging, malleable beau, who establishes a lumber business in Atlanta, she finally has a manlike opportunity for self-assertion. She experiments with new marketing techniques, perfects her advertising, and teaches herself the profit skills that her Klansman husband, off pursuing vengeance, does not possess. Exploiting a postbellum version of the 1930s breadline, convict labor, she thrusts herself into the "grasping opportunism" that was off-limits to women but that legitimized men like Rhett Butler in Atlanta society after the war.[75]

Scarlett refuses to be shamed so Mitchell does it for her. Indeed, Mitchell seems not to have understood the gender ironies in her own book. She consistently brands Scarlett amoral, punishing her with community scorn, personal turmoil, an unrequited love, and, ultimately, a destructive marriage to Butler in which she trades managerial control for a wealthy Atlanta lifestyle. Like Lewis, Mitchell was, not accidentally, an opponent of New Deal programs for their supposed encouragement of dependence. She seemed oblivious to the widespread suffering in Atlanta's female job market, particularly among black women.[76] But, as with Lewis, Mitchell's conservative posture resulted in the creation of a self-reliant heroine who mines the masculine in her nature to become a law unto herself, recognizing no control, not even her creator's. Like Ann Vickers, and unlike the more conscience-driven Margaret Flinders and Victoria Chance, Scarlett brings all men to their knees, symbolized not only by her sometime control of Ashley Wilkes and her marital/sexual alienation from Rhett but by the death of her daughter Bonnie, which both unmans Rhett and represents in its way Scarlett's ultimate refusal to mother.

Having cut Scarlett off from husband, (platonic) lover, and child but left her with property and ambitions still intact, Mitchell laments the unnatural role reversals the death of the slaveowning South had wrought. Yet neither in the 1930s nor in our own time has Mitchell's need to see the conditions that gave rise to Scarlett as tragic—or herself as stifled—obscured the deeper truth. The death of the South was the rise of the New Woman previously forbidden to exist there.

Scarlett managing her husband's lumber mill. Victoria covering the male-run Flint sit-down strike. Ann Vickers at the helm of a prison. Kitty Foyle profiting from women's desires to be pleasing to men. Margaret Flinders within ceaseless earshot of a demanding boss. Such varied but linked portraits aside, the woman professional in her business, government, reportorial, and social welfare roles was not a welcome subject in 1930s fiction. Most male and many female reformist writers dismissed her as antilabor; the majority of mainstream authors found her conventionally dull. Leftist revisions of the New Woman novel did attempt more balanced portraits of career-minded characters but, registering the many ways jobholding womanhood was undermined, offered heroines who (less strong-minded than their creators) responded apologetically to devaluation at work and home. All too often these characters are besieged by "worry like guilt" (Slesinger, *Unpossessed,* 162), even if, in the occasional Herbst novel, such worry is repressed. Their own competence is a reproach to them, their mates, their radical circles, and society at large. Slesinger's fitfully left-wing Margaret Flinders is mired in self-blame; Herbst's more political Victoria Chance, moving from clerical work to labor journalism, throws off self-censure, though not self-laceration, for a failed marriage.

Both validating and undermining misogyny, Morley, Mitchell, and the most ambivalent of the trio, Lewis, felt under no constraint to portray heroines who balance a lust for power with much of a social conscience. These popular authors thus liberated guilt-ridden female professionalism, but in the name of success-driven ascension. In their works, women seized the opportunity to move upward, in defiance of social norms. Though they rise to success in business with hardly a thought for the underclass, they represent the era's truly subversive professionals. For by their very pursuit of masculine power, Ann Vickers, Kitty Foyle, and Scarlett O'Hara challenged the back-to-the-home movement better than they know.

Yet their creators, taking away with one hand what they gave with the other, labeled such ambitions unfeminine. Ann unmans a husband, a suitor, and finally a lover; Kitty and Scarlett, both alone at their novels' ends, are tainted by promiscuity, real or imagined. From *The Unpossessed* to *Gone with the Wind,* authorial insecurities about female professionalism create a dialectic between erasure and celebration. Slesinger and Herbst gave woman's job performance a 1930s coloration, adulterating its effectiveness with doubts about her emasculating effect on often underachieving men. Producing narratives in crucial ways oblivious to (even contemptuous of) the Depression and women's job difficulties during it, Morley, Lewis, and Mitchell could praise feminine careerism only by locating it in a pre-Crash milieu, variously using the 1920s upward mobility plot, submerging the New Deal great woman in a Progressive Era vocation novel, or burying the 1930s feminine will to power in a Civil War fantasy.

Whether emphasizing the career woman's extreme self-deprecation or her overpowering singularity, whether undercutting or expanding on the Perkins and Thompson models of vocation, writers of imaginative literature demonstrated myriad personal and cultural difficulties in conceptualizing the 1930s professional woman. Their novels offer a composite homage to woman's intelligent ambition instead of her "instinctual" mothering—a welcome variant on so much of the fiction examined in earlier chapters. Still, to judge by the New Woman novel of the Great Depression, as in other 1930s subgenres on the female breadwinner, the truest achievement of the working woman, professional or not, was to remain one.

DEPRESSION FICTIONS

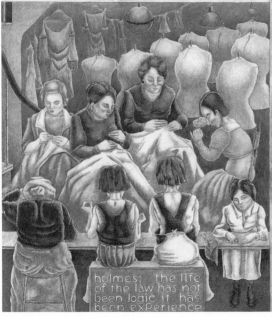

Sweatshop, George Biddle's homage to the female garment trade role, ca. 1935.
Art Gallery, University of Maryland at College Park.

That would be the end of [his skilled job] as he knew it. It would then be a job
for women, for women and hunkies.
—Wellington Roe, *Begin No Day* (1938)

A study by the National Industrial Conference Board . . . surveying the differences
in job classifications between men and women . . . [from] 1890 to 1930, found
evidence "almost entirely lacking" that the lower paid women workers had been
substituted for men or that women had "encroached" on so-called "male occupations."
It reiterated the conclusion after reviewing the data for the period 1930 to 1935.
—Mary W. M. Hargreaves, "Darkness Before the Dawn: The Status of Working
Women in the Depression Years," in *Clio Was a Woman* (1980)

Depression Era women, concludes historian Winifred Wandersee, "were discouraged both materially and psychologically from advancing themselves in the world of work."[1] At the core of the "new" objections to a sustained feminine job-site identity was the decades-old belief that women are at best transients in the labor force. For many of the predominantly masculine producers of fiction in the 1930s, as for the culture's other apologists for customary gender roles, women were intruders in the workplace. In homage to this view, a wide range of period fiction exploited the working woman rather than give her a voice of her own. As the country's hard times either gave rise to new prejudices or validated old ones, a resanctified womanhood was relegated, like its Victorian predecessors, to the home or, in a variant, the sphere of labor helpmeet. The old emphasis on woman's alarming or imperiled sexuality resurfaced with surprising vigor, whether in tales of sweat-shop labor, women strikers, white-collar girls, or womanless workplaces whose erasure of the working woman sent a clear message about the value of domesticity.

Taken as a whole, the fiction scrutinized in this book provides a gallery of homeloving or workplace earth mothers; their monstrous, promiscuous, or love-obsessed antitheses; picket-line adjuncts, even saints, but never agents; and too-manly New Women. A few radical texts by women and a small group of novels by male black authors, the latter informed by a critique of racism, provide alternative images. The era's prime triad of radical women, Olsen, Smedley, and Le Sueur, produced a composite critique of a mothering ideal "impossible to achieve on the level of social formation."[2] The stalwart agitprop mother—and the undernurtured activist daughter—are depicted as troubled. They are humanly flawed, not, as in many white males' texts, heroic or placid (or, in a demonic variant, monsters). As in the novels of Wright, Hughes, and McKay, such women are doubly oppressed, by society and by family. But, paralleling their white male counterparts, these African-American authors saw the working woman in relational terms—a sounding board for the injuries directed at, or inflicted by, black men. As in white men's texts, the ideal remained the solacing mother. Either her breadwinning work was recast as a symbol of commitment to the family or her rejection of supporting the home was sexually disquieting evidence of her non-nurturing role.

This is not to deny that texts with mother-centered images of women reflected the many real-life Depression Era mothers harried by financial and personal demands. Nor is it to impugn the validity of their devotion. But to the extent that the good mother was bound up with 1930s notions of "woman's place," the stereotype glossed over the family disruption so common in the era. More important, it rendered woman's economic and identity problems largely invisible; those who extolled the strong woman keeping the family together were the least interested in her personhood. Who cared about Ma Joad's inner life?

The historian Estelle Freedman, in studying the historiography of Depression Era womanhood, pointed out that generations of post-1930s social scientists have linked the period's working women, particularly careerist ones, with the decline of the family.[3] Fiction, too, rehearsed the widespread belief that the "return of the wife and mother to her 'natural' sphere . . . [would mean] a sign of the return of 'good times.' "[4] Yet society was not oblivious to the upsurge of labor activity among women, who, rather than leaving the workplace, held onto their jobs tenaciously and even slightly increased their numbers (though at the end of the Depression more women than men were out of work). The decade that should have driven women back to the home may even have strengthened their positions as workers.[5] But with some important exceptions, in the era's fiction it is difficult to find this female working class, much less a revolution-minded one. Even the literature of protest trumpeted that radical women should be helpmeets, whether on the home front or on the picket line. Events like the Gastonia walkout brought some textile town women into the labor focus; one northern female organizer brought in to rally the textile workers observed "a real transformation in the personality of women who became union members."[6] Yet despite their spontaneous militancy and the genesis of leadership roles among them, when they inhabit the Gastonia school of fiction, their understanding of revolutionary action is severely limited. They cede the labor stage to men.[7]

The maternal/sexual axis for working women characterized career women as well. Many actual white-collar marriages achieved (a measure of) middle-class status because the wife had a job, what was euphemistically called the era's "new marriage."[8] But in her literary refiguring, the great woman weakens the men who surround her or begins to sound like the rueful mother of a newborn in Jane Lazarre's *Mother Knot* (1976), guilty "because I leave him too often."[9] Even when a writer "celebrates the independence and career of the New Woman, he [or she] betrays an underlying ambivalence and hostility."[10] Black authors, aware of the few opportunities for nonwhite professionals, found the careerist white woman irrelevant to the issues bedeviling the mass of black women. But for white women authors, especially those on the Left, the type was real enough. In autobiographical texts by Slesinger and Herbst, the New Woman, more employable than her husband, is an emotional punching bag.

"A woman is nothing very important," reflects an unemployed man in a period novel of working-class life.[11] Placed in the context of the decade's jobs-for-women controversy, such a sentiment reveals that literature, with some notable exceptions, was enlisted in a widespread cultural campaign against changes in woman's traditional role. Even when the day's more radical-minded authors appeared to embrace a working class of both sexes, they did not. Put simply, in a time of supreme economic stress, strictures on feminine conduct narrowed. The urgency to sustain the nation's morale resurrected a controlling myth of womanhood. The irony is that with the revivified economy, absent soldiers, and attendant vocational necessities of World War II, in art as in life, the nation would be swiftly reconciled—at least for a time—to the woman at work.

NOTES

Preface

1. A sampling of the newer studies of women, work, and the Depression includes Alice Kessler-Harris, *Out to Work: A History of Wage-Earning Women in the United States* (New York: Oxford University Press, 1982), chap. 9, hereafter cited in text, and her "Gender Ideology in Historical Reconstruction: A Case Study from the 1930s," *Gender and History* 1 (Winter 1989): 32–49. See also Susan Ware, *Holding Their Own: American Women in the 1930s* (Boston: Twayne, 1980), chaps. 1, 2, and 5. Lois Scharf, *To Work and to Wed: Female Employment, Feminism, and the Great Depression* (Westport, Conn.: Greenwood Press, 1980), and Winifred Wandersee, *Women's Work and Family Values, 1920–1940* (Cambridge, Mass.: Harvard University Press, 1981), mainly address white-collar work. Two important new studies of New Deal art and gender ideology that analyze the iconography of working womanhood are Barbara Melosh, *Engendering Culture: Manhood and Womanhood in New Deal Public Art* (Washington, D.C.: Smithsonian Institution Press, 1991), and Ellen Wiley Todd, *The "New Woman" Revised: Painting and Gender Politics on Fourteenth Street* (Berkeley: University of California Press, 1993), hereafter cited in text. Much vital work on women laborers either touches on the 1930s or concentrates on the pre-Depression era. See, for example, Miriam Cohen, *Workshop to Office: Two Generations of Italian Women in New York City, 1900–1950* (Ithaca, N.Y.: Cornell University Press, 1992), and Lisa M. Fine, *The Souls of the Skyscraper: Female Clerical Workers in Chicago, 1870–1930* (Philadelphia: Temple University Press, 1990).

2. Standard studies of the masculine Depression include Irving Bernstein, *The Turbulent Years: A History of the American Worker, 1933–1941* (Boston: Houghton Mifflin, 1970); John A. Garraty, *The Great Depression* (Garden City, N.Y.: Doubleday/Anchor, 1988); Anthony J. Badger, *The New Deal: The Depression Years, 1933–1940* (New York: Noonday/Farrar, Straus & Giroux, 1989); and Robert S. McElvaine, *The Great Depression: America, 1929–1941* (New York: Times Books, 1984). Bernstein and Badger have no index entries for women workers. Garraty, who gives the topic two pages, and McElvaine (seven pages) focus only on the era's perception of the woman worker as undermining male dominance.

Similarly, although the new male leftism, literary, political, or both, is engaged in important revisionary scholarship, it passes over the Left feminine role. Some sample titles are James F. Murphy, *The Proletarian Moment: The Controversy over Leftism in Literature* (Urbana: University of Illinois Press, 1991); James D. Bloom, *Left Letters: The Culture Wars of Mike Gold and Joseph Freeman* (New York: Columbia University Press, 1992); Harvey Klehr, *The Heyday of American Communism: The Depression Decade* (New York: Basic Books, 1984); and Fraser M. Ottanelli, *The Communist Party of the United States from the Depression to World War II* (New Brunswick, N.J.: Rutgers University Press, 1991).

In feminist contrast, see Paula Rabinowitz, *Labor and Desire: Women's Revolutionary Fiction in Depression America* (Chapel Hill: University of North Carolina Press, 1991), hereafter cited in text. Barbara Foley, *Radical Representations: Politics and Form in U.S. Proletarian Fiction, 1929–1941* (Durham, N.C.: Duke University Press, 1993), has a lengthy section on "the Woman Question" and much discussion of women's texts. Constance Coiner's book *Better Red* (Oxford University Press, forthcoming), promises to be another important addition. See also Elsa Jane Dixler's fine Ph.D. dissertation, "The Woman Question: Women and the American Communist Party, 1929–1941" (Yale University, 1974), hereafter cited in text.

3. Unemployment figures for Depression women are usually understated, for many women classified in census data as "homemakers" were actually unemployed, and jobless girls aged sixteen to nineteen—an estimated 750,000 of them—often went uncounted. See Betty Lindley and Ernest K. Lindley, *A New Deal for Youth: The Story of the National Youth Administration* (New York: Viking Press, 1938), 6. See also *Sister of the Road: The Autobiography of Box-Car Bertha,* as told to Ben L. Reitman (1937; reprint, New York: Harper & Row, 1975); and Ware, 34.

4. Elaine Showalter notes that the "documentary devices and mixture of social consciousness and personal narrative struck [1930s] readers as less significant when the central protagonists were women." See her essay "Women Writers Between the Wars," in *The Columbia History of the American Novel,* ed. Emory Elliott et al. (New York: Columbia University Press, 1988), 834; hereafter cited in text. See, too, the scant offerings on working and working-class women or by leftist women in *Proletarian Literature in the United States,* ed. Granville Hicks (New York: International Publishers, 1935), and, in that tradition, *Our Lives: 32 Short Stories About American Labor,* ed. Joseph Gaer (New York: Boni and Gaer, 1948); *The American Writer and the Great Depression,* ed. Harvey Swados (Indianapolis: Bobbs-Merrill, 1966); *Years of Protest,* ed. Jack Salzman and Barry Wallenstein (New York: Pegasus, 1967); *New Masses: An Anthology of the Rebel Thirties* (New York: International Publishers, 1969); and *Writers in Revolt: The Anvil Anthology,* ed. Jack Conroy and Curt Johnson (Westport, Conn.: Lawrence Hill, 1973).

5. See especially the essay by Leslie Fiedler, "The Two Memories: Reflections on Writers and Writing in the Thirties," with its slighting references to women

writers, in *Proletarian Writers of the Thirties,* ed. David Madden (Carbondale: Southern Illinois University Press, 1968). Irving Howe, "The Thirties in Retrospect," in *Literature at the Barricades: American Writers in the 1930s,* ed. Ralph Bogardus (Tuscaloosa: University of Alabama Press, 1982), 15, remarks, for example, that "Edmund Wilson, Erskine Caldwell, Sherwood Anderson talked to hungry men in New York, listened to desperate strikers in North Carolina," excising the female Gastonia School entirely. Relevant, too, in this regard is Alfred Kazin's reminiscence of his 1930s colleague Tess Slesinger: "She was crowding me . . . almost off the edge of the earth" (*Starting Out in the Thirties* [1962; reprint, Boston: Little, Brown, 1965], 99).

6. See, for example, Paula Rabinowitz, "Women and U.S. Literary Radicalism," in *Writing Red: An Anthology of American Women Writers, 1930–1940,* ed. Charlotte Nekola and Paula Rabinowitz (New York: Feminist Press, 1987), 1–16, hereafter cited in text. The anthology's reprint gallery includes Tillie Olsen, Agnes Smedley, Meridel Le Sueur, Leane Zugsmith, Josephine Herbst, Tess Slesinger, Ruth McKenney, and the African-American writer Ramona Lowe, all treated here.

In addition to the book-length works by Foley and Rabinowitz (see note 2), a tiny sampling of the newer criticism includes Deborah Rosenfelt, "Getting into the Game: American Women Writers and the Radical Tradition," *Women's Studies International Forum* 9 (1986): 563–572, and Constance Coiner, "Literature of Resistance: The Intersection of Feminism and the Communist Left in Meridel Le Sueur and Tillie Olsen," in *Left Politics and the Literary Profession,* ed. Lennard J. Davis and M. Bella Mirabella (New York: Columbia University Press, 1990), 162–85. See also, among others, Alice Kessler-Harris and Paul Lauter, "Introduction," in Tess Slesinger, *The Unpossessed* (1934; reprint, Old Westbury, N.Y.: Feminist Press, 1984) (hereafter cited in text), who remark: "[Addressing] distinctly female experiences . . . women writers of the Left chose to flout male convention and to write about themes that fell outside the frameworks of their male peers" (xi). See also Suzanne Sowinska, "American Women Writers and the Radical Agenda, 1925–1940" (Ph.D. diss., University of Washington, 1992).

Recent male explicators of 1930s leftist women's fiction include Joseph R. Urgo, "Proletarian Literature and Feminism: The Gastonia Novels and Feminist Protest," *Minnesota Review* 24 (Spring 1985): 64–84; Paul Lauter, "Working-Class Women's Literature: An Introduction to Study," *Radical Teacher* 15 (1980): 16–26; and Alan Wald, "Culture and Commitment: U.S. Communist Writers Reconsidered," in *New Studies in the Politics and Culture of U.S. Communism,* ed. Michael E. Brown et al. (New York: Monthly Review Press, 1993), 284.

7. See the Feminist Press reissues of, among other titles, Myra Page's 1932 *Daughter of the Hills* (1977), Agnes Smedley's 1929 *Daughter of Earth* (1987), Josephine

Herbst's 1939 *Rope of Gold* (1984), Tess Slesinger's 1934 *The Unpossessed* (1984), Fielding Burke's 1932 *Call Home the Heart* (1983); the University of Illinois Press reissue of the Mary Heaton Vorse 1930 Gastonia novel *Strike!* (1991); the ILR Press republication of a Ruth McKenney Akron rubber strike tale, the 1939 *Industrial Valley;* and the Omnigraphics Press reissue of Clara Weatherwax's orthodox 1935 novel of male proletarianism, *Marching! Marching!* (1990). A forthcoming University of Illinois Press series on the radical novel, edited by Alan Wald, will feature other novels by Page, Herbst, and Lumpkin, as well as Josephine Johnson and others, although, as in other reprints of lost 1930s authors, male writers greatly predominate.

Nonleftist reprints, far less numerous, include the well-received 1937 Zora Neale Hurston novel of the southern folk, *Their Eyes Were Watching God* (New York: Harper/Perennial, 1990), and a male author's ambivalent 1933 ode to female professional achievement, Sinclair Lewis's best-selling *Ann Vickers* (Lincoln: University of Nebraska Press, 1994). All will be treated in this study.

8. A small sampling of the new studies includes Elinor Langer, *Josephine Herbst* (Boston: Little, Brown, 1984); Janice R. MacKinnon and Stephen R. MacKinnon, *Agnes Smedley: The Life and Times of an American Radical* (Berkeley: University of California Press, 1988); Abe C. Ravitz, *Leane Zugsmith: Thunder on the Left* (New York: International Publishers, 1992); Mickey Pearlman and Abby H. P. Werlock, *Tillie Olsen* (Boston: Twayne, 1991), hereafter cited in text; Elaine Neil Orr, *Tillie Olsen and a Feminist Spiritual Vision* (Jackson: University Press of Mississippi, 1987); Judith Mara Faulkner, *Protest and Possibility in the Writing of Tillie Olsen* (Charlottesville: University Press of Virginia, 1993); Rabinowitz, *Labor and Desire;* Coiner, *Better Red.*

9. Kessler-Harris, "Gender Ideology in Historical Reconstruction," 35.

10. Norman Cousins, "Will Women Lose Jobs?" *Current History and Forum* 41 (September 1939): 14.

11. Patricia Cooper, *Once a Cigar Maker: Men, Women, and Work Culture in the American Cigar Factories, 1900–1919* (Urbana: University of Illinois Press, 1987), 5–7.

12. Janet Zandy, "Preface," in *Calling Home: Working-Class Women's Writings, an Anthology,* ed. Janet Zandy (New Brunswick, N.J.: Rutgers University Press, 1990), 5.

13. See Laura Hapke, *Tales of the Working Girl: Wage-Earning Women in American Literature, 1890–1925* (New York: Twayne/Macmillan, 1992), chap. 1, and the first chapter of this study.

14. E. Ann Kaplan, *Motherhood and Representation: The Mother in Popular Culture and Melodrama* (London: Routledge, 1992), 23.

15. Warren French, "American Fiction and the 1930s," in *Dictionary of Literary*

Biography, vol. 9, pt. 3, ed. James J. Martine (Detroit: Gale Research Co., 1981), 258, conjoins the two forms. He also sees proletarian and nonproletarian novels as linked proof that "genteel literature was a casualty of the Depression." Chapter 4 of this book addresses these matters.

16. James T. Farrell, *Studs Lonigan: Judgment Day* (New York: Vanguard Press, 1935), 215–17.

17. Cited in Halford E. Luccock, *American Mirror: Social, Ethical and Religious Aspects of American Literature* (New York: Cooper Square Publishers, 1971), 116.

18. Dashiell Hammett, *Red Harvest* (New York: Knopf, 1929), 63.

19. Louis Adamic, "What the Proletariat Reads . . . ," *Saturday Review* 11 (1 December 1934): 321–22; Vera Buch Weisbord, *A Radical Life* (Bloomington: Indiana University Press, 1977), 229.

Chapter One. Old Whine, New Battles: Men's Needs, Women's Jobs

1. Henry T. Finck, "Employments Unsuitable for Women," *Independent* 63 (April 1907): 834. For a survey of the debate, see Laura Hapke, *Tales of the Working Girl: Wage-Earning Women in American Literature, 1890–1925* (New York: Twayne / Macmillan, 1992), chap. 1.

2. For two classics of period fears, see Edgar Fawcett, "The Woes of the New York Working-Girl," *Arena* 4 (1891): 26–35, and Ruth Batchelder, "The Country Girl Who Is Coming to the City," *Delineator* 72 (November 1908): 836–37; for a modern discussion, see Lois Scharf, *To Work and to Wed: Female Employment, Feminism, and the Great Depression* (Westport, Conn.: Greenwood Press, 1980), 12, hereafter cited in text.

3. Rebecca Farnham, *Women at Work: A Century of Industrial Change,* U.S. Department of Labor, Women's Bureau Bulletin no. 161 (Washington, D.C.: U.S. Government Printing Office, 1939), 6–7.

4. Quoted in Margery Davies, *Woman's Place Is at the Typewriter: Office Work and Office Workers, 1870–1930* (Philadelphia: Temple University Press, 1982), 77.

5. Mrs. John [Bessie] Van Vorst and Marie Van Vorst, *The Woman Who Toils* (London: Grant Richards, 1903), 27.

6. Winston Churchill, *The Dwelling Place of Light* (New York: Macmillan, 1917), 322.

7. Anzia Yezierska, *Bread Givers* (1925; reprint, New York: Persea, 1975), 172.

8. Lynn Y. Weiner, *From Working Girl to Working Mother: The Female Labor Force in the United States, 1820–1980* (Chapel Hill: University of North Carolina Press, 1985), 79. See also Alice Kessler-Harris, *Out to Work: A History of Wage-Earning Women in the United States* (New York: Oxford University Press, 1982), 224, hereafter cited

in text. She argues the minority view that, despite a decline compared to the 1920s, the Depression "solidified [women's] positions as workers" (272). For an opposing argument, see Susan Estabrook Kennedy, *If All We Did Was to Weep at Home: A History of White Working-Class Women in America* (Bloomington: Indiana University Press, 1979), chap. 8, hereafter cited in text.

9. *New York Times,* 12 August 1923.

10. Grace Hutchins, *Women Who Work* (New York: International Publishers, 1934), 28, hereafter cited in text. On white women's new possibilities in clerical and sales positions, see Dorothy M. Brown, *Setting a Course: American Women in the 1920s* (Boston: Twayne, 1986), 95. On black women's continued poor prospects, see Jacqueline S. Jones, *Labor of Love, Labor of Sorrow: Black Women, Work, and the Family, from Slavery to the Present* (1985; reprint, New York: Vintage Books, 1986), 200. White women still averaged 61 cents and blacks 23 cents to white men's dollar (Jones, 208).

11. Philip S. Foner, *Women and the American Labor Movement from World War I to the Present* (New York: Free Press, 1980), 256 (hereafter cited in text), records that the 1930 census found a 4.7 percent unemployment rate for women compared with 7.1 percent for men. Ruth Milkman, "Women's Work and the Economic Crisis," in *A Heritage of Our Own,* ed. Nancy F. Cott and Elizabeth H. Pleck (New York: Simon and Schuster, 1979), 518, reports that the gap had narrowed by 1940 to 8.6 percent of the male labor force and 7.5 percent of the female.

12. Nancy Woloch, *Women and the American Experience* (New York: Knopf, 1984), 441, hereafter cited in text.

13. Lorena Hickok, *One Third of a Nation: Lorena Hickok Reports on the Great Depression,* ed. Richard Lowitt and Maurine Beasley (Urbana: University of Illinois Press, 1981), 49, hereafter cited in text.

14. Elisabeth D. Benham, *The Woman Wage Earner: Her Situation Today,* U.S. Department of Labor, Women's Bureau Bulletin no. 172 (Washington, D.C.: U.S. Government Printing Office, 1939), 31, 1; Genevieve Parkhurst, "Is Feminism Dead?", *Harper's Monthly* 170 (May 1935): 744 (hereafter cited in text), gave a figure of four million; Hutchins, 181, estimated two to four million.

15. "M. W.," 19 February 1937 letter in *"Slaves of the Depression": Workers' Letters About Life on the Job,* ed. Gerald Markowitz and David Rosner (Ithaca, N.Y.: Cornell University Press, 1987), 156, hereafter cited in text. More on wages in hotel, restaurant, and domestic fields can be found in Hutchins, 99.

16. I am indebted to Jones, 199–208, for her fine discussion of black women's wages. The 1930 census lumped under "other races" Mexicans, Chicanas, Asians, Amerasians, and Native Americans. On that census and Chicana laborers, see Julia Kirk Blackwelder, "Women in the Work Force: Atlanta, New Orleans, and San

Antonio, 1930 to 1940," *Journal of Urban History* 4 (May 1978): 357n and passim. As with black females, the predominant work of these migrants or immigrants was as servants, laundresses, farm laborers, and, excepting American Indian women, factory workers. See Vicki Ruiz, "A Promise Fulfilled: Mexican Cannery Workers in Southern California," in *Unequal Sisters: A Multicultural Reader in U.S. Women's History,* ed. Ellen Carol DuBois and Vicki L. Ruiz (New York: Routledge, 1990), 264–74; essays by various hands in *Chinese Labor Immigration Under Capitalism: Asian Workers in the United States Before World War II,* ed. Lucie Cheng and Edna Bonacich (Berkeley: University of California Press, 1984); Evelyn N. Glenn, "Occupational Ghettoization: Japanese American Women and Domestic Service, 1905–1970," *Ethnicity* 8 (1981): 351–86; and Joan M. Jensen, "Native American Women and Agriculture: A Case Study," in *Unequal Sisters,* 51–65. A sad reference to tribal women "clean[ing] out motel rooms along Highway 66" in the 1930s appears in Leslie Marmon Silko's novel *Ceremony* (1977; reprint, New York: New American Library, 1986), 115.

17. On women's dominance in teaching and minuscule presence in more prestigious professions, see Scharf, 66, and Susan Ware, *Holding Their Own: American Women in the 1930s* (Boston: Twayne, 1983), 73, hereafter cited in text. See also Scharf, 75, 90–93, on school boards refusing employment to married teachers; on black women's low teaching salaries, see Hutchins, 77, 75.

18. Winifred Wandersee, *Women's Work and Family Values, 1920–1940* (Cambridge, Mass.: Harvard University Press, 1981), 93. By 1936, there were 250,000 teachers but nearly two million women in office work. See "Should White Collar Workers Organize?" *Independent Woman* 15 (November 1936): 342, 356.

19. Tess Slesinger, *The Unpossessed* (1934; reprint, New York: Feminist Press, 1984), 9.

20. *New York Times,* 12 August 1934.

21. On the codes, see Kessler-Harris, *Work,* 263, and Woloch, 448–49.

22. Amy Hewes, "Women Wage Earners and the N.R.A.," *American Federationist* 42 (February 1935): 160.

23. Quoted in Rose Pesotta, *Bread upon the Waters,* intro. Ann Schofield (1944; reprint, Ithaca, N.Y.: ILR Press, 1987), chap. 3; see also Hewes, 163. On similar injustices under work relief, see Helena Weed, "The New Deal Women Want," *Current History* 36 (November 1934): 183, hereafter cited in text; Miriam Cohen, "The New Deal," in *Women's Studies Encyclopedia,* vol. 3, *History, Philosophy, and Religion,* ed. Helen Tierney (Westport, Conn.: Greenwood Press, 1991), 337, hereafter cited in text; and Robert S. McElvaine, *The Great Depression: America, 1929–1941* (New York: Times Books, 1984), 183, hereafter cited in text. On the inadequate government work and training activities for jobless women, particularly com-

pared with those for men, see Joyce L. Kornbluh, *A New Deal for Workers' Education: The Workers' Service Program, 1933–1942* (Urbana: University of Illinois Press, 1987), chap. 5.

24. On employers' ploys to circumvent the codes when dealing with black women, see Woloch, 450, and Markowitz and Rosner, 152.

25. James R. Green, *The World of the Worker: Labor in Twentieth-Century America* (New York: Hill and Wang, 1980), 167.

26. See comments on woman's duty to her home in Eleanor Roosevelt, *It's Up to the Women* (New York: Frederick A. Stokes, 1933), 145, and on the impossibility of using women on mass projects "such as those suitable for men," in her remarks in *Proceedings of the Conference on the Emergency Needs of Women,* Federal Emergency Relief Administration, 20 November 1933, 11. A feminist first lady emerges, in contrast, in Blanche Wiesen Cook, *Eleanor Roosevelt,* vol. 1, *1884–1933* (New York: Viking Press, 1992).

27. Evelyn Seeley, "Our Feudal Housewives," *Nation* 146 (28 May 1938): 613–15. Comments a defiant character in an African-American novel of the time, "there ain't no use in learnin' books . . . to work in white folks' kitchens." See Langston Hughes, *Not Without Laughter* (1930; reprint, New York: Collier Books, 1969), 21.

28. Compare earnest surveyor of women's work Clare de Graffenreid, "The Condition of Wage-Earning Women," *Forum* 15 (March 1898): 18–82, with Poppy Cannon, "Pin-Money Slaves," *Forum* 84 (August 1930): 98, and Rita Halle, "Do You Need Your Job?" *Good Housekeeping* (September 1932): 171. Even Labor Secretary Frances Perkins seemed more interested in publishing pieces on past wage earners than addressing current problems. See her "Women in Industry: An Historical Survey," *Independent Woman* 16 (May 1937): 133, 152–54. Wrote Mary Heaton Vorse, complaining that even the numerous women on strike were underrepresented, there was "nothing in the papers about the fact that the working women of America have gotten fighting mad" (Mary Heaton Vorse, "Perkins, This Way!" in *Rebel Pen: The Writings of Mary Heaton Vorse,* ed. Dee Garrison [1934; reprint, New York: Monthly Review Press, 1985], 165).

29. Jane Allen, "You May Have My Job: A Feminist Discovers Her Home," *Forum* 87 (April 1932): 229. See also Worth Tuttle, "A Feminist Marries," *Atlantic Monthly* 153 (May 1936): 73–81, and Frank L. Hopkins, "Should Wives Work?" *American Mercury* 39 (December 1936): 415. In reality, one-third of married women were the sole family breadwinners, one-half shared the responsibility, and widowed, separated, and divorced women made up one-quarter of women in the labor force. See Mary Elizabeth Pidgeon, *Women in Industry: A Series of Working Papers to Aid Study Groups,* U.S. Department of Labor, Women's Bureau Bulletin no. 191 (Washington, D.C.: U.S. Government Printing Office, 1931), 59–60, hereafter cited in text.

30. Mary Doyle, "Working Girl," *Atlantic Monthly* 157 (May 1936): 552–62. See, in contrast, Fleta Campbell Springer, "The N.R.A. Goes into Action," *Harper's* 167 (October 1933): 606; Gerald W. Johnson, "What an Old Girl Should Know," *Harper's* 168 (January 1934): 613.

31. Elizabeth Slesinger, "They Say Women Are Emancipated," *New Republic,* 18 December 1933, 126, hereafter cited in text.

32. "Business Woman's Bookshelf," *Independent Woman* 15 (December 1936): 399. Incensed opponents of unionization boycotted an isolated *IW* symposium with a labor theme, "Should White Collar Workers Organize?"

33. Donald Robin Makosky, "The Portrayal of Women in Wide-Circulation Magazine Short Stories" (Ph.D. diss., University of Pennsylvania, 1966), 93–94.

34. "How It Feels, by a Social Worker," *Survey* 67 (February 1932): 29–30; Claire Howe, "Return of the Lady," *New Outlook* 164 (October 1934): 34–38; Ann Rivington, "We Live on Relief," *Scribner's* 95 (April 1934): 282–85; see also Edna C. McKnight, "Jobs—for Men Only?" *Outlook and Independent* 159 (September 1931): 12–13, 18.

35. *American Mercury* (September 1934): 53–56; Meridel Le Sueur, "Women Are Hungry," in *Ripening: Selected Work, Meridel Le Sueur,* 2d ed., ed. Elaine Hedges (1934; reprint, New York: Feminist Press, 1990), 144. See Thomas Minehan, "Appendix," in *Boy and Girl Tramps of America* (New York: Farrar and Rinehart, 1934), 253–63, in which he provides statistics on 1,377 boys but only 88 girls.

36. C. W. Bakke, *Citizens Without Work: A Study of the Effects of Unemployment upon the Workers' Social Relations and Practices* (New Haven: Yale University Press, 1940), 3.

37. Norman Cousins, "Will Women Lose Jobs?" *Current History and Forum* 41 (September 1939): 14.

38. James Steele, *Conveyor* (New York: International Publishers, 1935), 46, hereafter cited in text.

39. Sharon Hartman Strom, "Challenging 'Woman's Place': Feminism, the Left, and Industrial Unionism in the 1930s," *Feminist Studies* 9 (Summer 1983): 362–69, hereafter cited in text.

40. *Hard Times: An Oral History of the Great Depression in America,* comp. Studs Terkel (New York: Pantheon, 1970), 135, 137. On women's participation in needle trades and other strikes in the 1930s, see Hutchins, 247, Foner, 282–312, and Scharf, 118.

41. Quoted in Jeremy Brecher, *Strike!* (Boston: South End Press, 1971), 172. He offers a good discussion of women's role in automotive strikes, both as strikers and members of ladies' auxiliaries. See, in particular, 198–203, 208–9. For other labor-historical landmarks, see, on women's militance in San Francisco, Foner, 286, and in Gallup and Minneapolis, 291; for their activity in the Illinois coal

fields, see Elsa Jane Dixler, "The Woman Question: Women and the American Communist Party, 1929–1941" (Ph.D. diss., Yale University, 1974), 251, hereafter cited in text.

42. By 1936, for instance, 20 percent of the Firestone local of the United Rubber Workers were women; they struck in the 1937 Flint auto protests, and at the notorious 1937 "Memorial Day Massacre" in Chicago, when police fired into unarmed demonstrators, women were at the head.

43. Mary E. Frederickson, "Heroines and Girl Strikers: Gender Issues and Organized Labor in the Twentieth-Century American South," in *Organized Labor in the Twentieth-Century South,* ed. Robert H. Zieger (Knoxville: University of Tennessee Press, 1991), 102. On union misogyny see James J. Kenneally, *Women and American Trade Unions* (St. Albans, Vt.: Eden Press, 1981), passim. See also William H. Chafe, *The Paradox of Change: American Women in the Twentieth Century* (New York: Oxford University Press, 1991), 89, Hutchins, 261, and Woloch, 441. On United Mine Workers power John L. Lewis as a test case, see Dee Garrison, "Editorial Introduction," in Mary Heaton Vorse, "Perkins, This Way!" in *Rebel Pen: The Writings of Mary Heaton Vorse,* ed. Dee Garrison (1934; reprint, New York: Monthly Review Press, 1985), 162.

44. On textile organizers, see Staughton Lynd and Alice Lynd, *Rank and File: Personal Histories by Working Class Organizers* (Boston: Beacon Press, 1973), 83–84, hereafter cited in text. By the mid-1930s in the textile industry alone almost half of the nearly half a million workers were female.

45. Of relevance here is the comment of a trade union archivist regarding women textile and clothing workers in the 1930s: "There was no bias against women; they couldn't attend meetings because they had to go home to their children after work" (Interview with Walter Mankoff, ILGWU headquarters, New York City, 2 December 1992). The Nowicki interview appears in Lynd and Lynd; see Pesotta, *Bread,* passim. Pesotta eventually felt so thwarted by the union hierarchy that she resigned her vice-president's post.

46. See Kenneally, 168, and Strom, 369–70, on CIO policy toward female wage earners. On the idea of male union leader and "girl striker," see Frederickson, passim. On CIO sexism, including pictures of women workers in cheesecake poses for the *CIO News,* see Strom, 369–70.

47. Mary Inman, *In Woman's Defense* (Los Angeles: Committee to Organize the Advancement of Women, 1940), passim.

48. Sherna Gluck, "Socialist Feminism Between the Two World Wars: Insights from Oral History," in *Decades of Discontent: The Woman's Movement, 1920–1940,* ed. Lois Scharf and Joan M. Jensen (1983; reprint, Boston: Northeastern University Press, 1987), 280.

49. Irene Leslie, "It Is Necessary to Work Among Women," *Party Organizer* 9 (March 1936): 27.

50. Tillie Olsen, "The Strike" [1934], reprinted in *Calling Home: Working-Class Women's Writings, an Anthology,* ed. Janet Zandy (New Brunswick, N.J.: Rutgers University Press, 1990), 275. See also Dixler, 211, on party regular Anna Damon: "We did not put ourselves at the head of this strike movement to defend . . . working women."

51. On working-class women's issues treated by party organs, see Paula Rabinowitz, "Women and U.S. Literary Radicalism," in *Writing Red: An Anthology of American Women Writers, 1930–1940,* ed. Charlotte Nekola and Paula Rabinowitz (New York: Feminist Press, 1987), 6.

52. Edith Berkman, "Why I Am on Hunger Strike," *Equal Justice* [formerly *Labor Defender*] 8 (June 1932): 105; "Voices from Prison," *Labor Defender* 11 (May 1935): 20. The journal also featured pieces on female luminaries such as Mother Bloor.

53. Mark Naison, "Harlem Communists and the Politics of Black Protest," *Marxist Perspectives* 1 (Fall 1978): 30, 82.

54. On the popular CP ideology of the union wife who let her husband fight the labor battles while she organized food boycotts, see Mary Harrison Pierce, "Some Problems in Our Women's Work," *Party Organizer* 9 (October 1936): 18, and Strom, 371.

55. On period texts bolstering the perception that married women were responsible for male unemployment, see *New York Times,* 7 March 1930, and "Preface," *America's Working Women: A Documentary History—1600 to the Present,* ed. Rosalyn Baxandall, Linda Gordon, and Susan Reverby (New York: Random House/Vintage, 1976), 245. On legal moves to disfranchise women workers, especially the Economy Act of 1932, see Mary P. Ryan, *Womanhood in America from Colonial Times to the Present* (New York: New Viewpoints Press, 1975), 315, Parkhurst, 739, 743, and Woloch, 441. For an exposé of false assumptions about married women's prosperity, see Pidgeon, 59; Ruth Shonle Cavan and Katherine Howland Ranck, *The Family and the Depression* (Chicago: University of Chicago Press, 1938), 62.

56. James W. Tuttleton, " 'Combat in the Erogenous Zone': Women in the American Novel Between the Two World Wars," in Springer, 293; John Steinbeck, *The Grapes of Wrath* (1939; reprint, New York: Viking/Penguin, 1976).

57. Sylvia Jenkins Cook, *From Tobacco Road to Route 66: The Southern Poor White in Fiction* (Chapel Hill: University of North Carolina Press, 1976), 160, hereafter cited in text.

58. Charles Poore, "Books of the Times," *New York Times,* 14 April 1939, 27.

59. Robert G. Athearn, *The Mythic West in Twentieth-Century America* (Lawrence: University of Kansas Press, 1986), 88.

60. Mary Anderson, "On the Trail of the Migrant," *American Federationist* 39 (July 1932): 776–77, hereafter cited in text.

61. Carey McWilliams, *Factories in the Field: The Story of Migratory Farm Labor in California* (Boston: Little, Brown, 1939), 218; Vicki L. Ruiz, *Cannery Women, Cannery Lives: Mexican Women, Unionization, and the California Food Processing Industry, 1930–1950* (Albuquerque: University of New Mexico Press, 1987), 45.

62. William Stott, *Documentary Expression and Thirties America* (1973; reprint, Chicago: University of Chicago Press, 1986), 121. For an acidly dissenting view, see George Thomas Miron, *The Truth About John Steinbeck and the Migrants* (Los Angeles: Haynes Corp., 1939), 8–9. For a feminist critique, though one that does not deal with female wage earning, of Steinbeck's vision as patriarchally ideological rather than documentary, see Nellie Y. McKay, " 'Happy[?]-Wife-and-Motherdom': The Portrayal of Ma Joad in John Steinbeck's *The Grapes of Wrath*," in *New Essays on* The Grapes of Wrath, ed. David Wyatt (Cambridge: Cambridge University Press, 1990), 47–67. A 1938 Sanora Babb novel, whose publication was canceled for its supposed similarity to *Grapes of Wrath,* does acknowledge Okie women's routine presence in California fields. Equating work with maleness, she praises the women because they can "pick like [men]." See a recent Babb excerpt, "Whose Names Are Unknown," *Michigan Quarterly Review* 29 (Summer 1990): 365.

63. *Steinbeck: A Life in Letters,* ed. Elaine Steinbeck and Robert Wallstein (1952; reprint, New York: Viking/Penguin, 1975), 161–62.

64. Erskine Caldwell, *God's Little Acre* (1933; reprint, Savannah, Ga.: Beehive Press, 1977), hereafter cited in text.

65. Margaret Jarman Hagood, *Mothers of the South: Portraiture of the White Tenant Farm Woman* (Chapel Hill: University of North Carolina Press, 1939), 193.

66. Agnes Smedley, *Daughter of Earth* [original ed.] (1929; reprint, New York: Feminist Press, 1987), 208, hereafter cited in text.

67. Ruth McKenney, "Women Are Human Beings," *New Masses* 37 (10 December 1940): 9.

68. David P. Peeler, *Hope Among Us Yet: Social Criticism and Social Solace in Depression America* (Athens: University of Georgia Press, 1987), hereafter cited in text; Amy Godine, "Notes Toward a Reappraisal of Depression Literature," *Prospects* 5 (1979): 214.

69. Lois Rita Helmbold, "Beyond the Family Economy: Black and White Working-Class Women During the Great Depression," *Feminist Studies* 13 (Fall 1987): 633.

Chapter Two. Earth Mothers, Streetwalkers, and Masculine Social Protest Fiction

1. Until 1937 the FSA, set up in 1935 to document the Depression's effect on rural labor, was called the Resettlement Administration. Lange's description of the Nipomo woman is in Dorothea Lange, "The Assignment I'll Never Forget," *Popular Photography* 46 (February 1940): 126, hereafter cited in text.

2. Quoted in Frazer Ward, "Foreign and Familiar Bodies," in *Dirt and Domesticity: Constructions of the Feminine* (New York: Whitney Museum, 1992), 13.

3. Karin Becker Ohrn, in *Dorothea Lange and the Documentary Tradition* (Baton Rouge: Louisiana State University Press, 1980), 103, quotes Lange on the importance of captions and contends she titled her own photos. Her FSA colleague Marion Wolcott, however, quoted in F. Jack Hurley, *Marion Post Wolcott: A Photographic Journey* (Albuquerque: University of New Mexico Press, 1989), 57, said that Lange's husband, Paul Taylor, captioned her work. Lange's own word, at least on the *Migrant Mother,* should be final. In "An Assignment I'll Never Forget," 42, she wrote: "I have never captioned it other than with date or place."

4. John Steinbeck, *The Grapes of Wrath* (1939; reprint, New York: Viking/Penguin, 1976), hereafter cited in text. On his use of Lange, see Irving Bernstein, *A Caring Society: The New Deal, the Worker, and the Great Depression* (Boston: Houghton Mifflin, 1968), 262, hereafter cited in text.

5. John Steinbeck, *Their Blood Is Strong* (San Francisco: Simon J. Lubin Society, 1938), hereafter cited in text.

6. Milton Meltzer, *Dorothea Lange: A Photographer's Life* (New York: Farrar, Straus & Giroux, 1978), 135.

7. James Curtis, *Mind's Eye, Mind's Truth: FSA Photography Reconsidered* (Philadelphia: Temple University Press, 1989), 55. See also Alan Trachtenberg, "From Image to Story: Reading the File," in *Documenting America, 1935–1942,* ed. Carl Fleischhauer and Beverly W. Brannan (Berkeley: University of California Press, 1988), 68.

8. The 1936 *San Francisco News* photos and article are reprinted in Paul Taylor, "Migrant Mother: 1936," *American West* 7 (May 1970): 43. Interestingly, Taylor makes no allusion to Thompson as a worker. The more celebrated *Migrant Mother* photograph, its subject again not identified as a migrant worker, ran in *Midweek Pictorial,* 17 October 1936.

9. The five statistics are in Elisabeth D. Benham, *The Woman Wage Earner: Her Situation Today,* U.S. Department of Labor, Women's Bureau Bulletin no. 172 (Washington, D.C.: U.S. Government Printing Office, 1939), 48. See also Winifred Wandersee, *Women's Work and Family Values, 1920–1940* (Cambridge, Mass.: Harvard University Press, 1981), 45; Alice Kessler-Harris, *Out to Work: A History of Wage-Earning Women in the United States* (New York: Oxford University Press, 1982),

256; Jeanne Westin, *Making Do: How Women Survived the '30s* (Chicago: Follett, 1976), ix; Grace Hutchins, *Women Who Work* (New York: International Publishers, 1934), 40.

10. See the description under the *Migrant Mother* photograph in James N. Gregory, *American Exodus: The Dust Bowl Migration and Okie Culture in California* (New York: Oxford University Press, 1989), xiv, hereafter cited in text. Gregory gives Thompson's later work history, but though he had read the Lange reminiscence, he, too, does not identify Thompson as a pea field worker. Yet her own daughter in a recent interview made clear that Thompson, using her own example, taught her children that "you work for what you get" (*The Great Depression,* pt. 6. Prod. by Henry Hampton and Terry Kay Rockefeller [New York: Blackside Productions, 1993]).

11. William Stott, *Documentary Expression and Thirties America* (1973; reprint, Chicago: University of Chicago Press, 1986), illustrations section, not paginated.

12. Sean Dennis Cashman, *America in the Twenties and Thirties: The Olympian Age of Franklin Delano Roosevelt* (New York: New York University Press, 1989), 195, hereafter cited in text.

13. For Wolcott's photo of the packinghouse mother, see the beginning of chapter 3. For Wolcott's other photos of women workers, see Hurley, chap. 3; Eudora Welty, *Photographs* (Jackson: University Press of Mississippi, 1989), passim; and Lewis Hine, *Women at Work* (New York: Dover, 1981), 96–117.

14. When women were depicted, whether by male or female artists, they were most often engaged in laboring in the cotton field or doing the rural chore. In contrast, see the auto industry paintings of William Gropper, Michael Lensen's pictures of coal miners, or Maurice Glickman's construction workers. There were exceptions, such as George Biddle's *Sweatshop,* ca. 1935, created for the WPA's Federal Art Project. A photograph of it appears at the beginning of the concluding chapter of this book.

15. Marlene Park and Gerald E. Markowitz, *Democratic Vistas: Post Offices and Public Art in the New Deal* (Philadelphia: Temple University Press, 1984), 158. See their survey of worker murals produced for public buildings under the Fine Arts Section (1934–43). They note that even in historical murals, women "stand idly by on the sidelines. . . . Femininity and feminine presence seem to have been more important than historical accuracy" (34). New Deal murals on farm subjects often included women but almost always with children on their laps or by their sides. See Barbara Melosh, *Engendering Culture: Manhood and Womanhood in New Deal Public Art* (Washington, D.C.: Smithsonian Institution Press, 1991), chap. 3. Melosh, 217–27, also points out that female artists followed male artists' conventions.

16. David P. Peeler, *Hope Among Us Yet: Social Criticism and Social Solace in Depression America* (Athens: University of Georgia Press, 1987), 155, hereafter cited in text.

17. Jon Christian Suggs, "The Proletarian Novel," in *Dictionary of Literary Biography,* vol. 9, pt. 3, ed. James J. Martine (Detroit: Gale Research Co., 1981), 241.

18. Steinbeck, Farrell, Dahlberg, and Wright, to cite a few examples, have all been dubbed social and proletarian novelists. On the controversy over labeling Steinbeck, see Claude E. Jones, "Proletarian Writing and John Steinbeck," *Sewanee Review* 48 (October 1940): 445–56. On Steinbeck, Farrell, Dahlberg, and Wright as social novelists, see Peeler, 150, 151; on Farrell and Dahlberg as proletarian ones, see Walter Rideout, *The Radical Novel in the United States, 1900–1954* (Cambridge, Mass.: Harvard University Press, 1956), 190, 185, hereafter cited in text; on Wright as a contributor to proletarian literature, see Herbert Mitgang, "An American Master and New Discoveries," *New York Times,* 1 January 1992.

19. Rather than embrace a more narrow period view, I concur that proletarian fiction "reflects the life of any typical cross-section of the proletariat and need not be more revolutionary than the proletariat . . . at the time" (E. A. Schachner, qtd. Rideout, 167).

20. David Sprague Herreshoff, *Labor into Art: The Theme of Work in Nineteenth-Century American Literature* (Detroit: Wayne State University Press, 1991), 147. In a provocative essay arguing for the relative scarcity of strikes, Melvin Dubofsky, "Not So 'Turbulent Years': A New Look at the 1930s," in *Life and Labor: Dimensions of American Working-Class History,* ed. Charles Stephenson and Robert Asher (Albany: State University of New York Press, 1986), 205–23, implicitly suggests this as another distortion of the proletarian school.

On erasures of the female proletariat by women female authors, see Ruth McKenney, *Industrial Valley* (1939; reprint, Ithaca, N.Y.: ILR Press, 1992), for example, 113. Jeremy Brecher, *Strike!* (Boston: South End Press, 1971), 178, finds her study "over-dramatized" but, although he chronicles the role of women in a Goodyear sit-down strike (184), he does not mention her omission of it.

21. [Edwin Seaver], "Call for an American Writers' Congress," *New Masses* 14 (January–March 1935): 20. See also his "The Proletarian Novel," in *American Writers' Congress,* ed. Henry Hart (New York: International Publishers, 1935), 101.

22. Mike Gold, "Go Left, Young Writers!" (1929; reprinted in *Mike Gold: A Literary Anthology,* ed. Michael Folsom [New York: International Publishers, 1972], 189).

23. For a summary of the divisions within leftist critical ranks, particularly regarding the "hobo" and petty-bourgeois novels, see Daniel Aaron, *Writers on the Left* (1961; reprint, New York: Avon, 1965), 310–12. On a representative social novelist's attacks on proletarian authorship, see James T. Farrell, *A Note on Literary Criticism* (New York: Vanguard Press, 1936) (hereafter cited in text), and his "A Working-Class Novel," *Nation* 137 (20 December 1933): 714. See also "James T. Farrell," *Dictionary of Literary Biography,* vol. 9, pt. 1 (Detroit: Gale Research Co., 1981), 265.

One should, however, contextualize negative responses to writers like Conroy in the political debates of the Communist Party, particularly the split between Stalinists like Gold and Trotskyite dissenters like Farrell, a schism that became wider with the Moscow Trials beginning in 1936 and the Hitler-Stalin Pact of 1939. A final irony is that Conroy himself disliked being viewed as a cultural agent of the party. See Jack Conroy, "Introduction," *The Disinherited* (1933; reprint, Westport, Conn.: Lawrence Hill, 1982), x, hereafter cited in text.

24. Ralph Bogardus and Fred Hobson, "Introduction," *Literature at the Barricades: American Writers in the 1930s,* ed. Bogardus and Hobson (Tuscaloosa: University of Alabama Press, 1982), 7. See also essays by various hands in *Proletarian Writers of the Thirties,* ed. David Madden (Carbondale: Southern Illinois University Press, 1968), particularly Jack Conroy, "Robert Cantwell's *Land of Plenty,*" 74–84, and Erling Larsen, "Jack Conroy's *The Disinherited:* or, *The Way It Was,*" 85–95.

25. Rideout, 190–94, adds a fourth category, the "novel of middle-class decay," with which I do not agree. I concur with Peeler that Farrell, the only male practitioner named by Rideout, is a social novelist. In the case of Josephine Herbst, the only female one Rideout named, though early volumes of her trilogy chart the bourgeois Trexler family from the nineteenth to the early twentieth centuries, her Depression Era text *Rope of Gold* (1939) (discussed in chapter 6) focuses on middle-class radicals, particularly their marital problems. She gives the plot a feminist rather than a bourgeois-decline slant. Rideout offers no other examples.

26. Paula Rabinowitz, *Labor and Desire: Women's Revolutionary Fiction in Depression America* (Chapel Hill: University of North Carolina Press, 1991), 69, hereafter cited in text.

27. Barbara Foley, "Women and the Left in the 1930s," *American Literary History* 2 (Spring 1990): 163.

28. Amy Godine, "Notes Toward a Reappraisal of Depression Literature," *Prospects* 5 (1979): 212–14, hereafter cited in text.

29. Richard Pells, *Radical Visions and American Dreams: Culture and Society in the Depression Years* (New York: Harper & Row, 1973), 25.

30. See Carey McWilliams, *Factories in the Field: The Story of Migrant Farm Labor in California* (Boston: Little, Brown, 1939), 327.

31. Harvey Winick and Paul M. Kinsie, *The Lively Commerce: Prostitution in the United States* (Chicago: Quadrangle Books, 1971), 155.

32. *Steinbeck: A Life in Letters,* ed. Elaine Steinbeck and Robert Wallstein (1952; reprint, New York: Viking/Penguin, 1975), 178; *Working Days: The Journals of John Steinbeck,* ed. Robert DeMott (New York: Penguin, 1989), 86.

33. Theodore Pollack, "On the Ending of *The Grapes of Wrath,*" in *A Companion to* The Grapes of Wrath, ed. Warren French (New York: Viking Press, 1963), 226.

34. James T. Farrell, *Studs Lonigan, A Trilogy: Young Lonigan* (1932), *The Young*

Manhood of Studs Lonigan (1934), and *Judgment Day* (1935) (New York: Vanguard Press), hereafter cited in text.

35. Qtd. Edgar M. Branch, *James T. Farrell* (Boston: Twayne, 1971), 16, hereafter cited in text.

36. James T. Farrell, *Reflections at Fifty and Other Essays* (1954; reprint, London: Neville Spearman, 1956), 148n.

37. Charles Child Walcutt, *American Literary Naturalism: A Divided Stream* (Minneapolis: University of Minnesota Press, 1956), 241, hereafter cited in text.

38. Josephine Herbst, "Studs Lonigan in Conclusion," *New Masses* 15 (25 May 1935): 25. A brief exception, calling attention to Mrs. Lonigan as an "inversion" of the Irish-American saintly mother, is Donald Fanning, "Introduction," in James T. Farrell, *Studs Lonigan* (1935; reprint, Urbana: University of Illinois Press, 1993), xxiv.

39. Donald Pizer, "James T. Farrell and the 1930s," in Bogardus and Hobson, 73.

40. Mike Gold, *Jews Without Money* (1930; reprint, with the 1935 introduction by Gold, New York: Carroll and Graf, 1958), hereafter cited in text.

41. Daniel Aaron, "Introduction," in *The Disinherited* (New York: Hill and Wang, 1963), viii.

42. Clinton Simpson, "*The Disinherited,*" *Saturday Review of Literature* 10 (2 December 1933): 305.

43. Henry T. Finck, "Employments Unsuitable for Women," *Independent* 63 (April 1907): 836. For a spirited response to period detractors' arguments, see Mary Gay Humphreys, "The New Working-Girl," *Scribner's* 20 (October 1896): 502–13.

44. Mrs. John [Bessie] Van Vorst and Marie Van Vorst, *The Woman Who Toils* (London: Grant Richards, 1903), 38. See also *Thoughts of Busy Girls,* ed. Grace Hoadley Dodge (New York: Assell, 1892), purported essays by "reconstructed" wage earners that are probably the work of the Working Girls' Club founder Grace Dodge.

45. Leonard Erlich, "*Jews Without Money,*" *Saturday Review of Literature* 6 (19 April 1930): 944.

46. Sydney Stahl Weinberg, *The World of Our Mothers: The Lives of Jewish Immigrant Women* (New York: Schocken, 1988), 54, hereafter cited in text.

47. Tom Kromer, *Waiting for Nothing* (New York: Knopf, 1935), hereafter cited in text.

48. Edward Anderson, *Hungry Men* (1935; reprint, New York: Penguin, 1985); Nelson Algren, *Somebody in Boots* (1935; reprint, New York: Thunder's Mouth Press, 1987), hereafter cited in text.

49. James Benet, "New York's Vice Ring," *New Republic* 87 (10 June 1936): 126.

50. "Prostitution in New York City," *Nation* 142 (25 March 1936): 369. For a

dissenting view, complete with the story of a prostitute who chose her profession, see Walter C. Reckless, "An Unregimented Professional: Millicent's Own Story," in *Vice in Chicago* (Chicago: University of Chicago Press, 1932), 146–51, and chap. 6, passim. Paul R. Cressey in *The Taxi-Dance Hall* (Chicago: University of Chicago Press, 1932), 265n, also denied that Chicago women moved from taxi dancing to the vice trade.

51. Peter Roffman and Jim Purdy, *The Hollywood Social Problem Film: Madness, Despair, and Politics from the Depression to the Fifties* (Bloomington: Indiana University Press, 1981), 20, 22–24.

52. Andrew Bergman, *We're in the Money: Depression America and Its Films* (New York: Harper & Row, 1971), 52.

53. Jules Chametsky, "Edward Dahlberg, Early and Late," in Madden, 71.

54. Jacob A. Riis, *How the Other Half Lives* (1890; reprint, New York: Dover, 1971), 183.

55. Jack Conroy, "*Somebody in Boots*" (1935), reprinted in *New Masses: An Anthology* (New York: International Publishers, 1969), 237.

56. See Barbara Meil Hobson, *Uneasy Virtue: The Politics of Prostitution and the American Reform Tradition* (Chicago: University of Chicago Press, 1987), chap. 8.

57. Mike Gold, "Love on a Garbage Dump" (1928), reprinted in *Mike Gold*, 177–85, hereafter cited in text.

58. Robert Cantwell, *The Land of Plenty* (New York: Farrar and Rinehart, 1934), hereafter cited in text.

59. Mary McCarthy, *Intellectual Memoirs: New York, 1936–1938* (New York: Harcourt Brace Jovanovich, 1992), 7.

60. Albert Halper, *The Chute* (New York: Viking Press, 1937), hereafter cited in text.

61. John E. Hart, "Albert Halper," *Dictionary of Literary Biography*, vol. 9, pt. 2 (Detroit: Gale Research Co., 1981), 95.

62. Jean Collier Brown, *The Negro Woman Worker*, Women's Bureau Bulletin no. 165 (Washington, D.C.: U.S. Government Printing Office, 1938), 1, hereafter cited in text.

63. Cheryl Lynn Greenberg, *Or Does It Explode?: Black Harlem in the Great Depression* (New York: Oxford University Press, 1991), 20, 23, hereafter cited in text.

64. Claude McKay, *Home to Harlem* (1928; reprint, Boston: Northeastern University Press, 1987), hereafter cited in text; Wallace Thurman, *The Blacker the Berry* (1929; reprint, New York: Collier/Macmillan, 1970), hereafter cited in text; Arnold Rampersad, *I, Too, Sing America: The Life of Langston Hughes*, vol. 1 (New York: Oxford University Press, 1986), 58.

65. W. E. B. Du Bois said that on reading McKay, he felt in need of a bath. See Wayne F. Cooper, "Foreword," McKay, *Home to Harlem*, xviii.

66. By 1915 one million southern blacks had migrated, predominantly to northern cities; by 1930, more than two million. See Jacqueline S. Jones, *Labor of Love, Labor of Sorrow: Black Women, Work, and the Family, from Slavery to the Present* (1985; reprint, New York: Vintage Books, 1986), 112, 153.

67. Langston Hughes, *Not Without Laughter* (1930; reprint, New York: Collier/ Macmillan, 1969), hereafter cited in text.

68. Langston Hughes, *The Big Sea* (1940; reprint, New York: Knopf, 1986), 305.

69. Walt Carmon, "Away from Harlem," *New Masses* 6 (October 1930): 17–18.

70. Richard Wright, *Native Son* (1940; reprint, New York: Harper & Row/ Perennial, 1989), hereafter cited in text.

71. Robert Felgar, *Richard Wright* (Boston: Twayne, 1980), 80.

72. Sylvia H. Keady, "Richard Wright's Women Characters and Inequality," *Black American Literature Forum* 10 (1976): 125, 124.

73. Kathleen Ochshorn, "The Community of *Native Son,*" *Mississippi Quarterly* 12 (Fall 1989): 389.

74. Elsewhere Hughes positively acknowledged the existence of white women organizers and their ethnic, female rank-and-file followers when he collaborated on *Blood on the Fields,* a 1934 play about the California ACWU leader Caroline Decker. Wright made slighting references to white female workers' aspirations and values in "The Man Who Went to Chicago," an autobiographical essay in the original *American Hunger,* not published until 1961. See *Eight Men* (New York: Thunder's Mouth Press, 1961), 261–65. *Black Boy* (1937; reprint, New York: HarperCollins/ Library of America, 1991), 261, also contains a disparaging portrait.

75. Edith Kine, "The Garment Union Comes to the Negro Worker," *Opportunity* 12 (April 1934): 107–10; interview with Mary Sweet, in *First-Person America,* ed. Ann Banks (New York: Random House, 1980), 133–35. See also chapter 1 of this book.

76. Alfred Kazin, *Starting Out in the Thirties* (1962; reprint, Boston: Little, Brown, 1965), 13, hereafter cited in text.

77. Dorothy Dinnerstein, *The Mermaid and the Minotaur: Sexual Arrangements and Human Malaise* (New York: Harper/Colophon, 1976), 124.

Chapter Three. Feminine Social Protest Fiction and the Mother-Burden

1. Robert Thompson, "An Interview with Jack Conroy," *Missouri Review* 7 (Fall 1983): 158, hereafter cited in text. Consistent with his rough-and-ready persona, he barely entered a state college before he left it.

2. Alfred Kazin, *Starting Out in the Thirties* (1962; reprint, Boston: Little, Brown, 1965), 78, hereafter cited in text.

3. Jack Conroy, "Introduction," in *The Disinherited* (1933; reprint, Westport,

Conn.: Lawrence Hill, 1982), vi, 1982 edition hereafter cited in text; *Steinbeck: A Life in Letters,* ed. Elaine Steinbeck and Robert Wallstein (1952; reprint, New York: Viking/Penguin, 1975), 101–2. Steinbeck himself did a WPA stint in the early 1930s: a census of the dogs of Monterey. See his "A Primer on the Thirties," *Esquire* 80 (October 1973): 130.

4. Paula Rabinowitz, "Maternity as History: Gender and the Transformation of Genre in Meridel Le Sueur's *The Girl,*" *Contemporary Literature* 29 (Winter 1988): 542. Although I agree with Rabinowitz that Le Sueur celebrated a "mythic maternal power" (545) in *The Girl,* she and other scholars use the revised 1978 text, refashioned at the behest of West End Press. Le Sueur herself wrote her editor, John Crawford, that year that the women in it were "much more social and collective" in the revised version. See her excerpted letter in John Crawford, "The Book's Progress: The Making of *The Girl,*" in Meridel Le Sueur, *The Girl* (rev. ed., Albuquerque: West End Press, 1990), 138. Furthermore, because the original manuscript is inaccessible to scholars, I base my discussion on Le Sueur's published writings from the 1930s, including sections of her novella.

5. Gold, for example, published editorials and fiction in *New Masses,* Farrell reviews in the *New Republic,* Caldwell and Algren fiction in the *Anvil.*

6. See Meridel Le Sueur, editorial endnote, "Women on the Breadlines," *New Masses* 7 (January 1932): 7; on Smedley, see Walt Carmon, "Away from Harlem," *New Masses* 6 (October 1930): 18.

7. Paula Rabinowitz, "Writing Red: Women's Short Fiction of the 1930s," in *Writing Red: An Anthology of American Women Writers, 1930–1940,* ed. Charlotte Nekola and Paula Rabinowitz (New York: Feminist Press, 1987), 26.

8. Constance Coiner, "Literature of Resistance: The Intersection of Feminism and the Communist Left in Meridel Le Sueur and Tillie Olsen," in *Left Politics and the Literary Profession,* ed. Lennard J. Davis and M. Bella Mirabella (New York: Columbia University Press, 1990), 165, hereafter cited in text.

9. Elsa Jane Dixler, "The Woman Question: Women and the American Communist Party, 1929–1941" (Ph.D. diss., Yale University, 1974), 129, hereafter cited in text; A. Landy, "Two Questions on the Status of Women Under Capitalism," *Communist* 20 (September 1941): 821.

10. Margaret Cowl, "We Must Win the Women," *Political Affairs* 16 (June 1937): 551, hereafter cited in text. See also Ella Reeve Bloor's pamphlet-paean *Women in the Soviet Union* (New York: Workers Library Publishers, 1938).

11. William Z. Foster, *History of the Communist Party in the United States* (New York: International Publishers, 1952), 264.

12. Dixler's third chapter, "Housewives and Mothers," trenchantly questions the party's commitment to working mothers.

13. "Fight with the Workers for Immediate Relief" read a June 1933 *Working Woman* headline; see also *Daily Worker,* 21 August 1933, 4.

14. On the housewife-activist, see Dixler, 136–43; on milk strikes, Kim Chernin, *In My Mother's House: A Daughter's Story* (New York: Harper & Row, 1983), 94.

15. Mary Inman, *In Woman's Defense* (Los Angeles: Committee to Organize the Advancement of Women, 1940), hereafter cited in text. For an early plea to compensate housewives, see Flora McDonald Thompson, "The Work of Wives," *Outlook* 91 (April 1909): 994–96. Like Inman's, it was a cry in the wilderness.

16. Elizabeth Gurley Flynn, "Housewives—Our Country's Heroines," *People's Daily World* [formerly *Daily Worker*], 8 January 1939, 9.

17. Edward Newhouse, *This Is Your Day* (1937; reprint, New York: AMS Press, 1977), 39, hereafter cited in text.

18. Helen Coppell, "Out of the Hole," *Anvil* 1 (November–December 1933): 22.

19. Deborah Rosenfelt, "From the Thirties: Tillie Olsen and the Radical Tradition," *Feminist Studies* 7 (Fall 1981): 403. For a contrasting emphasis on Olsen's quest motif and the (unfinished) finale of *Yonnondio* as a journey to feminist spiritual transcendence, see Elaine Neil Orr, *Tillie Olsen and a Feminist Spiritual Vision* (Jackson: University Press of Mississippi, 1987), 168–70.

20. Joanne L. Goodwin, "An American Experiment in Paid Motherhood: The Implementation of Mothers' Pensions in Early Twentieth-Century Chicago," *Gender and History* 4 (Autumn 1992): 338.

21. Tillie Olsen, "A Note About This Book," in *Yonnondio: From the Thirties* (New York: Delacorte/Seymour Lawrence, 1974), n.p.; 1974 edition hereafter cited in text. The standard defense of the work as a recovered text appears in Catherine Stimpson, "Three Women Work It Out," *Nation* (30 November 1974): 565–68. See also "*Yonnondio: From the Thirties,*" *New Yorker* (25 March 1974): 140.

22. On the projected desertion, abortion, and death scenes, see Mickey Pearlman and Abby H. P. Werlock, *Tillie Olsen* (Boston: Twayne, 1991), 52, hereafter cited in text; on Will's hoboing, see Michael Staub, "The Struggle for 'Selfness' Through Speech in Olsen's *Yonnondio,*" *Studies in American Fiction* 16 (Autumn 1988): 138, hereafter cited in text.

23. Marleen Barr, "Tillie Olsen," *Dictionary of Literary Biography,* ed. Daniel Walden, vol. 28 (Detroit: Gale Research Co., 1984), 197.

24. See Tillie Olsen, "General Notes for *Yonnondio,*" folder 13, Berg Collection, New York Public Library.

25. Susan Porter Benson, "Women, Work, and the Family Economy: Industrial Homework in Rhode Island," in *Homework: Historical and Contemporary Perspectives*

on Paid Labor at Home, ed. Eileen Boris and Cynthia R. Daniels (Urbana: University of Illinois Press, 1989), 71.

26. Annie Gottlieb, "*Yonnondio: From the Thirties,*" *New York Times Book Review,* 31 March 1974, 5.

27. Robert D. Stolorow, Bernard Brandchaft, and George E. Atwood, "Bonds That Shackle, Ties That Free," in *Psychoanalytic Treatment: An Intersubjective Approach,* ed. Robert D. Stolorow, Bernard Brandchaft, and George E. Atwood (Hillsdale, N.J.: Psychoanalytic Press, 1987), 49. In contrast, for a representative feminist, and, to my mind, less reliable interpretation of Anna's behavior as "the grotesque shape of motherhood in . . . patriarchy," see Mara Faulker, *Protest and Possibility in the Writing of Tillie Olsen* (Charlottesville: University Press of Virginia, 1993), 44.

28. E. Ann Kaplan, *Motherhood and Representation: The Mother in Popular Culture and Melodrama* (London: Routledge, 1992), 4, hereafter cited in text.

29. Erika Duncan, "Coming of Age in the Thirties: A Portrait of Tillie Olsen," *Book Forum* 4 (1982): 211, hereafter cited in text. Nor is it surprising to find evasiveness about her relation to her own mother in a rare, brief description from *Mother to Daughter: Daughter to Mother, a Daybook,* comp. Tillie Olsen (Old Westbury, N.Y.: Feminist Press, 1984), 263.

30. Rebecca Harding Davis, *Life in the Iron Mills and Other Stories,* ed. and intro. Tillie Olsen (Old Westbury, N.Y.: Feminist Press, 1972).

31. Marion Glastonbury, "The Best-Kept Secret—How Working-Class Women Live and What They Know," *Women's Studies* 2 (1979): 177.

32. Bell Gale Chevigny, "*Yonnondio: From the Thirties,*" *Village Voice,* 23 May 1974, 39, calls Anna the book's "other center of vision."

33. Tillie Lerner, "The Iron Throat," *Partisan Review* 1 (April–May 1934): 3–9, hereafter cited in text.

34. On child development theories, particularly the self-other relationship and the mother-child dyad, as well as the "shift . . . from oedipal to preoedipal— that is, from father to mother," in psychoanalytic research over the past twenty-five years, see the summary in Jessica Benjamin, *The Bonds of Love: Psychoanalysis, Feminism, and the Problem of Domination* (New York: Pantheon, 1988), 11, 12, 247n–248n. See also D. W. Winnicott, "Ego Distortion in Terms of True and False Self," in *The Maturational Processes and the Facilitating Environment* (Madison, Wisc.: International Publishers, 1965), 141, 145–60, hereafter cited in text.

35. Lorraine Jennrich, "Some Experiments in Case Work in Motherless Families," *Proceedings of the National Conference of Social Work, Atlantic City, 1936* (Chicago: University of Chicago Press, 1936), 163.

36. Alice Miller, *Prisoners of Childhood* (New York: Basic Books, 1986), 69, 73, hereafter cited in text.

37. Two unpublished versions of the story are in the Berg Collection, New York Public Library. Though not dated, the note atop the first page of the second version reads "Begun at age 18 (?)," although it is believed Olsen began the stories in 1927, when she was only fourteen or fifteen; first and second versions hereafter cited in text as Berg 1 and Berg 2, respectively.

38. Olsen, who admired Katherine Mansfield's work, considered Nena a Mansfield type (Berg 2: 5, 7), a significant designation in that some of Mansfield's best stories were concerned with young women whose development was preempted, whose working-class mothers failed to empower them. See the pinched girls in "The Woman at the Store" (1912) and "The Doll's House" (1922).

39. Biographical data appear in Neala Schleuning Yount, " 'America: Song We Sang Without Knowing': Meridel Le Sueur's America" (Ph.D. diss., University of Minnesota, 1978), 28–34, hereafter cited in text.

40. Meridel Le Sueur, *Crusaders* (New York: Blue Heron Press, 1955), 39.

41. Blanche H. Gelfant, " 'Everybody Steals': Language as Theft in Meridel Le Sueur's *The Girl*," in *Tradition and the Talents of Women*, ed. Florence Howe (Urbana: University of Illinois Press, 1991), 183, hereafter cited in text.

42. Meridel Le Sueur, "Proletarian Literature and the Middle West," in *American Writers' Congress*, ed. Henry Hart (New York: International Publishers, 1935), 135–37.

43. Meridel Le Sueur, "I Was Marching," in *Ripening: Selected Work, Meridel Le Sueur*, 2d ed., ed. Elaine Hedges (1934; reprint, New York: Feminist Press, 1990), hereafter cited in text.

44. Tillie Olsen, "The Strike" (1934), reprinted in *Calling Home: Working-Class Women's Writings, an Anthology*, ed. Janet Zandy (New Brunswick, N.J.: Rutgers University Press, 1990), 280, hereafter cited in text.

45. "She heard only some of the words, the ones that her body's experience repeated to her, the class struggle, militant workers, the broad masses" (Meridel Le Sueur, "Tonight Is Part of the Struggle" [1935], reprinted in *Salute to Spring* [New York: International Publishers, 1940]). See also Linda Ray Pratt, "Woman Writer in the CP: The Case of Meridel Le Sueur," *Women's Studies* 14 (1988): 257.

46. Tom Kromer, *Waiting for Nothing* (New York: Knopf, 1935), 103–7.

47. Ashley Buck, "Now He Is Safe" (1940), reprinted in *Writers in Revolt: An Anvil Anthology*, ed. Jack Conroy and Curt Johnson (Westport, Conn.: Lawrence Hill, 1973), 21–25.

48. Meridel Le Sueur, "Annunciation" (1935), reprinted in *Salute to Spring*, 81–97, hereafter cited in text.

49. Meridel Le Sueur, "Biography of My Daughter" (1935), reprinted in *Salute to Spring*, 98–110, hereafter cited in text.

50. Agnes Smedley, *Daughter of Earth* (1929; reprint, Old Westbury, N.Y.:

Feminist Press, 1987), 1987 edition hereafter cited in text. (A 1976 Feminist Press edition is referred to in note 57.)

51. For biographical data on Smedley, I am indebted to Janice R. MacKinnon and Stephen R. MacKinnon, *Agnes Smedley: The Life and Times of an American Radical* (Berkeley: University of California Press, 1988), chaps. 1–6, hereafter cited in text.

52. Agnes Smedley, *Battle Hymn of China* (New York: Knopf, 1943), 10, hereafter cited in text.

53. On Smedley's supposed lack of sophistication, see Malcolm Cowley, Foreword to Agnes Smedley, *Daughter of Earth* (New York: Coward-McCann, 1935), vi; on her revolutionary's unattractiveness, see Cowley, *The Dream of the Golden Mountains: Remembering the 1930s* (New York: Viking Press, 1964), 225.

54. Agnes Smedley, "Cell Mates," *Call Magazine* [Sunday supplement, *New York Call*], "My Cell Mate: No. 1," 15 February 1920, 1; "My Cell Mate: No. 2," 22 February 1920, 1–2; "My Cell Mate: No. 3," 29 February 1920, 2; "My Cell Mate: No. 4," 14 March 1920, 2, hereafter cited in text.

55. Judith A. Scheffler, "Agnes Smedley's 'Cell Mates': A Writer's Discovery of Voice, Form, and Subject in Prison," in *Faith of a (Woman) Writer*, ed. Alice Kessler-Harris and William McBrien (Westport, Conn.: Greenwood Press, 1988), 204.

56. Agnes Smedley, "The Women Take a Hand" (1942), reprinted in Agnes Smedley, *Portraits of Chinese Women in Revolution* (Old Westbury, N.Y.: Feminist Press, 1974), 122.

57. Paul Lauter, Afterword to Agnes Smedley, *Daughter of Earth* (Old Westbury, N.Y.: Feminist Press, 1976), 416, hereafter cited in text.

58. Agnes Smedley, "Women Agricultural Workers" (1934), reprinted in *Portraits,* 115.

59. Agnes Smedley, "Five Women of Mukden" (1930), reprinted in *Portraits,* 33, 29. Manchurian Mukden was, however, a semicolony of Japan. For woman-enslaving attitudes in China itself, see "Youth and Women's Committees" (1930), reprinted in *Portraits,* 112; regarding a similar bondage for upper-class wives, see "Hsu Mei-ling" (1930), reprinted in *Portraits,* 36.

60. On mothers' attitudes see, for instance, 1973 interviews with the bookbinder Minnie Grabowetski (I-86), the Harlem domestic Mary Belle Stanley (I-31), and the homemaker Grace Gelo (I-25), City University of New York Oral History Research Project, New York City Immigrant Labor Oral History, Tamiment Library, New York University. See also interviews with Kitty McCulloch and Mary Owsley, in *Hard Times: An Oral History of the Great Depression in America,* comp. Studs Terkel (New York: Pantheon, 1970), 56, 62. Complaints about martyr mothers appear in quoted interviews in Glen H. Elder, Jr., *Children of the Great*

Depression: Social Change in Life Experience (Chicago: University of Chicago Press, 1974), 112–13.

61. See, for instance, *Hard Times Cotton Mill Girls: Personal Histories of Womanhood and Poverty in the South,* ed. Victoria Byerly (Ithaca, N.Y.: ILR Press, 1986), 23, 48, 53–54; interview with Elizabeth Miller, in *First-Person America,* ed. Ann Banks (New York: Random House, 1980), 165; Terkel, 55, 62. See also a 1939 Federal Writers' Project interview with Betty Piontkowsky, reprinted in *Calling Home,* 54.

62. Interview with Yetta Brier (G-21), Oral History Research Project, Tamiment.

Chapter Four. Love's Wages: Women, Work, Fiction, and Romance

1. Murray Kempton, *Part of Our Time: Some Ruins and Monuments of the Thirties* (New York: Simon and Schuster, 1955), 217, hereafter cited in text.

2. Maxwell Bodenheim, "To a Revolutionary Girl," *New Masses* 11 (3 April 1934): 8, hereafter cited in text. It is fashionable to speak of "woman's desire," a term encompassing but not limited to feminine romanticism. Modern feminists with a poststructuralist or psychoanalytic bent thus write of "desire coded as love . . . [as] the narrative repository of femininity" (Paula Rabinowitz, *Labor and Desire: Women's Revolutionary Fiction in Depression America* [Chapel Hill: University of North Carolina Press, 1991], 40, hereafter cited in text), and of woman's "missing desire which takes the form of adoring the man who possesses [agency]" (Jessica Benjamin, *The Bonds of Love: Psychoanalysis, Feminism, and the Problem of Domination* [New York: Pantheon, 1988], 86, hereafter cited in text). Critical of the cultural arrangements that continue to produce it, modern feminists see a widespread pattern of womanly displacement of creative energy onto loving, "a love in which the woman submits to and adores another who is what she cannot be" (ibid., 86). It is beyond the boundaries of this study to enter the debate on feminine passivity, emotional and sexual, other than to note that modern feminists have inherited a controversy that divided 1930s leftists. Compare, for instance, Bodenheim's verse or Mike Gold's essays on virile, woman-conquering politics with Mary Inman's fiery denunciations of romantic love in her *In Woman's Defense* (Los Angeles: Committee to Organize the Advancement of Women, 1940), hereafter cited in text.

3. Steinbeck had an unsuccessful meeting with another assertive woman journalist, Anna Louise Strong. He termed her a "Red" but was as put off by her gender as her politics. He would have probably abhorred Smedley, although there is no record that they met. See Jackson J. Benson, *The True Adventures of John Steinbeck, Writer* (New York: Viking Press, 1984), 425.

4. Agnes Smedley, *Daughter of Earth* (1929; reprint, Old Westbury, N.Y.: Feminist Press, 1987), 405. Marie's declaration appears in the closing pages of the original edition of *Daughter of Earth,* the culmination of a short-lived affair with Juan Diaz (in real life, Herenbala Gupta) and a lengthy "marriage" to Anand (Viren Chattopadhaya) that drove her to nervous collapse. For details, see Janice R. MacKinnon and Stephen R. MacKinnon, *Agnes Smedley: The Life and Times of an American Radical* (Berkeley: University of California Press, 1988), 42, 170, and chap. 6, passim.

5. Of the three, only Le Sueur lays the groundwork for, but stops short of, lesbian relationships. Party doctrine on homosexuality and lesbianism was not enlightened. Although, as Alan Wald observes, there are occasional gay and lesbian scenes in novels by 1930s leftists, they are usually presented homophobically (Letter to author, 23 June 1993).

6. The strike militant in radical fiction and the extent to which she transcends her biological and gender role is taken up in chapter 5.

7. Saul Levitt, "Pick Up," *New Masses* 26 (11 January 1938): 50. On the eight hundred thousand real-life couples who canceled or put off marrying during the Depression, see John F. Bauman and Thomas H. Coode, *In the Eye of the Great Depression: New Deal Reporters and the Agony of the American People* (De Kalb:: Northern Illinois University Press, 1988), 77, hereafter cited in text. For a fact-filled, one-page summary of the upsurge in contraception during the time, see Rosalind Rosenberg, *Divided Lives: American Women in the Twentieth Century* (New York: Hill and Wang, 1992), 109. Prefacing that summary, Rosenberg quotes a Studs Terkel interviewee: "Do you realize how many people [of the Depression generation] are not married?" (108).

8. Morgan Himelstein, *Drama Was a Weapon* (New Brunswick,N.J.: Rutgers University Press, 1963), 76.

9. Brooks Atkinson, "Garment Specialty," *New York Times,* 23 January 1938, sec. 11, 1.

10. Fannia Cohn, "Facing the Future," *American Federationist* 42 (November 1935): 1203, hereafter cited in text.

11. Jon Bloom, "Workers' Education," *Encyclopedia of the American Left,* ed. Mari Jo Buhle, Paul Buhle, and Dan Georgakas (New York: Garland, 1990), 850.

12. Gladys L. Palmer, *The Industrial Experience of Women Workers at the Summer Schools, 1928 to 1930,* Women's Bureau Bulletin no. 89 (Washington, D.C.: U.S. Government Printing Office, 1931).

13. Mike Gold, *Jews Without Money* (1930; reprint, with the 1935 introduction by Gold, New York: Carroll and Graf, 1958), 307.

14. *I Am a Woman Worker: A Scrapbook of Autobiographies,* ed. Andria Taylor Hourwich and Gladys L. Palmer (New York: Affiliated Schools for Workers, 1936),

hereafter cited in text. Interestingly, the authentic laboring voices of that collection disappear entirely in the tired, derivative historical summaries in *A Scrapbook of the American Labor Movement,* edited by Palmer and Hourwich and published in 1932 by the Affiliated Schools.

15. Lillian S. Robinson, "Working/Women/Writing," in *Sex, Class, and Culture* (Bloomington: Indiana University Press, 1978), 250.

16. I do, though, find Robinson's claim that these women authors "develop[ed] their potential as part of their class and its struggle—a commitment that they did not separate from self-actualization" (232) somewhat overstated. Still, they form a collective voice of self-assertion compared to interviews with women conducted for the Women's Bureau. See Amy Hewes, "Appendix," *Woman Workers in the Third Year of the Depression,* Women's Bureau Bulletin no. 103 (Washington, D.C.: U.S. Government Printing Office, 1933).

17. For stereotypes of empty-headed marriage hunters, see Dorothy Richardson, *The Long Day: The Story of a New York Working Girl* (1905; reprint, Charlottesville: University Press of Virginia, 1990); Mrs. John [Bessie] Van Vorst and Marie Van Vorst, *The Woman Who Toils* (London: Grant Richards, 1903), 38; and Frances Donovan, *The Saleslady* (Chicago: University of Chicago Press, 1929) and *The Woman Who Waits* (Boston: R. G. Badger, 1920). On working women's historic striving for identity through sexual expressiveness with men, see Kathy Peiss, *Cheap Amusements: Working Women and Leisure in Turn-of-the-Century New York* (Philadelphia: Temple University Press, 1986).

18. Hilda Smith, "The Bryn Mawr Summer School of 1927," *American Federationist* 34 (October 1927): 1220. A 1920s force at the Bryn Mawr Summer School, Smith was organizing educational programs for FERA (later the WPA Workers Education Service) by the New Deal Era. For a completely different view of women's motives for attending workers' colleges, in this case coeducational ones, see Benjamin Stolberg, *Tailor's Progress: The Story of a Famous Union and the Men Who Made It* (Garden City, N.Y.: Doubleday, Doran, 1944), 290–91.

19. Sallie Westwood, *All Day, Every Day: Factory and Family in the Making of Women's Lives* (Urbana: University of Illinois Press, 1984), 101, hereafter cited in text. See also Leslie Woodcock Tentler, *Wage-Earning Women: Industrial Work and Family Life in the United States, 1900–1930* (New York: Oxford University Press, 1979), 73, hereafter cited in text.

20. John Cawelti, *Adventure, Mystery, and Romance: Formula Stories in Art and Popular Culture* (Chicago: University of Chicago Press, 1976), 42, hereafter cited in text.

21. One period study quotes a woman wage earner who found proletarian novels "untrue." See Louis Adamic, "What the Proletariat Reads . . . ," *Saturday Review* 11 (1 December 1934): 322. Walter Rideout, *The Radical Novel in the*

United States, 1900–1954 (Cambridge, Mass.: Harvard University Press, 1956), 320n, does, however, cite a lone 1939 study, a doctoral dissertation on Flint, Michigan, blue-collar readers, to challenge Adamic's view.

22. The romance form that certain 1930s authors subverted concerned a heterosexual love relationship, star-crossed or otherwise, and sometimes replete with historical costumes (vide *Gone with the Wind,* 1936). In *The American Novel and Its Tradition* (Garden City, N.Y.: Doubleday, 1957), 20, Richard Chase, distinguishing the form from higher imaginative art such as *The Blithedale Romance,* curtly dismisses the Mitchell School as the "other stream of romance." But John Cawelti, in *Adventure, Mystery, and Romance: Formula Stories as Art and Popular Culture,* takes the form and its "antiromance" antithesis more seriously as cultural artifacts. See also Kay J. Mussell, "Romantic Fiction," in *Handbook of Popular Culture,* ed. M. Thomas Inge (Westport, Conn.: Greenwood Press, 1980), 317–43. In my view, Mussell wrongly places Hurst under the rubric (322).

23. Harry Salpeter, "Fannie Hurst: Sob-Sister of American Fiction," *Bookman* 73 (August 1931): 612, hereafter cited in text.

24. Mary Rose Shaughnessy, *Myths About Love and Women: The Fiction of Fannie Hurst* (New York: Gordon Press, 1979), 32, hereafter cited in text; Antoinette Frederick, "Fannie Hurst," in *Notable American Women,* ed. Carol Sicherman and Carol Hurd Green (Cambridge, Mass.: Belknap/Harvard University Press, 1980), 360–61, hereafter cited in text. Further biographical data appear in Virginia M. Burke, "Zora Neale Hurston and Fannie Hurst as They Saw Each Other," *CLA Journal* 20 (June 1977): 435–47, hereafter cited in text.

Modern revisionists have resurrected *Imitation of Life* (1933), but scant *Back Street.* See Lauren Berlant, "National Brands/National Body: *Imitation of Life,*" in *Comparative American Identities: Race, Sex, and Nationality in the Modern Text,* ed. Hortense J. Spillers (New York: Routledge, 1991).

25. On romance magazine formulae, see, for instance, Dena Hutto, "*True Story,*" in *American Mass-Market Magazines,* ed. Alan Nourie and Barbara Nourie (Westport, Conn.: Greenwood Press, 1990), 510–15. On *True Story*'s working-class readership, see Lizabeth Cohen, *Making a New Deal: Industrial Workers in Chicago, 1919–1939* (Cambridge: Cambridge University Press, 1990), 101–2.

26. Fannie Hurst, *Anatomy of Me* (Garden City, N.Y.: Doubleday, 1958), 241–42, hereafter cited in text.

27. "*Back Street,*" *Books,* 18 January 1931, 4; "*Back Street,*" *Saturday Review* 151 (March 1931): 347. The *Herald Tribune,* 18 January 1931, 4, called the Hurstian pages those "that would tempt nobody into sin."

28. "*Back Street,*" *Nation* 132 (19 February 1931): 195, hereafter cited in text; Archer Winsten, "*Imitation of Life,*" *Bookman* 76 (February 1933): 197; "*Back Street,*"

New Republic 65 (11 February 1931): 362. On Hurst's skill as a psychologist, see "*Imitation of Life*," *Books*, 5 February 1933, 4.

29. Fannie Hurst, "Are We Coming or Going?", *Vital Speeches of the Day*, 3 December 1934, 160. In *Today Is Ladies' Day* (Rochester, N.Y.: Home Institute, 1939), 36, she inveighed against "that aimless army of lobby-sitters and time-killers": sisters of Ray Schmidt all.

30. *Justice* 16 (April 1934): 6.

31. Fannie Hurst, *Back Street* (New York: Cosmopolitan Book Co., 1931), 42, hereafter cited in text.

32. Among other things, 1930s women needed to cope with disgruntled male family members who, like Walter Saxel, though for different reasons, alternately scorned and clung: Walters on the dole. The psychologist Lorinne Pruette found that such women retreated into "dreary little worlds of their own" (qtd. Nancy Woloch, *Women and the American Experience* [New York: Knopf, 1984], 444, hereafter cited in text).

33. Gay Wilentz, "White Patron and Black Artist: The Correspondence of Fannie Hurst and Zora Neale Hurston," *Library Chronicle of the University of Texas at Austin* 35 (1986): 22, hereafter cited in text.

34. "Powerhouse," *New Yorker* 34 (31 January 1959): 22.

35. Catharine Brody, *Babe Evanson* (New York: Century, 1928), 25, hereafter cited in text. For a modern novel in the Brody vein, though of far greater artistry, see Joyce Carol Oates, *Them* (New York: Fawcett/Crest, 1969).

36. Theodore Dreiser, *Dawn* (New York: Horace Liveright, 1931), 69.

37. Ruth McKenney, "Women Are Human Beings," *New Masses* 37 (10 December 1940): 6–7. See Richard Pells, *Radical Visions and American Dreams: Culture and Society in the Depression Years* (New York: Harper & Row, 1973), 229, for a discussion of mainstream films effectively satirizing the status quo. Such a satire, however, did not have the fervor of Bodenheim's poetic line in "Revolutionary Girl": the Hollywood film purveys "living death" to the imagination.

38. Catharine Brody, *Nobody Starves* (New York: Longmans, Green, 1932), 49–50, hereafter cited in text. A less effective Brody novel on a similar theme, *Cash Item*, appeared the next year.

39. Elsa Jane Dixler, "The Woman Question: Women and the American Communist Party, 1929–1941" (Ph.D. diss., Yale University, 1974), 90–92, hereafter cited in text.

40. James Rorty, "Nobody Writes Objectively," *New Republic* 12 October 1932, 239; Seth Singletree, "*Nobody Starves*," *Saturday Review of Literature* 157 (October 1932): 6.

41. Edward Newhouse, [autobiographical sketch], *Wilson Library Bulletin* 11

(May 1937): 588; "Depression's Wrecks," *New York Times Book Review,* 25 November 1934, sec. 5, 20; "Living in Hooverville," *New York Times,* 20 November 1934, 19.

42. Edward Newhouse, *You Can't Sleep Here* (New York: Macaulay, 1934), 197, hereafter cited in text.

43. Peter Roffman and Jim Purdy, *The Hollywood Social Problems Film: Madness, Despair, and Politics from the Depression to the Fifties* (Bloomington: Indiana University Press, 1981), 114; Andrew Bergman, *We're in the Money: Depression America and Its Films* (New York: Harper Colophon, 1972), 105–7.

44. "Review of *You Can't Sleep Here,*" *New York Times,* 25 November 1934, sec. 5, 20.

45. Mari Jo Buhle, "Leane Zugsmith," in *Women and the American Left: A Guide to Sources* (Boston: G. K. Hall, 1983), 193; Alfred Kazin, "The Other Side of the Counter," *New York Times,* 13 September 1936, sec. 6, 5; Leane Zugsmith, *A Time to Remember* (New York: Random House, 1936), hereafter cited in text. A similar reversal of Hurst informs "The Betrayal," in *Home Is Where You Hang Your Childhood and Other Stories* (New York: Random House, 1937). On the enthusiastic left-wing response to the novel, see (a disapproving) Walter Rideout, *The Radical Novel in the United States, 1900–1954* (Cambridge, Mass.: Harvard University Press, 1956), 314n, hereafter cited in text. On both Zugsmith's literary-political life (including her presidency of a left-wing consumer's organization) and *A Time to Remember* as proletarian fiction, see Matthew Josephson, "Leane Zugsmith," *Southern Review* 1 (July 1975): 530–52.

46. Susan Porter Benson, *Counter Cultures: Saleswomen, Managers, and Customers in American Department Stores, 1890–1940* (Urbana: University of Illinois Press, 1988), 188. On sales jobs as conforming to the "ideology of woman's proper place," see Ellen Wiley Todd, *The "New Woman" Revisited: Painting and Gender Politics on Fourteenth Street* (Berkeley: University of California Press, 1993), 252. On saleswomen's sporadic militance, see "Ohrbach Feast Spoiled by Two Comely Pickets," *Daily Worker,* 22 January 1935, 1, and "Writers to Aid Ohrbach Strike," *Daily Worker,* 25 January 1935, 3, hereafter cited in text.

47. Though Rideout calls the Zugsmith novel "proletarian" (235), he ignores the feminine conversions at its core and labels it instead a strike novel.

48. O. Henry, "The Trimmed Lamp," in *Collected Stories of O. Henry,* ed. Paul J. Horowitz (New York: Avenel/Crown, 1979), 828.

49. Leane Zugsmith, "A New Novel by Contributor Newhouse," *New Masses* 22 (16 February 1935): 23.

50. Henry Louis Gates, Jr., "Zora Neale Hurston: A Negro Way of Seeing," Afterword to Zora Neale Hurston, *Their Eyes Were Watching God* (1937; reprint, New York: Harper/Perennial, 1990), hereafter cited in text.

51. Sidney H. Bremer, *Urban Intersections: Meetings of Life and Literature in United States Cities* (Urbana: University of Illinois Press, 1992), 133. A fuller discussion of Hurston's use of folk heritage joins a biographical discussion in Robert L. Hemenway, *Zora Neale Hurston: A Literary Biography* (Urbana: University of Illinois Press, 1977), chap. 4, hereafter cited in text.

52. Zora Neale Hurston, *Dust Tracks on a Road: An Autobiography* (1942; reprint, New York: Harper/Perennial, 1991), 176, hereafter cited in text.

53. Jay S. Walker, "Zora Neale Hurston's *Their Eyes Were Watching God:* Black Novel of Sexism," *Modern Fiction Studies* 20 (Winter 1974–75): 521, hereafter cited in text.

54. Richard Wright, "Between Laughter and Tears," *New Masses* 22 (5 October 1937): 25.

55. Positive reviews of the novel appeared in the 13 October 1937 *New Republic* and the 26 September 1937 *New York Times.*

56. Philip S. Foner, *Women and the American Labor Movement from the First Trade Unions to the Present* (New York: Free Press, 1979), 302. For the deplorable wages in cigar factories, fish canneries, and food establishments, see also *Women in Florida Industries,* Women's Bureau Bulletin no. 80 (Washington, D.C.: U.S. Government Printing Office, 1939), 49–54.

57. Jacqueline S. Jones, *Labor of Love, Labor of Sorrow: Black Women, Work, and the Family, from Slavery to the Present* (New York: Vintage Books, 1986), 212.

58. Gretchen Sullivan Sorin, Beth Klopott, and Julie Reiss, "Bridges and Boundaries: A Visual Essay," in *Bridges and Boundaries: African-Americans and American Jews,* ed. Jack Salzman, Adina Back, and Gretchen Sullivan Sorin (New York: George Braziller, 1992), 204.

59. *The Black and the Red: Activists in Harlem in the Early Days of the Depression,* pt. 1 of "Grandma Was an Activist," WBAI and the Oral History of the American Left, Tamiment Institute Library, New York University, prod. 1982, Radio Arts Productions, hereafter cited in text. On the FERA camps, see Joyce L. Kornbluh, *A New Deal for Workers' Education: The Workers' Service Program, 1933–1942* (Urbana: University of Illinois Press, 1987), 87. On black women at, for instance, the Bryn Mawr Summer School, see Rita Heller, "Blue Collars and Bluestockings: The Bryn Mawr Summer School for Women Workers, 1921–1938," in *Sisterhood and Solidarity: Workers' Education for Women, 1914–1984,* ed. Joyce L. Kornbluh and Mary Frederickson (Philadelphia: Temple University Press, 1984), 116.

60. Hazel V. Carby, *Reconstructing Womanhood: The Emergence of the Afro-American Woman Novelist* (New York: Oxford University Press, 1987), 166.

61. Division remains on Hurston's stance on what she called the "Race Problem" (*Dust Tracks,* 151). Hemenway, Gates, and others argue for the "racial health" (Hemenway, xii) of her created literary world, empowering blacks; Carby, Dar-

win Turner, and Ann L. Rayson find in Hurston at best indifference, and at worst, antagonism, to the cause of blacks. See Darwin T. Turner, *In a Minor Chord* (Carbondale: Southern Illinois University Press, 1971), and Ann L. Rayson, "*Dust Tracks on a Road:* Zora Neale Hurston and the Form of Black Autobiography," *Negro American Literature Forum* 7 (Summer 1978): 39–45. These readers find both racial empowerment and unreality in Hurston's oeuvre.

62. Mary Jane Lupton, "Zora Neale Hurston and the Survival of the Female," *Southern Literary Review* 15 (Fall 1982): 49; Barbara Smith, "Sexual Politics and the Fiction of Zora Neale Hurston," *Radical Teacher* 8 (May 1978): 29, hereafter cited in text.

63. Jacqueline S. Jones, *The Dispossessed: America's Underclasses from the Civil War to the Present* (New York: Basic Books, 1992), 167, hereafter cited in text.

64. Jean Collier Brown, *The Negro Woman Worker,* Women's Bureau Bulletin no. 165 (Washington, D.C.: U.S. Government Printing Office, 1938), 8–9.

65. Hurston also reversed the assumptions of an earlier form of fiction about blacks, the late nineteenth-century melodrama of the tragic mulatta. Janie is a quadroon, but she neither attempts to join the white world nor is caught between it and the black one. See Judith R. Berzon, *Neither White Nor Black: The Mulatto Character in American Fiction* (New York: New York University Press, 1987), 99–106, for a discussion of the mulatta stereotype.

66. Lillie P. Howard, *Zora Neale Hurston* (Boston: Twayne, 1980), 71.

67. Simone de Beauvoir, *The Second Sex,* trans. H. M. Parshley (1952; reprint, New York: Bantam, 1970), 629.

68. For a once-popular, deeply superficial romancer who blithely solves all of her heroines' emotional and economic difficulties, see Viña Delmar, especially *Bad Girl* (New York: Literary Guild of America, 1928) and *The Marriage Racket* (New York: Harcourt, Brace, 1933).

Chapter Five. The Rising of the Mill Women: Gastonia and Its Literature

1. Ronald L. Filippelli, "Gastonia," in *Labor Conflict in the United States,* ed. Filippelli (New York: Garland, 1990), 196.

2. Dale Newman, "Work and Community Life in a Southern Textile Town," *Labor History* 19 (Spring 1978): 205, hereafter cited in text. Gastonia's movie house, in contrast, remained open.

3. A good account of southern paternalism before and during the Depression is in Jacqueline Dowd Hall et al., *Like a Family: The Making of a Southern Cotton Mill World* (Chapel Hill: University of North Carolina Press, 1987), chap. 4, hereafter cited in text. I am also indebted to that chapter's discussion of early modern

southern strikes, Elizabethton, and biographical data on the Gastonia heroine Ella May Wiggins.

4. On key events in Gastonia, see Philip S. Foner, *Women and the American Labor Movement from World War I to the Present* (New York: Free Press, 1980), chap. 12; Theodore Draper, "Gastonia Revisited," *Social Research* 38 (Spring 1971): 3–29; Otto Hall, "A Negro Organizer's Experience in Gastonia," *Labor Unity* (22 June 1929): 4, all hereafter cited in text.

5. Despite the Great Textile Strike of 1934, the largest of the southern protests, by the end of the decade only 7 percent of the South's 350,000 mill hands were unionized. See Susan Ware, *Holding Their Own: American Women in the 1930s* (Boston: Twayne, 1987), 44. When the CIO organized the textile mills in the mid-1930s, it was in the North that membership, including women's, increased. Jacqueline Dowd Hall, "Disorderly Women: Gender and Labor Militancy in the Appalachian South," *Journal of American History* 73 (1986): 372 (hereafter cited in text), argues for a "female protest tradition" informing strikes like Elizabethton but offers strikes including coal miners' wives and northern mill women as influences. Too, relatively few southern women were in manufacturing, another factor in their low level of sustained union participation.

6. Herbert J. Lahne, *The Cotton Mill Worker* (New York: Farrar and Rinehart, 1944), 104, hereafter cited in text.

7. Mary Anderson, *Women's Place in Industry in 10 Southern States,* U.S. Department of Labor, Women's Bureau Pamphlet (Washington, D.C.: U.S. Government Printing Office, 1931), 10, hereafter cited in text.

8. Elizabeth L. Otey, "Women and Children in Southern Industry," *Annals of the American Academy of Political and Social Science* 153 (1931): 163. See also Liston Pope, *Millhands and Preachers: A Study of Gastonia* (New Haven: Yale University Press, 1942), hereafter cited in text.

9. See, for example, *Hard Times Cotton Mill Girls: Personal Histories of Womanhood and Poverty in the South,* ed. Victoria Byerly (Ithaca, N.Y.: ILR Press, 1986), 76, hereafter cited in text; Otey, 164, cites a 50 percent figure for at least one southern state.

10. Jennings J. Rhyne, *Some Southern Cotton Mill Workers and Their Villages* (Chapel Hill: University of North Carolina Press, 1930), 95; Paul Blanshard, *Labor in Southern Cotton Mills* (New York: League for Industrial Democracy, 1927), 64.

11. Paul Blanshard, "One Hundred Percent American," *Nation* (8 May 1929): 555.

12. Tom Tippett, *When Southern Labor Stirs* (New York: Jonathan Cape, 1931), 77–78; *First-Person America,* ed. Ann Banks (New York: Random House, 1980), 163.

13. Mary Heaton Vorse, *Strike!* (1930; reprint, Urbana: University of Illinois

Press, 1991); Grace Lumpkin, *To Make My Bread* (New York: Macaulay, 1932); Dorothy Myra Page, *Gathering Storm: A Study of the Black Belt* (New York: International Publishers, 1932); Fielding Burke [Olive Tilford Dargan], *Call Home the Heart* (1932; reprint, Old Westbury, N.Y.: Feminist Press, 1983); Sherwood Anderson, *Beyond Desire* (New York: Liveright, 1932); William Rollins, Jr., *The Shadow Before* (New York: Robert M. McBride, 1934), all hereafter cited in text. For a useful discussion of female and male Gastonia writers, but one that, to my mind, overstates the women authors' feminism, see Joseph R. Urgo, "Proletarian Literature and Feminism: The Gastonia Novels and Feminist Protest," *Minnesota Review* 24 (Spring 1985): 64–84.

14. David J. Goldberg, *A Tale of Three Cities: Labor Organization and Protest in Paterson, Passaic, and Lawrence, 1916–1921* (New Brunswick, N.J.: Rutgers University Press, 1989), 103.

15. As is often the case in estimates of numbers of strikers, one source, in this case *The Encyclopedia of the American Left,* ed. Mari Jo Buhle, Paul Buhle, and Dan Georgakas (New York: Garland, 1990), 255, says thirty-five hundred, but another source, Draper, gives two thousand (14). Regarding the percentage of women strikers, most sources are mute, although Foner, 232, says they were in the majority.

16. Dorothy Myra Page, *Southern Cotton Mills and Labor* (New York: Workers Library, 1929), 76.

17. Fred Beal, *Proletarian Journey* (New York: Hillman-Curl, 1937), 123, 125–26 (hereafter cited in text), implies that he was caught up in the workers' urge to strike.

18. An account of the party's attempt at "dual unionism" appears in "Gastonia Sees Red," the ninth chapter of Beal's *Proletarian Journey.*

19. Sylvia Jenkins Cook, *From Tobacco Road to Route 66: The Southern Poor White in Fiction* (Chapel Hill: University of North Carolina Press, 1976), 86 (hereafter cited in text), comments: "What Gastonia [offered] was a historic confrontation of communism and capitalism."

20. A front-page photo appears under "Jailing a Woman Striker in Gastonia Strike Zone," with a caption about rough handling by a deputy-thug (*Daily Worker,* 12 April 1929). Another photo, on the 8 April front page, shows "one of the militant women textile workers in Gastonia, North Carolina, wresting a gun from a National Guardsman." Page 4 of the 15 April issue contains the headline "Gastonia Mill Girl Was Paid $20 Since Christmas"; page 6 contains a poem from Christene Patton, a "young Loray striker."

21. On the prescab Violet Jones, see Vera Buch Weisbord, *A Radical Life* (Bloomington: Indiana University Press, 1977), 196, hereafter cited in text. Jones,

who came to New York to raise money for the strikers and was lionized by the *Daily Worker,* soon proved more hindrance than blessing. See Beal, 151.

22. Though it surpassed the *New York Times*'s misogynistic references to Gastonia strikers, "some of them women" (see "Mill Strikers Clash with Southern Police," *New York Times,* 23 April 1929), the *Daily Worker* gave women headline equality, so to speak, only when they *were* the strike: "Cleveland Rayon Workers Refuse to Accept Cut in Wages: Girls Go Out on Strike," 8 April 1929.

23. In erasing feminine mass participation, the first wave of male Gastonia historians, Lahne, Rhyne, and Tippett, joins the moderns: Filippelli; Draper; and Harvey Klehr, *The Heyday of American Communism: The Depression Decade* (New York: Basic Books, 1984), 28–31. All merely give Wiggins a nod.

24. An important essay on how the new gender historians "rewrite" labor events such as the 1910–11 woman-fueled shirtwaist strike by pointing to the sexual division of labor in the garment trades, women's secondary roles in unions, and the female dimensions of the strike, is Ann Schofield, "The Uprising of the 20,000: The Making of a Labor Legend," in *A Needle, a Bobbin, a Strike: Woman Needleworkers in America,* ed. Joan M. Jensen and Sue Davidson (Philadelphia: Temple University Press, 1984), 167–82. (In the new feminist history, there lies, however, the potential danger of minimizing men's crucial involvement in labor militance.)

25. Two essays by Dee Garrison serve as exceptions to feminine erasure, one in the introduction to the reprinted *Strike!,* the other a chapter called "War in the South," in *Mary Heaton Vorse: The Life of an American Insurgent* (Philadelphia: Temple University Press, 1989), 213–32, hereafter cited in text.

26. Matilda Robbins, "My Story," typescript, Box 2, 66–69, Matilda Robbins Collection, Archives of Labor and Urban Affairs, Wayne State University.

27. Matilda Robbins, "From the Notebook of a Labor Organizer," typescript, Box 1, 5, ibid., hereafter cited in text.

28. Mary E. Frederickson, "Heroines and Girl Strikers: Gender Issues and Organized Labor in the Twentieth-Century American South," in *Organized Labor in the Twentieth-Century South,* ed. Robert H. Zieger (Knoxville: University of Tennessee Press, 1991), 85, hereafter cited in text. Publications by many of the CP women sent to Gastonia are listed in Jayne Loader, "Women in the Left, 1906–1941: A Bibliography of Primary Sources," *Michigan Papers in Women's Studies* 2 (1975): 9–82.

29. Mary Frederickson, " 'I know which side I'm on': Southern Women in the Labor Movement in the Twentieth Century," in *Women, Work and Protest: A Century of U.S. Women's Labor History,* ed. Ruth Milkman (London: Routledge & Kegan Paul, 1985), 171, hereafter cited in text.

30. Bertha Hendrix, "I Was in the Gastonia Strike" (ca. 1938), reprinted in *Calling Home: Working-Class Women's Writings, an Anthology,* ed. Janet Zandy (New Brunswick, N.J.: Rutgers University Press, 1990), 271–73.

31. Nancy F. Gabin, *Feminism in the Labor Movement: Women and the United Auto Workers, 1935–1975* (Ithaca, N.Y.: Cornell University Press, 1990), 8–9.

32. Susan A. Glenn, *Daughters of the Shtetl: Life and Labor in the Immigrant Generation* (Ithaca, N.Y: Cornell University Press, 1990), 228, hereafter cited in text. Ellen Kay Trimberger's assessment of fellow leftist Peggy Dennis, who never "envisioned a movement of women which made personal relations between women and men a central political issue," also applies to these Gastonia organizers. See Trimberger, "Women in the Old and New Left: The Evolution of a Politics of Personal Life," *Feminist Studies* 5 (Fall 1979): 432.

33. Mary H. Blewett, *We Will Rise in Our Might: Workingwomen's Voices from Nineteenth-Century New England* (Ithaca, N.Y: Cornell University Press, 1991), 15, 193. Glenn, 236ff., also addresses this issue.

34. Dolores Janiewski, "Sisters Under Their Skins: Southern Working Women, 1880–1950," in *Sex, Race, and the Role of Women in the South,* ed. Joanne V. Hawks and Sheila L. Kemp (Jackson: University Press of Mississippi, 1983), 19. Sophie Melvin (Gerson) remembered years later that "the man who set up the relief store [for the Gastonia strikers] was a member of the Ku Klux Klan" (Interview with Sophie Melvin-Gerson, 1976, Oral History of the American Left, Tamiment Institute Library, New York University).

35. Elsa Jane Dixler, "The Woman Question: Women and the American Communist Party, 1929–1941" (Ph.D. diss., Yale University, 1974), 124, hereafter cited in text.

36. Quoted in Alice Kessler-Harris, "Organizing the Unorganizable: Three Jewish Women and Their Union," *Labor History* 17 (Winter 1976): 11, hereafter cited in text.

37. Marie Van Vorst, *Amanda of the Mill* (Indianapolis: Bobbs-Merrill, 1905). Despite its antiproletarian stance, it does include passages anticipating the Gastonia School; the mill sang "its epic Labour and Toil at the cost of brain and body and soul" (89).

38. See Cook, 21–26, for a discussion of the poor white female in works by Ellen Glasgow, Edith Summers Kelly, and Elizabeth Madox Roberts. Such portraits do not, however, address the industrial experience.

39. Only "in another class of society," writes Van Vorst, would the discontented mill women "have been leaders, agitators for schemes of emancipation" (197).

40. Dee Garrison, "Introduction" to Mary Heaton Vorse, *Strike!,* xv, points out that the conclusion of the Vorse novel depicts a shooting and funeral in the Marion, South Carolina, strike; see also Cook, 93.

41. Meredith Tax, *The Rising of the Women: Feminist Solidarity and Class Conflict, 1880–1917* (New York: Monthly Review Press, 1980), 220, provides an early modern example of the sexualization of working women. During the 1910–11 shirtwaist strike, police and employers called the picketing women "whores because they were walking the streets shamelessly; they tried to insult them . . . as if the way to stop them from rebelling as workers was to put them back in their places as sexual objects."

42. Sinclair Lewis, "A Novel for Mr. Hoover," *Nation* 131 (29 October 1930): 374.

43. "Some Other Works of Fiction," *New York Times,* 2 November 1930, 6; Murray Godwin, "Good Proletarian Realism," *New Republic,* 10 December 1930, 113. A recent argument on how Vorse and the female Gastonia novelists supposedly solved the "binary opppositions" problem of male/female participation is in Barbara Foley, *Radical Representations: Politics and Form in U.S. Proletarian Fiction, 1929–1941* (Durham, N.C.: Duke University Press, 1993), 239–40.

44. Mildred Gwin Andrews, *The Men and the Mills: A History of the Southern Textile Industry* (Macon, Ga.: Mercer University Press, 1987), 90. This official history of Gastonia not only embraces management but also erases feminine participation in the strike.

45. Mary Heaton Vorse, "Grind My Bones," *New Republic,* 7 December 1932, 105.

46. "*To Make My Bread,*" *Bookman* 75 (November 1932): 739.

47. Deborah Rosenfelt, "Afterword," in Myra Page, *Daughter of the Hills* (1950; reprint, Old Westbury, N.Y.: Feminist Press, 1986), 253.

48. Clara Weatherwax, *Marching! Marching!* (1935; reprint, Detroit: Omnigraphics, 1990), hereafter cited in text. For a somewhat more enlightened female laborite, see the portrait of Vera in Clifton Cuthbert, *Another Such Victory* (New York: Hillman-Curl, 1936).

49. Quoted in Anna W. Shannon, "Afterword," in Fielding Burke, *Call Home the Heart,* 416, hereafter cited in text.

50. "*Call Home the Heart,*" *New Republic,* 18 May 1932, 27; Robert Cantwell, "Class-Conscious Fiction," *Nation* 134 (25 May 1932): 606.

51. See also Dorothy Ray Healey and Maurice Isserman, *California Red: A Life in the American Communist Party* (1990; reprint, Urbana: University of Illinois Press, 1993), 38: "Who could think of a revolutionary having a child?" For a far more emphatic interpretation than mine of Burke's novels as critiques of the role of marriage and family in capitalist oppression, see Kathy Cantley Ackerman, "Olive Tilford Dargan: Recovering a Proletarian Romantic" (Ph.D. diss., University of South Carolina, 1991).

52. In the sequel, *A Stone Came Rolling* (1935), Ishma reenters the labor fray as

an organizer in cotton and hosiery mills, but she again pays for her daring by her husband's murder at the hands of vigilantes.

53. Christian Suggs, "Introduction" to Weatherwax, *Marching! Marching!*, xxiii.

54. Carey McWilliams, quoted in Appendix A; see also Vicki Ruiz, *Cannery Women, Cannery Lives: Mexican Women, Unionization, and the California Food Processing Industry, 1930–1950* (Albuquerque: University of New Mexico Press, 1987), 38. See also Appendix C, 135–36, for a countervision of the maternal militant, viz.: "One woman jumped up [at the union meeting], tossed back her skirts, and laughingly exhibited a huge bruise [from falling on the dangerous factory floor] well above the knee, and in the general vicinity of her ass. The others howled [with] laughter." Still, when men entered strikes, women's issues were completely muted. See Elizabeth Nicholas, "Working in the California Canneries," *Harvest Quarterly*, nos. 3–4 (September–December 1976): 20.

55. Jacqueline Dowd Hall, "Private Eyes, Public Women: Images of Class and Sex in the Urban South, Atlanta, Georgia, 1913–1915," in *Work Engendered: Toward a New History of American Labor,* ed. Ava Baron (Ithaca, N.Y.: Cornell University Press, 1991), 243–72, hereafter cited in text.

56. Nancy Cott, "Afterword" in Sarah Eisenstein, *Give Us Bread but Give Us Roses: Working Women's Consciousness in the United States, 1890 to the Present* (London: Routledge & Kegan Paul, 1983), 162, hereafter cited in text.

57. Interview with Alice Caudle, in *First-Person America,* ed. Ann Banks (New York: Random House, 1980), 163.

58. Sherwood Anderson, "Elizabethton, Tennessee," *Nation* 128 (1 May 1929): 526–27; Sherwood Anderson, "Anderson on *Winesburg, Ohio,*" in Winesburg, Ohio: *Text and Criticism,* ed. John H. Ferres (1960; reprint, New York: Penguin/Viking, 1977), 15, both hereafter cited in text.

59. On Anderson's sometime Communism, see Cook, 126; Rex Burbank, *Sherwood Anderson* (Boston: Twayne, 1964), 129; "Sherwood Anderson," *Dictionary of Literary Biography,* vol. 9, pt. 1, ed. James J. Martine (Detroit: Gale Research Co., 1981), 30. Leftist ideologues received his Gastonia novel well enough—see Granville Hicks, "Red Pilgrimage," *New Republic,* 21 December 1932, 168—but it is now considered one of his poorest.

60. Alfred Kazin, "The New Realism: Sherwood Anderson," in Winesburg, Ohio: *Text and Criticism,* 325, 323.

61. See Kathy Peiss, *Cheap Amusements: Working Women and Leisure in Turn-of-the-Century New York* (Philadelphia: Temple University Press, 1986), passim, hereafter cited in text.

62. Florence Codman, "*The Shadow Before,*" *Nation* 133 (4 April 1934): 392; John Dos Passos, "*The Shadow Before,*" *New Republic,* 4 April 1934, 220.

63. See, for instance, James Oppenheim, *The Nine-Tenths* (1911; reprint, Upper Saddle River, N.J.: Gregg Press, 1968); Theresa Serber Malkiel, *Diary of a Shirt-*

waist Striker (1910; reprint, Ithaca, N.Y.: ILR Press, 1990); Arthur Bullard [Albert Edwards], *Comrade Yetta* (New York: Macmillan, 1913).

64. Walter Rideout, *The Radical Novel in the United States, 1900–1954* (Cambridge, Mass.: Harvard University Press, 1956), 174. Among the garment trade strike fiction that did appear was Beatrice Bisno's *Tomorrow's Bread* (Philadelphia: Jewish Publication Society of America, 1938), a semibiographical homage to her father, the Chicago Cloakmaker's Union president Abraham Bisno, and his later ILGWU struggles with other male leaders; and Dorothy Meyersburg's *Seventh Avenue* (New York: E. P. Dutton, 1941), published at the end of the Depression, which sided with the bosses. Other attempts to limn female firebrands such as Carleton Beals's *The Stones Awake* (Philadelphia: J. B. Lippincott, 1936) restrict the discussion to Mexican revolutionaries.

65. Benjamin Stolberg, *Tailor's Progress: The Story of a Famous Union and the Men Who Made It* (New York: Doubleday, Doran, 1944).

66. Sharon Hartman Strom, "Challenging 'Woman's Place': Feminism, the Left, and Industrial Unionism in the 1930s," *Feminist Studies* 9 (Summer 1983): 379, hereafter cited in text.

67. Coverage of Elizabethton focused on men; see, for instance, "Three New Strikes in Southern Mills," *New York Times,* 16 April 1929, 3; "Dynamite Home of Textile Worker," *New York Times,* 25 May 1929, 31; "Strikers Put on Trial," *New York Times,* 23 May 1929, 3.

Chapter Six. With Apologies for Competence: Women, Profession, Tales of Conflict

1. Frank Stricker, "Cookbooks and Lawbooks: The Hidden History of Career Women in Twentieth Century America," *Journal of Social History* 10 (Fall 1976): 1, hereafter cited in text. Lacunae in record keeping make the figure on black women professionals, 5 percent of all black women, less reliable. See Jean Collier Brown, *The Negro Woman Worker,* Women's Bureau Bulletin no. 165 (Washington, D.C.: U.S. Government Printing Office, 1938), 11–12, hereafter cited in text.

Stricker excludes most clerical workers from the category of "career women," yet, because by 1930 a substantial number of college graduates engaged in business as secretaries and clerical workers, I follow 1930s methods of occupational classification and do not exclude them. See, for instance, Susan Kingsbury, *Economic Status of University Women in the U.S.A.,* Women's Bureau Bulletin no. 170 (Washington, D.C.: U.S. Government Printing Office, 1939), 6.

2. "Women in Business II," *Fortune* 12 (July 1935): 50–55, hereafter cited in text. See, in particular, the profile of Isabelle T. Yeaman, 51.

3. Susan M. Kingsbury, "A Study of the Economic Status of University Women," *American Association of University Women Journal* 32 (1939): 225.

4. Helen Law, "A New Job for the College Girl," *Review of Reviews* 81 (1930): 76.

5. Ishbel Ross, "Girls Must Work," *Ladies' Home Journal* 53 (June 1936): 32–33. See also Eunice Fuller Barnard, "College Girl: 1932–33," *Scribner's Magazine* 94 (January 1933): 51.

6. Mary W. M. Hargreaves, "Darkness Before the Dawn: The Status of Working Women in the Depression Years," in *Clio Was a Woman: Studies in the History of American Women*, ed. Mabel E. Deutrich and Virginia C. Purdy (Washington, D.C.: Howard University Press, 1980), 180. By 1930 women made up 95 percent of stenographers, and the number of women in all clerical jobs had increased eightfold since 1900. See Margery Davies, *Woman's Place Is at the Typewriter: Office Work and Office Workers, 1870–1930* (Philadelphia: Temple University Press, 1982), 79, and David Brody, *Workers in Industrial America*, 2d ed. (New York: Oxford University Press, 1993), 20. Again, statistics on black women in offices and stores are incomplete. See Brown, 12–13, on figures for selected cities with large black populations.

7. Tess Slesinger, *The Unpossessed* (1934; reprint, Old Westbury, N.Y.: Feminist Press, 1984), hereafter cited in text. Weekly salaries of skilled clerks ranged from the median $25 to the senior clerk's $50. See Grace Coyle, "Women in the Clerical Occupations," *Annals of the American Academy of Political and Social Science* 143 (May 1929): 180–87, and Ethel Erickson, *The Employment of Women in Offices*, Women's Bureau Bulletin no. 120 (Washington, D.C.: U.S. Government Printing Office, 1934).

8. Mary McCarthy, *The Company She Keeps* (London: Weidenfeld and Nicolson, 1942), 19. Black women formed only 1.3 percent of clerical workers to white women's over 30 percent by 1940. See Jacqueline S. Jones, *Labor of Love, Labor of Sorrow: Black Women, Work, and the Family, from Slavery to the Present* (New York: Vintage Books, 1986), 200.

To judge by the fiction produced by women of the Harlem Renaissance and appearing in the African-American journal *Opportunity* in the Depression years—Dorothy West's 1940 dispirited black caseworker in "Mammy" (compared with her hopeful typist in her 1926 story "The Typewriter"), and Marita Bonner's 1933 story of limited job options, "Triad on Black Notes"—McCarthy's college heroine did not know how ungrateful she sounded.

9. Carol Hymowitz and Michaele Weissman, *A History of Women in America* (New York: Bantam, 1978), 307, hereafter cited in text.

10. Barbara Miller Solomon, *In the Company of Educated Women: A History of Women and Higher Education in America* (New Haven: Yale University Press, 1985), 179–81. See also Marion Cuthbert, *Education and Marginality: A Study of the Negro Woman College Graduate* (1942; reprint, New York: Garland, 1987), 46, 43. Black women professionals are only noted in Charles S. Johnson's otherwise thorough *The Negro College Graduate* (Chapel Hill: University of North Carolina Press, 1938),

and are omitted entirely from the 1935 Census Bureau Survey, *Negroes in the United States, 1920–1932,* the 1939 Women's Bureau report on the economic status of university women, and Gerda Lerner's important *Black Women in White America: A Documentary History* (New York: Vintage Books, 1972). The claim that compared with white women, "disproportionate numbers" of black women entered law, medicine, dentistry, and nursing (Paula Giddings, *When and Where I Enter: The Impact of Black Women on Race and Sex in America* [New York: William Morrow, 1984], 147), seems inflated. In 1930, only 2.1 percent of black doctors, dentists, or lawyers were women; little more than one thousand black women were in social work. See Jeanne Noble, "The Higher Education of Black Women in the Twentieth Century," in *Women and Higher Education in American History,* ed. John Mark Faragher and Florence Howe (New York: Norton, 1988), 84. White women formed 4.4 percent of physicians and 2.1 of lawyers, but because more white than black men entered those fields, the figure represents a percentage of a much larger total (Susan Ware, *Holding Their Own: American Women in the 1930s* [Boston: Twayne, 1987], 73, hereafter cited in text). Black women graduates outnumbered their male peers in the 1930s (Noble, 88) but chose careers in black colleges, high or elementary schools, or what New Dealer Mary McLeod Bethune called "social uplift" work for the black race (Lerner, 582). None of these arenas provided incomes or recognition commensurate with those in white society. Black women did, however, make strides under various WPA arts and writers' projects. See Barbara Blumberg, *The New Deal and the Unemployed: The View from New York City* (Lewisburg, Pa.: Bucknell University Press, 1979), 80–82.

11. Among the yea-sayers, see Alice Kessler-Harris, *Out to Work: A History of Wage-Earning Women in the United States* (New York: Oxford University Press, 1982), 260; Ware, *Holding Their Own,* 71; Kingsbury's two studies, passim. Stricker, 10, takes a middle-of-the-road position. Lois Scharf, *To Work and to Wed: Female Employment, Feminism, and the Great Depression* (Westport, Conn.: Greenwood Press, 1980), 86, who presents the statistics, finds substantial job losses, as does Barbara J. Harris, *Beyond Her Sphere: Women and the Professions in American History* (Westport, Conn.: Greenwood Press, 1978), 137–42.

Because occupational data for blacks were often kept separate from those for whites, I have been unable to ascertain whether the cited statistics include the kind of women profiled, for instance, in Gwendolyn Etter-Lewis, *My Soul Is My Own: Oral Narratives of African-American Women in the Professions* (New York: Routledge, 1993).

12. Winifred Wandersee, *Women's Work and Family Values, 1920–1940* (Cambridge, Mass.: Harvard University Press, 1981), 95–97, hereafter cited in text. On negative public attitudes toward married professional women, see Bernard Sternsher and Judith Sealander, "Introduction," in *Women of Valor: The Struggle Against the Great*

Depression as Told in Their Own Life Stories, ed. Sternsher and Sealander (Chicago: Ivan R. Dee, 1990), 6; Hargreaves, 181; and Solomon, 179. The New Deal's codes excluded the 1.5 million professional women, but by the early New Deal in the WPA Women's and Professional Division, clerical jobs at least were increasing. See also chapter 1 of this book.

13. On the inclusiveness of the term as early as the mid-1910s, see Lois Rudnick, "The New Woman," in *1915, The Cultural Moment: The New Politics, the New Woman, the New Psychology, the New Art and the New Theater in America,* ed. Adele Heller and Lois Rudnick (New Brunswick, N.J.: Rutgers University Press, 1991), 69–81. Rudnick's expansion of the term to include not only political and sexual radicals but also working-class women seeking leisure-time freedom seems broad. For an argument against mistaken views of the New Woman's supposed moral emancipation, see Estelle B. Freedman, "The New Woman: Changing Views of Women in the 1920s," *Journal of American History* 61 (September 1974): 372–93. On the manifold meanings of the term in the 1930s, see Ann Wiley Todd, *The "New Woman" Revised: Painting and Gender Politics on Fourteenth Street* (Berkeley: University of California Press, 1993), xxviii, hereafter cited in text.

For discussions of New Woman fiction, including the upward mobility novel, see chapter 1 of this book; Carolyn Forrey, "The New Woman Revisited," *Women's Studies* 2 (1974): 37–56; Maureen Honey, "Gotham's Daughters: Feminism in the 1920s," *American Studies* 31 (Spring 1990): 25–40. See also Anzia Yezierska, "Hunger," in *Hungry Hearts and Other Stories* (New York: Persea, 1985), 41. One of the last 1920s New Woman authors, Ruth Suckow, in *Cora* (New York: Knopf, 1929), writes that her heroine "had discovered now that she liked to appear before these people [at working girls' clubs and business schools] . . . capable, poised, well-dressed, successful" (132). See also Ursula Parrott, *Ex-Wife* (1929; reprint, Feminist Press, 1990); Booth Tarkington, *Alice Adams* (New York: Odyssey Press, 1921).

14. Mary P. Ryan, *Woman in America from Colonial Times to the Present* (New York: New Viewpoints Press, 1975), 255, hereafter cited in text. See also Miriam Cohen, "The New Deal (1933–1941)," in *Women's Studies Encyclopedia,* vol. 3, ed. Helen Tierney (Westport, Conn.: Greenwood Press, 1991), 335–37, for a brief analysis of the Progressive roots of female New Deal social thought.

15. Eunice Fuller Barnard, "The College Girl Puts Marriage First," *New York Times Magazine,* 2 April 1933, 8–9. See also Lillian Symes, "Still a Man's Game: Reflections of a Slightly Tired Feminist," *Harper's Monthly* 158 (May 1929): 678–86; and Todd, passim.

16. James M. Cain, *Career in C Major* (1936; reprint, New York: Knopf, 1944), hereafter cited in text. On the even more popular, three-million-reader-strong *Saturday Evening Post* and its mass-magazine approach to curbing feminine vocation, see Maureen Honey, "Images of Women in the *Saturday Evening Post,*" *Journal*

of Popular Culture 10 (1976): 352–58. In leftist male novels like Newhouse's *You Can't Sleep Here,* Rollins's *The Shadow Before,* Farrell's *Studs Lonigan: Judgment Day,* Halper's *The Chute,* and Cantwell's *Land of Plenty,* women professionals are prudish authority figures, unconflicted scabs, or willing extensions of their male bosses. In Thomas Bell's autobiographical ode to a young Bronx couple, *All Brides Are Beautiful* (1936), the novel's focus is on a left-wing man's frustration at being supported by his bookstore clerk wife; women are once again implicated in masculine unemployment.

On actual leftist professional women, see Nathan Glazer, *The Social Basis of American Communism* (New York: Harcourt, Brace, 1961), 138–42, and Alice Dodge Woolson interview, in "Grandma Was an Activist," pt. 3, *On the Line: Radical Women in the Labor Movement,* WBAI and the Oral History of the American Left, Tamiment Institute Library, New York University, prod. 1982, Radio Arts Productions. Woolson was a white-collar worker, a Vassar graduate, and a Norman Thomas devotee. See Irving Bernstein, *The Turbulent Years: A History of the American Worker, 1933–1941* (Boston: Houghton Mifflin, 1970), 770 (hereafter cited in text), on the more common phenomenon of unorganized white-collar workers.

17. Plots about black women professionals, whether pulled by marital and vocational stresses or carving out careers alone, are common in pre-Depression texts by Jesse Fauset and Nella Larsen but do not resurface until postwar works such as Ann Petry's *The Street* (1946; reprint, Boston: Houghton Mifflin, 1974).

18. Rachel Maddux, "No Smoking, No Spitting," in *The Way Things Are: The Stories of Rachel Maddux,* ed. Nancy A. Walker (Knoxville: University of Tennessee Press, 1992), 63, hereafter cited in text. All Maddux stories are from this edition.

19. See, for instance, McCarthy's derision of the Book-of-the-Month Club, common to those sympathetic to radical fiction, in *The Company She Keeps,* 71. McCarthy also satirized Frances Perkins in one story about a woman who was "somebody in the New Deal . . . a rococo suffragette" (65).

20. Sinclair Lewis, *Ann Vickers* (Garden City, N.Y.: Doubleday, Doran, 1933), hereafter cited in text.

21. William H. Chafe, *The American Woman: Her Changing Social, Economic, and Political Roles, 1920–1970* (New York: Oxford University Press, 1972), 100.

22. Jill Conway, "Women Reformers and American Culture, 1870–1930," *Journal of Social History* 5 (Winter 1971–72): 167, hereafter cited in text. See also Winifred Wandersee, " 'I'd Rather Pass a Law Than Organize a Union': Frances Perkins and the Reformist Approach to Organized Labor," *Labor History* 34 (Winter 1993): 5–32, hereafter cited in text. Wandersee's article is an attempt to restore Perkins to labor history, which has routinely omitted her or "placed her in the background of labor disputes" (7n). Wandersee also cuts through the adulatory approach of previous biographers such as George Martin in *Madam Secretary: Frances Perkins*

(Boston: Houghton Mifflin, 1976). On revisionist views of Perkins's feminism, see Susan Ware, *Beyond Suffrage: Women in the New Deal* (Cambridge, Mass.: Harvard University Press, 1981), hereafter cited in text.

23. Conway applies the term to Julia Lathrop, a colleague of Perkins's settlement days, but it could apply just as well to Perkins herself.

24. On the sexual neutralizing of the type, see Carroll Smith-Rosenberg, "The New Woman as Androgyne," in Smith-Rosenberg, *Disorderly Conduct: Visions of Gender in Victorian America* (New York: Knopf, 1985), 245. The term "Lady in Lavender," 282, was often used judgmentally.

25. The headline, its punctuation revealing doubt that a woman can have a public role, read, "Miss Perkins Does 'Man-Sized' Job in Labor's Behalf," *Newsweek,* 29 July 1933, 16.

26. Marguerite Young, "Frances Perkins: Liberal Politician," *American Mercury* 33 (August 1934): 403; "Labor's Leading Lady," *Business Week,* 1 March 1933, 12; see also Wandersee, "I'd Rather," 8n.

27. Nancy Woloch, *Women and the American Experience* (New York: Knopf, 1984), 425, hereafter cited in text. A few modern historians characterize Perkins as assertive and sharp-tongued (Sean Dennis Cashman, *America in the Twenties and Thirties* [New York: New York University Press, 1989], 154), but her alleged acerbity seemed eclipsed by her amiability, forced or not. Note the serene tone in her book *The Roosevelt I Knew* (New York: Viking Press, 1946).

28. See Ray Tucker, "Fearless Frances," *Collier's* (28 July 1934): 16.

29. Ernest R. Groves, "The Personality Results of the Wage Employment of Women Outside the Home and Their Social Consequences," *Annals of the American Academy of Political and Social Science* 143 (May 1929): 342.

30. Tess Slesinger, "The Mousetrap," in *On Being Told That Her Second Husband Has Taken His First Lover and Other Stories* (1935; reprint, Chicago: Ivan R. Dee, 1990). All Slesinger short stories are quoted from this volume and hereafter cited in text. On the guidebooks' compliance ideology, see, for example, Frances Maule, *She Strives to Conquer: Business Behavior, Opportunities and Job Requirements for Women* (New York: Funk & Wagnalls, 1934), esp. chap. 9. Compare the title and tone to those of the more assertive collection of a decade before, *Careers for Women,* ed. Catherine Filene (Boston: Houghton Mifflin, 1920).

31. On the few other women correspondents of national importance but of lesser note than Thompson, see Marion Marzolf, *Up from the Footnote: A History of Women Journalists* (New York: Hastings House, 1977), 55, hereafter cited in text. On Thompson, see Margaret Case Harriman, "The It Girl," *New Yorker,* 20 April 1940, 24–29, and Peter Kurth, *American Cassandra: The Life of Dorothy Thompson* (Boston: Little, Brown, 1990), both hereafter cited in text. An example of the

awed, muted hostility of male period interviewers is Jack Alexander, "The Girl from Syracuse," *Saturday Evening Post,* 18 May 1925, 9ff., hereafter cited in text.

32. Dorothy Thompson, "Is America a Paradise for Women?", *Pictorial Review,* June 1929, 60, hereafter cited in text.

33. "It's a Woman's World," *Ladies' Home Journal* 57 (July 1940): 25, hereafter cited in text. On the article prompting Thompson's response, see Tess Slesinger, "They Say Women Are Emancipated," *New Republic,* 13 December 1933, 125–27, hereafter cited in text.

34. On Thompson's bisexuality, see Paul Boyer, "Dorothy Thompson," in *Notable American Women: The Modern Period,* ed. Barbara Sicherman and Carol Hurd Green (Cambridge, Mass.: Belknap/Harvard University Press, 1980), 684, hereafter cited in text. See also Vincent Sheean, *Dorothy and Red* (Boston: Houghton Mifflin, 1963), 214–16, hereafter cited in text.

35. Elaine Showalter, "Introduction," in *These Modern Women: Autobiographical Essays from the Twenties,* ed. Showalter (New York: Feminist Press, 1989), 5. For details about Slesinger's education, I am indebted to Shirley Biagi, "Forgive Me for Dying," *Antioch Review* 35 (Spring–Summer 1977): 225, hereafter cited in text. On Herbst's schooling, see Elinor Langer, *Josephine Herbst* (Boston: Little, Brown, 1984), 46.

36. See Showalter, 4, for details of Kirchwey's achievements. On Herbst's 1920s editorial work, see Josephine Herbst, "The Year of Disgrace," in *The Starched Blue Sky of Spain* (1960; reprint, New York: HarperCollins, 1991), 77–79, hereafter cited in text.

37. Josephine Herbst, *Rope of Gold* (1939; reprint, New York: Feminist Press, 1984). As aspiring writers, both supported themselves in assorted postcollegian semiprofessional jobs—for Slesinger, retailing, for Herbst, 1920s bookselling jobs at Gimbel's and Brentano's, interspersed with stints in stenography and casework. See, respectively, Janet Sharistanian, "Afterword," in *The Unpossessed,* 362, and Langer, 56.

38. Paul Lauter and Alice Kessler-Harris, identical introduction in both *Rope of Gold* and *The Unpossessed,* xiv.

39. Charlotte Nekola, "Writing Red: Women's Short Fiction of the 1930s," in *Writing Red: An Anthology of American Women Writers, 1930–1940,* ed. Charlotte Nekola and Paula Rabinowitz (New York: Feminist Press, 1987), 12–13; Paula Rabinowitz, *Labor and Desire: Women's Revolutionary Fiction in Depression America* (Chapel Hill: University of North Carolina Press, 1991), 137–50, hereafter cited in text. See also Barbara Foley, "Women and the Left in the 1930s," *American Literary History* 2 (Spring 1990): 150. An argument for Slesinger's radicalism is in Deborah Rosenfelt, "Getting into the Game: American Women Writers and the Radical

Tradition," *Women's Studies International Forum* 9 (1986): 364. For a more convincing view of Slesinger as "neither a theoretician nor a partisan," see Sharistanian, 367, and Biagi, passim. On Herbst's qualified radicalism, see Diane Johnson, "Introduction," in Herbst, *The Starched Blue Sky of Spain*, xvi.

40. For a counterview of the importance of the Menorah Circle, see "Preface," in *American Proletarian Culture: The Twenties and Thirties,* ed. Jon Christian Suggs (Detroit: Gale Research Co., 1993), 161.

41. "Call for an American Writers' Congress," *New Masses* 14 (22 January 1935): 20.

42. On Herbst, see Walter Rideout, *The Radical Novel in the United States, 1900–1954* (Cambridge, Mass.: Harvard University Press, 1956), 190, and Walter Rideout, "Forgotten Images of the Thirties: Josephine Herbst," *Literary Review* 27 (Fall 1983): 28–36, hereafter cited in text.

43. See, for example, Tess Slesinger, "Memoirs of an Ex-Flapper," *Vanity Fair* 43 (December 1934): 26–27, 74, 76.

44. On Herbst's distrust of dogma, see Dee Garrison, *Mary Heaton Vorse: The Life of an American Insurgent* (Philadelphia: Temple University Press, 1989), 273, hereafter cited in text. On her enduring dislike of the "proletarian novel" label as "narrow . . . and part of the [1930s] jargon," see the excerpt from her 1968 letter in the introduction to *Proletarian Writers of the Thirties,* ed. David Madden (Carbondale: Southern Illinois University Press, 1968), xvii.

45. For a good brief discussion of Herbst's German period, see Sharistanian, 438.

46. Rabinowitz, *Labor and Desire,* argues that Margaret Flinders "cannot be both a [radical] intellectual and a mother" (162) and that "Herbst reconciles the dilemma of the female intellectual subject by linking Victoria to the male worker" (167) as a labor reporter. Yet Rabinowitz does not mention the corollary conflict that both women experience.

47. Stanley Aronowitz, *False Promises: The Shaping of American Working Class Consciousness* (New York: McGraw-Hill, 1973), 292.

48. According to Sharistanian, "Afterword," 371.

49. T. S. Matthews, *"The Unpossessed," New Republic,* 23 May 1934, 52, hereafter cited in text.

50. J. Donald Adams, *"The Unpossessed," New York Times Book Review,* 20 May 1934, 6.

51. See also a Margaret-scorning Philip Rahv, "Storm Over the Intellectuals," *New Masses* 14 (May 1934): 26. To him, she is "aching to absorb [Miles] and have his child."

52. "A Passport to Realengo 18" (1935), reprinted in *Writing Red,* 199–202.

53. There were two previous volumes about the pre-Depression Trexlers, *Pity*

Is Not Enough (New York: Harcourt, Brace, 1933) and *The Executioner Waits* (New York: Harcourt, Brace, 1934).

54. From "The Enemy" (1936), reprinted in *Writing Red,* 104.

55. Philip Rahv, "A Variety of Fiction," *Partisan Review* 6 (Spring 1939): 111. For the same point about Slesinger's novel, see the Ferner Nuhn review of her work, *Nation* 138 (May 1934): 598.

56. Sinclair Lewis, *It Can't Happen Here* (Garden City, N.Y.: Doubleday, Doran, 1935), 246–47. On Lewis's inability to identify with the proletarian novel, see James M. Hutchisson, "'Babbitt in Overalls': Sinclair Lewis' Abandoned Labor Novel," *South Dakota Review* 29 (Winter 1991): 5–22. On Lewis's sometime praise of a strike novel, see his "A Novel for Mr. Hoover," *Nation* 131 (29 October 1930): 374.

57. A useful biography is Mark I. Wallach and Jon Bracker, *Christopher Morley* (Boston: Twayne, 1976), hereafter cited in text. Lewis's *Elmer Gantry* was a Book-of-the-Month Club selection in 1927.

58. On Morley and the Book-of-the-Month Club, see Joan Shelley Rubin, *The Making of Middlebrow Culture* (Chapel Hill: University of North Carolina Press, 1992), 133–38; on the club and proletarian literature, see 147, hereafter cited in text.

59. Christopher Morley, *Kitty Foyle* (New York: Grosset and Dunlap, 1941), 268, hereafter cited in text. Alice P. Hackett, *Fifty Years of Best Sellers, 1895–1945* (Boston: R. R. Bowker, 1945), 159, lists *Kitty Foyle* as one of 1939's top ten.

60. James D. Hart, "Christopher Morley," *Oxford Companion to American Literature* (1941), 2d ed., rev. (New York: Oxford University Press, 1948), 499.

61. Rose Feld, *"Kitty Foyle," Books,* 29 October 1939, 3.

62. See Alice Kessler-Harris, "Gender Ideology in Historical Reconstruction: A Case Study from the 1930s," *Gender and Ideology* 1 (Winter 1989): 42, hereafter cited in text.

63. "Helena Rubinstein," in *Current Biography, 1943,* ed. Maxine Black (New York: H. W. Wilson, 1943), 642, hereafter cited in text.

64. "Typewriters and Clubs," *New York Times,* 4 February 1900, 22.

65. Publishing data are in Mark Schorer, *Sinclair Lewis: An American Life* (New York: McGraw-Hill, 1961), 580; and James Lundquist, *Sinclair Lewis* (New York: Ungar, 1972), 105.

66. Karl Schriftgiesser, *"Ann Vickers," Boston Transcript,* 28 January 1933, 1; see also Mary Ross, [Review of *Ann Vickers*], *Survey Graphic* 22 (February 1933): 114.

67. Caroline Bird, *The Invisible Scar* (New York: David McKay, 1966), 288. For a view of the novel as solely an attack on women and suffrage, see Boyer, "Thompson," 684.

68. Susan Suleiman, *Authoritarian Fictions: The Ideological Novel as a Literary Genre* (New York: Columbia University Press, 1983).

69. Barbara Melosh, *Engendering Culture: Manhood and Womanhood in New Deal Public Art* (Washington, D.C.: Smithsonian Institution Press, 1991), 20.

70. Nicole Hahn Rafter, "Prison Reform Movement, 1870–1930 (U.S.)," in *Women's Studies Encyclopedia,* Vol. 3, *History, Philosophy, and Religion,* ed. Helen Tierney (Westport, Conn.: Greenwood Press, 1991), 362.

71. On Mitchell's New Womanly attempts, see Darden Asbury Pyron, *Southern Daughter: The Life of Margaret Mitchell* (New York: Oxford University Press, 1991), chaps. 8 and 9, hereafter cited in text.

72. On Mitchell's fearful personal stance, see Helen Taylor, *Scarlett's Women: Gone with the Wind and Its Female Fans* (New Brunswick, N.J.: Rutgers University Press, 1989), 50. On Victorian lady novelists, see Elaine Showalter, "Desperate Remedies: Sensation Novels of the 1860's," *Victorian Newsletter* 49 (Spring 1976): 1–5.

73. Publishing information is in Louise Y. Gossett, "Margaret Mitchell," in *Notable American Women, 1607–1950,* Vol. 2, ed. Edward T. James et al. (Cambridge, Mass.: Belknap/Harvard University Press, 1971), 552–54.

74. Marion J. Morton, " 'My Dear, I Don't Give a Damn': Scarlett O'Hara and the Great Depression," *Frontiers* 5 (1981): 52–56. Morton's is the only interpretation of *GWTW* as a Depression text I have been able to locate.

75. Anne Jones, " 'The Bad Little Girl of the Good Old Days': Sex, Gender, and the Southern Social Order," in *Recasting:* Gone with the Wind *in American Culture,* ed. Darden Asbury Pyron (Miami: University Presses of Florida, 1984), 113.

76. Julia Kirk Blackwelder, "Quiet Suffering: Atlanta Women in the 1930's," *Georgia Historical Quarterly* 61 (1977): 112–24. Unemployment in Atlanta, notes Blackwelder, was more than 10 percent higher than statewide joblessness (113).

Conclusion. Depression Fictions

1. Winifred Wandersee, *Women's Work and Family Values, 1920–1940* (Cambridge, Mass.: Harvard University Press, 1981), 5.

2. E. Ann Kaplan, *Motherhood and Representation: The Mother in Popular Culture and Melodrama* (London: Routledge, 1992), 3.

3. Estelle B. Freedman, "The New Woman: Changing Views of Women in the 1920s," *Journal of American History* 61 (September 1974): 382.

4. Robert S. McElvaine, *The Great Depression: America, 1929–1941* (New York: Times Books, 1984), 184.

5. Alice Kessler-Harris, *Out to Work: A History of Wage-Earning Women in the United States* (New York: Oxford University Press, 1982), 272. She reports that in 1930 women were 24.3 percent of all workers compared to 25.1 percent in 1940 (258).

6. Interview with Sophie Melvin-Gerson, 1976, Oral History of the American Left, Tamiment Institute Library, New York University.

7. Barbara Foley, *Radical Representations: Politics and Form in U.S. Proletarian Fiction, 1929–1941* (Durham, N.C.: Duke University Press, 1993), 233, makes a similar point.

8. Caroline Bird, *The Invisible Scar* (New York: David McKay, 1966), 287.

9. Jane Lazarre, *The Mother Knot* (1976; reprint, Boston: Beacon Press, 1986), 155.

10. Barbara Melosh, *Engendering Culture: Manhood and Womanhood in New Deal Public Art* (Washington, D.C.: Smithsonian Institution Press, 1991), 21.

11. Daniel Fuchs, *Summer in Williamsburg* (1934; reprint, New York: Basic Books, 1937), 274.

INDEX